1000 HANDY
GARDENING HINTS

1000 HANDY GARDENING HINTS

**Consultant Editor
Alan Titchmarsh**

Contents

First published in Great Britain in 1983 by
Octopus Books Limited
59 Grosvenor Street
London W1

Sixth impression, 1985

© 1983 Hennerwood Publications Limited

ISBN 0 86273 059 7

Printed and bound in Great Britain by
Collins Glasgow

Joy Larkcom

Horticultural journalist; market gardener specializing in organic methods; author of three books on vegetable gardening.

Vegetables
and
Herbs

The site

1

What would be the ideal site for a vegetable garden?

Most vegetables need to be in the sun for as much of the day as possible, so the ideal site is an open one, where vegetables are not shaded by buildings or tall trees. However, it should not be too exposed, for winds, even light winds, prevent plants from growing as well as they might. In very exposed gardens some sort of windbreak should be erected or planted. A level site is certainly preferable to a sloping one as it is much easier to work. On a sloping site cultivate across, rather than down the slope: this will minimise erosion. Poorly drained sites are unsuitable for vegetables and herb growing unless the drainage can be improved.

2

Vegetables are not growing well in my windy garden, but I am reluctant to plant windbreaks of trees or hedges, as they will create shade and take moisture and nutrients from the soil. What alternatives are there?

Special windbreak materials, made of synthetic netting, are available, which can be battened to posts. Although fairly costly, a 1.5-1.8 m (5-6 ft) windbreak around your plot would give dramatic results. Make sure the posts are anchored firmly in the ground (corner posts may need to be reinforced) as the netting takes a tremendous strain in high winds. Netting, which filters the wind, makes a far better windbreak than a solid wall or fence, which can create damaging turbulence on its leeward side.

3

Why is it important to rotate vegetables in a garden?

The main reason for rotation (growing particular vegetables in a different part of the plot each year) is that certain soil pests and diseases, such as clubroot and eelworm, which are exceptionally difficult to control, attack plants belonging to the same botanical family. If these plants are grown for several successive years in the same piece of soil, the pests and diseases can build up very seriously. The four main groups of vegetables to rotate are brassicas (cabbages, cauliflowers, broccoli, brussels sprouts, kale, turnips, swedes, Chinese cabbage); legumes (peas and beans); onions (including leeks, shallots, and garlic); and potatoes and tomatoes. Grow plants from these groups on the same ground only one year in three or, preferably, four. It is sound gardening practice, wherever possible, to avoid growing *any* vegetable on the same ground in consecutive years.

4

I'm laying out a vegetable garden for the first time, and wonder what size of bed is most suitable?

Traditionally vegetables were grown in large plots, often 6-9 m (20-30 ft) wide and as long as the garden allowed. The vegetables were arranged with a lot of wasted space between rows. Today we know that vegetables can be grown far closer than traditional spacing without any adverse effects; indeed, there is a trend towards abandoning rows and growing vegetables with equal spacing between the plants in each direction. This compactness lends itself to smaller, narrow beds, say 0.9-1.5 m (3-5 ft) wide, which can be any length you like. The small beds look very attractive, and all the work can be done from the path without treading on the ground; the narrowest beds, in particular, are easily covered with low polythene tunnels.

The soil

5

What is the best type of soil for growing vegetables?

The ideal soil is a medium loam, but vegetables will grow on a wide range of soils, from light sandy ones to heavy clays, so long as they are *fertile*. Vegetables are greedy and never do well on poor, starved soils. Digging in plenty of well-rotted manure or compost is the best way of making the soil fertile: aim at two bucketsful per square metre (square yard) each year. Soil bacteria break manure and compost down into humus, from which plant foods are released. Humus makes light soils more moisture-retentive, improves the drainage of heavy soils, increases the amount of air in the soil, and encourages earthworms, which play a key role in creating fertile soil.

6

My garden is on very sandy soil. What vegetables are best suited to such conditions?

The great advantage of sandy soil is that it is airy and well-drained, and so warms up rapidly in spring. It is excellent for early (and later) crops of carrots, ordinary radishes, beetroot, early salads, garlic, the first sowings of dwarf French beans and peas, and long-rooted vegetables such as parsnip, scorzonera, salsify, and winter radishes. Unless you can work in plenty of organic matter and are prepared to water heavily in summer, it is best to avoid brassicas, maincrop potatoes, runner beans, and plants such as celery, celeriac, fennel, and rhubarb, which require a great deal of moisture throughout their growing period.

7

Can you explain how soil acidity affects different vegetables?

Soil acidity is measured on the pH scale (see 739). Most British soils are slightly acid. The following vegetables prefer slightly acid soil in the range from pH 5.5 to 7.0: beans, brussels sprouts, cabbage, cucumbers, marrows, parsley, parsnip, peas, radish, swede, sweet corn, tomato, and turnip. Potatoes and rhubarb prefer more acid soils (pH 5.0 to 6.0); while asparagus, beetroot, carrot, cauliflower, celery, leeks, lettuce, onions, and spinach prefer more alkaline soils (pH 6.5 to 7.5). On peaty soils vegetables can tolerate somewhat lower levels of acidity than on normal, mineral soils. Excess acidity, the commonest problem, is remedied by liming (see 743).

8

We have just moved into a new house, the 'garden' of which is a pile of builder's rubble. We are anxious to start growing vegetables. Should we import topsoil?

Topsoil is expensive and that offered for sale is often of poor quality and lifeless. Instead, invest in a large load of farmyard manure, spent-mushroom compost, sewage sludge, or seaweed. Spread it over your garden in the autumn in a layer 150 mm (6 in) thick. You will be surprised how it will work into the ground during the winter. In spring fork it in as much as possible, apply a base fertiliser, and plant potatoes and Jerusalem artichoke tubers to help break up the ground. For other sowings and plantings, make mini-trenches, about 150 mm (6 in) deep, filled with commercial potting compost and covered with about 50 mm (2 in) of soil. Start with lettuces, radish, cress, mustard, salad rape, spring onion, carrots, and dwarf beans: once *something* is growing, fertility begins to build up.

9

What is the difference between organic and inorganic fertilisers?

The essential difference between them is that organic fertilisers are 'natural' (derived from plants or animals), while almost all inorganic fertilisers are manufactured. For practical purposes fertilisers can be divided into bulky manures and concentrated fertilisers. The bulky manures are all organic. They are essential for keeping the soil in good heart, and they also release plant nutrients slowly. Most of the concentrated fertilisers are inorganic salts such as ammonium and potassium nitrate, superphosphate, or mixtures such as Growmore. They are used in much smaller quantities, release the nutrients more rapidly, but do little to improve the soil structure. The traditional concentrated organic fertilisers, such as dried blood, hoof-and-horn, and bonemeal, are expensive sources of nutrients today, but organic seaweed extracts are very useful for vegetables.

10

Can vegetables be grown organically and, if so, what are the advantages?

All vegetables were grown organically before the introduction of artificial fertilisers, when manure was plentiful. If you want to grow organically today you must be prepared to build up the soil fertility by very frequently working organic matter into the soil. Feed the soil, not the plants, is the organic grower's maxim! Seaweed extracts and home-made liquid fertilisers (made by soaking bags of soot, manure, or comfrey in a tub of water) can be used to boost plant growth during the season. One of the arguments against artificial fertilisers is that they may encourage sappy, over-vigorous growth. This makes plants much more susceptible to pest and disease attack and less tolerant of adverse weather conditions.

11

How can I be sure my vegetables are getting enough nitrogen, phosphorus, and potassium (potash)?

Nitrogen (chemical symbol N), in particular, but also phosphorus (P)

and potassium (K) are the elements vegetables require in the largest quantities (*see also* 755). Nitrogen, which is obtained by the breakdown of humus, is the most likely to be in short supply because it is washed out of the soil in winter. Poor growth and yellowing foliage are signs of nitrogen deficiency. In soils of average or below average fertility, the natural supply of nitrogen can be supplemented by a top dressing of a balanced fertiliser when planting in spring or during the growing season. For vegetables with very high nitrogen requirements, such as potatoes, cauliflower, beetroot, spinach, brussels sprouts, leeks, and spring and summer cabbage, apply Growmore (which also contains P and K) at the rate of $270\text{-}340 \text{ g/m}^2$ (8-10 oz/sq yd). Use half that amount for less-demanding vegetables. Adequate reserves of P and K can be maintained in the soil by working in 5 kg/m^2 (10 lb/sq yd) of farmyard manure or 2.5-5 kg/m^2 (5-10 lb/sq yd) of garden compost every autumn.

12

My father used to lime his vegetable garden religiously every autumn. Was that necessary?

Probably not: there was a tendency to over-lime in the past. Most soils need liming about every third year, if then. Signs that liming are necessary include poor growth, a 'sour' look, with moss and unrotting vegetation on the surface, or a problem with clubroot. If a soil test then indicates that the pH is below 6.5, apply ground limestone at the rate of 270 g/m² (8 oz/sq yd) on sandy soil, 540 g/m² (1 lb/sq yd) on loamy soil, and 810 g/m² (1½ lb/sq yd) on clay soil.

Digging, sowing & planting

13

As I've never grown vegetables before, could you advise me on what garden tools are essential?

Essential tools are a full-sized 4-pronged garden fork, a rake, a hand trowel, a hand fork, a dibber, and a hoe. A small onion hoe is very useful for close weeding among vegetables; otherwise, choose between a Dutch and a draw hoe. Make yourself a garden line with nylon cord attached to stout tent pins. A wheelbarrow and watering can are almost essential. Always buy the best quality tools you can afford, and try them out first to make sure they feel right.

14

Is it better to dig soils in the spring or the autumn?

It depends on the soil. Heavy soils are best dug over roughly in the autumn, before Christmas if possible; the action of the winter frosts will break down clods. Light soils, whose structure is easily damaged by winter weather, can be manured in winter and dug over in January or February.

15

How necessary is it to dig deeply, and what is the best way of doing it?

If your vegetable garden soil is heavy, 'double dig' about once in three years (see 730).

Seeds & seedlings

16

A lot of vegetable seeds are marked F₁. What does this mean, and are they worth growing?

F_1 is a term used to define varieties obtained by a complicated, costly breeding process in which two carefully selected parent lines, which have been inbred for several generations, are crossed. The seed is therefore more expensive than ordinary seed, but because of its 'hybrid vigour', the plants are of exceptional quality. The only drawback for the amateur gardener is that, owing to their uniform quality and vigour, the vegetables will all ripen at the same time, unless they are sown in batches at intervals—which involves extra work.

Do not bother to save the seed of F_1 vegetables: it will not produce plants that resemble their parents.

17

Can I keep left-over seed for sowing next year?

It depends on the seed and how it is kept. Seeds deteriorate rapidly in moist and warm conditions (for instance, in garden sheds and hot kitchens). Always keep seed somewhere cool and dry, preferably in an airtight tin or box, with a bag or a dish of cobalt chloride-treated silica gel in it to absorb any moisture. When this gel turns pink, put it in an oven, dry it until it turns blue, and put it back in the box. Do *not* keep parsnip and scorzonera seed; and keep peas and beans only for two years. Marrows, cucumbers, most brassicas, tomatoes, beetroot, spinach, and lettuce generally remain viable for three or four years if stored carefully. Seed stored in air-sealed foil packs or glass jars keeps fresh longer than seed in ordinary packets.

18

How should I prepare a seedbed?

A seedbed is any ground where seeds are being sown. The rough surface must be raked to a fine tilth (*see* 720) after it has been forked over in spring, to make sowing easy. Rake the soil several times in each direction, drawing small stones and clods to one side. Heavy or wet soil may need to be broken down in stages. A multi-pronged cultivator is useful for breaking down clods initially; then allow the soil to dry out a few days before raking, leave it again, rake it again, and so on. Small clods can sometimes be crumbled up by hand, or broken by walking lightly over the ground before raking. Dry soil may need watering before it can be raked to a tilth. After light soils are dug over in spring, cover them with a light mulch (*see* 706) of straw. This keeps the surface in a beautifully moist condition until it is time for sowing your seeds.

19

How deep should seeds be sown?

Roughly speaking, the larger the seed, the deeper it should be sown. Small seeds such as carrots, leeks, lettuce, and onions can be about 13-19 mm ($\frac{1}{2}$-$\frac{3}{4}$ in) deep; slightly larger seeds such as cabbages and marrows 19-25 mm $\frac{3}{4}$-1 in) deep; sweet corn and peas 25-38 mm (1-1$\frac{1}{2}$ in) deep; beans 38-50 mm (1$\frac{1}{2}$-2 in) deep. Tiny seeds, and seeds such as celery which require light to germinate, should be sown on the surface. They are best sown in seed boxes, so they can be watched over and kept moist (but not wet) until germination occurs.

20

I get poor germination from outdoor sowings in hot weather. Can you tell me why?

Results are often poor in dry conditions because seeds dry out before they start to germinate. Here is a useful tip. Make your drill in the usual way, then, using a can with a fine spout, water just the drill fairly heavily. Let the water sink in, sow the seeds in the moist drill, press them in gently, then cover them with *dry* soil, firming it afterwards. The dry soil acts as a mulch, preventing the moisture from evaporating. You will then find germination will be very rapid.

Seeds of butterhead varieties of lettuce will not germinate if the soil temperature is above 25°C (77°F). The problem can be overcome in hot weather if you sow between 2 and 4 o'clock in the afternoon, so that the critical germination stage occurs in the cool of the evening. Water the drill to lower the soil temperature, and shade the soil after sowing.

21

When does one broadcast seed, and how is it done?

Broadcasting is useful, especially in small areas, for growing seedling crops such as mustard, rape, cress, sugar-loaf chicories, lettuce, and even spinach. The less-well-known Mediterranean rocket (*Eruca sativa*), a tasty, spicy, easily grown salad plant, is also ideal for broadcasting. These can be grown closely and cut when 50 mm (2 in) high for salads: they will re-sprout to give several subsequent cuttings. Rake the soil smooth, and sprinkle the seed evenly but thinly on the surface. Then rake the soil again, first in one direction then at right angles to the first direction, and cover the seedbed with clear polythene until the seeds germinate. Try to avoid broadcasting on ground where annual weeds have set seed, as weeding will be difficult.

22

I never seem to have time to thin seedlings properly. Can thinning be simplified—or eliminated?

Under good conditions seedlings grow fast and soon become checked, over-crowded, and susceptible to disease if they are not thinned. It is a very important, and often neglected, garden task. The secret is to sow *very thinly*. Sow radishes, for example, 25 mm (1 in) apart. Most other vegetables can be 'station sown'—that is, in clusters of 3 or 4 seeds together, with a gap between clusters. If the plants will eventually be, say, 150 mm (6 in) apart, make the stations 75 mm (3 in) apart; this will make thinning much easier. Start thinning as soon as the seedlings are large enough to handle; thin so that each seedling stands just clear of its neighbour. Do not pull up surplus seedlings;

nip them off at the base just above ground level. This causes much less disturbance.

In many cases thinning can be avoided by raising plants in seed trays, pots, or peat blocks and planting them out.

23

Why is one always told to remove thinnings? I should have thought they could be left on the ground to rot.

The point is that some pests are attracted to their 'host' plant by its scent. Crushed or bruised foliage smells much stronger (even though we might not be aware of it) and can prove a great giveaway. This is particularly true of the carrot fly, a serious garden pest; it is attracted like a magnet to a row of carrots by the scent of thinnings, and then lays its eggs on the top of the young carrot roots. So bury the thinnings as deep as possible in the compost heap.

24

Why must some vegetables be sown indoors?

Sowing 'indoors' means sowing under cover, whether in heated or unheated greenhouse, in a heated propagator, under cloches or frames, or even on a window sill indoors. This gives plants an earlier start, and therefore a longer growing season. It is useful for several types of crops: first, for tender vegetables such as tomatoes, peppers, cucumbers, sweet corn, and French beans, which cannot be planted outside until all risk of frost is past; second, for plants such as celery, celeriac, and maincrop onions, which need a long growing season to reach their full potential, and so will do best if they are planted early; third, to get exceptionally early crops of ordinary vegetables, such as lettuces, cabbages, and cauliflowers.

25

Should vegetables and flowers be treated differently when sown in pots or boxes?

Most common vegetable seed is robust, relatively large, and germinates easily, so it can be sown directly into potting compost, rather than being started in a fine sowing compost (exceptions are delicate seeds such as celery and celeriac). Because relatively few vegetable plants are required at any one time, they can be sown thinly and it may be unnecessary to prick them out into pots. Cauliflowers or lettuce, for example, can be sown in a tray of potting compost, with the seeds 25-38 mm (1-1½ in) apart, and then planted out directly when they are large enough. Large seeds such as cucumbers, marrow, sweet corn, and French beans can be sown in small individual pots or seed trays divided into sections, and so planted out with minimum root disturbance.

26

What are soil blocks, and why are they recommended for raising vegetable seedlings?

Blocks are made by compressing potting compost with small hand tools, which make a hole in the top of the block where the seed is sown. The seed germinates, and having no competition, grows into an exceptionally strong plant with a fine root system. There is minimal root disturbance when the block and its seedlings are planted out as one. Vegetables which normally do not transplant well, such as Chinese cabbages, can be successfully transplanted when grown in blocks. If soil conditions are unsuitable for planting, the plants can remain in soil blocks, without harm, for longer than would be possible in a seed tray.

27

I've started using soil blocks for vegetables, but find it hard to sow the smaller seeds individually. Have you any suggestions?

Try putting the seeds on a piece of paper and gently pushing one at a time into the holes. Alternatively, get a small piece of broken glass, put the seeds in a saucer, and moisten the tip of the glass. You will find you can pick up a single seed on the tip of the glass (rather like spillikins!). The seed will drop off when you touch the glass against the hole. You can always sow several seeds in each block, nipping off at just above ground level extra seedlings once they have germinated to leave one plant per block. (Do not *pull* the seedlings out, otherwise the plant blocks may disintegrate).

28

Can you explain the term 'hardening-off'?

Plants which have been raised in protected conditions indoors need to be 'toughened up' over a period of 10 to 14 days before planting out or they will suffer a severe check. Start this hardening-off by gradually increasing the ventilation in the greenhouse, frames, under cloches, or wherever your plants are. Next, move indoor plants outside during the day, or into cold frames or cloches where available, initially bringing them indoors at night, and later closing up the cloches or frames. Expose the plants to increasingly longer periods outdoors, until they have no protection day or night. They are then ready for planting. Hardening-off is particularly important for plants raised in peat-based composts, which encourage softer, lusher growth than soil-based composts.

29

What is the best size at which to plant out vegetables?

As a general rule, the smaller they are the better, with the proviso that if they are too small they will be especially vulnerable to pests. Plant lettuce seedlings when they have about four true leaves (do not count the first tiny 'seed' leaves), fennel when it has two true leaves, brassicas when they are 100-125 mm (4-5 in) high, tomatoes and peppers when the first flowering truss is visible. Root vegetables such as beetroot, parsnip, and parsley can be transplanted only when they are very small, before the roots start to swell.

30

Have you any general hints on planting vegetables?

Everything should be done to minimise the shock of transplanting and to avoid damaging the delicate root hairs. Whether the plants are in a seedbed, seed tray, or soil blocks, water them thoroughly a couple of hours before moving them. Then, using a trowel, make a hole in the prepared ground large enough to accommodate the roots (water the ground first if it is very dry). Dig up the plant carefully, holding it by the leaves, *not* by the roots. With one hand hold the plant in the hole, with the other tuck the soil around the roots, firming it gently with your fingers; the lowest leaves should be just above soil level. Finally, give a leaf a gentle tug: if the plant wobbles, make it firmer. Then water it gently. In very hot weather young plants such as brassicas will wilt. Shade them with conical 'sun hats' made of newspaper for a couple of days until they perk up.

Prepare hole

Fill in hole

Insert plant

Water gently

Watering

31

What equipment do I need for watering my vegetables?

If you have a small plot all you need is a watering can, with one ordinary rose and a finer rose for watering small plants. For larger areas, the choice is wide. Hoses are useful, preferably with nozzles which can be adjusted to alter the force of the spray. Automatic sprinklers, joined to an indoor or garden tap by a hose, water quite large areas of ground but have to be moved fairly frequently; a drawback is that the spray is apt to drift in strong winds. A useful system is 'layflat tubing', consisting of plastic hose perforated with tiny holes. This is laid on the ground between plants and connected to a tap; water seeps through the holes.

32

Can you give me any tips on watering vegetables?

The key words here are *gently* and *thoroughly*. Water gently because coarse, heavy droplets can damage seedlings and leaves. Water thoroughly because it is the roots which need the water, and not until the surface layer of soil is saturated will moisture seep through to the layers below. It takes a lot of water to wet the soil thoroughly. Poke your finger into the soil after a shower: you will be surprised how dry it is immediately beneath the surface! Occasional, really heavy waterings are far more beneficial to vegetables than frequent light ones. Peas, beans, cabbages, and other brassicas, for example, can safely be given as much as 22 l/m^2 (4 gal/sq yd) per week in a dry period.

33

I'm told that peas need to be watered heavily when they start to flower and the pods are forming. Is this true?

Yes, this is their 'critical period', when water is most needed. Unless there has been heavy rain, watering then will increase the crop dramatically. The same holds true of other 'fruiting' vegetables such as beans, tomatoes, sweet corn, cucumbers, and marrows. Leafy vegetables, such as cabbages, summer cauliflower, lettuce, and spinach need several heavy waterings while growing, but their 'critical point' is about two weeks before maturing. Even if watering was impossible earlier, water them heavily at this stage, at the rate of about 22 l/m^2 (4 gal/sq yd).

34

Are there any methods by which I can reduce the need for watering?

Several courses of action may help, as follows: 1. Work plenty of organic matter into the soil to help it retain moisture. 2. Dig deeply from time to time, so that the roots can penetrate deeper and extract moisture from lower reserves. 3. Keep the soil surface mulched (far more moisture is lost through evaporation than through drainage) and, when you plant, water and mulch the soil (*see* 706) immediately. 4. Erect artificial windbreaks around the vegetable garden or between rows, as strong winds increase evaporation. 5. Remove weeds, which compete for moisture; but hoe only shallowly, as deep hoeing brings moisture to the surface which then evaporates. 6. Plant your seedlings farther apart than usual, so that each plant has a larger area from which to draw moisture.

Weeding

35

I find weeding hard work as well as a bore. Is it really necessary?

Weeds need to be removed because they compete with vegetables for water, soil nutrients, space, and light. Some are apt to harbour pests and ordinary diseases. More seriously, weeds such as chickweed, groundsel, shepherd's purse, and hairy bitter cress act as hosts during the winter to several virus diseases. In summer these diseases are spread by aphids to cucumbers, marrows, tomatoes, and lettuce—with disastrous consequences. For some reason weed competition is much more serious *between* rows than within rows; and, generally speaking, it starts to become serious about three weeks after a sown crop has germinated.

36

Is there any truth in the saying 'One year's seeding is seven years' weeding'?

By counting the numbers of weed seeds in the soil, scientists have recently verified this old saying. In any piece of ground where weeds have gone to seed there will be up to 54,000 weed seeds per square metre (45,000 per square yard)! When the ground is cultivated, about half these seeds are lost in the first year: some will germinate on the surface; some will die; some will be exposed and eaten by birds. If no further weeds go to seed, the remaining weed seed population will be halved again the following year, and again the following year, and so on until by the seventh year it will have declined to 1 per cent of its original level. The moral for gardeners is: *never* let weeds go to seed. Remember, one fat hen plant can produce 70,000 seeds!

37

I want to grow vegetables in ground which at present is full of weeds, including docks, thistles, nettles, bindweed, couch grass, and ground elder. How can I clear it?

These are perennial weeds which can last from one season to the next, although once the ground is cultivated regularly they are generally little of a problem. The hard way to get rid of them is to dig them up: dandelion, ground elder, bindweed, and couch roots can regenerate themselves even from small pieces; docks, however, will not grow again if you remove the top 100 mm (4 in) of root. The easy way is to use what is called a translocated weedkiller, such as glyphosate, which is watered on the foliage and absorbed into the plant, killing it slowly. If you use this, follow the manufacturer's instructions precisely: it may be necessary to wait three or four weeks before sowing or planting.

38

Can I safely put weeds on my compost heap?

With the one (crucial!) exception of weeds which have gone to seed, the answer is 'yes'. It is worth doing because weeds, like other plants, contain valuable minerals. Cut large perennial roots such as docks into small pieces; and dry out the roots of creeping perennials such as couch and bindweed in the sun before adding them to the heap. Any that do manage to revive and sprout can be picked out easily when the compost is eventually used.

39

How can I cut down on hand weeding and hoeing in my vegetable garden?

Try equidistant spacing—lettuce, for example, grown 250-300 mm (10-12 in) apart in each direction—so that when your plants are mature, they will completely cover the ground, keeping light from any weeds and so preventing them from germinating or developing. Hand weeding or hoeing will be necessary only in the early stages. This method will not work with narrow-leaved vegetables such as onions, but these (and virtually all other vegetables) can be mulched (*see* 706) after planting.

40

What is the best time to mulch my vegetables?

The thing to remember is that mulching (*see* 706) preserves the *status quo*, so never mulch when the soil is very cold, very wet, or very dry: it will simply remain that way. In practice, the easiest time to mulch is after planting, especially in spring when the soil is nicely warmed up. If you mulch in summer, after planting, water dry soil thoroughly beforehand.

Keeping pests & diseases at bay

41

How can I prevent pests and diseases from attacking my vegetables?

They cannot be prevented completely, but healthy plants, grown in a good environment, are less likely to be attacked and will recover faster. Concentrate on making the soil fertile, ensuring that plants have adequate moisture and are not overcrowded, that they are hardened off well before planting out, and that they are not forced unduly. Garden hygiene is also very important: keep beds and paths clean, put lids on water tanks and tubs, and remove weeds, rotting debris, and any other rubbish, as these are likely to harbour pests and diseases, especially in winter. Burn any diseased material promptly.

42

Is it true that certain vegetable varieties are resistant to pests and diseases?

Plant breeders are constantly developing varieties with *some* resistance to *specific* pests and diseases. A disease may then develop new strains which overcome the resistance, so that more new varieties have to be bred! Several cucumber varieties have resistance to mildew, gummosis, and fusarium; some tomatoes have resistance to cladosporium, tomato mosaic virus, and fusarium; some new lettuces have resistance to certain strains of downy mildew. A number of potato varieties have considerable resistance to eelworm, and these are invaluable if your soil is infested with eelworm; the potato 'Stormont Enterprise' has some slug resistance. Consult current seed catalogues for up-to-date information on resistant varieties.

Cloches, frames & tunnels

43

I want to make good use of my cloches. Can you suggest a cropping plan?

The most economic way of using cloches is 'strip cropping', in which cloches are moved backwards and forwards between two strips of land. (It is easiest, of course, if the strips are adjacent.) Start by sowing dwarf hardy peas or dwarf broad beans under cloches in October or November on Strip A. Leave them cloched until April or early May; then move the cloches on to a summer crop, such as bush tomatoes, peppers, cucumbers, or melons planted on Strip B. In August sow late-autumn lettuce or quick-maturing carrots on Strip A, and cover them with cloches in September, when the summer crop is finished. When these are harvested in late autumn, move the cloches back onto hardy peas or broad beans, this time sown on Strip B.

44

Have you any general hints on choosing cloches?

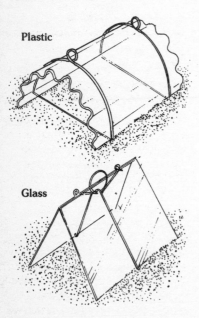

Plastic

Glass

The main choice is between glass and plastics. Glass transmits light well and conserves heat better than plastics, especially at night. Its disadvantages are awkwardness in erecting and handling, the risk of glass breakages, and the relatively high cost. Plastics are excellent for protecting plants but they are lighter and easily blown away; so look for cloches which can be anchored securely—either with legs which stick several inches into the soil, or with loops on the roof through which string can be run and attached to stakes at either end of the row. Cloches can rapidly become overheated so some means of ventilation is advisable. If you buy plastic, make sure it has been treated with ultra-violet inhibitors: it lasts much longer than untreated plastic.

45

I've just moved house and in my garden there is an old-fashioned, wooden-sided permanent frame. What can I use it for? I have no greenhouse.

In spring you will find the frame very useful for early crops of lettuce, radish, or carrots, or for raising seedlings. (It may be necessary to stand your seed boxes or pots on other upturned seed boxes, so the young plants are not drawn up towards the light.) In summer a frame is ideal for melons or cucumbers, which can be trained horizontally. Because of the limited amount of light it admits, this type of frame is less suitable than cloches for winter crops, but it can be used for overwintered seedlings of summer cauliflower, lettuces, autumn-sown varieties of onions, and so on, or for forcing chicory or blanching endives.

46

What are the pros and cons of low plastic tunnels?

These tunnels, consisting of sheets of film stretched over semi-circular hoops about 300-375 mm (12-15 in) high, are the cheapest form of protection for garden crops. They have the mobility of cloches, but are less durable. The film, unless it is treated with ultra-violet inhibitors, lasts only for about one season, although the steel hoops last much longer. Tunnels are easily ventilated, watered, and weeded by pushing up the plastic on one side; but they are less well insulated than cloches—the sides can often be blown upward by winds unless they are anchored in some way. They are, of course, soon outgrown by tall crops; but overall they make a useful substitute for cloches.

47

I can't afford a greenhouse. Would you recommend a 'walk-in', polythene tunnel for growing vegetables?

Polythene tunnels, widely used in commercial horticulture, are very suitable for vegetables. They are far cheaper than greenhouses, so large patches of ground can be covered. They require no foundations, are quickly erected, and—very important—are easily moved to a fresh site when the polythene needs replacing after

three years. This prevents the build-up of soil sickness and obviates the need for soil sterilisation, which arises when tomatoes and cucumbers are continually grown in a greenhouse. Use the tunnel for tender crops in summer, and for lettuce, endives, Swiss chard, celery, and winter salads from autumn to spring.

What to grow, and where

48

How do I decide what vegetables to grow?

Start by asking questions which will help you to draw up a short-list of what is most worth growing for you. For example, is your main objective to save money? If so, avoid cheap vegetables such as main-crop potatoes, carrots, onions, and cabbage, and concentrate on highly productive vegetables such as purple sprouting broccoli and Swiss chard. Then ask yourself what is available locally. If the choice is limited, grow unusual vegetables such as sugar peas, calabrese (green broccoli), green peppers, and celeriac. Do you particularly want fresh, well-flavoured produce? If so grow salad crops, spinach, early carrots, new potatoes, sweet corn, unusual varieties of tomato—all of which lose quality when shop-bought.

You must also take your location and soil into account. It is very difficult to grow sweetcorn and outdoor varieties of tomatoes, peppers, and aubergines in the north and in other cold areas. Very heavy soils are best suited to hungry crops, such as brassicas, while lighter soils are preferable for carrots and other root crops.

Other points for consideration are whether you will store your produce in a freezer, and—of course—the particular preferences in vegetables of the various members of your family.

49

What vegetables can I grow in my flower beds without them looking out of place?

Provided the soil is fertile enough (vegetables generally need richer soil than flowers), there is plenty of choice. Use herbs such as chives, parsley, thyme, marjoram, and winter savory for edgings, especially variegated and coloured forms such as silver thyme and gold marjoram. The frilly salad-bowl lettuces and red lettuces, beetroot, and the red-leaved and red-stemmed ruby chard are all decorative. Carrot seed can be mixed with annual flower seed and broadcast together to make a pretty patch. For dramatic effects grow single plants of the handsome grey-leaved cardoon or the closely related globe artichoke; for pretty blue

flowers, try borage; for feathery softness, grow fennel and asparagus. Runner beans, which were originally introduced for their ornamental qualities, can be trained up a tripod of canes at the back of a border.

50

What can I grow in a very dry corner of my vegetable garden?

Not many vegetables really like dry conditions, so work in plenty of compost in order to make the soil gradually become richer and more moisture-retentive. New Zealand spinach and pickling onions will grow in dry places; but, provided the site is sunny, it is probably best suited to herbs such as marjoram, thyme, sage, and winter savory.

51

What can be grown to fill the 'hungry gap' between February and May?

The 'hungry gap' is actually something of a misnomer: there are plenty of vegetables which can be harvested at that time—for example, Jerusalem artichokes, celeriac, parsnips, Hamburg parsley, purple sprouting broccoli, late brussels sprouts, savoy cabbages, curly kale, overwintered spinach, chard, leeks, and giant winter radishes. In the south-west of England winter cauliflowers are ready between December and February; elsewhere late-winter and early-spring types can be grown that mature in March, April and May.

There is also a wide choice of salads, which will be of better quality if protected in some way: winter and spring lettuce, Italian and sugar-loaf chicories, endives, corn salad, land cress, Mediterranean rocket, sorrel, winter purslane (*Claytonia*), mustard, rape, and cress.

52

Can you suggest some intercropping schemes so that I can get more from my small garden?

Try fast-growing crops such as radish, cress, spring onions, or small lettuces (such as 'Tom Thumb' or 'Little Gem') in the same row as slow-growing roots such as parsnips, Hamburg parsley, salsify, or scorzonera. 'Station-sow' the roots about 125 mm (5 in) apart, at the same time sowing (or planting, if appropriate) the faster crops between the 'stations'. The radishes, lettuces, and so on will be used long before their space is required by the growing parsnips. When widely spaced brassicas such as brussels sprouts or purple sprouting broccoli are planted out, you can sow radishes, cress, or spring onions or plant lettuces, corn salad, or land cress between them. Almost anything, including dwarf beans and trailing marrows, can be grown beneath the tall plants of sweet corn.

The cabbage family

53

What sort of conditions do brassicas need?

Brassicas (members of the cabbage family) need fertile, well-drained, moisture-retentive soil, dug thoroughly and preferably manured several months in advance: they are best planted into firm soil. (You can, for instance, plant them immediately after lifting peas, without even forking the soil.) Acid soils should be limed to discourage the serious brassica disease, clubroot.

Good anchorage is an important factor. On light soils, plant brassicas in drills about 75 mm (3 in) deep, gradually filling the drills as the plants grow to increase stability. For the same reason, earth up the stems of cabbages and cauliflowers as the plants gain height, and stake tall brassicas such as brussels sprouts and purple sprouting broccoli.

54

Can you suggest a sowing programme that will provide cabbage all year round?

For spring cabbage, sow outdoors in late July or early August, planting them where they are to grow in September. Suitable varieties include 'Harbinger', 'Durham Early', and 'Offenham'.

They will be ready between March and May.

For summer cabbage start sowing in April and May, planting from May to June. Suitable varieties are 'Hispi', 'Stonehead', and 'Minicole'. These will be ready from July to October.

For winter cabbage, sow in mid-May, planting towards the end of June, using any savoys, 'January King', or 'Celtic'. These will be ready from about December to February.

55

I get poor results with cauliflowers. Can you suggest what I may be doing wrong?

First, sow the right variety at the right time for your particular area: check on this in a good seed catalogue. Secondly, aim to grow your cauliflowers very steadily: they hate suffering any kind of check to their growth. Raise them in soil blocks, if possible, and transplant them when they are still small—about 6 weeks old.

They need plenty of moisture throughout growth, but especially in the early stages. However, they need less nitrogen than many other brassicas: too much makes them produce leaf rather than curd. Cauliflower seedlings are often attacked by cabbage-root fly. Protect the stem with a disc of foam carpet underlay, slipped around the stem at soil level after planting. It should be about 150 mm (6 in) in diameter, with a slit from the outside to a small central hole as wide as the stem. Alternatively, dip the transplants in calomel before planting.

56

Can you give me advice on growing calabrese for freezing?

Calabrese (green sprouting broccoli) freezes beautifully, retaining its colour and flavour. Sow in April or May, preferably directly in the soil as it dislikes transplanting (plants raised in soil- or peat-blocks or in small pots can be transplanted safely as there will be little disturbance). It needs moderately fertile soil and plenty of moisture, so that it can grow fast: it should be ready in about 10 weeks. Cut the large central head first. About a month later a second crop of smaller side shoots appears.

Space the plants about 300 mm (12 in) apart for the highest yields. If you grow them closer, however—say, 200-225 mm (8-9 in) apart—the side shoots will be suppressed and smaller terminal shoots will mature all together, which is useful for freezing. 'Green Comet' and 'Premium Crop' are recommended for freezing.

57

I'm told you can get a second crop from a cabbage stalk. How is this done?

This is an old gardening trick which works best on spring and early summer cabbages. When you cut the cabbage head, leave the stalk in the ground, and cut a shallow cross about 6 mm (¼ in) deep on the top of the stalk. Provided the soil is fertile and there is plenty of moisture, several buds will appear below the cross and develop into cabbage heads by late summer. As many as six new heads may be produced, crammed together on the old stalk.

Onions & root vegetables

58

It seems easier to raise onions by planting sets than by sowing seeds. Are there any disadvantages?

Sets are specially produced miniature onion bulbs. They can be planted early in spring (when the ground is still unsuitable for sowing), are easy to handle, and the food reserves in the set give the onions a head start over ones raised from seed. They are also less susceptible to attack from onion fly. The principal drawback is that they are more likely to bolt (run to seed) than seed-grown onions. To minimise this risk, select the smallest sets or use heat-treated ones (which cannot be planted until late March). Sets are more expensive than seed, and at present are available only in a few common onion varieties.

59

What exactly are Japanese onions and what are their advantages?

The Japanese onions are very hardy, autumn-sown onions, maturing in the onion 'gap' in June and July, before the spring-sown crop is ready. Sowing time is critical: sow in the first week of August in the north of England, in the second and third weeks of August in the midlands, south, and south-east, and in the last week of August in the south-west and Wales. Sow the seeds 25 mm (1 in) apart in rows 225 mm (9 in) apart, thinning to 50 mm (2 in) apart in spring. One of the earliest varieties is 'Express Yellow'; heavier varieties include 'Imai' and 'Kaizuka'. Japanese onions are unsuitable for storing.

60

My onions never keep well. Can you give me any advice?

Obviously, first make sure you are growing storing varieties, such as 'Sturon', 'Hygro', or the 'Rijusburger' types. Good harvesting is the key to successful storage. When the onion leaves die back naturally (do *not* bend them over; this damages them), ease them out of the soil, place them in wooden trays, and dry them in the sun for several days. Dry them as fast and as thoroughly as possible, bringing them indoors to finish if the weather turns wet. Handle them with great care: storage rots start from tiny cuts and bruises. Store them somewhere dry but frost-free with plenty of air, plaited in ropes, suspended in nets or nylon stockings, or laid in single layers in seed trays.

61

I am told spacing is very important in growing beetroot. Is this so?

Yes. The precise spacing depends on when you are sowing, but *never* crowd your beetroot. Very early beetroot, sown under cloches in late February or early March (using a bolt-resistant Detroit variety), needs to grow very fast. Sow in rows 175 mm (7 in) apart, thinning to 100 mm (4 in) between each plant. The main summer crop, sown in May and June, can be in rows 300 mm (12 in) apart, thinning to 25 mm (1 in) between plants. For late-autumn and storage beet, sown in late June and early July, the rows should be 200 mm (8 in) apart, thinning to 90 mm (3½ in) apart in the rows. For pickling beet, aim to harvest no more than $215/m^2$ (20 per square foot); this involves rows 75 mm (3 in) apart, with plants thinned to 56 mm (2¼ in) apart in the rows.

62

Every year carrot fly ruins my carrots. What can be done?

There is no guaranteed chemical remedy for the amateur gardener,

but various preventive measures can be taken. Very early sowings (February and March) and late sowings (June) avoid the worst attacks. The Amsterdam and Nantes types of carrot, which are less 'leafy', are less susceptible than maincrop varieties. Sow away from tall plants and hedges, which may shelter adult flies. The flies are said to fly low, so try growing carrots in raised boxes or tubs, or with 200 mm (8 in) high boards around the beds; or put cloches over them in the early, more vulnerable stages. Sow very thinly, and when the time comes for thinning out, do this in the evening, when the flies are not about, and remove all thinnings (*see* 23). Lift all carrots by mid-October to prevent the late batch of grubs developing, and burn any damaged roots and rubbish.

63

I want to try some unusual root crops. Can you suggest a few?

How about Hamburg parsley, which gives you both a root and green parsley leaf in winter; Jerusalem artichoke, a marvellous winter standby and an excellent grower on rough ground; the long thin 'twins' salsify and scorzonera, which do best on light soil; and celeriac, with its subtle celery flavour? Another possibility (though not strictly a root crop) is kohl-rabi, a very-fast-growing brassica, which can be sown directly in the ground from February (in mild districts) until August or early September.

These underrated crops are all very nutritious, and are delicious on their own, in stews or soups, grated raw in salads, or cooked and eaten cold, which brings out their flavour superbly.

64

What are the differences between early, second early, and maincrop potatoes?

The main difference is in the length of time they take to mature. Earlies will mature in about 100 to 110 days; second earlies in about 110 to 120 days; and maincrop potatoes in 125 to 140 days. The earlies tend to be the lowest yielding, but there is no reason why you should not sow earlies late, or maincrop potatoes early—you will just have to wait longer for the crop!

65

What is the best way of storing root vegetables?

Very hardy roots such as parsnips, Hamburg parsley, and celeriac can be left in the soil and covered with straw or bracken, so that they will be easier to lift in hard frost. Beetroot, swedes, carrots, and turnips can be stored in sheds in boxes in layers of sand, peat, or sieved ashes, or outdoors in clamps. Start a clamp with a 200 mm (8 in) layer of straw, pile

the roots on top, cover them with another 200 mm layer, then leave them to sweat for two days before covering them with 150 mm (6 in) of soil. Store potatoes somewhere dark and frost-free, in double-thickness paper or hessian sacks. *Never* store diseased or damaged roots.

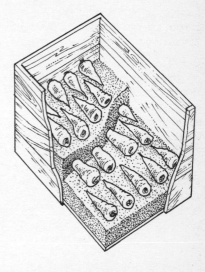

Peas & beans

66

My French beans often fail to germinate. Any advice?

The commonest cause of such failure is sowing in cold, wet soil: the beans rot or are attacked by pests and diseases. It really pays to start beans off indoors, sowing them in potting compost in seed trays, in single pots, or in the individual cells of polystyrene trays. Put the seeds on damp newspaper for at least 12 hours until they swell, then sow them. Harden-off (*see* 28) the seedlings before planting them outside—and then only after all danger of frost is past. This method may sound laborious, but it will give you excellent results.

67

Does spraying runner beans with water help them to set?

No: it has been proved to have no effect. Runner-bean flowers are insect-pollinated, and the insects are brought out by warmth. So grow runners in sheltered rather than exposed positions (erect a windbreak if necessary) to encourage insects. They are also more attracted to the white-flowered runner bean varieties, such as 'Mergoles', 'Desirée', 'White Achievement', and 'Fry', than to the pink- or red-flowered varieties. The flowers are occasionally nipped off by birds, so net your beans at flowering time if this is a problem. Once the pods have started to set, pick them regularly to encourage further setting.

68

What are sugar peas?

Sugar, or mangetout ('eat-all'), peas are a kind in which the pod is eaten, usually when you can just see the immature peas forming inside it. Some varieties have flat,

sickle-shaped pods; others, such as 'Sugar Snap', are round. (Most sugar peas can be shelled like ordinary peas if they are allowed to mature fully.) They are grown like other peas, and with their sweet, superb flavour are a gastronomic treat. Cook them like French beans, ideally steaming them to retain the flavour. Because it is the pods that are eaten, you get more bulk from a row of mangetout than of ordinary peas—with the added bonus of no shelling!

69

Is it worthwhile sowing broad beans in November? It seems that the spring-sown varieties usually manage to catch up.

It's a bit of a toss-up, and in most areas of the country one might as well wait until spring, particularly as the spring-sown beans are often sturdier because they grow under better light conditions. If you live in the north, however, it may well be best to sow them under cloches in November to give them a good start. In the south you can start them under cloches in January. Use dwarf varieties such as 'the Sutton' if sowing under cloches, and remember to allow access to pollinating insects. Remove the cloches in late spring.

Tender vegetables

70

Do you recommend the all-female varieties of cucumber which are now available?

Yes, these are a very useful development. With the old-fashioned varieties of greenhouse or frame cucumbers you have to remove all the male flowers because, once the flowers are pollinated, they become mis-shapen, swollen at the ends, and bitter. This is not necessary with the all-female varieties, apart from removing the occasional male flower which may appear. (You can recognise the female flower by the embryonic fruit behind the petals). The outdoor ridge cucumbers, incidentally, *can* be pollinated, with no adverse effects.

71

When should I 'stop' my tomatoes?

Stopping tomatoes—that is, nipping out the growing point about two leaves above the top flower truss—concentrates the plant's energies into maturing the remaining trusses before the cold weather comes. Outdoor tomatoes are usually stopped after three trusses in the north, and after four or five in the south; generally speaking, this means in late July or early August. Indoor tomatoes are stopped after seven or eight trusses, or—if they are growing well—you can leave them until there is no more greenhouse space. Remember that on all upright tomatoes the sideshoots must be nipped out throughout growth; this is unnecessary with bush tomatoes.

72

Is it possible to grow peppers and aubergines outdoors in this country?

You are likely to be really successful only in the south—and even there, the plants will probably need (and will certainly benefit from) cloche protection, especially in the early stages. Grow them in a sunny, sheltered spot. Start them indoors in heat in late February or early March, pot them up in small pots, harden them off well (*see* 28), and plant them out from mid-May onwards after all risk of frost is past. Nip out the tops when the plants are about 375 mm (15 in) high to make them bushy, and stake them if they are top heavy.

Reliable varieties are the aubergine 'Moneymaker F1', and the F_1 hybrid peppers 'Early Prolific', 'Ace', and 'Canapé'.

73

Can you give me any advice on growing sweet corn?

Sweet corn needs a long growing season, so is suitable only for the south of England. Grow it in a sheltered, sunny position. As the seed will not germinate in cold soil, it is best sown indoors in April in soil blocks or small pots, so that there will be minimum root-disturbance when it is planted out. Alternatively, sow it outdoors (from the end of May onwards) under cloches (or even under jam jars), which can be removed after germination. Plants should be spaced about 350 mm (14 in) apart, and grown in blocks rather than in long rows, so that they will be cross-pollinated by the wind.

The cobs are mature when the tassels have turned brown and the cobs, hanging at an angle of about 60 degrees to the stem, will snap off easily. If the cobs have to be worked to and fro before they come away, it indicates that they are not fully ripe and should be left for a little longer.

74

I want to grow courgettes rather than marrows. Any advice?

'Courgette' is French for 'little marrow': courgettes are simply marrows that are picked while they are immature; they are at their most tasty when they are 100-125 mm (4-5 in) long. Any marrow variety can be used, but the F_1 hybrid bush varieties are best for courgettes. The seeds germinate poorly under cold conditions, but the plants grow rapidly once the soil warms. Sow them indoors in individual pots at the end of May, or outdoors (preferably under cloches) from mid-May onwards, in well-prepared, well-manured soil. Allow about 900 mm (3 ft) between plants. Male flowers often appear long before the female: be patient! Keep picking the small courgettes to encourage further cropping; any that are left too long will develop into marrows.

Salad, leafy & perennial vegetables

75

I would like to grow good-quality lettuce all the year round; I have an unheated greenhouse. What varieties do you suggest?

An excellent sweet, crisp lettuce is 'Little Gem', which can be harvested from spring to autumn. Make the first sowing indoors in early February for planting outside; it will be ready in June. Continue sowing and planting outside until August. From September, the sowings are made in the greenhouse; they will be ready the following April or early May. Sow again in October and early November, and overwinter these indoors as seedlings for planting out in spring. They will be ready for harvesting in May.

A good winter lettuce for unheated greenhouses is 'Dandie'. Sow it in succession from early September to November, planting it 225 mm (9 in) apart, for cutting from late autumn to spring. The key to maintaining a succession of any variety is to make the *next* sowing when the seedlings from the previous sowing emerge.

76

I'm a vegetarian, so I'm partial to interesting salads all year round. What can you suggest for the winter months?

If you have an unheated greenhouse, plant endives, sugar-loaf chicory, and Chinese cabbage in October. Keep cutting them about 25 mm (1 in) above ground level, and you will find they survive low temperatures and re-sprout to give supplies over several months. Outdoors you must grow hardier plants, such as land cress, corn salad (lamb's lettuce), winter purslane (*Claytonia*), red Italian chicory, and Mediterranean rocket—all of which will survive several degrees of frost. (If you *can* grow these under cover, however, they will be of better quality.) Other possibilities are Witloof chicory and giant winter radishes. Make lovely salads by mixing all these together, along with chopped red and green cabbage and sprouted seeds.

77

I have a tiny garden and love fresh salads. What would it be best to grow?

Have you thought of seedling crops, which are wonderfully productive and highly nutritious? Instead of growing cress on a windowsill, broadcast a small patch, say one metre square, in the garden. Cut the cress when it is about 50 mm (2 in) high. It will grow again: provided you keep it well watered, it may give you up to five cuts! Mustard, rape, Mediterranean rocket, coriander, sugar-loaf chicory, even lettuce can be grown in this way.

78

Is it difficult to grow Witloof chicory?

It is much easier than you might think. Sow it very thinly in late May or early June, and then thin to 150 mm (6 in) apart. Keep the plants weeded during summer. In late October or November, lift the roots, cut off the foliage an inch above the crown, and store the roots horizontally, in boxes of peat or sand, in a shed. To get the white 'chicons' the roots must be 'forced' in a dark and warm (50-60°F) place. Force a few at a time. The easiest way is to plant three roots in soil in a 225 mm (9 in) flower pot. Over this place an upturned pot of the same size, covering the drainage holes with aluminium foil to exclude light. Keep the soil moist, and put the pots somewhere warm indoors. The chicons should be ready in three or four weeks.

79

I no longer have the space, time, or energy to grow celery in a trench. Are there any alternative methods?

I suggest you try self-blanching celery. It is not quite as crunchy or as hardy as trenched celery but is less trouble to grow and makes a very good substitute. One of the best white-stemmed varieties is 'Lathom Self Blanching'. Recommended green-stemmed varieties are 'Green-snap' and 'Tendergreen'. You must grow self-blanching celery in blocks, with plants about 225 mm (9 in) apart; this close spacing helps to blanch the stems a little more. The celery can be cut from July until the first frosts of the autumn.

80

Can you describe the different types of spinach?

First there is the ordinary, annual spinach (*Spinacia oleracea*) in summer and winter forms. Summer (round-seeded) spinach is sown in spring, and the hardier winter (prickly-seeded) type in autumn for a winter crop. They are small leaved and run to seed quickly.

Leaf beet (*Beta vulgaris*) is simply a form of beetroot grown for its leaves. The various types include Swiss chard (also known as seakale beet), a biennial, which has attractive large leaves and usually a widened stem and midrib which are also edible; and perpetual spinach (or spinach beet), with a less pronounced stem and midrib.

New Zealand spinach (*Tetragonia tetragonoides*) is a quite different, half-hardy plant which trails over the ground; it is particularly useful in dry situations.

Probably the leaf beets—and

especially Swiss chard—are the best value. Sow them in spring, and again in July and August, to keep yourself continually supplied.

81

Why is asparagus grown on raised beds?

The main reason is to improve the drainage: although asparagus will do well on an extraordinarily wide range of soils, from heavy clays to sand, it *must* have good drainage. Moreover, when you grow asparagus in raised beds or ridges you get a longer blanched 'handle'. Provided your drainage is good, however, there is no reason why you should not grow asparagus on the flat. If you are starting a bed, use one-year-old rather than older crowns; they establish themselves more easily than two-year-old crowns. Even so, you will have to wait until their third season before you can start cutting the shoots lightly.

This crop certainly needs patience, and if you want to go in for asparagus, even on a small scale, it would be a good idea to set aside a corner of the vegetable garden specifically for it.

82

My old rhubarb plant is very unproductive. What should I do?

Your plant is probably suffering from a very common rhubarb complaint—neglect! When the leaves die down in autumn, dig it up and, using a spade, divide the crown into two or three pieces, each with a bud and good piece of root. Prepare a new site in an open position, digging in generous quantities of well-rotted manure or compost, and plant the pieces at least 1.5 m (5 ft) apart. During the summer keep them well watered, and in spring and autumn each year mulch them, again with a very generous layer of farmyard manure or compost. To keep them productive, old plants need dividing every five years or so.

Herbs

83

What is the best way of getting chives established?

You can raise chives (*Allium*) either from seed or by dividing old clumps. Sow seed in the spring, and when the seedlings are several inches high, plant them out in clumps of up to half a dozen seedlings together, spacing the clumps about 225 mm (9 in) apart. They soon spread into larger clumps. Mature clumps can be divided and replanted at any time from spring to late autumn. Remember that the natural habitat of chives is damp meadows, so if they are to thrive they need humus-rich soil and plenty of moisture.

84

I always seem to have difficulty getting parsley to germinate. Have you any hints?

Parsley (*Petroselinum*) is naturally slow to germinate, and if the soil dries out the seed may *never* germinate. Use the 'summer-sowing' trick: make your drill, water the drill *only* until it is moist, sow the seed in the drill, and cover it with dry soil. This dry covering will prevent evaporation, so the soil will keep moist for a long time. You can also sow parsley in seed boxes (or, better, in soil blocks), provided you plant it out while the roots are still small.

By the way, have you tried the broad-leaved parsley? It has a very good flavour and seems to be much easier to grow than the more popular curly type.

85

I grow most of the common culinary herbs—sage, rosemary, thyme, parsley, etc, and want to branch out. Have you any suggestions?

A marvellous summer herb is basil (*Ocimum basilicum*), which needs to be started indoors and undoubtedly is best if it can be protected with cloches. Then the marjorams (*Origanum*) are a lovely group: the sweet or knotted marjoram (*O. marjorana*) is an annual, while the pot (*O. onites*) and wild (*O. vulgare*) marjorams are hardier and make neat evergreen clumps.

The savories (*Satureia*) are also worth growing. Sow the annual summer savory (*S. hortensis*) each April, and grow the perennial winter savory (*S. montana*) in a pot: it makes a pretty and useful house plant! All these are excellent culinary herbs.

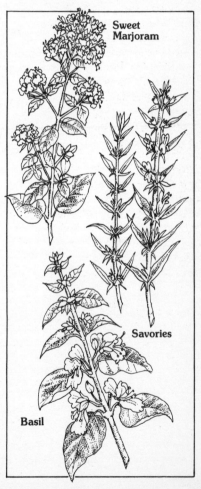

Sweet Marjoram

Savories

Basil

86

What herbs can be grown for use fresh in winter?

Chervil (*Anthriscus cerefolium*) is an excellent winter herb: sow it in August or September; it will withstand most winters outside. As a substitute for chives, grow either Welsh onions or perennial onions (both *Allium* spp.). Raise Welsh onions from seed or by dividing old clumps in spring or autumn, and use both the leaves and the flattened bulbs. Perennial onions, which look like pale chives, must be raised by division. Sow parsley in July for a winter supply, but remember that it tends to die back in cold weather unless protected with cloches.

Other evergreen herbs are the thymes (*Thymus*), rosemary (*Rosmarinus officinalis*), which needs protection in cold areas, pot marjoram, and winter savory. All these, and chervil, are more productive in winter if grown in frames or under cloches.

87

What herbs can be grown in a shaded site?

Provided it is not heavily shaded and the soil is reasonably moist and fertile, you can grow any of the numerous mints (*Mentha*), angelica, and lovage (*Levisticum officinale*)—but bear in mind that this last can grow 2 m (6½ ft) tall—or sweet cicely (*Myrrhis odorata*). Chervil and parsley will grow better in partial shade in the summer.

Arthur Billitt

Journalist and widely respected authority on every aspect of fruit-growing; frequent broadcaster on radio and television.

Fruit

Apples

88

After a fine show of blossom and an excellent set of fruit, our 'James Grieve' tree has shed more than half its tiny fruitlets. What went wrong?

'James Grieve' is a very reliable cropper but, like many other varieties, is unable to swell every fruitlet (the tiny apple) that it may set as a result of pollination. Whenever the crop potential exceeds the ability of a tree to sustain it, nature steps in to relieve the stress, invoking what is called the 'June drop'. When it is over there will still be plenty of fruit for you, but bear in mind that the 'June drop' in fact continues well into July.

89

We have a 'Cox's Orange Pippin' tree, about 20 years old, which has developed several nasty-looking lumpy areas of rough bark around the top of its trunk. What treatment is necessary to clean it up?

It is evident that canker has started to attack. 'Cox's Orange Pippin' is susceptible to this disease, especially if the soil is badly drained. Scrape the rough bark away right down to clean wood, then treat the exposed area with a wound paint to prevent re-infection and to encourage healthy bark to grow over the treated area.

90

We are thinking of planting a row of cordon apples to screen off our vegetable garden; the row would run almost north and south. What distance apart should we plant them?

This is an excellent idea. Make sure that the trees are on the dwarfing rootstock 'Malling 9', and plant them 900 mm (3 ft) apart. It is preferable to buy maidens (one-year-old trees) rather than older ones, and if possible avoid planting tip-bearing varieties (those that carry most fruit at the end of the stems). Cordons should be planted at an angle of 45 degrees; if they slope from south to north they will get the full benefit of the sunshine.

91

Is it always necessary to keep the ground under apple trees clean? We have a large garden, part of it devoted to an orchard, and want to arrange things so that we don't have too much work.

If the trees are either half or full standards and well-established, there is no reason why you should not grass the whole area down. All you need to do is to allow the grass and weeds to grow; then, when the overall height is about 75 mm

(3 in), go over it with a rotary lawn mower; repeat the operation from time to time. In this way you will get a 'tumbledown' sward.

92

According to my gardening books, sulphate of potash is good for practically all kinds of fruit. I have given our apple trees plenty over the last few years, but now the leaves are yellowish with green veins. What is wrong?

Sulphate of potash is valuable if applied in moderation, along with the other principal plant foods, nitrogen and phosphorous. When you use Growmore (a balanced fertiliser) you are applying all three. By using too much potash you have created a magnesium deficiency—a condition clearly indicated by the leaf colouring. An application of commercial Epsom salts (magnesium sulphate) at the rate of about 68 g/m^2 (2 oz/sq yd) to the soil under the trees should help to put matters right.

93

Our garden is very small and we can find room for only one apple tree. Our friends tell us that unless we plant several we shall get blossom but no fruit. Is this true?

It is true that most apple varieties need another variety for pollination—and it must be a variety that blossoms at the same time. However, the nursery trade has an answer to your problem. You can buy what are called 'family trees'—standard trees on a single stem, with three varieties grafted on top. They may all be cookers or dessert varieties, but in either case the selection will have been carefully made to ensure pollination.

94

We are planning to plant four apple trees—three dessert varieties and one cooker. Which ones would you recommend for northern England—our summers are usually cool?

To start the dessert season in September you will find 'James Grieve' a most reliable cropper; when picked ripe from the tree it is delicious. To follow in October, plant 'Red Ellison' for its aromatic, aniseed flavour. Then for keeping until November choose 'Lord Lambourne'; you will welcome its good-flavoured crisp flesh. If you can accommodate only one cooker, make it 'Lord Derby', which defies the cold and sets its fruit without pips.

95

We have several apple trees, including 'James Grieve', 'Charles Ross', and 'Cox's Orange Pippin'; but the fruit—when we get any—is always small. In addition, the leaves often have a pale yellow look about them. What's the trouble?

The combination of small apples and pale-coloured foliage indicates that the trees are being starved of nitrogen. First, clear the ground under the trees, get rid of any grass or weeds, then start feeding the soil with Growmore fertiliser, which will supply nitrogen plus phosphate and potash. The best time to apply it is late February or early March. A foliar feed (that is, a plant food sprayed onto the foliage) during the growing season will also help.

96

My mother treasures an apple tree she has raised from a 'Cox's Orange Pippin' pip, but after eight years it is still growing bigger without showing any signs of fruiting. Any ideas?

This is a common experience with seedlings; each one is an individual with a unique genetic make-up. If and when your mother's tree does decide to crop, the apples will certainly be very different from those of a 'Cox's Orange Pippin'. It would be a near miracle if its apples were worth eating; and,

whatever their quality, it would be necessary to bud or graft the plant onto a dwarfing rootstock to restrict its growth.

97

I have been in the habit of pruning our young apple trees every July and again in November/December. Now, with the trees 10 years old, some of the varieties seem to have almost completely stopped cropping. Why?

There could be several reasons. July is too early to start summer pruning: it can cause fruit buds to break into growth when they should still be dormant. These buds are not replaced, so the following season's crop is lost. Some of your apples may be tip-bearing varieties (see 90); if so, there will be fruit buds towards the ends of the young branches —but perhaps you have been cutting these off in November or December.

98

Our 'Egremont Russet' apples are often covered with small brown specks. These are more than just skin blemishes—the flesh below the specks is also brown. Is this a disease?

It is not a disease but a disorder known as 'bitter pit', to which 'Egremont Russet' is particularly susceptible. It is undoubtedly related in some way to nutrition, and a low level of boron in the soil may be responsible. Experience has shown that domestic borax applied annually to the soil at the base of the trees at the rate of 34 g/25 m² (1 oz per 30 sq yd) helps to eliminate it. To obtain even distribution, apply the borax in solution with a watering can fitted with a rose.

99

Why has our old 'Bramley' tree suddenly stopped fruiting, even though it still blossoms normally? It did well until our neighbour severely cut back some of his apple trees to let more light into his and our garden.

To crop successfully a 'Bramley Seedling' tree should have nearby at least two suitable pollinators which blossom at the same time; otherwise it does not set its fruit. It is evident that your neighbour's trees previously provided the pollen, and they will do so again if allowed to re-grow their fruiting wood. The extra light and air, however, will certainly benefit the health of your tree.

100

Our old 'Bramley' tree has developed a crack in its bark from top to bottom of the trunk. What do you think could have caused this?

A crack of this sort usually follows a severe winter when the residual sap below the bark freezes. It is somewhat akin to the bursting of a waterpipe. If the bark alongside the crack shows signs of being loose, use a few large-headed tacks to hold it in close contact with the trunk wood. Paint the exposed wood with a bituminous wound dressing.

101

We have a standard 'James Grieve' tree planted in our lawn, and although the apples are always highly coloured and sweet, they are usually rather small. We have recently cleared a circle of soil around the tree to free it from grass competition. Will that help?

A fruit tree growing in grass is always liable to be short of nitrogen, which encourages growth. When nitrogen is in short supply, the apples will be small and highly coloured. Clearing away some of the grass will help. Keep the circle weed-free, apply water in dry weather, and do not forget a February application of Growmore fertiliser applied to the whole area beneath the branches of your tree.

102

Is there any answer to the biennial cropping problems of our apple trees? We have two varieties, 'Superb' and 'Rev. W. Wilks'.

It has been suggested that de-blossoming one half of a tree

would set up a rhythm whereby the two halves fruited in alternate years; in practice, however, it seldom works out that way. The best bet is to plant two trees of each variety. De-blossom one of each of the pairs this year while allowing the other to fruit. The de-blossomed trees will form fruit buds for next season.

103

We are in the process of making a garden in Kent. We would very much like to plant a 'Cox's Orange Pippin' tree but have no space for another variety to pollinate it. Is there any chance that a 'Golden Hornet' crab-apple we planted not far away in our ornamental garden will act as a substitute?

You are lucky: 'Golden Hornet' is a very widely used pollinator for 'Cox's Orange Pippin'. But the distance between the two trees must not be more than about 15 m (50 ft). Two eating-apple varieties that also make suitable pollinators for 'Cox's' are 'Discovery' and 'James Grieve'.

104

Several of our young bush apple trees have branches that now almost touch the ground. Should we shorten them?

When the branches bow down naturally it is a good sign, because from then on a tree usually fruits regularly and well. In fact, if the young branches had remained upright I would have recommended that you bent them down and anchored them to the ground, for this is a way to induce good fruiting habits. If the fruits actually touch the ground, however, cut back the affected branches to allow other younger ones to take their place.

105

We are re-planning our garden. We already have a 'John Downie' crab apple, which is a dual-purpose tree, providing blossom in spring and fruit in the autumn for making jelly. Is there a cooking apple worthy of planting in an ornamental garden?

Few of the best cooking apples are noted for their blossom, but 'Arthur Turner' is an exception and in a class by itself when it comes to blossom time. It is certainly worth a place on that score alone, and its upright growth habit is also a good point. From August to October it will provide large apples with fair cooking qualities.

Pears

106

Our new garden is very exposed on the north-east side, but in our fruit-planting scheme we would like to include pears. We are in the process of growing a shelterbelt of trees to the north-east, so would it be wiser to wait until the cold winds are blocked out before planting the pear trees?

Pears easily suffer from wind damage: the bruised foliage turns black, and this loss of leaf area affects tree growth and fruit production. Delay your planting until the wind problem is solved, when the calmer and warmer conditions will increase your chances of success.

107

We have a couple of very old pear trees whose varieties are unknown but whose flavour is very good. A friend of ours would like to grow the same pears in her garden, so last winter we dug out some rooted shoots from around the trees. We have now grown them on in pots, but the foliage looks different. What has happened?

The shoots you have dug up are suckers thrown up from the rootstock, which may well be a seedling pear rootstock of no fruiting merit. Only by budding or grafting scions from the upper part of your tree onto a rootstock could you help your friend.

108

Could you suggest two varieties of pears, not too difficult to grow, that would be suitable for planting in our small Surrey garden?

'Conference' is an obvious choice; it is a reliable cropper, and when fully ripe in October and November the fruit is juicy and sweet. It also makes a good pollinator for my second choice, 'Louise Bonne de Jersey', another good cropper. Its medium-sized pears ripen in October, are an attractive yellowish-green flushed with red, and are deliciously flavoured. These two pears make an ideal combination for a small southern garden.

109

'Doyenne du Comice' is our favourite pear, but we are told that it is one of the most difficult to grow. What would be our chances of success here in Cheshire?

In your district it would need some protection to provide extra warmth during the growing season. Trained as an espalier (that is, with pairs of opposite horizontal branches) on a south- or west-facing wall or fence, it might thrive, provided it had the company of two good pollinators flowering at the same time; 'Beurre Hardy' and 'Glou Morceau' would be suitable for this.

110

We have several pear trees, including a 'William's Bon Chrétien' which seldom fails to crop, but we have been very disappointed with the quality of its ripe fruit.

'William's Bon Chrétien' pears must be picked *before* they are ripe, otherwise the flesh goes gritty and rather dry. Next time, when they are mature and full-sized but still green (about September), pick them carefully and store them in a closed container such as a cardboard shoe box. Inspect them daily, so that you can enjoy them at their peak of ripeness; thereafter, they deteriorate rapidly.

Plums

111

We have two plum trees, a 'Victoria' and a 'Czar'; they both blossom and usually produce a small crop, but a lot of the plums drop before they are fully formed. Is it because our soil is sandy?

Most sandy soils tend to be low in calcium, and in the absence of sufficient available calcium the

trees will go through a difficult time when the stones are being formed. If there is not enough to go round, some of the plums will be shed.

An application of garden lime over the whole area during the winter will probably solve your problem. In spring, mulching (*see* 706) with well-rotted manure or compost will also help.

112

Can you tell us if our native Hertfordshire is a good county for plums; and if so, which would be two of the best dessert varieties for us to grow? Our garden has a south-facing wall about 9 m (30 ft) long.

Fortunately, plums can be grown almost anywhere in the country. Some of the top-class dessert varieties need a little extra protection, but your wall would help to supply the warmth that makes all the difference when plums are grown as trained trees. The two varieties I would recommend are 'Kirke's Blue' and 'Golden Transparent'.

113

Why do my plum trees have so many bare branches with leaves bunched together at the ends? After six years I am still waiting for the trees to crop.

You are evidently plagued by bullfinches. The damage is done early in the new year, when these birds attack any unopened buds they can reach safely, so it is only those at the end of the branches that are left to develop. The best answer would be a fruit cage covered with netting—but this is not practical with free-standing plum trees. You could try spraying with a bird repellent, but you will have to repeat the application after heavy rain.

114

Some five years ago we planted a 'Merryweather Damson' tree. It is now beginning to crop but the fruits are more like plums than damsons, with little or no damson flavour. Did we plant the wrong variety?

You did if you want damsons of the traditional flavour and colour. One of the best is 'Shropshire Damson'. It makes a small tree, needs no routine pruning, is self-fertile, and in general is very well suited for garden planting.

115

Several years ago we planted a 'Monarch' plum tree. It has cropped well, but we are disappointed with the quality of the fruit. What we wanted was an early blue plum for stewing and for dessert. Can you recommend one?

'Rivers' Early Prolific' would fit the bill; but it needs a pollinator, so I

would advise you to keep your 'Monarch', which flowers at the same time. 'River's Early Prolific' is a small blue plum which stews well as soon as it colours. When fully ripe it is sweet and full of superbly flavoured juice. It also freezes well.

116

Several of our plum trees have got out of hand, with lots of dead and crossing branches. When is the best time to wade in with a saw to tidy them up?

The dead branches can be removed at any time—the sooner the better. Early May is the safest time for taking out living wood, but be sure that all the cuts are cleanly made, as close to the trunk as possible, and that the wounds are immediately and carefully dressed with a proprietary wound sealant.

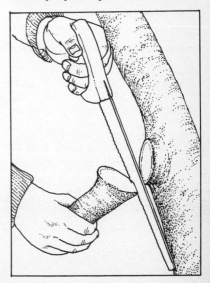

117

Being fond of greengages, we planted a 'Jefferson Gage' and an old-fashioned 'Green Gage', but neither of them has succeeded in producing more than a few fruits.

The old-fashioned 'Green Gage' is never a good cropper and it must have a pollinator along with it which flowers at the same time. 'Jefferson Gage' is a reliable cropper but it, too, needs pollination. Your problem is one of blossom timing: the 'Jefferson Gage' finishes before the 'Green Gage' starts. 'Oullin's Golden Gage' blossoms as late as 'Green Gage', while 'Coe's Golden Drop' flowers as early as 'Jefferson Gage'.

118

Two years ago we planted a 'Warwickshire Drooper Plum' tree in our lawn, hoping it would be both ornamental and useful, but it does not seem at all happy.

All plum trees do better when planted in clean, cultivated ground. To help your tree to get going, make sure that it is allowed a circle about 2 m (6½ ft) in diameter completely free of grass and weeds. Your soil will probably be short of lime, so start with an application of garden lime and follow this up with Growmore fertiliser in February or early March, at a rate of 65-100 g/m^2 (2-3 oz/sq yd).

119

One of our plum trees—a 'Victoria' which has done well for several years—is now looking sick. Several of the branches have leaves with a silvery sheen on them. What can we do to bring it back to health?

That silvery sheen is most likely a sign of silver leaf, a disease covered by an order which requires the removal and burning of all the dead and infected wood before the middle of July. No doubt there will be dead wood in your tree, so get it out as quickly as possible and burn it. If you do cut into living, healthy wood paint the wounds immediately with a proprietary wound sealant. To improve the health of the tree apply Growmore fertiliser in late February or early March.

Strawberries

120

Which strawberry variety would you recommend for a small garden? How do I make a start on bed preparation?

'Cambridge Favourite' is a good cropper with an acceptable strawberry flavour. Choose if possible a well-drained soil in a sunny position. Prepare the ground some weeks ahead of planting time, making sure that it is free from perennial weed roots such as those of couch grass, convolvulus, ground elder, nettles, and docks. Dig the soil to the full depth of your spade and incorporate some moisture-holding material such as well-rotted compost or manure. If neither is available, peat will make a useful substitute. Be sure to buy healthy plants, if possible ones with a Ministry of Agriculture certificate. The best planting time is late July to early September.

121

Although our greenhouse is unheated, would it be possible for us to force some early strawberries?

The simple answer is 'yes', but you will need to start with some healthy, well-rooted plants in early September. Two of the best varieties for forcing are 'Tamella' and 'Royal Sovereign'. In September pot the plants into 125 mm (5 in) pots using a peat-based potting compost or John Innes Potting compost No 3; leave a space between the compost and the top of the pot to allow for watering and feeding. Stand the pots outdoors on a solid base after potting: do *not* put the pots on soil, as they would be an invitation to worms seeking winter quarters. Water only if the compost starts to dry out.

Early in March spray the plants to kill greenfly, remove any dead leaves, and bring the pots into the greenhouse, placing them on a shelf where the light is good. Feed the plants with a high-potash liquid fertiliser every fortnight from now on. You will harvest your fruits several weeks before outdoor plants begin to crop.

122

We planted 'Royal Sovereign' strawberries in October, with high hopes of picking some fruit in June. We harvested only the odd strawberry per plant. Why?

By October the soil is getting cold, and consequently your plants no doubt made little root before winter. Next time, plant before the end of August; when the plants will have time to make not only strong root systems but also strong crowns to house the overwintering embryo fruit-blossom trusses. 'Royal Sovereign' needs the best possible treatment, so make sure that the ground is well prepared with some good compost underneath.

123

We are able to get clean straw for nothing, but a neighbour tells us that it would be better to use plastic sheeting to prevent soil splashing up on the fruit. Which is the better material for the job?

Clean straw is the traditional material, spread out around the plants to protect the fruits. Plastic sheeting has the advantage of absorbing heat and controlling weed growth, in addition to keeping the strawberries clean in wet weather. It is also easier to remove and store than straw, which should be burnt after use.

124

Three years ago we bought a plastic strawberry barrel and planted it up with some well-rooted 'Cambridge Favourite' plants. Only the plants at the top survived; and now it has happened again. Advice, please.

The problem with growing strawberries in barrels is unequal distribution of the water: the plants at the top are all right, but those lower down may be either too dry or too wet; in addition, the soil lower down tends to become compacted. A length of plastic drainpipe drilled with holes can be pushed down the centre of the barrel from top to bottom to make watering easier.

125

Our garden is always inclined to be wet. The soil is not bad, but underneath it is clay. We have tried growing strawberries, but in a wet winter we lose a lot of plants. Is there anything we can do about it?

Your clay subsoil is undoubtedly the cause of the problem. It is

preventing good drainage, with the result that stagnant water is killing the roots. Improved drainage would be the answer, but elaborate schemes are not always possible in a small garden. Try growing on the top of raised ridges—a method frequently used in high-rainfall areas and on heavy clay soils. You may also cure the problem if you break up the clay with a spade and add lots of sand and grit.

126

We have gone to a lot of expense in covering our strawberry bed with a permanent fruit cage. There are no holes in the netting, but we still find birds inside the cage from time to time. Have you any ideas on the subject?

Young blackbirds have a habit of scratching a way in *under* the netting, and once inside they do a lot of damage. To keep them out make sure that the bottom of the netting is buried at least 150 mm (6 in) below ground, curved outwards and pegged down.

127

Last year we covered a row of strawberries with large plastic cloches, hoping for protection against a possible late spring frost. It came—and most of the blossoms were frozen. Can you explain why?

Plastic-covered cloches provide protection from cold winds, but when the night temperatures fall rapidly, those under plastic are sometimes lower than the ground temperatures *outside* the cloches. Additionally, the flower trusses would probably be touching the plastic. A safe precaution would be to cover the cloches with hessian or similar material.

128

Our garden is in a frost pocket, and more often than not our early strawberry flowers suffer from black eyes; consequently we lose a lot of fruit. We have tried putting straw down before blossoming starts but this has not improved matters. What can we do?

In a situation such as yours strawing-down should be delayed until the fruit starts to swell. Once the ground is straw-covered it cannot absorb and store as much heat during the day, with the result that the night temperature around the open blossom is likely to be lower. Try protecting the plants with glass-covered cloches.

129

We have always understood that strawberries do best on soils with a pH slightly below 7. Our well-drained medium-type soil is, according to our tests, pH 6.5. Would a little lime be beneficial?

Your well-drained medium loam with pH 6.5 (*see* 739) should be

fine, but there is an additional question: is the calcium in the soil *available* to the plants? Lack of colour in the foliage often indicates a low availability of calcium, so if the foliage colour is poor make a light application of garden lime.

130

Our 'Cambridge Favourite' strawberry plants still look healthy after two seasons cropping. Would you advise hanging on to them for another year?

'Cambridge Favourite' is one of the most vigorous varieties, but I would expect the fruit to be on the small side in the third year. However, as your plants are still in good health the yield would justify keeping them for another season.

131

For the last 10 years we have been taking runners from our own strawberry plants (variety unknown), but now for some reason our new bed is not doing well, in spite of the usual careful preparation of the ground. Can you help?

All strawberries grown for cropping sooner or later degenerate, usually owing to viruses invading the stock. This has no doubt happened in your case. Start again with plants covered by a Ministry of Agriculture health certificate—but get rid of your diseased plants first by burning them.

132

As it is possible now to buy strawberry plants all the year round, we bought some recently in small netted blocks. The soil was dry at the time and several plants have not survived in spite of regular watering. Do they need to be grown on into larger plants before planting out?

I have found it is best to pot them on into 88 mm (3½ in) pots using a peat-based potting compost, and I remove the small nets before potting on (even though some manufacturers state that the nets can be left intact). After two or three weeks of intensive care the plants begin to look much better and have developed larger and more efficient root systems, which cut out the risks of losses.

Gooseberries

133

We have two gooseberry bushes which are now very old, and we would like to plant some new ones. Which variety would you recommend for dessert rather than pie fruit?

The first choice on most soils would be 'Whinham's Industry'. It is a vigorous grower and a reliable cropper, with dark red berries that are full of flavour and juice when

ripe. 'Leveller', with its much larger yellow-green berries, would do well on really fertile soil. Another large yellowish-green gooseberry with good flavour is 'Whitesmith'.

134

Our gooseberry bushes are difficult and painful to pick. Is it possible to grow them, like trees, on short trunks rather than as prickly shrubs?

Gooseberries can be bought on what is called a 'leg'. The longer the leg the more space between the bottom branches and the ground. Why not grow your own long-legged bushes by taking strong 450-600 mm (18-24 in) cuttings of young wood in the autumn? Remove with a sharp knife all the buds except three or four at the top; then make a slit in the soil with a spade and insert the cutting with at least half its length below ground; firm around the cutting. They will be ready for transplanting the next autumn on a leg at least 300 mm (12 in) long.

135

In our district sparrows are a problem. Early in the season they attack the gooseberry buds, leaving far more on the ground than they eat. What is the practical, inexpensive answer?

Gooseberry buds start to move soon after Christmas, and that's the time to do any pruning necessary, not before. Immediately after pruning, cover the bushes with netting; but make sure that it is held well clear of all branches, otherwise the sparrows will sit on the netting and peck out the buds they can reach.

136

My gooseberries did well to start with, but now the growth is poor. The leaves are small and most have brown margins. What is wrong?

The small leaves with brownish margins indicate that the plants are short of potash, and until this deficiency is corrected growth and cropping is likely to be poor. Make a start by applying 65 g/m² (2 oz/sq yd) of sulphate of potash around the bushes. In the future give them a Growmore fertiliser feed every February. It may be two years before the foliage is completely normal.

137

I have read with interest about cordon gooseberries. Are they difficult to grow, and how many years could I expect to crop them?

Cordon gooseberries are very easy to grow and take up little space. You must start with one-year-old plants with good strong leaders. Plant them sloping at an angle of 45 degrees, towards the north if possible; canes will be needed for supports. Each autumn prune back

the laterals to within 75 mm (3 in) of the main stem. With care and feeding there is no reason why cordons should not crop well for 10 years or more.

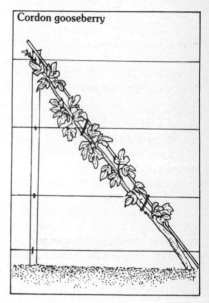

Cordon gooseberry

Currants

138

I find it difficult to understand why the pruning of redcurrants and blackcurrants is so different?

Redcurrants fruit on old wood, whereas blackcurrants fruit on last season's growth. The best results are obtained with redcurrants if the pruning is restricted to the removal of the weaker branches and any necessary thinning out. Blackcurrants, however, crop best when, immediately after fruiting, as much as possible of the old fruiting wood is removed without sacrificing the strongest young growths.

139

We have recently seen advertisements offering two- and three-year-old blackcurrant bushes for sale. Which would you advise to buy?

In the case of blackcurrants it would be better to plant one-year-old bushes; they would have more vigour than either two- or three-year-olds. Whatever its age, it is advisable to prune a newly planted blackcurrant bush hard—almost to the ground. The time to do this is early in March. It is this pruning that ensures production of strong new wood for fruiting the following season.

140

Our main interest in growing blackcurrants is for their Vitamin C content—although we enjoy them cooked and like the jam, too. Which variety would you suggest we grow?

As with other fruits, there are varietal differences, and it is generally accepted that 'Baldwin' is the blackcurrant with the highest Vitamin C content. This is

fortunate as it is a compact grower well suited to garden culture. It is a proven cropper and it flowers late, so it has a better chance than most varieties of escaping the spring frosts. The fact that it also ripens late may not be important if it is Vitamin C you want.

141

Our blackcurrants 'Boskoop Giant' are now eight years old and produce very little new growth, with the result that the fruiting wood is now at the tips of the branches. Each year we have mulched with peat around the bushes, so why don't they grow well?

Blackcurrants need more than peat: they are hungry feeders, and your bushes are evidently short of nitrogen—and maybe of potash and phosphates as well. When fruiting is finished this season, cut the old wood back hard to produce an open framework and stimulate new growth. Then in February apply Growmore fertiliser at the rate of 130 g/m^2 (4 oz/sq yd). Repeat this application each year.

142

Our redcurrant bushes always lose their leaf colour in July or August, but the ribs of the leaves always stay green. Are they suffering from some disease?

By July and August redcurrant bushes tend to lose lustre in their foliage, but the fact that the leaf ribs of yours remain green indicates a shortage of magnesium, one of the trace elements (see 756). Commercial Epsom salts applied in the spring at the rate of 65 g/m^2 (2 oz/sq yd) should improve matters.

143

We would like to grow white currants. Are they difficult? If not, what variety would you recommend for a small Middlesex garden?

White currants are not at all difficult, and they seem to have returned to favour in recent years. Like redcurrants they fruit on the old wood. 'White Versailles' is an excellent cropper—the berries are large, and the plant is certainly the best white variety for any district.

144

The new blackcurrant variety 'Jet' is said to be frost-resistant. Would you agree that it is the best one for us to plant in Yorkshire?

Its reputation for being frost-resistant may stem from the fact that it blossoms much later than other varieties, and so often escapes the frosts altogether. 'Jet' has a flavour of its own, very different from the traditional blackcurrant flavour. Include it as a trial, but remember that the more conventional 'Baldwin' always does well in the north.

Cherries

145

In a town garden is there any way in which we can grow cherries and defeat the birds at ripening time?

This is an age-old problem to which a fruit cage is the only real answer. The new 'Colt' rootstock has the reputation of being dwarfing, but cherries grown on it without additional treatment will soon be too tall to be housed in a fruit cage. I suggest that you plant maiden trees (one-year-olds) budded on the 'Colt' rootstock in a cage, or be prepared to cover the trees just before ripening time. In the first year the trees will make long young branches. In the autumn bend these down towards the ground and hold them in position with string and small stakes. Keep them tied for about a year. In time you will have low-growing umbrella-shaped trees that will be easy to cover with some form of netting.

146

On a visit to Switzerland we enjoyed the local cherry jam. Would it be possible to grow cherries for jam-making in a suburban garden?

The Swiss climate suits cherries—especially the black varieties they use for jam-making. 'Morello' cherries do well in this country and are self-fertile. When fully ripe they are dark red and acceptable for dessert dishes. For jam-making the fruit must not be over ripe. Like all cherries, 'Morello' needs protection from the birds.

Other fruits

147

We intend to plant two peach trees in our Sussex orchard 48 km (30 miles) from the coast. The summers are usually good. What variety should we buy?

In the south of England it is possible to grow peaches successfully as free-standing orchard trees. At your distance from the sea the risk of wind damage should be slight, and you certainly have one of the best climates for the job. Plant 'Peregrine', which is the best outdoor variety. For peach-tree enthusiasts in rather less favourable areas, 'Duke of York' and 'Hale's Early' should do reasonably well.

148

We have tried growing apricots of the variety 'Farmingdale' in our Essex garden. In spite of all our efforts, and the advantage of a 2.4 m (8 ft) high south-west-facing wall, we have not been successful. What do you suggest?

'Farmingdale' is a good variety, and your Essex climate is better than most for outdoor apricots. The problem with apricots is their time of flowering—February to early March. Between then and May, frost all too often destroys either the blossom or the young fruitlets. Nightly covering with old lace curtains could provide the necessary protection.

149

We would like to grow a grapevine in our 3.7 × 2.4 m (12 × 8 ft) greenhouse, which is unheated but in a good sunny position. Is it practical, and if so what variety would you recommend?

It is practical provided you plant the vine in the centre of the border on the *less* sunny side of the greenhouse. The most reliable variety is 'Black Hamburgh'. Do not be tempted to crop it until the third year. Remember that it will be growing in a small space, so it will be essential to keep up to date with the trimming. A book on the subject would help.

150

We have tried without much success to grow melons in a cold greenhouse, which is a 3 × 2.4 m (10 × 8 ft) cedarwood model. We raise our own plants of the 'Ogen' variety from seed. Can you suggest where we are going wrong?

Melons do best when grown on a mound of old turf. Make the mound during the winter, with all the grass turned inwards. 'Ogen' needs fairly hot weather so try 'Sweetheart', an F_1 hybrid, and be ready to plant out not later than mid-May. Train the plants on single stems up canes, and pinch out the side shoots two leaves beyond each set female flower. Pollination of the female flowers is essential. This can be done by hand, or by the bees if you leave the greenhouse door open on warm days. Feed your plants weekly with a liquid tomato fertiliser.

151

We very much want to grow our own green figs, but we have no space for a greenhouse. The best we can offer is a south-west-facing wall in our London suburban garden. What are our chances?

Fairly good if you start with a pot-grown 'Brown Turkey' fig, the best outdoor variety. Restriction of root growth is essential otherwise the plant will soon become rampant. Sink a 182-litre (40-gallon) drum into the ground and plant in that, making sure that there are large drainage holes in the bottom. The old practice of putting in a barrier of well-beaten chalk or lime rubble 1 m (3¼ ft) below the soil surface is an alternative method and gives less problems than a container while keeping growth in check.

Cane fruits

152

We have got an 'Oregon Thornless' blackberry which for three years has fruited well but which now is a mass of tangled growth. What should we do with it?

Like all blackberries the 'Oregon Thornless' throws up long and strong new growths each year. It is these that bear the fruit the following season. When fruit-picking has finished, start clearing away the old canes. As yours are tangled up it is a job to do carefully and a bit at a time. Avoid damaging the new young canes— you will need at least six of the strongest for tying in to the support wires.

153

Instead of swelling and ripening, many of our 'Malling Promise' raspberries shrivel and dry up. We have given them good treatment, with always plenty of compost as a mulch after the winter digging. What more can we do?

You must avoid cultivating the soil anywhere near the plants in future. Raspberries are surface-rooting, and the roots spread out quite a long way. If these are broken the plants are unable to cope with the extra stress at fruiting time. Restrict your cultivations to the use of a Dutch hoe, then your mulching will work wonders.

154

We are disappointed with our 'Malling Admiral' raspberries: the berries are wonderful to look at but they have little or no flavour. Is there anything we can do to improve them?

It is often suggested that an application of sulphate of potash will enhance fruit flavour—but that is true only if the variety has some natural flavour of its own. Unfortunately, 'Malling Admiral' has little flavour compared with, say, 'Malling Jewel' or 'Malling Promise'. Without doubt, 'Malling Jewel' is still the best raspberry for flavour.

155

In February we planted a row of 'Malling Promise' canes. They grew fairly well, but in July the crop was very disappointing and now the new growth is inclined to be weak. Would a fertiliser feed help?

'Malling Promise' canes (and any other summer-fruiting raspberry) planted in February should have been cut down to 100 mm (4 in) in March. This treatment encourages strong root systems and new cane growth for fruiting the following season. Failure to do this has left your new canes weak. Cut all

growth down next March. You will lose a season's cropping but the sacrifice will be worthwhile in the long run. Make an application of Growmore fertiliser next spring.

156

We have a south-east-facing fence which is 12 m (40 ft) long and about 1.8 m (6 ft) high. Would it be suitable for growing loganberries, and if so how many should be planted?

Loganberries trained either on or in front of the fence should do well. Two plants would be sufficient; this would allow each one 3 m (10 ft) of growing space on either side. You would need three strands of horizontal wiring spaced about 450 mm (18 in) apart, into which the canes could be tied.

157

I would like to put raspberries on the bench in the local show, and if possible win a prize with them. What is the best variety for this purpose?

The most beautiful looking raspberry is 'Malling Delight'. Well-grown fruits of this variety could win you a first at any show. They are nearly as large as loganberries, but sadly lack that really good raspberry flavour. Plant only a few canes of 'Malling Delight', and fill the rest of the row with a good-flavoured variety such as 'Malling Jewel'.

158

Would you recommend cutting down the canes of my autumn-fruiting raspberries immediately after harvesting?

The short answer is 'no'. Fruiting usually finishes towards the end of October, and that is the time to tidy up by removing any broken or damaged canes. The rest of the pruning should be done early in March, when all the canes can be cut down almost to ground level. In July remove all weak growth, so that only strong canes are left for fruiting in August and September.

159

We plan to plant a few autumn-fruiting raspberries and would appreciate your advice on suitable varieties.

At present there are only four suitable autumn varieties, as follows. 'Zeva' is the easiest to manage, and its canes are strong enough to stand without support; it produces the largest berries, and its flavour is good. 'September' always requires thinning early in the season, and even the strongest canes need support; its medium-sized berries have an excellent flavour. 'Heritage' berries are small and their flavour is only fair, but the fruit is firm and very suitable for freezing. 'Fall Gold', true to its name, produces golden raspberries of excellent flavour, but it is inclined to be a poor cropper and is subject to mildew on its fruit.

160

We are puzzled (but relieved!) that the blackbirds are not interested in our September raspberries—although they will strip our row of 'Malling Promise' unless it is netted. Can you explain this?

This has surprised many gardeners. Apparently when blackbirds are given the opportunity, they are selective feeders; in the autumn they seem to prefer, if available, the fruits of the hedgerows to our cultivated fruits. Another reason may be that the damage in summer is done mainly by fledglings, which have grown up by autumn.

161

I have seen advertisements for Japanese wineberries. Before ordering any I would like to know whether or not they are a proposition for a garden where space is at a premium.

Japanese wineberries require a lot of space, plus posts and wires for supporting the fruiting canes. Compared with other cane fruits the crop yields are only moderate. The berries are a very attractive bright red, are carried in fairly large trusses, and their flavour is unique, if slightly acid. The colourful canes are extremely prickly, and die-back appears to be a frequent problem. Nevertheless the plants are, I think, worth experimenting with for those who have space to spare.

General

162

The gardening experts tell us to spread the roots out when we plant fruit trees. Last spring we bought two apple trees in containers and did just that—and yet a little while later they both died. Why?

The advice you mention applies to trees lifted directly from the nursery and planted during the dormant season (November to March). Container-grown trees can be planted at any time during the year, but by spreading out the roots and thereby removing the nutrient-rich compost in which they had been grown, you gave the trees little chance of surviving at a time when they should have been in full growth.

163

I have tried growing a 'Brown Turkey' fig outdoors without much success. The plant produces plenty of growth but few ripe figs. Now I have a plant in its third year in a 300 mm (12 in) pot. Its growth is controlled, but the figs drop before they are full size. Why?

After three years in a 300 mm (12 in) pot it must be well and truly pot-bound. To a certain extent this is desirable, but now it should be put into a somewhat larger container so that you can feed and water it adequately. Lacking sufficient water means that the compost has dried out, and that has caused the figs to drop before they were mature.

164

Fertilisers are expensive and we want to get the fullest value from them. What is the best time of year to apply them to apple and pear trees?

Late February or early March is undoubtedly the best time. By then the fruit buds are beginning to swell; the soil is still moist, and so the first rain carries the fertilisers down to within reach of the roots, and the response within the tree is immediate. If applied later in the season, unless they were thoroughly watered in, the fertilisers might well stay above the reach of the roots for a long time.

165

Four years ago we planted a 'Black Hamburgh' grapevine in our 3.7 × 2.4 m (12 × 8 ft) greenhouse. We managed all right at the start and had some fruit last year, but now we are faced with masses of growth and practically no sign of fruit. How do we tame it?

Most crucially, do *not* cut into any old wood: if you do the wound may bleed for the whole of the season. Thin out the new growth by taking out all the sub-laterals (subsidiary sideshoots) and shortening the laterals somewhat. During the growing season take off all the sub-laterals regularly. In the autumn, when the vine is completely dormant, prune all the laterals back to within two buds of the main stem (the rod). In the spring select the laterals with flower trusses and stop these laterals at two leaves beyond the blooms; and subsequently rub out all secondary lateral growth.

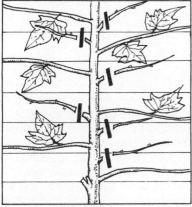
Removing sub-laterals

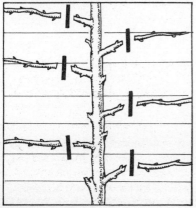
Autumn pruning

166

We are advised to plant cordon fruits at an angle of 45 degrees. This seems strange as trees and bushes grow naturally upright. What is the reason?

By planting cordon fruits with their stems sloping at an angle of 45 degrees the upward sap flow slows down. This results in a higher ratio of fruit buds, with less emphasis on wood growth.

167

I have always had a desire to grow my own walnuts. Could you suggest a relatively quick-growing and cropping variety?

All walnuts are slow growers, and they usually take several years to establish themselves, especially in areas subject to spring frosts, which do a lot of damage to the young growth. Varieties such as 'Leeds Castle', 'Lady Irene', or 'Northdown Clawnut' are worth considering, but do not expect walnuts for at least 15 years.

168

It is all very well for the experts to talk about the risk of 'soil sickness' if you replant strawberries or raspberries in the same ground—but what else can one do in a fruit cage which cannot be moved?

Soil sickness is a real problem and crop rotation is the obvious answer, but you are right to say that this is difficult to arrange in a small fruit cage or when space is very limited. A compromise which can work is to site the replanting between the previous rows. During the preparations dig in a liberal amount of well-rotted compost or manure, and just prior to planting apply a dressing of fish, blood, and bone fertiliser.

169

Would you recommend foliar feeding for fruit as a complete alternative to soil-applied fertilisers?

No. Foliar feeding is useful and can greatly help plants under stress during the growing season; but it should be regarded as a first-aid treatment rather than the complete nutritional answer. It is mainly nitrogen which is easily absorbed by the leaves: potash and phosphates are not. Start with a balanced fertiliser such as Growmore in the spring, which you will find is not only better but also cheaper than a foliar feed.

170

When I was young my mother used to make quince jelly, which had a wonderful flavour. Is it possible to buy a quince tree, and if so how long would I have to wait for a crop large enough for making jelly?

Much depends on where you live. Quinces do best in the southern half of the country, and they dislike

cold winds during the growing season. On a well-drained soil a one- or two-year-old tree would take about three years to settle down before fruiting. The secret of making good jelly is to use fully ripe fruit, so do not start picking until late October. 'Vranja' is a good self-fertile variety.

171

I have just moved into a house with a very neglected garden full of couch-grass and other vigorous weeds. I want to grow strawberries and other soft fruits, but can the site be cleared without resorting to weedkillers?

Yes, but it would be advisable to devote a whole season to the job. The most effective method would be winter-digging one spade deep before Christmas, turning the whole lot in in order to deny the couch-grass above-ground growth. Follow this with regular and persistant surface cultivations from early spring onwards, so that at no time are the weeds allowed to grow above ground level. Denied their normal growth the weed roots will soon die.

If you *must* use a chemical weedkiller, a dalapon-based herbicide should be effective. Apply it in diluted form over the whole affected area, and then dig in the couch-grass.

172

Although our garden is not shaded by trees, it gets very little sunshine. Would it be possible for us to plant fruit trees with any chance of success?

It would not be wise to plant either apples or pears: they would grow but the cropping prospects would be poor. However, a 'Victoria' plum or a 'Morello' cherry would tolerate the conditions. Both these varieties are self-fertile, so will fruit without the need for another pollinator. In addition, both are suitable for training as fan trees on a wall or fence.

173

We have just finished building a new house on a sloping site and are planning a terraced garden, including a site for a fruit cage to house strawberries and raspberries. The most convenient spot for the fruit cage would be at the bottom end but a friend has advised us against it. Why?

Cold air, like water, flows downhill; consequently, when a spring frost did occur, the blossom on your strawberries would be at great risk at the lower end of the garden. Take your friend's advice, and site the fruit cage on the high ground.

174

I have been in the habit of summer-pruning our apples and pears in July, after which we get a lot of soft growth. Why?

July is usually too early for summer pruning. If done at that time there is a risk of some of the dormant fruit buds breaking into growth. When this happens the prospects for the following years crop are reduced. If you do your summer pruning in August it has the desired effect of swelling the fruit and leaf buds without causing them to break into growth.

175

We are very pleased with the design of our soft-fruit cage, but we have come up against two problems: first, how do we get rid of weeds at the base of the netting; and second, how do we eliminate the risk of snow damage?

Unless dealt with, weeds soon build up; but to avoid the job of lifting up the netting to get them all through the growing season, apply one of the herbicides containing glyphosate. This is a simple, effective, once-a-season operation.

As far as snow damage is concerned, your best bet is, at the end of October, to roll the top netting from both ends of the cage to the centre rod and tie it firmly; leave it there until May, when the risk of snow has past.

Janet Browne

Gardening writer and consultant; author or co-author of nine books on gardening topics; Horticultural Correspondent of *The Times*.

Flowers

Flower types

176

Can you explain exactly what hardy annuals are?

Hardy annuals are plants that grow from seed, flower, and then die in one growing season, usually between spring and late autumn. They are referred to as hardy because they can be sown directly out-of-doors in the positions in which they are to flower. There are many hardy annuals listed in seed catalogues; they are very useful for making colourful summer beds and borders and for filling spaces among perennial (longer living) plants, such as shrubs.

177

What is the difference between a hardy annual and a half-hardy annual?

Hardy annuals can spend their entire life out-of-doors, but the half-hardy annuals will not germinate from seed in cold conditions. The latter, therefore, must be raised by sowing the seed in warm conditions (in a greenhouse, frame, or the home) and then gradually hardening them off (see 28) as young plants before they are set outdoors in their flowering positions in bed or border. Many of the most popular bedding plants are half-hardy annuals.

178

What do seed catalogues mean by the term 'biennial'?

Biennial plants are those that are raised from seed in one year for flowering the next. As most are hardy and are bedding plants, the seeds are sown outdoors during the first summer in a seedbed. The young plants are set in their flowering positions in autumn or the following spring, and after they have finished blooming in the autumn they are discarded. Some biennials, such as poppies (*Papaver*), honesty (*Lunaria*) and forget-me-not (*Myosotis*), will often seed themselves.

179

What are half-hardy perennials and how should they be looked after?

A half-hardy herbaceous perennial plant is one that will not stand cold conditions and needs some protection during the winter. Most of them are, in fact, treated as summer bedding plants. Typical garden flowers of this type are the pelargoniums (often wrongly called geraniums) and most florist's chrysanthemums, which need to be dug up and kept in a frost-free place during the winter. Certain tuberous plants, such as dahlias and tuberous begonias, also require the same treatment.

Other herbaceous plants of doubtful hardiness in very exposed gardens can be protected *in situ* during the winter by covering them with straw or bracken held in place with twigs or wire netting.

Bear in mind that some plants are commonly termed hardy in mild areas, while these same plants will succumb to winter conditions in other, colder areas.

180

How does an herbaceous perennial differ from other perennials?

All plants that live for a long time, in the right climatic conditions, are called perennials. They include trees and shrubs as well as herbaceous perennials (sometimes known as hardy perennials). Trees and shrubs have woody stems, whereas herbaceous perennials do not. Most of the latter die down at the end of their flowering period, new top growth and flowers appearing the following season. The length of life of herbaceous perennials in the flower garden can vary from a few seasons to many years.

181

I often see the term 'bulbous plants' when reading about flowering plants. What does this mean?

Bulbous plants are those with fleshy roots, stems, or underground leaves which act as food-storage organs and from which the above-ground stems, leaves, and flowers arise. They are

divided into four groups: bulbs, corms, rhizomes, and tubers. The groups are botanically different and in some cases require different growing techniques. (*See* Bulbs, 489-579, for bulbs and corms.)

182

What is a rhizome and how should it be looked after?

A rhizome is a horizontally growing, fleshy, swollen stem that grows at the surface of the soil or 'creeps' underground. The most common hardy rhizomatous plants are the flag (border) iris and the lily-of-the-valley (*Convallaria*). Rhizomes produce the plant's top growth from their upper portion and the roots from their base. The plants are easily propagated in autumn by lifting the rhizomes and cutting them into sections, so that each piece has buds on the upper surface and roots on the basal part. As regards conditions, lilies-of-the-valley grow in moist soil in partial shade, while irises usually prefer a drier, more sunny position.

183

When people talk about dahlia tubers are they referring to those unusually thick roots?

Yes, those roots are correctly called root tubers. They are fleshy food organs which provide foods for the stems, leaves, and flowers from upper surface 'buds'. They also produce roots below to produce more food in order to create new tubers. Dahlia tubers are the ideal means of raising new plants each year, as they are easily divided; in doing this you must make sure that each tuber has at least one shoot bud attached to it. Because dahlias are half-hardy plants, they must be kept in a frost-free place during the winter and propagated in the spring.

Other common tuberous flowering plants are winter aconite (*Eranthis*), tuberous anemone, day lily (*Hemerocallis*), and herbaceous peony (*Paeonia*).

Bedding plants

184

What is a bedding plant?

It is any type of flowering plant that is set out in a bed or border to give a few months' display of colour. Bedding plants are used mainly in summer and in spring. They can either be planted in beds on their own or used to fill gaps among herbaceous and other plants. After flowering, they are lifted and destroyed (if they are biennials) or given winter protection (if they are half-hardy perennials, such as pelargoniums or chrysanthemums).

185

How should I prepare the soil for bedding plants?

If the soil is in good condition, fork it over lightly and, to keep the surface level, rake it in several directions; this will also give it a good crumbly structure. Add a general-purpose fertiliser such as Growmore during forking. If the soil is poor or heavy, you will also need to add organic matter, such as well-rotted manure, peat, shredded bark, or compost, before setting out spring bedding plants. Remove all weeds, by hand or by hoeing.

186

How do I set out bedding plants?

First make sure the soil is fairly moist around the roots of the plants to be moved. If it is not, water and leave for a few hours. Also ensure the soil in the bed or border is neither too wet to work nor too dry. Start by planting the back (or the middle if it is an island bed), and stand on a board laid across it to prevent the soil compacting too much.

Bedding plants in boxes should have their roots 'teased' apart by gently and carefully pulling them away from each other; those in clay or plastic pots must have the pots removed (best done with rigid pots by giving them a firm tap on the base with the trowel handle). Bedding plants in peat pots can be planted as they are, but make sure that the pots are quite sodden first. Make a planting hole of the correct depth with the trowel and set the plant in it, making sure the roots are not cramped or twisted. Firm the soil down with the hands or trowel handle. The depth of planting should be to the same depth as the original soil mark on the stem; plant apart to the distance recommended on the seed packet. Hoe carefully among the plants to remove footprints, and then spray them with water. Water regularly, night or morning, until the plants are established and growing strongly.

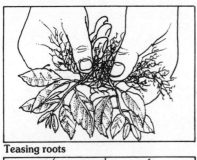
Teasing roots

Plant gently

Remove footprints

187

Can you suggest some half-hardy biennial and perennial plants for my summer bedding scheme?

For summer bedding, easily grown half-hardy biennials, or plants treated as such, include fibrous-rooted begonias (*B. semperflorens*), sweet william (*Dianthus barbatus*), and foxglove (*Digitalis purpurea*). Useful half-hardy perennials include certain chrysanthemums (especially *C. indicum* and *C. morifolium* varieties), various pelargoniums (*Pelargonium* × *hortorum*, *P.* × *domesticum*, and *P. peltatum* varieties), and varieties of *Canna*.

188

Could you suggest some good half-hardy annuals for brightening up my summer flower beds?

Seed catalogues list a large number of half-hardy annuals from which you should be able to meet your needs. Particularly popular are the many varieties of asters, antirrhinums, Prince of Wales' feathers (*Celosia cristata 'Pyramidalis'*), cosmea (*Cosmos*), pinks (*Dianthus*), busy-lizzie (*Impatiens*), Californian poppies (*Eschscholzia californica*), godetias, lobelias, marigolds, nemesias, tobacco plant (*Nicotiana*), petunias, salvias, stocks (*Matthiola*), tagetes, zinnias, and butterfly-flower (*Schizanthus*).

189

I have noticed that many summer bedding plants are on sale in the shops in April. Surely this is too early to plant them in the open?

In all except the most sheltered gardens in the country, the answer is 'yes'. Most summer bedding plants should not be planted out until all danger of frost is past, and this can be as late as the end of May or even early June. It is not advisable to buy such shop plants until you are nearly ready to plant them; otherwise, they will get straggly and root-bound in their containers, even if they are protected against frost and properly hardened off.

190

What should I do with my bedding geraniums after they have finished flowering in the autumn?

Bedding geraniums (*Pelargonium*) should be dug up in the autumn and planted in compost in pots or boxes. Keep the plants in a cool, well-lighted, not too warm place, and water them very occasionally to prevent the compost from drying out completely.

191

How can I increase my half-hardy pelargoniums?

If you have a good stock of healthy plants, the easiest way to increase

pelargoniums is by cuttings taken from over-wintered plants in March. With a sharp knife, cut off 75 mm (3 in) long shoot tips just below a node (leaf joint); remove all but the topmost pair of leaves and insert the cuttings to half their depth in small pots of seed compost. Water in the cuttings and keep them in a moderately warm, brightly lit place, such as a window-sill, until they have rooted. When they are growing well, transplant them to larger pots containing a stronger compost. Gradually harden them off (*see* 28) before planting them where they are to flower in May.

192

How can I tell when my cuttings of pelargoniums have rooted?

There are two ways. First, if it is obvious that new top growth is being produced and, second, by very gently pulling the cutting upwards with the fingers; if it moves freely it has not rooted and should be firmed back carefully, but if it remains firm, it has rooted.

193

My seed catalogues list hybrid geranium (*Pelargonium*) seeds. Are these easy to grow?

The pelargoniums now listed include some excellent new hybrids. They are easy to raise from seed sown between December and March, but they do require a high germination temperature, about 18-21°C (65-70°F). This means that, to economise on heating costs, you would be well advised to use an electrically heated seed propagator (*see* 853). The techniques for seed sowing, growing-on, and so on are the same as for other seed-raised plants (*see* 860-77).

194

As dahlias are half-hardy plants, what should one do with them during the winter?

Dig up the dahlias after flowering, or following the first autumn frost, and cut back the top growth to about 150 mm (6 in). Place the tubers upside down for a few days in a cool place to allow any moisture from the stems to drain away. Then remove all the soil, cut off any diseased or damaged portions, and place the tubers, with their stems upright this time, in a shallow box of dry peat or sand, and keep them in a dry, frost-free place for the winter. For details of inducing growth the following spring, *see* 884.

195

How can I protect my cannas during the winter, and can I increase my stock of them?

Lift the cannas in autumn, dry them for a few days, cut the top growth down to 150 mm (6 in), and remove loose soil; then set them in boxes of slightly moist peat. Store in a frost-free place and keep the peat only just moist.

In early spring, place the fleshy roots (rhizomes) in a rich peaty soil in a warm place to start them into growth. As the shoots appear, increase the stock of plants by dividing the rhizomes, so that each piece has a new shoot and some roots. Pot them individually, and keep the temperature at about 13°C (55°F) until April. Gradually harden-off the cannas before planting out in late May.

196

What do I do with my half-hardy chrysanthemums after they have been used in summer bedding schemes?

Dig up the plants and cut the top growth back to about 150 mm (6 in). Place the chrysanthemum stools (rootstocks) into a box of soil compost and store them in a cool but frost-free place for the winter months. Water the soil occasionally to keep it just moist. Label each stool with the name of the variety if you have mixed them in the boxes.

197

When and how should my bedding chrysanthemums be propagated?

Start the over-wintered chrysanthemum stools into growth in a warm greenhouse in early spring, or in a cold frame in late spring. This will encourage production of new young shoots.

When these are about 50 mm (2 in) long, cut them off the plant with a very sharp knife, as close to the stool as possible. Remove any leaves at the base of the cuttings, then insert them in boxes of a potting compost, about 50 mm (2 in) apart each way. Firm them in with the fingers and sprinkle them lightly with water. Keep them warm and in a shady place until new growth indicates that the cuttings have rooted. Transplant them to pots or other boxes as they grow larger, and then gradually harden them off for planting out in May.

198

How can I produce my own half-hardy annual bedding plants for summer?

Sow half-hardy annual seeds in boxes of seed compost in a warm place, such as a greenhouse, propagating unit, or the home, from January to March. When they are large enough to handle they are pricked off (transplanted) into boxes of a stronger soil compost, and kept growing in warm conditions until April. They are then hardened off gradually, until ready for planting out in May.

199

What is the best way to harden-off half-hardy plants raised from seeds or cuttings?

Half-hardy plants need to be hardened off very slowly from the temperature in which they were raised to the cooler atmosphere in which they are to be grown outdoors. This is best done by gradually reducing the heat in the place where they are started into growth, or by moving them to a cooler place in the greenhouse or in your home.

After a week or two, place them in a cold frame with the light (lid) closed for the first few days; alternatively, use a coldish room in the house. Then open the light of the frame, making sure that the plants do not suffer any chilling draught; if the plants have been raised in the home, stand them outdoors under cloches in a sheltered place during the day, but bring them indoors at night.

Finally leave the plants unprotected, but still in their containers, for 7-10 days before planting them in the ground.

200

How can I raise spring bedding plants, and when should the work be done?

Suitable plants for spring bedding include forget-me-not (*Myosotis*), double daisies (*Bellis perennis*), wallflowers (*Cheiranthus*), aubrietas, and primroses and polyanthus (*Primula*), as well as many bulbous plants such as daffodils, tulips, hyacinths, crocuses, and snowdrops (all of which are dealt with in the Bulbs chapter, 489-579).

The double daisies, wallflowers,

forget-me-nots, and aubrietas are raised from seed sown in a seed bed in early summer. Primroses and polyanthus are best sown in a heated greenhouse or warm room in late winter or in a cold frame in April or May.

The plants are put into the prepared bed or border in the autumn. The tallest-growing ones should be at the back, and the heights gradually reduced to the lowest-growing plants at the front. Thereafter, of course, you will have to wait for several months before the plants break into flowering colour the following spring.

201

Can you explain what a seed bed is and how it is prepared?

A seed bed is a piece of ground that is kept solely for raising hardy plants from seed. It should if possible be sited in a sheltered position which gets plenty of light but not too much direct sun. To prepare it, fork the ground over, dig in some humus-forming material such as well-rotted manure, compost, shredded bark, or peat, and add a general-purpose fertiliser. Then tread it down, and finally rake it in at least two directions to break the soil down to a fine crumbly texture (tilth: *see* 720), so that the surface has no earth clods or large stones. This preparation is best done when the soil is neither too wet nor too dry but just moist, so that the particles bind together when squeezed.

202

How do I sow and look after seedlings in a seed bed?

Sow seed in rows 100-150 mm (4-6 in) apart. Put pegs at either end of where the row is to go, tie string tightly to the pegs so that it rests on the surface of the soil, and with the side of a hoe make a very shallow V-shaped drill (furrow) by drawing the hoe backwards, against the string to keep the drill in a straight line. Scatter the seeds very thinly in the drill and rake the soil back over them. Finally put in labels to show what seeds are sown where.

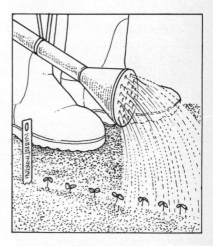

If the soil dries, water it thoroughly using a sprinkler or a watering can with a fine-rose sprinkle head. Remove any weeds to prevent competition with the young plants.

When the seedlings are 50-75 mm (2-3 in) tall they should

be thinned and transplanted. Ease the seedlings out of the ground with a hand fork and replant them in well-prepared soil 150-200 mm (6-8 in) apart. The best way to make a hole for the little plants is with a dibber or a hand trowel. Firm in the soil around each plant and water it thoroughly. Keep them watered every morning if the soil gets dry and until the plants are growing strongly again. There is no need to discard any seedlings unless they are diseased or damaged.

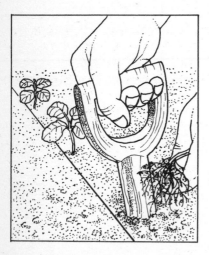

203

Could you describe the method of digging up spring bedding plants and setting them in the bed or border?

Use either a small garden fork or a hand fork to lift (dig up) the plants. Do this on a cool, preferably cloudy day, so that the roots do not dry out and the plants wilt. Move them to their new positions and get them planted as quickly as possible. Make the planting holes with a hand trowel, setting the plants to the intervals recommended on the seed packet and to the same depth as the soil mark visible on the stem. Firm the soil around the roots, and water in. Continue to water as necessary until the plants are established.

204

I am at present planning a bedding scheme. Do I really need to plot in detail on graph paper exactly what bedding plants and hardy annuals are to be placed where and at what planting distances?

It is certainly wise, if you are an inexperienced gardener, to draw a rough plan of the bed to be sown or planted so that a decision can be made as to what flowers to grow and how many of each type will be needed. It can also help you to create a harmonious colour scheme, and to arrange that when one group of plants is not in flower a neighbouring group is, so ensuring that your bed or border always has a focal point. In addition, if a formal 'carpet' effect of bedding plants of mainly low-growing subjects is to be created, any possible monotony can be spotted and relieved by a single or a group of taller-growing 'dot' (feature) plants.

Hardy annuals

205

Can you suggest some good hardy annuals to sow for summer colour?

It is always interesting to browse through seed catalogues and select some of the lesser-known hardy annuals. The following, however, are a few of the most deservedly popular: alyssum, anchusa, pot marigold (*Calendula officinalis*), candytuft (*Iberis*), clarkia, cornflower (*Centaurea cyanus*), hound's tongue (*Cynoglossum*), star-of-the-veldt (*Dimorphotheca aurantiaca*), viper's bugloss (*Echium lycopsis*), godetia, gypsophila, larkspur (*Delphinium annual*), mallow (*Lavatera trimestris*), poached-egg flower (*Limnanthes douglasii*), love-lies-bleeding (*Amaranthus caudatus*), night-scented stock (*Matthiola bicornis*), mignonette (*Reseda odorata*), nasturtium (*Tropaeolum majus*), love-in-a-mist (*Nigella damascena*), poppies (*Papaver*), annual scabious (*Scabiosa atropurpurea*), sunflower (*Helianthus annuus*), and sweet pea (*Lathyrus odoratus*).

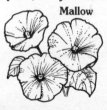
Mallow

Cornflower

206

Do I need to make any special preparation of the soil before sowing my hardy annuals?

It is desirable to fork over the soil to a depth of about 100 mm (4 in), adding some organic matter, such as compost, peat, shredded bark, or well-rotted manure. After this, tread down the soil and rake it in several directions to remove clods of earth and create a fine seed-bed type of tilth.

207

When is the correct time to sow hardy annuals?

This varies, depending on the species or variety, but in general hardy annuals are sown where they are to flower in April. In particularly warm parts of the country some of the hardiest annuals can be sown the previous autumn, and the resulting plants will flower earlier than if they had been spring-sown. The best advice, however, is to follow the instructions on the seed packets.

208

What is the best way to sow hardy annual flowers?

Once the ground is prepared, use a pointed stick to mark out on the soil the 'drift' areas each type of plant is to occupy. For the best effect, these areas should be irregular in shape and allowed to overlap. Broadcast the seeds by scattering them very thinly, or make shallow drills (as in a seed bed) within each 'drift' area and sow in these. Lightly rake the soil to cover the seeds. Be sure to label each 'drift' with the name and variety of the plant sown. When the plants are 25-50 mm (1-2 in) high, thin them to the recommended distance apart and firm the soil around the remaining seedlings.

As to general conditions, sow the seeds when the soil is moist— neither soaking wet nor dry. Water regularly and thoroughly, with a fine spray, until the seedlings are growing healthily. When thinning, remove any weeds, otherwise they will compete with your annuals.

209

Can I use thinnings of hardy annuals elswhere or must I discard them?

If they are replanted immediately these seedlings can certainly be used to fill gaps in other borders and beds. If you have no room, a neighbour may welcome them.

210

What sort of general maintenance do my annuals need while they are growing and flowering?

They should be watered thoroughly and regularly during periods of drought and it is obviously good practice to keep the bed weeded. It may also be necessary to stake the taller plants with canes, twigs, or proprietary plant supports, especially in very windy areas. Plants such as tall-growing sweet peas (*Lathyrus*) and sunflowers (*Helianthus*) should be tied to their supports. Another important job is to remove dead flower-heads (except from everlasting flowers or those grown for their decorative seed heads, such as poppies and grasses), to prevent seed forming and to encourage the plants to continue flowering freely over a long season.

Herbaceous perennials

211

What exactly is a herbaceous border, and how should it be planted?

Traditionally, a herbaceous border was at least 3 m (10 ft) wide and about 10 m (35 ft) long, usually backed by an evergreen hedge, and planted entirely with herbaceous perennials. As this is impractical today in most gardens, herbaceous borders tend to be much smaller and of irregular shape to give more interest. They are usually planted with clusters of each type of plant, in groups of three to five; the tallest are at the back and the lowest at the front. The clumps of plants are intermingled to a certain extent to give an informal effect.

The plants are selected to harmonise in terms of colour and give different times of flowering, so there is always something of interest in the border in the spring, summer, and autumn. Which herbaceous plants are selected from the huge number available is a matter of personal taste and colour harmonies. Plant breeders have recently introduced a wide range of low-growing varieties suitable for the smaller border.

212

How must I prepare the ground to make a new herbaceous border?

As your plants are likely to be in the ground for a long time, it pays to prepare the soil thoroughly. Remove all weeds, especially the perennial types with deep roots, by digging, hoeing, or with a suitable weedkiller. Then fork the soil to a depth of at least 150 mm (6 in), adding humus-forming matter such as well-rotted manure or compost, rotted bark, granulated peat, or hop manure. Lime may also be needed if the soil is very acid (peaty) or in generally very poor condition. It should be applied in autumn or spring, one month before planting or adding humus-forming matter, or two or three months after manuring (lime and manure must *never* be applied at the same time).

If possible, leave the freshly dug

soil for a couple of months to allow it to settle, then scatter a general-purpose fertiliser over it and rake the ground to give a reasonably crumbly surface suitable for planting.

213

Can you recommend a planting plan for my herbaceous border?

Using a sheet of graph paper draw on to it (to scale) the shape of the border. Then select your plants from a catalogue or book which not only describes the plants but also gives an indication of their height and spread. Allow for the plants to be grouped in clumps of three or five and draw a rough semi-circle on the plan for each clump, giving the plants the spacing they will ultimately require. The very tall plants will go at the back of the border (or centre if it is an island bed); the heights of the remaining subjects are gradually reduced until you are left with the low-growing edging plants.

If you use a set of colour crayons to draw the semi-circles, it will help to give you an idea of a colour scheme. Write into each semi-circle the name of the plant and its period of flowering, so that you can make sure that you will not be left with large non-flowering areas at any time. If you plan in this way, you will buy the right number of plants in the colours you like best and will be able to place them in the correct positions in the ground.

214

Are herbaceous plants fussy about whether the soil is acid or alkaline?

Nearly all herbaceous perennials grow well in most soils, provided they are neither very acid nor very alkaline. By manuring and liming regularly, the soil can usually be kept at a fairly neutral pH (*see* 739), while applications of fertiliser will supply the nutrients the plants need.

215

When is the best time to plant herbaceous plants, and how are they set out?

The best time is spring or autumn, although those grown in containers can be planted at any time of year provided they are kept well watered. If you buy by mail order, the nurseryman will send you the plants at the right time for planting, although the roots will probably have little or no soil on them. If you cannot get them planted on arrival, store them in a cool place in damp peat or put them in a trench in the garden. However, do try to plant them out as quickly as possible provided that the ground is workable. If the plants seem dry on arrival, soak the roots in water for 24 hours; if any are damaged in transit, let the nurseryman know immediately.

Planting is best done with a trowel. Set the plants in holes large enough to accommodate the roots without cramping them. Work from the back of the border (or centre of an island bed), spacing the plants to suit their final growing size and according to your planting plan. Always plant to the same depth as the soil mark on the stems. Hoe carefully to remove footmarks, and water in the plants with a thorough but gentle sprinkling. Do not forget to label each clump of plants.

As the border may look a little empty while the herbaceous perennials are maturing, fill the spaces temporarily with bulbs, bedding plants, or annuals to give summer colour—but be careful not to crowd out the perennials.

216

Is it better to buy herbaceous plants from a garden centre or (by mail-order) from a nursery?

The answer depends really on what you want. If you need an 'instant' border and are not too fussy about which particular species or varieties you grow, good well-established container-grown plants from a garden centre can be set out at any time during the season. The plants must be carefully and regularly watered if they are planted during the summer. This will get them established and encourage them to make new growth.

The advantage of buying by mail-order is that you generally have a much larger choice of plants, species, and varieties from which to choose, and can therefore create a more interesting final effect; many nurseries have made a name for themselves by specialising in a particular range of plants. The main disadvantage of mail-order is that you are generally confined to plants suitable for spring or autumn planting. There is generally little difference between the two methods of buying in terms of cost.

217

My garden is somewhat exposed to winds. How can I prevent the stems of my perennials from breaking?

It is always advisable, even in a sheltered garden, to stake tall or weak-growing plants. Single-stemmed plants, such as delphiniums, should each have a bamboo cane and be tied with twine at intervals as they grow. Less tall but floppy-growing plants can be supported with 'pea sticks' (tree and hedge trimmings) of different heights, so that the plants grow through the twigs and support themselves. Short-growing floppy plants will require only the twiggy top-growths of those pea-sticks.

Alternatively, a number of different kinds of proprietary plant supports are available, usually made of wire and often in various shapes for different plants. It is best to put the plant supports in position in spring and remove them in autumn.

If your garden is so exposed that these regular types of supports are inadequate, grow the lower-growing or dwarf varieties of tall plants; many have been introduced recently and are just as effective as their taller counterparts.

If it is at all possible, create windbreaks with fencing and hedges. This will not only help to protect your plants but make the garden a pleasanter place to sit in. If high winds are the norm, a fence should act as a filter rather than as a barrier. Not only is a solid fence likely to be blown down; it is also apt (like a wall) to set up turbulence on the lee-side, and so cause as much havoc in beds and borders as direct winds.

218

How can I get rid of the weeds in my new herbaceous border?

The real answer is to keep hoeing, because it is vital to prevent annual weeds from seeding. Deep-rooted perennial weeds, however, such as docks and dandelions, should have their entire roots taken out; a long-bladed knife is a good tool for this job. It is possible in theory to use a systemic weedkiller by painting the solution on to the weeds with a brush, but this is time-consuming and great care is needed to keep the chemical away from the cultivated plants.

Once the ground is clear of weeds, and when the soil is moist, apply a 50 mm (2 in) layer of mulch (see 706); this will help to suppress the weeds.

219

Is it necessary to water herbaceous-plant borders?

All plants benefit to a greater or lesser degree from artificial watering during extended dry periods, and herbaceous plants are no exception. Whatever method of applying the water is used—sprinkler, hose, or watering can—make a thorough job of it every few days if necessary, so that the water reaches a depth of 300 mm (12 in) for large plants and 150 mm (6 in) for smaller ones. Merely sprinkling the plants does more harm than good: if regularly practised it will encourage the parched roots to grow nearer the surface in search of moisture.

220

Do herbaceous perennials need dead-heading?

Yes: to keep the border looking tidy, to prevent plants wasting their energies on seed production, and to encourage them to flower again (unless, of course, you require the seeds for propagation or the seed heads for decoration).

Use secateurs, a sharp knife, finger and thumb, or a flower-gathering type of implement for dead-heading most types of plants; shears should be used on edging or ground-cover plants such as aubrieta, perennial alyssum, and similar mat-forming subjects whose heads are too small and too numerous to remove individually.

221

Should I feed the plants in my herbaceous border?

Yes: apply fertilisers at least twice a year—a general one in the spring and bonemeal in the autumn. Both should be applied at the rate recommended by the manufacturer, and then hoed or forked into the soil. Booster feeds of a liquid fertiliser are often beneficial during the growing season.

To keep the soil in good heart, fork in mulching materials or manure each autumn; apply lime if the soil is sour, badly drained, or very peaty.

222

My herbaceous border tends to look a mess in the autumn. What's the best way to tidy it up?

After the first autumn frosts, cut back the stems of all but evergreen or winter-flowering herbaceous plants to about 100 mm (4 in) above the ground. Remove, clean, and store plant supports. Remove all weeds, then lightly fork over the border to a depth of 100 mm (4 in) to loosen the soil and incorporate the early summer mulch. When doing this take care not to damage the plants' roots. Leave the soil surface rough. Ensure the plant labels are left in position. Manure or lime can be added (but *not* both at the same time) while you are forking and worked-in later.

223

I have read that it is necessary to fork over the herbaceous border in the spring. Why is this?

For the same reasons, in the main, that it should be forked over in the autumn: to aerate the top soil, to incorporate manure or lime, to remove footmarks after putting plant supports in position, to mix in a general fertiliser, and to remove weeds. After this, the ground is usually ready for mulching.

224

How (and when) should I increase my herbaceous perennials?

Most herbaceous plants can be increased by division in mild weather in autumn (after cutting back) or in early spring, when they are dormant (that is, not in active growth). Dig up the plants and, if they have a matted root system, pull this apart by hand, or split them by levering two garden forks back to back to break the clump into pieces. Replant the new outside pieces of root and discard the older inner portions.

If the roots are tuberous or rhizomatous—for instance, iris, solomon's seal (*Polygonatum*), bergenia, bergamot (*Monarda*), peony (*Paeonia*), day lily (*Hemerocallis*), or anemone—lift them in spring and cut them into sections with a sharp knife, so that each has growth buds and roots.

Herbaceous plants can also be increased by basal cuttings, tip cuttings, root cuttings, and some are grown from seed. Layering is sometimes used during the summer, especially for border carnations (*Dianthus*).

225

I have 'inherited' a very overgrown and weedy herbaceous border. What do you suggest I do to renovate it?

Regretfully, the only really practical answer is virtually to start from scratch. The border is probably best dealt with in sections. Dig up all the plants and weeds, get rid of the latter, divide the former if you want to keep them, fork the bed, adding compost, lime (if needed), and fertiliser, and then replant.

To keep herbaceous plants happy and in good health, this sort of operation should be undertaken about every three to five years and is well worth the effort involved.

226

Are there any herbaceous plants that flower during the winter?

Regrettably, very few. Four that *are* useful for this purpose, however, are: kaffir lily (*Schizostylis coccineum*), from September to November; stylosa iris (*Iris unguicularis*), from October to March, Christmas rose (*Helleborus niger*) from January to

February, and *Bergenia* 'Silver Light' from February to March. Putting cloches over the last three will encourage earlier flowering and protect the blooms from severe winter weather.

227

In my exposed garden I find that many of my favourite plants, such as bear's breeches (*Acanthus*), African lily (*Agapanthus*), Peruvian lily (*Alstroemeria*), red-hot poker (*Kniphofia*), penstemon, cape figwort (*Phygelius*), and kaffir lily (*Schizostylis*), rarely survive our cold winters. Can I protect them *in situ* or do they have to be lifted and kept in a frost-free place?

Such plants can usually be left in place in the ground provided they are protected with a 50-100 mm (2-4 in) covering of leaves, straw, or bracken from late autumn to mid- to late spring. Fix the protective material in place with twiggy sticks or pegged-down netting.

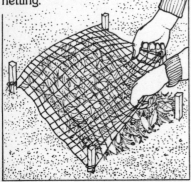

Window boxes & hanging baskets

228

How should I prepare and fill decorative stone containers into which I want to place bedding plants?

All containers, whether of wood or stone, should have 'crocks' (pieces of broken pots or irregular shaped stones) placed over the drainage holes to ensure free drainage. A layer of coarse peat mixed with charcoal should follow, if you really want to do the job properly; or you can go straight ahead and fill to the half-way mark with John Innes Potting compost No 2. Continue to fill up with the potting compost as you plant. If you are going to stand pots of plants in a large container, fill up the container around the pots with peat/charcoal mix instead of the potting compost.

229

How does one prepare and plant a hanging basket?

Stand the basket on a bucket or a large plant pot, and line it with moss (sphagnum moss if you can get it); suitable alternatives to moss include carpet underlay, black polythene, or special compressed peat liners. Make holes in the liner where necessary, and push the roots of the plants through from outside the basket. Then plant the centre of the basket, surrounding the roots with John Innes Potting compost No 2 as you go along. Water the basket thoroughly after planting and keep it in a warm, bright place for a few days. This procedure should be followed each time you replant the basket.

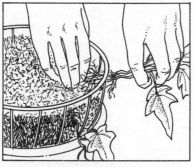

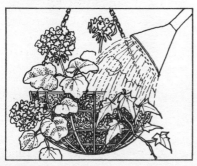

230

Can you suggest some suitable plants for hanging baskets, and tell me how to care for them once they are planted?

As hanging baskets are usually sited at or above eye level, try to include trailing plants as well as some central upright ones. Useful plants for this purpose are hardy and half-hardy bedding plants such as busy-lizzie (*Impatiens sultanii* varieties), pendulous begonias, ivy-leaved pelargoniums (*Pelargonium peltatum* varieties), wandering jew (*Zebrina pendula*), lobelia, catmint (*Nepeta*), bellflower (*Campanula isophylla*), petunias, tagetes, and verbena.

The plants will need watering regularly—even twice a day when it is very hot—and a fortnightly liquid feed will be helpful. Dead head as necessary to keep a successional display of blooms. Unfortunately, hanging baskets are not good containers in which to plant winter displays outdoors, as they tend to be buffeted by wind, snow, or driving rain.

231

What plants can I grow for an all-year-round effect in window boxes and other containers?

Dwarf conifers and ivies will grow well in window boxes and containers and will give permanent green or variegated foliage effects. To make the most of containers, however, you should plant them twice a year with spring and summer bedding plants (bulbs are also useful for spring colour). Any bedding plants that are not too tall can be used, as well as the trailing ones recommended for hanging baskets. When you change the plants, refresh the top 50 mm (2 in) of compost. Feed, water, and dead head regularly, as described above for hanging baskets.

Ornamental foliage plants

232

I would like to grow some ornamental grasses for their foliage and flowers. What kinds would you suggest?

As most ornamental grasses are evergreen (although their leaves may be of various shades of green, blue, yellow, or variegated) they are ideal plants for mixing with other perennial types to act as foils for bright colours; their flower heads are also much in demand with flower arrangers. Heights of decorative grasses vary from as low as 150 mm (6 in)—for example, the blue fescue (*Festuca glauca*)—to as tall as 2.7 m (9 ft) if you grow *Miscanthus sacchariflorus*, with its attractive grey-green leaves.

Other popular ornamental grasses include pampas grass (*Cortaderia richardii*), *Luzula*

nivea and *L. maxima variegatus*, feather grass (*Stipa gigantea*), and quaking grass (*Briza maxima*).

233

I would like to grow some ferns in the shady parts of my herbaceous border for their foliage effect. What are some interesting types?

Ferns are much more popular than they used to be for garden planting, and their fronds (leaves) vary in shape and colour quite considerably. A variety of interesting types to grow include the hardy maidenhair fern (*Adiantum pedatum*), hart's-tongue ferns (especially the unusual *Asplenium scolopendrium* 'Crispum'), several species of our native lady fern (*Athyrium filix-femina,* common polypody (*Polypodium vulgare* 'Pulcherrimum'), *Polystichum* species and varieties with different leaf forms, the ostrich-feather fern (*Matteuccia struthiopteris*), and the ever-adaptable male fern (*Dryopteris filix-mas*).

234

Bamboo canes are expensive to buy. Can I grow my own?

You *can* grow them for canes—but you will need a large garden and plenty of space for the plants. Bamboos are shrubby grasses and almost all grow more than 3 m (10 ft) tall. They are graceful, however, have attractive leaves, make good screens, and are generally easy to grow, although they prefer a reasonably moist soil and a site that is not too exposed. The most commonly grown are species of *Arundinaria*; the 600 mm (2 ft) high 'Shibataea Kumasasa' is an attractive small variety for borders. Bamboo canes are harvested in the autumn and dried in a cool place, either laid flat or hung from twine so that they dry straight.

Plants for a purpose

235

Are there any annual climbing flowers that I can grow to hide a temporary but unsightly shed?

Sweet peas (*Lathyrus*), climbing nasturtiums (*Tropaeolum*), cup-and-saucer vine (*Cobaea scandens*), and canary creeper (*Tropaeolum peregrinum*) are easily grown annuals suitable for such a purpose, as is the half-hardy morning glory (*Ipomoea purpurea*). You should give the plants something to climb up, such as trellis, horizontal wires, or netting. These plants are particularly attractive for decorating walls, pillars, and pergolas, especially where a permanent plant would impede house decoration and maintenance.

236

I have a long narrow border, about 450 mm (18 in) by 4.5 m (15 ft), along the side of my driveway. What permanent plants do you suggest I grow that would make it colourful during the summer but would allow the car door to be fully opened?

A useful selection of low-growing perennials for this purpose would include aubrieta, dwarf michaelmas daisies (perennial asters), *Primula denticulata* hybrids, lily-of-the-valley (*Convallaria majalis*), *Veronica gentianoides, Geum borisii*, yarrow (such as *Achillea* 'Moonshine'), montbretia (*Crocosmia* × *crocosmiiflora*), *Anemone* 'Bressingham Glow', doronicums, species and hybrids of pinks (*Dianthus*), dwarf phlox, pansies, violas, and violets (all *Viola* species and hybrids), candytuft (such as *Iberis* 'Little Gem'), cerastium, and cinquefoil (*Potentilla*). Between them these plants will give flower and leaf interest from late spring to early autumn.

237

Could you suggest some good ground-cover plants which will swamp the weeds in my flower borders?

Ground-cover plants will not swamp existing weeds: it will therefore be essential to remove all weeds before setting them out. It is equally important to continue weeding until the ground coverers have become well-established, for it is only then that weeds will be suppressed.

Some effective evergreen ground-cover plants are bugle (*Ajuga*), alyssum, rock cress (*Arabis*), thrift (*Armeria*), wormwood (*Artemisia*), aubrieta, snow-in-summer (*Cerastium*), coral flower (*Heuchera*), candytuft (*Iberis*) dead nettle (*Lamium*), creeping jenny (*Lysimachia*), catmint (*Nepeta*), self-heal (*Prunella*) soapwort (*Saponaria*), saxifrage (*Saxifraga*), comfrey (*Symphytum*), tellima, foam flower (*Tiarella*), and waldsteinia. These plants, being low-growing, also make useful front-of-border edging plants if kept under control.

238

Can you give me the names of some really tall-growing herbaceous plants for the back of my border that will screen an untidy neighbouring wall and fence during the summer?

There are not many herbaceous plants suitable for this purpose, and you would probably be best advised to put in a background screen of climbers, or shrubs that can be trained as climbers (*see* 325-402). The tallest-growing herbaceous plants include delphinium, *Crambe cordifolia*, foxtail lily (*Eremurus robustus*), mallow (*Lavatera olbia*), coneflower (for instance,

Rudbeckia 'Autumn Sun'), *Ligularia przewalskii,* and the perennial climbing sweet-peas (*Lathyrus latifolius* and *L. rotundifolius*). All grow to about 1.5 m (5 ft).

239

I am a keen flower-arranger and want to create an area devoted to flowers that are good for cutting. Which plants would you advise as being most suitable?

Many border plants fall into this category, but for a 'cutting' border the following are among the most useful: yarrow (*Achillea*), knapweed (*Centaurea*), blanket flower (*Gaillardia*), chalk plant (*Gypsophila*), *Heliopsis scabra* 'Golden Plume', gay feather (*Liatris*), sea lavender (*Limonium latifolium*), pyrethrum, scabious (*Scabiosa*), globe thistle (*Echinops*), iris, peony (*Paeonia*), phlox, golden rod (*Solidago*), coneflower (*Rudbeckia*), thalictrum, African lily (*Agapanthus*), lady's mantle (*Alchemilla*), cupid's dart (*Catananche*), crocosmia, leopard's bane (*Doronicum*), chrysanthemums, dahlias, everlasting flowers (*Helichrysum* and *Anaphalis*), and grasses for seed heads.

240

Which cultivated perennial plants will attract butterflies?

Some attractive garden plants that butterflies appreciate are yarrow (*Achillea*), michaelmas daisies (*Aster novi-belgii*) valerian (*Centranthus*), fleabane (*Erigeron*), sneezeweed (*Helenium*), scabious (*Scabiosa*), ice plant (*Sedum spectabile*), and golden rod (*Solidago*). (For butterfly-attracting shrubs, *see* 347.)

241

Could you suggest some flowers that will thrive in a shady border?

Plants that grow well in fairly dense or light shade include monkshood (*Aconitum*), japanese anemone (*Anemone* × *hybrida*), masterwort (*Astrantia*), Christmas rose and Lenten rose (*Helleborus niger* and *H. orientalis*), Virginian cowslip (*Mertensia*), solomon's seal (*Polygonatum multiflorum*), bugle (*Ajuga*), columbine (*Aquilegia*), astilbe, bergenia, brunnera, plantain lily (*Hosta*), dead-nettle (*Lamium*), lungwort (*Pulmonaria*), and wood-lily (*Trillium*).

242

I like scent in the garden. Can you tell me the names of some of the most popular sweet-smelling flowers?

Lily-of-valley (*Convallaria*: flowers in April/May), many border carnations and pinks (*Dianthus* species: all summer) catmint (*Nepeta*: summer to mid-autumn), many irises (early summer), verbena (summer to first frosts), violets (early spring to autumn, depending on species and varieties), mignonette (*Reseda*: all summer), and some sweet peas (June to September)—all these have beautiful fragrance.

243

We have just acquired a house and garden close to the sea and would like to know which plants will grow well with our salt-laden winds.

A surprisingly large range of plants can be grown by the sea, especially if windbreaks, in the forms of hedges or 'filter' fencing (*see* 2), are used to reduce the force of the winds and their salt content. Some good perennial plants for seaside gardens include sea holly (*Eryngium*), red-hot poker (*Kniphofia*), sea lavender (*Limonium latifolium*), thrift (*Armeria*), chamomile (*Anthemis*), aubrieta, montbretia (*Crocosmia*), pinks (*Dianthus*), crane's-bill (*Geranium*), rock or sun rose (*Helianthemum*), perennial varieties of lobelia, catmint (*Nepeta*), African lily (*Agapanthus*), yarrow (*Achillea*), spurge (*Euphorbia*), stonecrop (*Sedum*), woundwort or betony (*Stachys*), centaurea, and michaelmas daisy (*Aster novi-belgii*), as well as many silver-leaved plants (*see* 245).

244

Which plants have interesting leaves which last over a long period and can give variation to a flower border?

Among the most popular for this purpose are species and varieties of New Zealand flax (*Phormium*), with spiky leaves of different colours; green, blue-green, and variegated hostas; reddish bergenia; bear's-breeches (*Acanthus*), which are large, green, deeply toothed; purple tellima; peltiphyllum, with its large 'parasol' leaves; thyme (*Thymus*), yellow, grey, or green; purple forms of bugle (*Ajuga reptans*); and stonecrops (*Sedum*) and house-leeks (*Sempervivum*), which have various shades of reds, greens, and yellows.

245

I would like to grow some silver-leaved plants. Could you suggest a few?

Silver-leaved plants make an attractive, cool foil to other border plants, and some worth considering include: artemisia, lamb's-ears (*Stachys lanata*), yarrow (*Achillea*), garden ragwort (*Senecio cineraria*), blue fescue grass (*Festuca glauca*), *Salvia argentea*, mullein (*Verbascum olympicum*), *Ballota pseudo-dictamnus*, pearl everlasting (*Anaphalis*), *Helichrysum petiolatum*, *Centaurea gymnocarpa*, cardoon (*Cynara*),

pinks and carnations (*Dianthus*), campion (*Lychnis coronaria*), and scotch thistle (*Onopordon*). For silvery shrubs, see 344.

246

I am finding it difficult to grow plants on a bank that is in full sun and where the soil dries out quickly. Can you suggest some suitable plants?

Among useful plants for such an area are yellow (*Achillea*), alyssum, rock cress (*Arabis*), thrift (*Armeria*), aubrieta, pinks (*Dianthus*), flax (*Linum*), mesembryanthemum, catmint (*Nepeta*), stonecrop (*Sedum*), houseleek (*Sempervivum*), mullein (*Verbascum*), toadflax (*Linaria*), and sea holly (*Eryngium*).

247

Can you suggest any flowers I could grow in an area of very moist ground which adjoins a neighbour's stream?

Obviously many bog plants would be suitable; herbaceous perennials that enjoy such conditions include: monkshood (*Aconitum*), goat's beard (*Aruncus*), astilbe, *Inula magnifica*, loose-strife (*Lythrum salicaria*), globe flower (*Trollius*), monkey flower (*Mimulus*), spearwort (*Ranunculus lingua*), marsh-marigold (*Caltha*), rodgersias and ligularias (sometimes listed as *Senecio*), and the generally hardy arum lily (*Zantedeschia aethiopica*).

248

Can you suggest some plants for covering the ground beneath deciduous shrubs, particularly roses?

Nothing too invasive should be used, and the ground must first be cleared of weeds. Plants used for this purpose should not detract too much from the shrubs. Useful plants include: viola (*Viola gracilis*), violetta (*V. x williamsii*), speedwell (*Veronica prostrata*), dwarf cinquefoil (*Potentilla*), pinks (*Dianthus*), crane's-bills (*Geranium*); also spring-flowering bulbs and dwarf annuals, such as candytuft (*Iberis*), ageratum, alyssum, and nemophila. All these are good for general ground-cover purposes and also for the front of borders.

General flower gardening

249

What is the difference between a formal and an informal flower border?

Essentially, formal beds are oval, circular, square, or rectangular, and have regularly curving or straight edges, whereas informal beds have irregular shapes and irregularly curved edges. A formal border is usually one in which the plants are set out in geometric patterns, whereas informal beds generally have the plants in drifts (irregular clusters). Avoid star or triangular-shaped beds when you are planning your garden (it is difficult to plant the points of such figures), and make curved edges as sweeping as possible if the lawn is alongside—it will make grass-cutting much easier.

250

When people talk about mixed borders, what exactly do they mean?

A mixed border is one which can contain any kind of plant, including trees, shrubs, and ornamental vegetables, as well as the more commonly grown herbaceous perennials, bedding plants, annuals, biennials, and bulbous plants. The year-round interest created in such borders is one of their chief assets.

251

I find dead-heading flowers with secateurs very time-consuming—and the heads invariably fall to the ground and look messy. Is there any way of speeding up this job and also doing it more tidily?

There are now available both short- and long-handled secateur-type implements that include a special device which holds the dead flower head between the blades until the handles are released. Thus, you can snip off the flower head, keep the handles closed until the implement is over the rubbish container, then release the handles; the heads fall straight in. These tools are also useful for gathering flowers for floral arrangements, and in fact they are generally sold for this purpose.

252

What is an immortelle?

This is another name for a so-called everlasting flower. There is a number of such flowers which, when dried, will keep their colour for months or even years, and are extremely useful for flower arrangements. The flowers usually have a dry, strawy texture. They are best picked just before they are in full bloom, and they are then hung in bunches by their stems in a cool airy place to allow them to dry out completely. The stems are often quite weak, so it may be necessary to use florists' wires to hold up the flower heads.

Examples of immortelles are strawflower (*Helichrysum*), statice (*Limonium*), helipterum (sometimes known as acroclinium), moluccella, and xeranthemum. They are frequently sold in packets of mixed seeds, which sometimes include grasses and poppies (for their seed heads). They are best treated as hardy annuals. Many other garden flowers produce attractive seed heads for dried-flower arrangements, but they are not strictly immortelles.

253

What does the term 'pinching out' mean?

'Pinching out' or 'stopping' means removing the growing shoot-tips of plants such as carnations (*Dianthus*), antirrhinums, and wallflowers (*Cheiranthus*). This encourages the growth of sideshoots, which will make for bushier plants with more flowers. The growing tips are usually pinched out between finger and thumb, and the job can be done more than once to encourage flower-bud formation, especially with chrysanthemums.

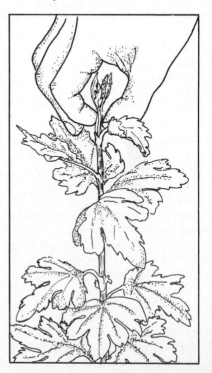

254

How can I stop cats scratching up seeds after they have been sown?

If the area is not too large, stick twigs in the ground or put in some stakes and criss-cross thick black cotton between them. Large areas, particularly where birds as well as cats are a nuisance, are best protected with netting supported on stakes or twigs. Repellent sprays based on ammonium aluminium sulphate can be tried, but they will have to be re-applied from time to time—more frequently in wet weather.

255

I find the way plants are classified a bit confusing. Could you explain the meanings of terms such as 'species', 'variety', 'cultivar', and 'hybrid'?

A plant's botanical name consists of at least two words: the first is always the generic name (a genus being a group of closely related plants); the second is usually the specific name (a species being one member of such a group). An example is the genus *Pelargonium*, of which the species *Pelargonium peltatum* is the botanical name for what is commonly known as ivy-leaved geranium. Genus and species names are customarily printed in *italics*. Just as a group of species makes up a genus, so a group of genera goes to make up a

plant family. Pelargoniums belong to the geranium family, the Geraniaceae.

A variety is a plant that differs from the species of which it is a member—but not by enough to warrant its classification as a different species. If it arose in the wild it is known as a natural variety; if it is the result of deliberate cross-pollination by a plant breeder it is often called a cultivar (short for 'cultivated variety'). Cultivar names are usually printed in quotation marks: *Pelargonium peltatum* 'Mexican Beauty' is a popular cultivar of ivy-leaved geranium.

Hybrids are obtained by the interbreeding of two (or more) species, usually of the same genus. They are indicated by a multiplication sign between the generic and hybrid names, thus: *Pelargonium × hortorum*. This, as it happens, is the collective name for a race (group) of hybrids known collectively as zonal pelargoniums. Individual hybrids of this race are indicated by the generic name followed by a cultivar name in quotation marks: *Pelargonium* 'Du Barry'.

Seed catalogues often categorise plants as F_1 hybrids. The term indicates a strain bred from two specially selected parents (*see* 16).

Michael Gibson

Author of four books on roses and a reg-
ular contributor to the gardening press; a
Vice-President of the Royal National Rose
Society.

Roses

Rose types

256

What is meant by a single, a semi-double, and a double rose bloom?

Strictly speaking a single rose flower should have only five petals, but the term is often used for blooms that have rather more than this and that ought to be known as semi-double. Both the single and semi-doubles almost always open wide to show off their stamens. One cannot set an exact limit on the number of petals in a double rose; there may be as few as 20 or as many as 100 or more. In some cluster-flowered and most large-flowered varieties (see the new rose classification, 264) the petals of double roses form a high, conical centre, with the outer petals reflexing (turning back).

257

Why does the number of petals vary from one variety to another?

This is a natural phenomenon, in which, however, man has played a part. When two different five-petalled wild roses interbreed, a new rose (hybrid) with more petals than either of them may be the result. Further crosses will produce more petals still, and the extensive hybridizing carried out by rose breeders over the years has resulted, among other things, in the very double roses of today.

258

What is a cabbage rose?

The term was coined to describe a group of ancient roses known as the centifolias. The word 'centifolia' means 100 leaves (early gardening writers often wrote of leaves when they meant petals), and there may well be 100 petals or more in the very double centifolia blooms. As these are globular at first and some of them very large, many people thought they looked like cabbages.

259

What is a moss rose?

These were popular roses in Victorian and Edwardian times and were sports (see 260) from the centifolias. They resemble them in every way except that their flower stems and buds are covered with green (sometimes brown) glands, which at a distance have some resemblance to moss.

260

What is a rose sport?

This is a mutation—a deviation from type. It occurs when a rose variety, owing to a genetic change (which may well be a throwback to earlier generations), grows one or more shoots which differ from the rest. They may either produce flowers that are different in colour (as was the case in 1962 when 'Chicago Peace' sported from 'Peace'), or they may have so much extra vigour that the rose becomes a climbing version of a bush rose. The word 'Climbing' in a rose variety listed in a catalogue always refers to a sport. Examples include 'Climbing Iceberg' and 'Climbing Cécile Brunner', sports respectively of a cluster-flowered (floribunda) variety and a shrub rose.

261

When were the first bright-yellow roses introduced into gardens?

In 1910, when 'Rayon d'Or' was put on the market by Joseph Pernet-Ducher, a French nurseryman and rose breeder. Until that time there had been only a few bright-yellow wild roses and some pale, creamy-yellow tea roses grown in gardens. All other Western varieties were white, pink, red, mauve, maroon, purple, or a mixture of these. After years of trying, Pernet-Ducher managed to cross a Persian wild rose, *R. foetida persiana*, which was of the brightest yellow imaginable, with a hybrid perpetual, and the yellow garden rose was born. The Persian rose, incidentally, was very susceptible to blackspot. This was little of a problem in gardens before the cross was made, but the weakness was passed on to a greater or lesser extent to many modern roses.

262

What is a tea rose?

Tea roses came from China about the middle of the 19th century. They, like other China roses, were recurrent, but they had much more refined flowers than the hybrid perpetual roses then fashionable in the West. A cross between the two types produced the first hybrid tea, 'La France', in 1867. The name tea rose is supposed to derive from their scent, said to resemble that of a newly-opened crate of tea.

263

Why are the names for classes of roses being changed?

Most of the early classification of roses into different groups was done in a very haphazard way, through lack of knowledge and of proper international co-ordination between the various authorities in different countries. The result has been confusion for the average gardener, some of the names used being very misleading. In addition, breeding between the various rose groups has made it progressively more difficult to tell which is which: it is, for instance, very hard to tell whether some modern roses are large-flowered floribundas or small-flowered hybrid teas.

The World Federation of Rose Societies therefore decided to introduce new, more descriptive names to replace some of the old ones, although these are not yet accepted by everybody.

264

How does the new classification work?

Take floribundas to start with. These were called hybrid polyanthas before they were known as floribundas; later, because of their constantly developing form, which changed both their flower shape and habit of growth, the group had to be subdivided into three types. The majority were still called floribundas; those with larger flowers resembling those of the hybrid tea became known by the clumsy name of floribunda, hybrid tea-type; and the exceptionally tall ones with big flowers were called grandifloras (although this name was not very widely used in the United Kingdom). Under the new classification, all these will be called cluster-flowered roses. Hybrid teas, in which often there is one large flower per stem, are now called large-flowered roses.

Most of the traditional group names such as gallica, damask, alba, and centifolia are retained because they are unlikely to have new and different-looking varieties added to them; but collectively they are to be known as old garden roses. The term shrub rose is now applied only to varieties outside these old groups which have been raised since the late 19th century. Climbers, ramblers, and miniatures remain as group names, but species roses are now known collectively as wild roses.

265

Can I grow wild (species) roses in my garden?

Yes—if you do not mind that their flowering period is so brief. Perhaps the best wild rose is 'Canary Bird', from China, which gives a more spectacular and longer-lasting display than most. Others which can be recommended are *R.* × *dupontii* (white), *R. moyesii* 'Geranium' (red, with fine hips later), 'Golden Chersonese' (yellow, very early), *R. virginiana* (pink, with fine autumn foliage colours), and *R. glauca* (syn. *R. rubrifolia*; pink flowers and purple-grey leaves).

Choosing bedding roses

266

Could you suggest some large-flowered and cluster-flowered roses in various colours that would be suitable for bedding?

The choice is immense, but the following are a few of my personal favourites: RED, LARGE-FLOWERED 'Alec's Red', 'Ernest H. Morse', 'Fragrant Cloud', 'John Waterer', 'Mister Lincoln', 'National Trust', 'Precious Platinum'. CLUSTER-FLOWERED 'City of Belfast', 'Evelyn Fison', 'Lilli Marlene', 'Memento', 'Rob Roy', 'Stargazer', 'Topsi', 'Trumpeter'. PINK,

LARGE-FLOWERED 'Blessings', 'Honey Favourite', 'Gavotte', 'Mischief', 'Mullard Jubilee', 'Pink Favourite', 'Silver Lining', 'Wendy Cussons'; CLUSTER-FLOWERED 'City of Leeds', 'Dearest', 'Elizabeth of Glamis', 'English Miss'. YELLOW, LARGE-FLOWERED 'Adolph Horstmann', 'City of Gloucester', 'Grandpa Dickson', 'King's Ransom', 'Peace', 'Peer Gynt', 'Simba', 'Sunblest'. CLUSTER-FLOWERED 'Allgold', 'Arthur Bell', 'Bright Smile', 'English Holiday', 'Kim', 'Korresia', 'Pot o' Gold', 'Sunsilk'. ORANGE, LARGE-FLOWERED 'Cheshire Life', 'Doris Tysterman', 'Just Joey', 'Troika'. CLUSTER-FLOWERED 'Dame of Sark', 'Golden Slippers', 'Living Fire', 'Orange Sensation', 'Redgold', 'Woburn Abbey'. WHITE, LARGE-FLOWERED 'Elizabeth Harkness' (buff-white), 'Pascali'. CLUSTER-FLOWERED 'Iceberg', 'Margaret Merril', 'Moon Maiden' (buff-white). COLOUR BLENDS, LARGE-FLOWERED 'Alpine Sunset', 'Champion', 'Chicago Peace', 'Double Delight', 'My Choice', 'Piccadilly', 'Rose Gaujard', 'Silver Jubilee', 'Tenerife', 'Tycoon'. CLUSTER-FLOWERED 'Escapade', 'Fragrant Delight', 'Iced Ginger', 'Matangi', 'Molly McGredy', 'Pink Parfait', 'Playboy'.

267

Which are the most strongly scented varieties?

Many roses other than those listed below have some fragrance. Bear in mind that scent may vary in strength at different times of the day and according to the humidity of the atmosphere; moreover, the sense of smell varies greatly from one person to another. That said, the following are among my favourite strongly scented forms. LARGE-FLOWERED 'Alec's Red', 'Alpine Sunset', 'Champion', 'Double Delight', 'Ernest H. Morse', 'Fragrant Cloud', 'Just Joey', 'Mister Lincoln', 'Mullard Jubilee', 'My Choice', 'Precious Platinum', 'Silver Lining', 'Tenerife', 'Wendy Cussons'. CLUSTER-FLOWERED 'Arthur Bell', 'Dearest', 'Elizabeth of Glamis', 'Fragrant Delight', 'Golden Slippers', 'Korresia', 'Margaret Merril', 'Orange Sensation'.

Climbers & ramblers

268

How should I train a climbing or rambling rose?

Use climbers rather than ramblers on walls: lack of air circulation there will encourage mildew on ramblers, which are more prone to this disease than climbers. Tie in your climber to horizontal wires about 450 mm (18 in) apart that are stretched between vine eyes driven into the brickwork; the wires should be about 75 mm (3 in) away from the wall surface. Train the shoots *along* the wires (never straight upwards); this will encourage flowering shoots to form low down and along their entire length, not just at the ends. When growing a rambler or a climber on a pillar, again do not take the shoots straight up, but bend them around the pillar in a spiral before tying them in; this, too, will encourage side shoots.

269

How can I make a rambler or climber grow up a tree?

This is one of the loveliest ways of growing them, but you must choose a variety with really long shoots. Plant the rose at least 1-1.2 m (3-4 ft) away from the trunk: the farther away the better, since there will be less competition for food from the tree roots and the soil will be less dry. Train the rose canes towards the tree along poles or strong canes. Once it reaches the lower branches the rose will hook its thorns into and over them and ramble upwards with very little further help. Plant on the windward side of the tree if possible: the long shoots will then be blown into, rather than away from, the tree. Suitably vigorous are 'Albéric Barbier', 'Albertine', 'Félicité et Perpétue', 'The Garland', and 'Wedding Day' among the ramblers; and 'Climbing Cécile Brunner', 'Lawrence Johnston', and 'Paul's Scarlet Climber' among the climbers.

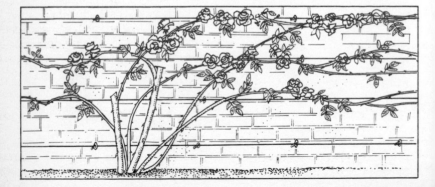

Siting & planting

270

What is the best garden site for my roses?

Almost anywhere as long as the soil is well drained and the plants will have full sun for most of the day. Avoid narrow, potentially draughty spaces—for instance, between closely adjoining houses.

271

What is the ideal soil for roses?

A good, well-drained, medium loam, not too acid and not too alkaline, is the aim—although roses are in fact very tolerant. Heavy clay retains moisture, which roses like, but some clays do not drain well and these will need lightening and breaking up. Light soils may drain too readily, so that the nutrients in them are all too quickly washed away.

272

How do I improve soil that is not ideal?

Only with very heavy, badly-drained clay should it be necessary to carry out double digging (see 730). If you do this, incorporate chopped turves and plenty of well-rotted manure (if you can get it) or well-rotted compost in the top spit, and add

two or three handfuls of bone meal or hoof-and-horn meal per square metre (square yard). Peat can also be used to improve the soil structure; but remember that it contains no plant nutrients, so if you use it you may need to add fertiliser. Peat may make soil more acid, while nitro-chalk makes it more alkaline and provides nitrogen for vigorous growth.

On light and medium soils it should be necessary to dig over only the top spit—one spade's depth—but manure, compost, and/or peat should be worked into it. This must be done two or three months before the roses are to be planted, so that the soil can settle down again, air pockets left by the digging have time to fill in, and the humus-forming materials can begin their work. Your roses will be many years in their new home, so this work should not be skimped.

Very few roses will thrive on chalk with a thin layer of soil over it. So dig out as much of the chalk as is physically possible for you and fill in the hole or holes with soil, peat, and other humus-forming materials. Lining the holes with polythene, which is sometimes recommended, can cause drainage problems after a time.

273

Can I plant my new roses in the bed from which I have removed older ones?

Not unless the soil is changed first—which can be a daunting job if it is a large bed. The old soil may have become what is known as 'rose sick', and even if manure or fertilisers are added, the new bushes will never do well, although other types of plants will be quite happy in it. Better to choose another site. If you just want to plant the odd new rose or two as replacements in an existing bed, dig out as much soil as possible without damage to the roots of nearby bushes, making if possible a hole at least 450 mm (18 in) deep and 750 mm (30 in) across.

274

How close together can I plant my roses?

This depends to some extent on the vigour and habit of growth of the different varieties. However, a good average distance between plants for large-flowered and cluster-flowered bedding roses is 450-600 mm (18-24 in). Vigorous climbers may need more space.

275

I have ordered some roses by post from a reputable nursery. How can I tell if they are good, healthy plants?

Each new rose should have a minimum of two strong canes (but preferably three or four) at least as thick as a pencil; they should be firm, healthy, and the bark unwrinkled. The roots should be plentiful and fibrous, and the neck (the section of stem between the roots and the point from which the shoots are growing) should be of thumb thickness at least.

276

I may not be able to plant my new roses immediately they arrive. How should I store them?

Roses, if ordered during the summer, will usually be despatched from the nursery in November, which is the best month for planting them. If planting is likely to be delayed longer than a week, leave them unopened in a cool, frost-proof shed. For longer periods, heel them in; that is, dig a trench, unpack the roses, and put them in the trench, covering the roots—or even the whole of the bushes—with plenty of soil. But do plant your roses as soon as possible.

277

Are there any special problems in planting climbing roses?

Follow the procedure as for bush roses, but if they are to go against a wall remember that the soil will be very dry there as bricks, stone, and masonry all absorb moisture. You should plant at least 450 mm (18 in) away from the wall, positioning each rose at the inside edge of its hole and fanning the roots outwards, away from the wall and towards moister earth. The shoots can be trained in towards the wall when they begin to grow.

278

How do I plant bush roses?

For the best results and quick
rooting, prepare a planting mixture
of granulated peat and soil in equal
proportions; about one shovelful
per plant will be needed, and mix
into it one handful per plant of
bone meal. Do your planting on a
frost-free day and make sure the
soil is not waterlogged. Dig the
holes wide enough for the roots to
be well spread out, and deep
enough for the budding union
(from which the shoots grow) to be
located *just* below the soil surface.
Cut away any weak, twiggy, or
diseased growth down to a healthy
bud, cut back long, thick roots by
about two thirds to encourage fine
feeding roots to sprout from them;
if the bushes look dry, soak them
in a bucket of water for an hour.

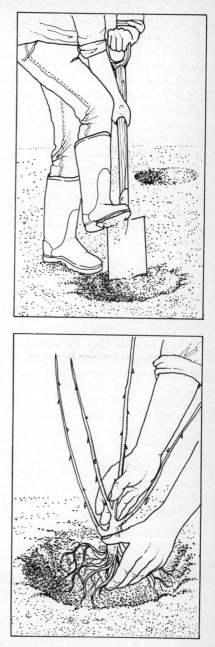

If the way the roots are growing
allows for this, place the bush in
the centre of its planting hole and,
holding it upright, spread the roots
out evenly without straining any of
them into unnatural positions. If, as
is often the case, they all run in
one direction, plant more of them
to one side of the hole. Check the
depth of the budding union with a
cane placed across the hole and
adjust the depth as necessary. Put
in your shovelful of planting
mixture and firm it round the roots.
Fill the hole with soil and tread it
firmly but not so heavily on heavy
soils as to expel the air). Water well
if the soil is dry. Firm the soil again
after the first frosty spell.

279

**I have been given a
container-grown rose as a
present. How should I plant it?**

This will already be established in
the soil in the container, so it can
be planted out at any time, even
when it is in flower. Make your
planting hole a good deal larger
than the root ball. Remove the
rose from the container, loosen the
outer soil of the root ball a little,
and place the rose in the centre of
the hole to check the depth; if this
is correct, fill in around the root
ball with planting mixture and
tread firm. Water well.

280

**Are there any special problems
in planting standard roses?**

Two things are especially
important. First, plant no deeper
than the soil-mark, which should
be visible on the stem: with the
type of rose used as rootstock for
standards, deeper planting will only
encourage undesirable suckers.
Second, drive in the supporting
stake *before* planting: if you do this
after planting you may damage the
roots. The top of the stake should
just reach into the head of the
standard to give it support. When
the rose is planted attach the stem
to the stake with special rose ties.
Leave them quite loose for a week
or two to allow the rose to settle
down in the soil. When tightening
them up later, remember to leave
room for stem growth.

Feeding

281

**What type of fertiliser should I
choose, and when should I
apply it?**

Any of the proprietary,
ready-mixed rose fertilisers will be
perfectly satisfactory, with bone
meal as a good alternative. They
are easy to apply, but use gloves
(preferably rubber) when handling
them. About a month before spring
pruning (*see* 285), sprinkle a small
handful of fertiliser evenly around
each rose bush and lightly hoe it
in. Repeat the process before the
end of July (later application would
encourage soft autumn growth
which could not ripen before being
killed by winter frosts). For mulch
feeds, *see* 283 and 706.

282

**I read that roses benefit from
foliar feeding. What is this?**

This entails spraying the leaves
with a specially formulated liquid
fertiliser. In the normal way,
nutrients travel from the soil, via
the roots, to the leaves, where they
are turned into plant foods.
Feeding the leaves directly
amounts to taking a short cut.
Opinions differ as to how effective
foliar feeding is. Certainly the
benefits are not as long-lasting as
those from normal feeding; so this
kind of feeding has to be done

more often—additional work the average gardener will not welcome. On the other hand, the speed with which plants take up foliar feeds is useful for the rapid correction of the effects of soil deficiencies, which are usually indicated by the yellowing of leaves in various ways.

283

What benefits would I get by mulching a rose bed?

A mulch 100-125 mm (4-5 in) deep spread over the bed after the ground has had a good soaking will help to smother weeds, keep the soil temperature reasonably even, and prevent the soil from drying out. Apply it in spring, when the ground has begun to warm up; but do not delay it until the time when many brittle new shoots have begun to form: these could easily be snapped off as you spread the mulch. If the mulch is of well-rotted stable manure or well-rotted compost it will provide additional plant foods and humus as it breaks down. Peat or granulated bark look tidier, but they do not feed the soil.

Pruning

284

Why must I prune my roses?

To get rid of weak, spindly, and diseased shoots; to encourage

strong new shoots to grow from the base of the plant each year (these bear the best flowers); to open out the centre of the bush to increase air circulation through it (this helps to check disease); and to create a pleasingly symmetrical outline to the plant.

285

When should I prune?

For large-flowered and cluster-flowered bush roses the traditional months are March in the south of England and April in the north, when growth is just beginning; but pruning can safely be done at any time from November onwards in the south, provided you are prepared if necessary to remove some frost-damaged growth in spring.

The most important rule is: *never* prune during a frosty spell. Prune ramblers after flowering, probably late in August, to divert vigour to new flowering-shoot development for the following summer. Prune climbers in October, when flowering of the recurrent varieties is over.

286

How should I prune my large-flowered bush roses?

Cut away completely all diseased, weak, and spindly shoots; remove all dead stumps left from earlier prunings, using a fine-toothed saw if they are woody and thick. If there are many canes criss-crossing in the centre, remove a few to open out the bush. If two shoots are growing so that they rub together, remove one of them. Finally, cut the remaining shoots back to about 200-250 mm (8-10 in). Harder pruning than this will produce larger but probably fewer flowers, but it will not harm the rose in any way.

287

How exactly do I make a pruning cut?

Pruning is easiest with secateurs; keep them sharp and clean or they may pass on disease from one rose to another. (Cheap secateurs may become distorted after a time, and blunt ones will not make a clean cut; this is an important failing, because jagged ends on a shoot may attract disease.)

Make your pruning cut about 6 mm (¼ in) above a bud on a shoot; the cut should slope down towards the side away from the bud. Cutting to an outward-facing bud encourages the bush to spread outwards, but do not worry if you cannot find one exactly where you want to cut; often a bud lower down will grow away more vigorously in the direction you want, and you can always trim back to it later on.

288

How should I prune my cluster-flowered rose?

Follow the procedure for large-flowered varieties (above), but leave the main shoots 300-350 mm (12-14 in) long. If these pruned shoots have side shoots, the latter need not be removed provided they are substantial, but you should cut them back by about two thirds.

289

How should I prune my climbers?

As distinct from ramblers, these are the roses, often recurrent, that carry small clusters of comparatively large flowers on a permanent framework of strong shoots. You need to cut back their side shoots to one or two buds from the point where they branch out from the main shoots. If the plant has become bare at the base, cut one of its main shoots hard back to encourage new growth from ground level.

290

How should I prune my ramblers?

These are non-recurrent (once-flowering) roses that bear large clusters of small flowers, the best carried on long flexible shoots that grow mainly from the base of the plant each year. Pruning consists of cutting out completely the shoots that have finished flowering and tying in the new shoots in their place. If in some years there are only a few of these, some of the old shoots (which can still produce a number of flowers) may be left in place, but you should shorten their side shoots by about two thirds.

291

How should I prune my miniature roses?

With those kinds that produce a thick tangle of tiny, wiry shoots, thin some of these out. Remove dead or diseased shoots, and trim back the rest by about two thirds. It may be difficult if not impossible to find a bud to cut to, especially on the very small miniatures, so just clip them over so that the plants look neat and tidy.

292

How should I prune my shrub roses?

These vary so enormously in size and type (see 319) that no general instructions can be given. Wild (species) roses should not be pruned at all, other than for removal of dead or diseased branches. Most of the old garden roses, such as the once-flowering gallicas, damasks, albas, and centifolias, together with the recurrent bourbons, will give more flowers if they have their side shoots shortened by about two thirds in winter. Those modern shrub roses that are, in fact, giant

cluster-flowered types should be pruned like their smaller cluster-flowered cousins used for bedding, but reduce their height by only about two thirds. The rugosa family needs little if any pruning, although on the less-dense-growing kinds a few main canes can be cut back every two or three years to encourage them to bush out.

293

What is meant by the term autumn pruning?

Tall-growing large-flowered and cluster-flowered bush roses may have their roots loosened in the soil if they are blown about by winter gales, and in sticky clay their movement may form a funnel of compressed earth, exposing the budding union. Water can collect in this funnel and may cause trouble if it freezes because the budding union is the most vulnerable part of the plant. To lessen the chance of windrock, cut back these roses by about one third in late October or early November.

294

Should I prune my newly planted roses in the same way as the established plants?

Prune them even more drastically, so that a really strong framework of new shoots will be built up from the beginning. It takes considerable determination with new purchases, but leave the shoots only 50-75 mm (2-3 in) long. Prune autumn-planted new roses when you do your established ones; prune spring-planted ones at planting time. Do *not* prune climbers at all in their first year, as they take longer to establish.

Keeping roses healthy

295

A friend seems to spend half his gardening life dealing with rose pests and diseases. I want to grow roses, but is it possible to buy varieties that are likely to be trouble-free?

It is certainly true that some varieties are inherently healthier than others. However, it is not possible to be very precise about the healthiest roses, for their resistance to disease can depend on the conditions under which they are grown, the type of soil, how well they are looked after, and even the part of the country in which the grower lives.

Unfortunately, regarding the last factor, there is not a set pattern of 'healthy' and 'unhealthy' localities. A wise gardener looks around other local gardens, parks, and nursery display beds to see how the roses are doing before he buys any for his own garden. One or two varieties often stand out with

shining, healthy foliage in the midst of a sea of mildew on those surrounding them. It can be taken for granted, however, that a rose that is well looked after and that grows strongly will be less likely to suffer badly from disease.

Despite what has been said above, there *are* certain roses that have been shown to be reasonably disease-free in most parts of the country. Among the best of these are the LARGE-FLOWERED 'Adolph Horstmann', 'Alec's Red', 'Alexander', 'Alpine Sunset', 'Blessings', 'Double Delight', 'Ernest H. Morse', 'Grandpa Dickson', 'Just Joey', 'My Choice', 'Peace', 'Piccadilly', 'Pink Favourite' (outstanding), 'Silver Jubilee', 'Sunblest', 'Troika', and 'Wendy Cussons'. Of the CLUSTER-FLOWERED varieties, the healthiest ones include 'Allgold', 'Anne Harkness', 'Arthur Bell', 'City of Belfast', 'Dame of Sark', 'Fragrant Delight', 'Korresia', 'Living Fire', 'Margaret Merril', 'Mantangi', 'Mountbatten', 'Queen Elizabeth', 'Rob Roy', 'Southampton', 'Trumpeter'.

Healthy CLIMBERS include 'Mermaid', 'Compassion', and 'Aloha'. And among the rugosa family of shrub roses disease is virtually unknown.

296

How do I go about spraying roses?

Except where a few exceptions are cited in the five answers that follow this, spray only when the first signs of a disease or pest are seen. Always follow the directions given by the spray manufacturers very carefully. In some sprays the constituents are ready-mixed to deal with disease and pests at the same time. Others can be mixed by the buyer, but do not do this unless your supplier or the manufacturer states that it is safe to do so, or you may scorch your leaves. Sprays with the longest-lasting effect (several weeks) are the systemics, which enter the plant tissue and so cannot be washed off by rain. Evening is the best time to spray; *never* spray in hot sunshine, or scorched leaves may be the result. Always use only enough spray to wet the leaves adequately on both sides: drenching the bushes is a waste of spray.

297

How can I recognise and deal with blackspot?

This fungus shows as round, black spots with fringed edges on the leaves, at first usually on the lower, older ones, towards the end of June or in early July. If neglected, the spots rapidly enlarge, the rest of the leaf yellows, and it will drop to the ground. Such defoliation weakens the plant, and the fungus spores will spread rapidly to neighbouring bushes. Spray with fungicide based on benomyl, triforine, thiophanate-methyl, bu-pirimate-triforine (almost

certainly the best), or fenarimol. In bad blackspot areas—your neighbours will soon tell you if you are in one—preventive spraying may be needed every 10 days or so from the second half of June onwards. Always remove affected leaves that drop on the beds. Spray the dormant bushes and surrounding earth with Bordeaux mixture two or three times in winter to kill over-wintering spores.

298

How do I recognise and deal with mildew?

This is a greyish, powdery-looking covering, usually first seen on young leaves and the flower stalks. It will spread rapidly over the whole bush and to others. It is not fatal, but if bad it will distort the foliage and flowers and it is very unsightly. Spray at first signs with the fungicides listed for blackspot (above) and give the same winter treatment to the beds.

299

How do I recognise and deal with rose rust?

This is much less common than mildew and blackspot, and many varieties seem immune to it. First signs are small orange pustules under the leaves, and these gradually turn black. Rust can be a killer if neglected, but the only really effective remedy, an oxycarbon spray, is not at present available in the small quantities needed by the average gardener. However, zineb, mancozeb, thiram, or maneb are worth trying.

300

How do I recognise and deal with sap-sucking pests?

These include aphids or greenfly, which are tiny green (sometimes brown) insects that cluster on young shoots, leaves (often on the undersides), and flower stems, and increase with incredible rapidity. There may also be froghoppers, which are larger greenish-yellow insects which hide in easily-seen blobs of foam. Spray both with derris (*not* systemic), manazon, fenitrothion, dimethoate, or formothion.

301

How do I recognise and deal with leaf- and petal-eating pests?

These include chafers (green flying beetles which nibble petals and anthers), thrips or thunder-flies (tiny brownish insects, more common in hot weather, which nibble flower buds), and the trotrix moth and other caterpillars. Some of the last hide in rolled-up leaves, and the lacky moth caterpillar makes a silken 'tent'. With a mild infestation, caterpillars can be removed by hand. Otherwise spray both these and chafers with trichlorphon or fenitrothion; the latter will deal with thrips as well. The leaf-rolling sawfly lays eggs in the leaf margins, and the leaf rolls into a tapered cylinder that protects the grub. To deal effectively with this pest, you must act before the leaf rolls. Spray it in late April and again in early May with trichlorphon or fenitrothion if infestation has been bad in previous years; otherwise, simply pick off the affected leaves and burn them.

General maintenance

302

What should I do if I take over a garden with badly neglected roses?

They are likely to be unpruned, may well have been badly pruned in the past, probably will be disease-ridden with many dead stumps, and there may be suckers as well. If the suckers are growing a great deal more strongly than the roses, it is probably not worth trying to rescue the plants. If, on the other hand, some of the roses are still producing strong new canes, prune them perhaps a little harder than usual in spring and leave them alone otherwise. Any that look as if they are on their last legs should be cut back almost to ground level and dead stumps round the base removed. This treatment may easily activate invisible dormant buds and completely rejuvenate the bushes.

The following summer will provide the answer, and any roses that do not survive this drastic pruning would not have been worth keeping anyway.

303

I am told I should remove suckers from my roses. How do I distinguish a sucker from an ordinary shoot, and how do I get rid of it?

A sucker is a shoot coming from the rootstock on to which your variety is budded. Thus, any shoot that forms below the budding union is a sucker. If it rises from the soil more than 75 mm (3 in) from the base of the plant it is almost certainly a sucker. A useful, but not infallible, indication of a sucker is if it has seven leaflets per leaf, rather than the usual five; the leaves are usually of a different shape, and of a lighter green, than those on the rest of the plant; and the thorns may also be different. Do *not* remove a sucker by cutting it with secateurs: this will have the same effect as pruning and encourage it to grow more strongly. The best method is to grip the sucker tightly and give it a sharp tug. This should pull it away cleanly from the rootstock, and also remove any dormant sucker buds that are clustered about its base.

304

What is meant by dead-heading?

This is the removal in summer of unsightly spent and faded flower heads in order to prevent hips from forming. If they are allowed to form, much of the plant's growing strength will be channelled into their development, and there will be less flowers later. Do not pull off the old flowers. Cut with secateurs back to a healthy leaf-axil bud 75-100 mm (3-4 in) down the stem, which will then more quickly produce a stronger shoot to carry new blooms. Do *not* dead-head those shrub roses or wild (species) roses that you are growing partly for their autumn display of hips. You will not get any if you do.

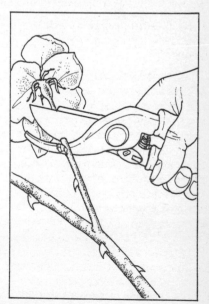

305

What is meant by disbudding?

It means pinching out, as soon as they are large enough, some or all of the side-flower buds if there is a cluster at the top of a shoot. This, of course, means that you will have fewer flowers, but those buds that remain will produce much larger blooms. Disbudding is done mainly by exhibitors, who need to produce large blooms. For normal garden display, however, disbudding is seldom necessary, and then only on the few varieties (such as 'Pink Favourite') in which the buds are likely to be packed so closely that the blooms cannot open properly.

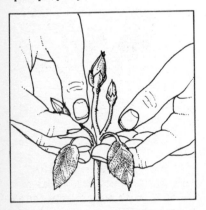

306

Are there any special jobs to do before winter sets in?

Cutting back to prevent windrock (*see* 293) has been dealt with already. The most important other task is to clear the beds of all fallen leaves, in which disease spores can over-winter. Put them on the bonfire, not on the compost heap. (*See also* 307).

307

Do my roses need special protection in the winter?

In the United Kingdom this should not generally be necessary, but in those northern districts subject to bitingly cold winds some earthing up around the base of the plants may be advisable. In addition, straw or bracken may be woven into the heads of standard roses, which are particularly vulnerable.

Growing methods

308

Can I grow roses in tubs?

Yes, provided that the tubs have plenty of drainage holes and are at least 300 mm (1 ft) deep and 450 mm (18 in) in diameter for the average-sized bush rose; more vigorous roses such as climbers will need larger tubs. The growing medium can be half and half of peat and garden soil, or you can use a John Innes potting compost; you will need to add fertiliser at least three times during the growing season. Careful attention must be given to watering as tubs dry out quickly in hot, dry weather.

309

Can I grow roses under glass?

Yes, and you should have your first blooms in May; but the bushes must then be stood outside in their pots for the rest of the summer. They are brought back into the greenhouse in October, when pruning should be done.

310

Can I grow roses from cuttings?

Yes, but it will take four or five years to achieve a full sized plant, and some roses will never have the vigour of those budded on a rootstock. This applies particularly to the large-flowered bush roses, which are also the most difficult to grow from cuttings.

311

How do I take cuttings of roses?

At any time from late August onwards, preferably during a showery spell, dig a narrow trench 150 mm (6 in) deep in a place shaded from the mid-day sun. Sprinkle coarse sand along the trench bottom. Select a firm, ripe shoot on your rose, and from the central portion cut one or possibly two lengths, each of approximately 225 mm (9 in). Make the lower cut just below and the upper one just above a leaf-axil bud. Remove all but the top pair of leaves, then place the cuttings upright against

one side of the trench and about 75 mm (3 in) apart. Fill the trench with soil and tread it firm (and firm it again in the winter after frosty spells).

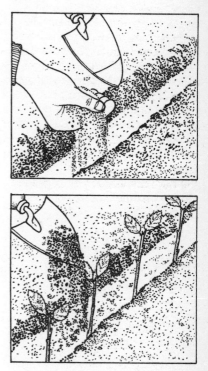

In spring new shoots will form and, perhaps, flower buds later. Remove these buds to concentrate the growing strength in the shoots and roots, so that the rose will be ready for planting in its final home by the autumn. (Wetting the ends of the cuttings and dipping them in hormone rooting powder before putting them in the trench may give them a better start, especially on heavy soils.)

312

Can I use roses as ground-cover plants?

While some rose varieties do grow naturally outwards rather than upwards, it must be said that few of them grow densely enough to smother weeds completely, as a ground-cover plant should. They are, however, useful for trailing over rough banks and other difficult places. Varieties to try include 'Max Graf', 'Snow Carpet', 'Swany', 'Rosy Cushion', 'Raubritter', and 'Fairyland'. Many new varieties are coming on to the market, as this type of rose is increasing in popularity.

313

Can roses be grown with other plants?

The rather formal upright habit of the large- and cluster-flowered bedding roses which most people grow means that they do not always blend easily with other plants. However, most of the shrub roses, both old and new, have a much less formal habit. They will mix very happily with other shrubs, such as mock orange (*Philadelphus*), cinquefoil (*Potentilla*), heathers, sun rose (*Cistus*), Mexican orange (*Choisya*), and lavender; and in mixed borders they blend especially well with grey-leaved plants such as anaphalis, Jerusalem sage (*Phlomis fruticosa*), senecio, or nepeta.

Roses as hedging

314

What are the advantages of using roses rather than other shrubs for hedges?

Mainly that they will provide almost continuous colour throughout the summer and well on into the autumn. If you are using upright-growing roses of the cluster-flowered type, staggered planting will be of advantage if you want a substantial rather than a purely decorative hedge, but with most of the shrub and old garden roses this will not be necessary. When choosing varieties for hedging, remember that most of the old garden roses, and the more modern rugosas and hybrid musks, need to be allowed a width of 1.5 m (5 ft) or more, so they are not suitable for a place where space is limited.

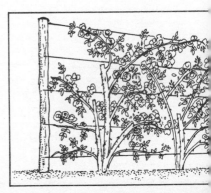

315

I want to create a rose hedge no more than about 1.2 m (4 ft) high. Can you suggest suitable varieties?

The following 18 make good low hedges: 'Alexander', 'Angelina', 'Anne Harkness', 'Ballerina', 'Chinatown', 'Dame of Sark', 'Dorothy Wheatcroft', 'Escapade', 'Eye Paint', 'Frau Dagmar Hartopp' (syn. 'Fru Dagmar Hastrup'), 'Iceberg', 'Lavender Lassie', 'Marjorie Fair', 'Mountbatten', 'Peace', 'Rob Roy', 'Southampton', 'The Fairy'.

316

What about varieties for taller hedges?

Here are 11 attractive varieties: 'Cornelia', 'Fountain', 'Fred Loads', 'Nymphenburg', 'Penelope', 'Pink Grootendorst', 'Queen Elizabeth', 'Roseraie de l'Hay', 'Salley Holmes', 'Scabrosa' and 'Schneezwerg' ('Snow Dwarf').

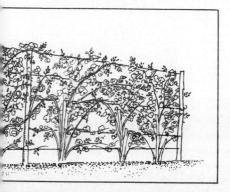

Old garden & shrub roses

317

I have been told that the old garden and shrub roses have only one flowering period every year, at about midsummer. Is that the case?

This is true of almost all the old garden roses with the exception of most bourbons, the hybrid perpetuals, and the China roses; it is also true of the wild (species) roses (*see* 265). However, a high proportion of the modern shrub roses raised during the present century are fully recurrent.

318

I have read that shrub roses are too big for a small garden like mine. Is this true?

Not by any means. Some of the modern ones developed in the past century will reach only 1.2 m (4 ft) or less; 'Yesterday', 'Frank Naylor', and 'Saga' could be added to them. Of the older roses, most of the gallicas and China roses grow within this limit, as do a few examples from among all the other groups. Particularly suitable are the alba roses 'Félicité Parmentier' and 'Königin von Dänemarck'; while the species or wild rose 'Canary Bird' can be kept to a moderate size if grown as a standard.

319

Are there any special advantages in growing shrub roses?

Yes, they greatly increase the uses to which roses in the garden can be put, for they provide many additional types of flowers, new and beautiful colour combinations, different and often very attractive foliage, and, in some cases, a fine display of decorative hips. They enable you to use roses for hedges of all sizes, you can grow them in a shrub border either on their own or mixed with other shrubs, or you can use them for specimen planting in a lawn or to fill up a difficult corner. Choose roses like 'Frühlingsgold', 'Frühlingsmorgen', or 'Nevada' for this.

320

Which are the best roses to grow for decorative hips?

For the sheer size of their hips, which can be over 25 mm (1 in) in diameter and as red as tomatoes (which they much resemble), pick members of the rugosa family that have single flowers, such as 'Frau Dagmar Hartopp', *R. rugosa alba*, and 'Scabrosa'. As they are recurrent, the hips of the first flush of flowers appear with the later blooms. Many of the wild (species) roses have hips varying in colour from red through orange to yellow, and some even of black. *R. roxburghii* has prickly hips resembling the fruit of the horse chestnut, while those of *R. pomifera* resemble large red gooseberries. Perhaps the most spectacular hips are those of *R. moyesii* and its various hybrids; they are bottle-shaped, bright red, and each may be up to 50 mm (2 in) long.

Miniature roses

321

How does a miniature rose differ from other kinds?

The earliest varieties, the true miniatures, were no more than 150-225 mm (6-9 in) high; many, like 'Cinderella', had fully double, scented flowers with 50 or more tiny petals. Most were red or pink, and in order to increase the colour range, breeders crossed them with the larger cluster-flowered varieties. They achieved their object, but at the expense of the original daintiness and small stature. Many modern so-called miniatures have flowers of such a size and growth so robust that it is difficult to tell them from dwarf cluster-flowered kinds. Typical examples are 'Angela Rippon', 'Starina', 'Anna Ford', and 'Magic Carousel', all of which will grow to 300 mm (12 in) or more. One of the easiest ways of keeping miniature roses small is to grow them from cuttings rather than buy plants budded on to rootstocks.

322

How can I use miniature roses to the best advantage?

The fact that they are usually sold in pots has led to the belief that they are fragile indoor pot-plants. In fact, they are perfectly suitable as garden plants: they are as hardy as other roses and, indeed, need the fresh air of outdoors. Their cultivation requirements are the same as for any other rose.

They are ideal for a patio when planted in tubs, troughs, or stone sinks, or for rockeries provided that they can have a good root run with plenty of soil between the rocks. Or you can try them in a terraced bed around a sunken garden, which will bring them nearer to eye level. Miniature standards and climbers are available to add variety to such a planting, and the larger varieties (see 321) can be used to line a path or drive.

323

Can I grow miniature roses indoors?

Not permanently unless you are prepared to instal special fluorescent strip lighting for them and provide the humidity they need: in the average house the light is insufficient and the air is much too dry. If the plants are placed in a window, the sun's heat coming through the glass will be too great. But roses in their pots can safely be kept in a cool greenhouse; then, when the buds are beginning to show colour, they can be brought into the house. They must be taken outside at once after flowering or the leaves will yellow and drop off.

324

Which are some of the best miniature roses for colour, robustness and health?

My favourites include: 'Angela Rippon' (pink), 'Baby Darling' (deep pink), 'Cinderella' (white, flushed pink), 'Colibri' (orange), 'Darling Flame' (orange vermilion, yellow reverse), 'Easter Morning' (ivory white), 'Eleanor' (pink), 'Judy Fischer' (cerise-pink), 'Little Flirt' (orange-red and yellow bicolour), 'Magic Carousel' (white, edged pink), 'New Penny' (pink), 'Orange Sunblaze', 'Perla-de-Montserrat' (pink), 'Pour Toi' (white), 'Red Sunblaze', 'Rise 'n' Shine' (yellow), 'Starina' (vermilion).

'Cinderella'

'Baby Masquerade'

Graham Rice

Technical writer on the staff of *Practical Gardening* magazine; author of St Michael Down-to-Earth Guide on *Pruning*.

Shrubs
and
Climbers

Choosing shrubs

325

How do shrubs differ from other garden plants?

Whereas herbaceous plants—the familiar annuals and perennials of a mixed border—have soft stems, shrubs have woody stems and branches that live throughout the year. Shrubs differ from trees mainly in growing habit: while most trees develop a single main stem (trunk) that branches out at some height above the ground, a shrub has branches near (or even below) the soil surface.

326

What is a sub-shrub, and should I treat it any differently from an ordinary shrub?

A sub-shrub is a plant that is woody at the base but has annual stems like those of a herbaceous plant. These stems die back every year to the older woody growth. The rose-of-sharon (*Hypericum calycinum*) is a good example. The stems should be cut back every spring, not to ground level but to the woody shoots at the bottom.

327

What is the difference between a heath and a heather?

Heathers (also known as ling) belong to the botanical genus

Calluna, while the heaths are species of *Erica*; both are members of the Ericaceae family. It is heather which forms most of the extensive moorlands in this country. Leaves of heathers tend to be very small and closely packed; the flowers are on one side of the stem, and are smaller than those of the heaths. Both show a preference for acid, peaty soil in full sun; although several of the most popular ericas, including *E. herbacea* (syn. *E. carnea*), will thrive on chalky soil.

328

Some of the shrubs I see in gardens and read about in books are not available in my local garden centre, so how do I get hold of them?

The answer is to go to specialists. Some will exhibit at the regular Royal Horticultural Society Shows in London, others will advertise in the gardening magazines. Many of the private gardens that open under the National Gardens Scheme also have small numbers of plants for sale, and you often find gems there.

329

My soil is exceptionally limy. What shrubs will do best in these conditions?

There's plenty to choose from. If the site is sunny try rock roses (*Helianthemum*), with red, yellow, or white flowers; sun rose (*Cistus*) with purple and white flowers; berberis (orange); buddleias (purple, lilac, or white); potentillas (red, orange, yellow or white); and lilacs (purple, lilac, or white). In shade, go for aucubas (with red fruits); euonymus (variegated foliage); Oregon grape (*Mahonia aquifolium*) with yellow flowers and purple fruits; and the periwinkles (*Vinca*), with blue or white flowers.

330

I have an acid soil in which rhododendrons do well. What other shrubs can I plant with them?

The number one choice must be the pierises with their lily-of-the-valley-like flowers and scarlet young shoots. Try in particular 'Forest Flame'. There are also camellias, pernettyas, with their large berries in reds, pinks, and whites, heaths and heathers (*Erica* and *Calluna*), most magnolias, and the pink-flowered calico-bush (*Kalmia latifolia*).

331

The soil in the garden of my new house has been made very hard by all the traffic from the builders' equipment. Are there any shrubs that will put up with these conditions?

Cotoneasters will grow well, as will buddleias, flowering currants (*Ribes*), weigelas, rose-of-sharon (*Hypericum calycinum*), and

potentillas. If you can dig a good-sized hole and add plenty of organic matter when planting, it will help. It might also be worth hiring a heavy-duty rotary cultivator to loosen the soil before re-planting.

332

My city garden is dark and shady from the houses and trees around me. What are the best shrubs to grow?

In the drier spots both the deciduous and evergreen berberis will thrive as long as it is not *too* dark; evergreen euonymus and other evergreens such as spotted laurel (*Aucuba japonica*), butcher's broom (*Ruscus aculeatus*), skimmias, and the periwinkles (*Vinca*) will also survive. In moist sites, try Japanese maple (*Acer palmatum*), camellias, rhododendrons, the guelder rose (*Viburnum opulus*) with its white flowers and red berries, the various elders (*Sambucus*), and hydrangeas.

333

I have a dry sunny bank where the soil is gravelly, and I would like to plant some shrubs there. Any ideas?

Thorough preparation of the soil will help a wide range of shrubs thrive in these conditions. Best bets are rock roses (*Helianthemum*)—a range of different colours could look very dramatic on their own;

sun roses (*Cistus*), prostrate cotoneasters, such as *C. horizontalis* or 'Skogholm Coral Beauty', the coloured foliage varieties of sage, and aromatic lavender.

334

My garden slopes in one corner to a rather wet patch where nothing except weeds seem to thrive. Are there any shrubs that will grow there?

Very few shrubs will grow in this situation, but if there is nothing you can do to improve the drainage, I suggest you try the dogwoods (*Cornus*), especially the varieties of *C. alba* which have bright stems in winter. Willows (*Salix*) will do well too; try *S. caprea*, with grey leaves and woolly catkins, and *S. purpurea* 'Eugenei' with yellow-green stems and grey-pink catkins. The varieties of elder (*Sambucus*) with variegated or yellow leaves are also worth growing.

335

My seaside garden is constantly buffeted by salty winds off the sea, and many of my favourite shrubs are scorched. Are there any that will flourish in these conditions?

You can help protect your plants by screening them when they are young with plastic windbreak netting and by planting windbreaks of plants such as evergreen oak

(*Quercus ilex*), hawthorn (*Crataegus*), and willows (*Salix*). Shrubs which will tolerate salt spray include shrubby veronicas (*Hebe*), escallonias, firethorns (*Pyracantha*), and snowberries (*Symphoricarpos*).

336

What plants can you suggest that will grow well in the cold winds that seem to be so destructive in my exposed garden?

You can help by planting a windbreak, but there are plenty of attractive yet very hardy plants to choose from. Both evergreen and deciduous berberises, all the cotoneasters, all the hollies (*Ilex*), buddleias, all the elaeagnuses, with their bright foliage, plus deutzias, philadelphuses, and spiraeas.

337

I have a small trough in which I want to grow some rock plants. What shrubs would be suitable to go with them?

First choice should be a tiny juniper (*Juniperus communis* 'Compressa'), which grows into an upright column about 600 mm (24 in) high at the rate of about 25 mm (1 in) a year. The dwarf form of Canadian spruce (*Picea glauca* 'Albertiana Conica') with grass-green foliage and a neat cone shape, is also very small. Among shrubs try the dwarf willows, such as *Salix reticulata* and *S. boydii*, and the tiny shrubby veronicas *Hebe buchananii* 'Minor' and *H.* 'Carl Teschner'. The dwarf purple-leaved berberis (*Berberis thunbergii* 'Atropurpurea Nana'), is a little vigorous for a trough, but it can be pruned.

338

Can you suggest one or two scented plants to put outside the window so that the scent wafts indoors?

The three I would strongly recommend are the June/July-flowering mock orange (*Philadelphus*), especially the hybrid 'Belle Étoile'; May/June-flowering lilacs (*Syringa*), especially double ones like *S. vulgaris* 'Katherine Havemeyer' and 'Mme Lemoine', which flower for longer; and lastly the July-to-October-flowering butterfly bush (*Buddleia davidii*), which will attract butterflies.

There are also many attractive shrubs with fragrant foliage. Apart from herbs such as rosemary, sage and thyme, there are the myrtles (*Myrtus*), the sweet briar (*Rosa rubiginosa*), lavender, *Perovskia atriplicifolia* 'Blue Spire' with a sage-like scent, and the Jerusalem sage (*Phlomis fruticosa*).

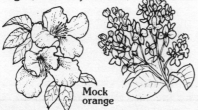

Lilac

Mock orange

339

Although my small garden is colourful for most of the year it looks rather dull in winter. What shrubs can I plant to brighten the cold months?

Winter-flowering heaths, which are tolerant of slightly limy soil would be my first choice. Varieties of *Erica herbacea* (syn. *E. carnea*) *E.* × *darleyensis*, and *E. mediterranea* fall into this category; they come in many colours, especially purples, reds, pinks, and whites. Witch hazel, with bright yellow flowers and a strong scent is another must; *Hamamelis mollis* 'Pallida' is the finest variety. Lastly I would suggest the evergreen laurustinus (*Viburnum tinus*), in particular the dwarf, bush variety 'Eve Price', with pink flowers.

340

In the local parks there are lots of trees whose leaves turn lovely shades in the autumn. Are there any smaller trees or shrubs that also have lovely autumn colours?

The following are especially fine; the figures quoted show the approximate height and spread reached after 10 years. The Japanese maples (*Acer palmatum*) make a wonderful show, and the varieties 'Dissectum', 0.6 × 1.2 m (2 × 4 ft), and 'Osakazuki', 1.5 × 1.5 m (5 × 5 ft), are especially fine. Deciduous azaleas, 2 × 2 m (6 ½ × 6½ ft), are all very reliable when it comes to autumn colour; and try some of the viburnums, such as *Viburnum plicatum* 'Lanarth', 1.8 × 2.4 m (6 × 8 ft).

341

I don't have much time to look after my garden so most of it is grass. In the few beds I have I would like to grow plants that are colourful all the year round and so make the most of the small amount of planting space. Can you suggest some?

There are three types of plants that fill the bill here: the most colourful evergreens; plants that flower for a long period; and plants with more than one season of interest. Of the evergreens, I should go for the best of all variegated shrubs, *Elaeagnus pungens* 'Maculata', or one of the variegated hebes such as *Hebe × andersonii* 'Variegata', which also has lilac flowers.

Long-flowering plants apart from recurrent roses include Mexican orange blossom (*Choisya ternata*), which flower late April-November, and potentillas in red, pink, yellow, or white (June-November). Among plants with more than one season of interest are pyracanthas, with white flowers in June and red or orange berries in September-March; and *Berberis thunbergii* 'Atropurpurea', with purple foliage (March-November), yellow flowers (May), red berries (August-September), and good autumn colour (October-November).

342

There are a lot of variegated shrubs to be had these days. Can you tell me which are the best and easiest to grow?

The best, brightest, and easiest is *Elaeagnus pungens* 'Maculata', which is evergreen. Other good ones are the variegated dogwoods *Cornus alba* 'Elegantissima' and *C. a.* 'Spaethii', with white and yellow variegations respectively; and the hollies (*Ilex*) especially the 'Golden King', 'Golden Queen', and 'Argentea Marginata' varieties of English holly (*I. aquifolium*).

343

I grow annuals and other flowers for arranging, but I would also like to grow some shrubs for cutting. Can you suggest a few?

Yes—but bear in mind that most shrub flowers do not last long after they have been cut. For blue-tinged silvery foliage, grow the cider gum (*Eucalyptus gunnii*), but you must cut it back every spring for a constant supply of the best leaves. Also with silver foliage is *Artemesia aborescens*, which has feathery leaves; but this plant is not completely hardy in colder areas. For yellow and gold leaves grow the bushy honeysuckle (*Lonicera nitida* 'Baggesons Gold') or the golden mock orange (*Philadelphus coronarius* 'Aureus'). For variegated leaves the privets (*Ligustrum*) take a lot of beating;

they come in white and gold forms and can be cut back every spring to increase the supply.

344

Why do some shrubs have silvery fur on their leaves?

Most of these plants come from hot dry areas of the world and the silvery hairs or 'wool' on the leaves help prevent too much water being lost from the foliage. As there is often very little water in the soil, the plants need to retain as much water as possible. It follows that most of these plants grow best in warm, sunny conditions, with a well-drained soil. Good examples include Jerusalem sage (*Phlomis fruticosa*), common wormwood (*Artemisia absinthium*), and cotton lavenders (*Santolina*).

345

I notice that the shoots on my dogwood are red at the tips, and they look delightful in the winter. What can I do to encourage them, and are there any other plants whose shoots colour up this way?

The red-stemmed dogwood (*Cornus alba*) in its several varieties, notably 'Westonbirt', is a very decorative winter shrub, but it needs regular pruning to keep the colour at its best. Cut all its stems back to 75-100 mm (3-4 in) of soil level every spring. Among other shrubs with vivid shoot colours, the varieties of the white willow (*Salix*

alba) with red shoots should be treated in the same way, while the white-stemmed bramble (*Rubus cockburnianus*), with blue-tinged white shoots, must be cut down every one year.

346

What shrubs can I plant at the top of my 900 mm (3 ft) high garden wall that will hang down and clothe the bare brickwork?

The creeping cotoneasters are ideal, in particular *Cotoneaster microphyllus* and *C. dammeri*. Others to try are the shrubby candytuft (*Iberis sempervirens*), with dense white flowers; the low brooms (*Cytisus* × *kewensis* with cream flowers, *C.* × *beanii* with yellow flowers, and *Genista lydia* with yellow flowers). The creeping ceanothus (*Ceanothus thyrsiflorus* 'Repens'), with blue flowers and glossy evergreen leaves, would also be ideal in this situation.

347

What plants can I put in the garden to encourage butterflies to settle?

The butterfly bush (*Buddleia davidii*) in its many varieties is undoubtedly the best, but you can ring the changes by also planting lavenders, privets (*Ligustrum*)—allow these to flower by not clipping them—and lilacs (*Syringa*), all of which are attractive to butterflies. *(See also 240.)*

348

Which of all the shrubs that produce berries make the best show?

This is a difficult one. The fruits of varieties of *Pernettya mucronata* come in a range of reddish shades and white and have the great advantage that they are rarely eaten by birds. The guelder rose (*Viburnum opulus*) has lovely translucent red fruits, but these *are* popular with birds. The strawberry tree (*Arbutus*) looks very striking with its red strawberry-like fruits, which the birds usually leave; while the berries of the firethorns (*Pyracantha*) in reds, yellows, and oranges are also impressive.

349

My front-garden path makes a right-angle turn—and all the delivery men step on the flower bed there to cut off the corner. What can I plant to discourage them?

You need something either small and spiny or small and tough. One of the dwarf berberises might give the paper boy an unpleasant surprise, while gorse (*Ulex europaeus*) could make him keep his distance. Periwinkles (*Vinca*) and rose-of-sharon (*Hypericum calycinum*) are very resilient.

On the whole, however, your best plan might be to plant up a tub with attractive shrubs on that corner; this would oblige all callers to walk around it.

350

I like using willow catkins in flower arrangements. Can you suggest some shrubs that bear attractive catkins?

Three spring to mind. *Garrya elliptica* is an evergreen winter-flowering shrub with olive-grey catkins up to 225 mm (9 in) long; it grows well on north and east walls. The second is *Itea ilicifolia*, which has holly-like evergreen foliage and creamy yellow catkins which may grow almost 300 mm (12 in) long; it must have full sun and well-drained soil for it is slightly tender. Much more resilient is the corkscrew hazel (*Corylus avellana* 'Contorta'), which has spirally twisted stems that are hung with sulphur-yellow catkins in late winter.

351

I have a small courtyard garden and wish to grow some shrubs in pots. What are the best varieties?

Heathers do well in pots; even if your soil is limy, you can provide an acid soil and so grow the summer-flowering ones. All the hebes (shrubby veronicas) are happy in tubs, as are the less-vigorous berberis—but mind the thorns! For winter colour plant the evergreen euonymuses, especially variegated ones such as 'Emerald Gaiety', 'Aureopictus' and 'Silver Queen'. New Zealand flax (*Phormium*) is stunning with its long, narrow leaves in many colours, and so are yuccas, with their rosettes of long needle-pointed leaves.

352

Are there any shrubs that I can plant which will be appreciated by my bees?

In the early part of the year flowering currants (*Ribes*) and the goat willow (*Salix caprea*) will be popular. Later there are many shrubs to choose from including the butterfly bush (*Buddleia davidii*), Californian lilac (*Ceanothus*), firethorn (*Pyracantha*), lilac (*Syringa*), gorse (*Ulex*), and daisy bush (*Olearia*).

Choosing climbers

353

The side wall of my house faces almost due north, and although it is not exposed to the wind it does not get any sun. Can you suggest some easy-to-grow climbers that would clothe it and not involve too much work?

Ivies (*Hedera*) will do well there: *H. helix* 'Goldheart', a small-leaved variety with a yellow blotch on each leaf, plus the two large-leaved variegated ones, *H. canariensis* 'Variegata' and *H.*

colchica 'Dentata Aurea', will brighten the wall all the year round. Some climbing roses will also do well, including 'Danse du Feu' ('Spectacular') 'Golden Showers', 'Guinée', and 'Mme Alfred Carrière'. Other flowering climbers to go for include *Hydrangea petiolaris*, most of the clematises, and the winter and summer jasmines. Most vine-family creepers, such as virginia creeper and boston ivy (both *Parthenocissus*), also make a good show.

354

The front of my house faces south, so it gets very sunny and warm and the soil is rather dry. I have tried honeysuckle there but it does not thrive. Is there anything that will put up with these conditions?

A south wall gives you a good opportunity to try out one or two slightly tender plants. The passion flower (*Passiflora*) will be ideal, as will the florist's mimosa (*Acacia dealbata*) and *Fremontia californica*, with its pretty, bright butter-yellow cups all summer long. Wisteria enjoys sun and warmth; and especially suited will be the ceanothuses native to California, in particular the sky-blue *Ceanothus* × 'Gloire de Versailles' and the deeper *C.* × 'Topaz'. If you particularly want to grow honeysuckle I suggest you try one of the sun-tolerant varieties, such as *Lonicera* × *brownii* 'Fuchsioides'.

355

My garage wall faces almost due east and gets a lot of cold wind. What climbers would put up with these conditions?

The vine family will make a brave show in the face of easterly gales, as will the common honeysuckles. The roses listed for north walls (see 353) will make a good show and to these can be added 'Étoile de Hollande', 'Gloire de Dijon', 'Mme Grégoire Staechelin' ('Spanish Beauty'), and 'Maigold'. The large cotoneasters, plus *Cotoneaster horizontalis*, can also be tried, as can pyracanthas, especially *Pyracantha* × *watereri*. Varieties of chaenomeles should also thrive.

356

We have a west-facing wall alongside the patio where we like to sit out in the evenings. What climbers or wall shrubs could I put there which would be at their best in summer?

Roses are a good choice and come in a tremendously varied range of colours and scents. Clematis hybrid varieties flower in summer and autumn, among the best being 'Hagley Hybrid', 'Jackmanii Superba', 'Mrs Cholmondeley', and 'Comtesse de Bouchaud'. You could also try jasmines, especially *Jasminum officinale*, the common white jasmine, and also many honeysuckles. For something a little out of the ordinary I suggest

you try the trumpet vines (*Campsis*), the potato vines (*Solanum*)—especially the beautiful white variety (*S. jasminoides* 'Album')—and annual climbers such as sweet peas (*Lathyrus*) and canary creeper (*Tropaeolum peregrinum*).

357

An old apple tree in my garden is no longer very productive, but it would make an attractive feature if I trained a climber through it. What should I choose?

Vigorous climbing roses (see 269) are ideal. Clematises too, look very good in this situation, but avoid the most vigorous, such as *Clematis montana*. The smaller-flowered ones usually look better than the larger-flowered hybrids; try *C. macropetala* and *C. orientalis*. Other good plants to train through trees include the staff vine (*Celastrus orbiculatus,* syn *C. articulatus*), with orange fruits in autumn and winter, and the wisterias.

358

I want to plant something scented to ramble over my front door. What can you suggest?

For winter I would go for *Abeliophyllum distichum*, with its almond-scented pink flowers, or the winter sweet (*Chimonanthus praecox*, syn. *C. fragrans*). For spring, plant *Azara microphylla*, which has vanilla-scented yellow flowers, wisteria, or the early Dutch honeysuckle (*Lonicera periclymenum* 'Belgica'). For summer and later in the year you would be advised to choose the pineapple-scented broom (*Cytisus battandieri*), the white *Jasminum officinale*, or the creamy white Chinese gooseberry (*Actinidia chinensis*).

359

I would like to grow some climbers in pots on my patio. Which varieties do best in pots?

Many climbers are too vigorous for pots, but the summer- and autumn- flowering clematises, which can be cut back every spring, will thrive. You could also try slightly tender climbers, such as the white potato vine (*Solanum jasminoides* 'Album') and the Chilean glory flower (*Eccremocarpus scaber*); the pots or tubs can be moved into a garage or greenhouse in winter to protect them against frost. Other possibilities are some of the less-vigorous roses, such as 'Nozomi'.

360

I have a wall three storeys high on one side of part of my garden and I'd like to grow something up it as it looks rather daunting. What do you suggest?

For a wall this size you really need something self-clinging: it would be very difficult to put wires up and tie the shoots in as often as would be necessary. Virginia creeper (*Parthenocissus quinquefolia*) and Boston ivy (*P. tricuspidata*) with their lovely autumn colour, will just keep on climbing (but *see* 397, 402). *Hydrangea petiolaris* is also a ready climber, and although it will take a very long time to reach the top, it should eventually get there. Ivies are ideal; Irish ivy (*Hedera hibernica*) is one of the quickest, but whichever variety you choose, remember that those with large, plain green leaves will cover the area more quickly than the smaller-leaved variegated types.

361

At the bottom of my garden are some old timber and corrugated iron sheds. I haven't got the time to dismantle them, but could I plant something that would rapidly cover them up?

The plant usually recommended for this purpose is the Russian vine, also known with justice as the mile-a-minute vine (*Polygonum baldschuanicum*). This can grow up to 6 m (20 ft) a year and will also stand hard pruning if it outgrows its space. I would not recommend ivies because they collect so much debris that the whole lot might collapse; but virginia creeper and the vigorous spring-flowering clematises, such as *Clematis montana*, or the American honeysuckle (*Lonicera × americana*) should all be suitable for your purpose.

362

Some of the stems of my clematis have fallen down and are growing along the ground, where they seem to be doing quite well. Can this or any other climber be used as ground cover?

Clematises make very good ground-cover plants, as do the yellow-veined honeysuckle (*Lonicera japonica* 'Aureo-reticulata') and the climbing hydrangea (*Hydrangea petiolaris*); many roses, especially ramblers, can also be used in this way.

363

I have an ugly tree stump in the garden which is too big to dig out. Can you think of a sprawling climber of some sort that would cover it but would not rampage too much?

The less-vigorous ivies are ideal for this job. Choose one of the varieties of common ivy (*Hedera helix*) with prettily marked leaves,

such as 'Glacier' in grey and white, 'Buttercup' with young leaves entirely yellow, or 'Adam' with white-margined green leaves. Try also the dutchman's pipe (*Aristolochia macrophylla*), with enormous leaves and yellow and purple pipe-shaped flowers. *Schizophragma hydrangeoides*, with its hydrangea-like similar flowers in creamy white, does very well on old stumps and is self-clinging.

Planting & maintenance

364

Planting time for shrubs always used to be spring or autumn for evergreens and anytime when dormant for deciduous varieties. Now that most kinds are available as container-grown plants, do these restrictions still apply?

Container-grown shrubs can be planted at any time of the year, but the fact remains that those planted at the traditional planting times will need the least attention. If you plant in summer, for instance, you must pay particular attention to watering, for if the rootball—which is usually of peat compost—is allowed to dry out, it will be very difficult to wet it again thoroughly; it will tend to drain very rapidly, and the plant will suffer.

365

I am planting up a large area with shrubs this winter. Should I plant them closer than is really necessary and so get good effect fairly soon, or should I plant at final spacings?

The problem with planting fairly close with the idea of thinning out later is that, when thinning becomes necessary, it may be difficult to bring yourself to do it! Rooting out thriving plants is not easy and you may find that those which remain have become spindly as a result of having to compete for light.

I suggest that, provided you buy good-quality plants, you plant them at their final spacings and fill the gaps with ground-cover plants. The latter will keep down the weeds, look attractive, and not impede the growth of the shrubs. Annuals and bedding plants are cheap infilling alternatives.

366

I sent off for some shrubs last winter, but when they arrived the ground was frozen. I was not sure what to do with them. Could you advise me?

Most shrubs and climbers, and especially deciduous ones which are sent out by mail order, are despatched with bare roots, not in containers. If they dry out they will die. When they arrive, and if there is no soil at all on the roots, stand them in a bucket of water for a day or two in a cool but frost-free place until the soil is in a fit state to receive them. Alternatively, store them for longer periods with their roots in moist peat.

Those that arrive with some soil on the roots, probably wrapped in netting, are best watered carefully with a can fitted with a fine rose, and stored in moist peat. As soon as possible after their arrival, dig a trench in a vacant bed of soil, lay in their roots, and replace the earth. 'Healed-in' like this the shrubs will stay in good condition for many weeks until the planting site is frost-free fully prepared, and in good condition.

367

We are recommended to use farmyard manure when planting shrubs, but I cannot get it locally. What is the best alternative?

Good farmyard manure, well-rotted, is probably the best organic material to use to improve soil structure and encourage the development of humus (see 708); but there is a number of more easily available alternatives and I suggest you use whichever of these is easiest to obtain.

Garden compost is easy to make, and a couple of home-made bins will produce a continuous supply. The contents of used growing bags are worth having, and you can sometimes get this material in bulk from commercial tomato growers. Spent mushroom compost, which usually contains at least some stable manure, is very good, although it contains chalk and may have an undesirable effect on lime-hating plants. There is also peat; but if you use it you should add two or three handfuls of bonemeal or Growmore fertiliser to each bucketful. Lastly, there are the proprietary brands of bulky organics; although they are mostly good, they are rather expensive.

368

I would like to train some climbers on the wall of my house but do not want to use too many nails. What is the best way to go about it?

There are two good ways. For small areas you can put up trellis; for larger areas it is better to put up a permanent wire-support system. Trellis can be attached to the wall with screws and plastic plugs after you have drilled holes with a masonry drill. To support wires, plug the wall and screw large vine eyes into the brickwork 1-1.2 m (3-4 ft) apart and at vertical intervals of 450-600 mm (18-24 in). Plastic-covered wires can then be threaded through the vine eyes and tensioned by means of eye bolts at one end.

369

To get some extra height in my borders I want to grow some clematis or climbing roses. What is the best way to support them?

Rustic poles make the most unobtrusive supports. They should be about 3 m (10 ft) tall and must be hammered at least 450 mm (18 in), and preferably 600 mm (24 in), into the ground. Paint them with a good wood preservative (*not* creosote) first. A few cross-pieces will help support the plants that can be trained along them. Clematis can be supported on tubes of special clematis netting: 2 m (6½ ft) lengths of netting are nailed to 2.4 m (8 ft) stakes, which are hammered 600 mm (2 ft) into the ground. This support is really suitable only for those late-summer-flowering varieties which can be cut back in spring to keep them to a reasonable size.

370

A wound has appeared at the base of a shrub in my border and it refuses to heal. What can I do about it?

It sounds as if the base of the stem has been damaged in some way, probably by hoeing. Take care when working through the border not to hit stems. The wound can be repaired by cutting away any rough parts with a sharp knife and painting the wound with a proprietary wound paint.

371

How can I protect my lobster-claw (*Clianthus*) and mimosa (*Acacia dealbata*) from frost in the winter?

The simplest way to protect shrubs in general is to attach netting to the wall above the plants and then to roll it down and fix it to the soil in front of the plants whenever frost threatens. This will provide a surprising amount of protection—but remember to remove it on warmer days.

372

Are there any particular problems involved in planting a climber to run up into a tree?

There are a number of important points. Pick a self-clinging variety—one with thorns, tendrils, or suckers—or a twiner. Plant the climber about 1 m (3¼ ft) away from the trunk so that the tree does not take all the moisture from the shrub's soil. Prepare the soil well with plenty of organic matter, and provide supports to lead the shoots into the tree. It may be necessary to tie a stake to a branch to keep it secure. *See also* 269.

373

A branch on my birch tree has broken in a gale, but it is still partly attached to the tree. What should I do?

Generally speaking, trying to repair a broken branch is not a good idea. The break is usually so ragged that the fibres could never be fitted together again and the wound will never heal properly. It is usually far safer to remove the branch cleanly, and paint with a bituminous wound dressing (*see also* 1047).

374

What can I do to help my hardy fuchsias to over-winter successfully?

In the coldest areas you have no option but to take cuttings and overwinter the plants in a greenhouse or conservatory. In warmer areas you can help them survive by not cutting the stems down in autumn, by making some holes around each plant with the tines of a fork to help water drain away, and by piling leaf mould, ashes, or soil around the base of the plant to protect it. Some varieties, incidentally, are hardier than others, the toughest being *Fuchsia magellanica*, *F.* 'Riccartonii', and *F.* 'Mrs Popple'.

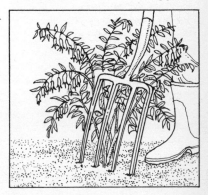

375

I planted a camellia a few years ago and it has done very well. Unfortunately, when I build my house extension the camellia will be in the way. Can I move it, and if so how should I go about it?

Camellias and other fibrous-rooted evergreens such as rhododendrons can be moved quite safely, at the right time of year—in September-October or April-May. If you have plenty of warning (say, six months) of the need to move, cut a circle around the plant by slitting the soil vertically with your spade. For a plant up to 1.2 m (4 ft) high, the cut should be about 300 mm (12 in) from the stem; for plants taller than 1.8 m (6 ft) it should be about 600 mm (24 in) from the stem. The slit, which should be to the depth of the spade blade, will cut some outer roots and encourage others to grow nearer the centre of the rootball.

Prepare the new site with plenty of organic matter, such as peat, and then, immediately before moving, thin out the shoots a little to compensate for the unavoidable root loss. Lift the shrub gently, keeping as much soil as possible on the roots (wrap them in polythene if necessary). Plant it carefully, replace the soil, water it in well, and stake it unless it is in a very sheltered spot; if the site is especially windy, put up a plastic wind-break. Keep a vigilant eye on the soil, watering it as necessary.

376

We are always recommended to dead-head flowers and house-plants. Should shrubs also be dead-headed?

Ideally, shrubs and climbers should be dead-headed, too, except those grown for their fruits; but the fact is that with most shrubs it is not practicable. It is, however, definitely worth doing with buddleias as it prolongs their flowering season; and it is always recommended for rhododendrons, although on all but the smallest specimens it is a long, fiddly job. Hydrangeas should also be dead-headed—but not until spring, as the old flowers help to protect the following year's flower buds.

377

I think that I ought to be feeding my shrubs to get the best out of them, but I am not sure exactly what I should do. Can you advise me?

The best way to feed shrubs once they have been planted out is to mulch them with a layer of organic matter spread around the base of the stem, usually in spring when the soil is moist (see 283).

Leaf mould or well-rotted weed-free compost is a suitable material; but the simplest way to go about mulching is to rake all the fallen leaves on to the border in autumn and let them rot down. This also helps keep the soil moist. However, bacteria use up a lot of soil nitrogen when they rot down the leaves; so to make sure that this nutrient is not in short supply, scatter a handful of sulphate of ammonia over each square metre (square yard) of soil in spring.

378

I have a large lawn. Can I spread my lawn-mowings as a mulch under shrubs?

There is a problem with using lawn-mowings. Most lawns contain weeds and weed grasses, particularly annual meadow grass, and if mowings containing the seeds of these unwanted plants are spread on the border, it will soon be full of weeds as well. It is better to compost the mowings, either on their own with a special activator or mixed sparingly with other material in the compost heap.

379

In my small city courtyard I have a number of shrubs and climbers in tubs and urns. My problem is that they seem to dry out very quickly. What can I do about it?

Some types of container dry out more quickly than others. Terracotta and concrete containers lose water through the sides and so need watering more frequently than others. Wooden containers are better in this respect, especially if painted, while plastic glass-fibre containers lose none.

The best thing to do is rig up a

semi-automatic watering system using a narrow-bore plastic pipe connected to a water tap. Nozzles are fitted to the pipe at intervals so that when the tap is turned on water trickles out into each pot.

380

I grow a number of shrubs and climbers in pots. How and when should I feed them?

In the growing season feed them every two weeks with a balanced liquid fertiliser, or use a proportionately weaker feed every time you water them. If you have a semi-automatic watering system for them, you can buy a diluter that will automatically put feed into the water supply.

381

Can you explain how to prune flowering shrubs?

There are two basic groups of flowering shrubs. One group flowers in summer and autumn on the tips of shoots that grew earlier the same season. The group includes buddleias, large-flowered and cluster-flowered roses, caryopteris, St John's wort (*Hypericum*), and some clematis hybrids. These must be pruned hard back in spring as growth is beginning, so as to encourage development of strong new shoots.

The second group includes plants that flower in spring on shoots which grew the previous season. This group includes mock orange (*Philadelphus*), forsythias, flowering currants (*Ribes*), weigelas, and beauty bush (*Kolkwitzia*). It is less vital to prune these; it is done immediately the flowers are over, and it involves removing the branches that carried the flowers. Shoots that will flower the following spring will already be growing and *must* be left unpruned.

Problems: shrubs

382

At Christmas I always like to have some holly with red berries. The problem is that my holly bush never seems to have any, although bushes belonging to my neighbours do. What is wrong?

Hollies (*Ilex*) come in male and female varieties and only the female ones bear berries. What is more, they have to be pollinated by males if fruiting is to be successful. It sounds to me as if you have a male bush and your neighbours have females, so your tree is pollinating theirs. I suggest you buy a variety like 'J.C. van Tol' or 'Golden King' (both of which, just to confuse matters, are actually female).

383

My camellia 'Donation' grows well but does not flower. What can I do about it?

Camellias need a moist, free-draining soil on a site that is sheltered from the strongest sun and, more particularly, sheltered from the early morning sun in winter. They are not tender plants but the flower buds are often damaged through thawing out too quickly. They then go brown and drop off. This happens when bright morning sun strikes the buds after a frosty night. I suggest you either move your camellia or plant another evergreen on its eastern side to shade it in the morning.

384

How do I make my hydrangeas bear blue flowers?

If your hydrangeas are pink, the chances are that you live on an alkaline, limy soil and they are unlikely to go blue even if you plant blue-flowered varieties such as 'La France' or 'Lorelei'. The answer is to dig in plenty of peat when planting, to mulch with peat every spring, and to apply a special blueing powder containing aluminium sulphate. Watering with what are called sequestered minerals can also help. On limy soil hydrangeas and some other shrubs cannot take up certain plant food. But if these are made available in their sequestered form, the plants can absorb them.

385

The magnolia I bought at the garden centre last year has not flowered. Should I take it back and complain?

Some magnolias flower very early in life, but others do not. If the plant you have is *Magnolia stellata* you have cause to be worried as this compact variety does tend to flower quite happily when young. *M. soulangeana*, however, sometimes takes quite a few years before doing its stuff. A regular mulch will help keep it happy, but there's little more you can do other than wait.

386

Couch-grass seems to be creeping farther and farther through my hydrangeas. Do I have to dig them all out to get rid of it?

Couch-grass is a particular problem with shrubs such as hydrangeas, St John's wort (*Hypericum*), and mock orange (*Philadelphus*) that produce dense basal growth. Until recently you had to do exactly that, but now there are two ways of dealing with it. A new weedkiller containing alloxydam-sodium has recently come onto the market which kills couch-grass and similar creeping grasses but not broad-leaved plants. You can spray it over shrubs or herbaceous plants and it will not harm them but *will* kill the couch. Alternatively, use the weedkiller

glyphosate, which comes as a gel, with a brush in the lid of the tub, and can be painted on the couch leaves. If you get any on your shrubs it will damage those, too, so be careful in applying it.

387

How can I stop the birds eating the berries on my pyracanthas and other shrubs?

Training a cat to sit by the bush is perhaps the best answer! There are various spray-on repellants which deter but do not harm birds, but heavy rain much reduces their effectiveness. If you look around your area you may find that one particular colour or variety is less popular with birds than the others; in some areas, for instance, yellow-berried varieties are never touched by the birds.

388

I have a problem with bindweed. It climbs up through my philadelphus, and although I keep pulling it out I can never get rid of it. What should I do?

The trouble with bindweed is that its roots are very deep and full of food reserves. You can kill it by repeatedly pulling or hoeing the tops off, since you will thus prevent it from producing food. But if it is right in amongst a shrub I would suggest a different approach. Unwind the bindweed from the stems of the shrub and then treat them with a weedkiller. Either paint the shoots with glyphosate gel or mix up some 2,4-D lawn weedkiller in an old jar or basin and dip the stems in the solution. The weedkillers will be carried right down to the root and kill the weed for good. Be careful not to get any chemical on the leaves of the shrub.

389

I have a hibiscus which had beautiful blue flowers when I bought it but, although it has seemed to be healthy since I put it in, I never get any flowers. Is there a reason for this?

It sounds as if your hibiscus is not in the right position. *Hibiscus syriacus* demands full sun, and unless it gets it, it is unlikely to flower. In colder areas the plant needs the additional protection of a warm, south-facing wall.

390

The leaves on my pieris are going yellow around the edges and the bush doesn't seem to be growing very strongly. What is wrong with it, and what should I do?

This sounds like a classic case of lime-hating plant growing in soil with too much lime in it. You can help by watering with sequestrene, which will improve the health and colour of the pieris; but if the soil is basically not suitable, you are fighting a losing battle.

391

Weed seeds from my neighbour's garden keep blowing into mine and coming up amonst my shrubs. What can I do?

There are three answers: have a firm but friendly chat with your neighbour; plant ground-cover plants amongst your shrubs (but you will have to continue to weed until they are established); or put down a weed preventer such as simazine. One application of this chemical will prevent weed seedlings coming up for a whole year, but do *not* put it around newly planted bushes.

392

The ceanothus that has been growing on my wall for about 10 years has recently started to go back. The shoots at the base suddenly go limp and die off, and I have noticed a stain creeping up the stem from about soil level.

I think this is probably root trouble. My guess would be that the soil is very wet deep down. This may be due to a fractured drain or broken gutter or downpipe, or possibly to a nearby soakaway. Check all these possibilities. The only alternative I can think of is that the area was used as a dump before the house was built, or during the building, and that something toxic was left there. Your local council may be able to help.

393

I have a spotted laurel, and one of its branches has suddenly gone dark brown and then black for no apparent reason. Why?

This is a difficult one. Most spotted laurel (*Aucuba japonica*) plants seem to do this at one time or another, and there does not seem to be any logical reason for it. As soon as you notice this happening, cut out the affected part; new shoots will soon fill the space. It is believed to be caused by a physiological imbalance in the plant, possibly combined with a badly drained soil.

394

Some of the shoots on my brooms have grown very flat with lots of short side shoots. Can you tell me what causes this, and is there anything I can do about it?

This is caused by buds not forming properly in the tip of the shoot, and it is called 'fasciation'. It can be caused either by damage to the shoot tip or, sometimes, by damage from pests, or by conditions which promote exceptionally rapid growth. The answer is simply to cut the shoot out entirely.

395

I'm worried about the possibility of my children being made ill by eating berries and leaves in the garden. Can you tell me which shrubs are poisonous, so that I can avoid buying them?

The main ones to avoid are: yew (*Taxus*), box (*Buxus*), cotoneaster, laburnum, mezereon (*Daphne mezereum*), ivy (*Hedera*), and sea buckthorn (*Hippophae rhamnoides*). Do not forget that some trees and perennials are poisonous, too.

Problems: climbers

396

The passion flower over my front door grows very vigorously but produces no flowers or fruit. What can I do?

The one thing that the passion flower (*Passiflora*) requires above all else is sunshine: without a sunny position and warmth lasting well into late summer, it will not flower and may well be killed in the winter months. A south wall is the only place where it will succeed in most parts of the country; it must be open to sun all day. Over-rich soil will often produce a mass of foliage and stems at the expense of flowers, so go easy on the manure and fertiliser.

397

The house I have just moved into has ivy all over one wall. Will it do the wall any harm?

Ivy can harm walls, but only certain walls. If the house is relatively new then the mortar between the courses of bricks will probably be hard enough not to be damaged. Pebble-dashed surfaces and older houses with very soft mortar can be damaged by the aerial roots, but if you remove an established ivy a lot of mortar can be pulled out with it.

I would advise leaving it in place, bearing in mind that it deflects water from the wall, so keeping it very dry. An annual clipping over with shears in April will take some of the strain off the mortar. The important thing is not to let the ivy get into window frames or gutters, behind fascia boards, or on to the roof. If you are planting ivy against a wall with soft mortar, rig up a wire or trellis support system which can take the weight of the stems.

398

I put up a new fence along one side of my garden and planted some climbers. Very soon they began to look ill and they are not doing very well at all. Could it be that the wood preserver from the fence has affected them?

If you put creosote on your fence, this is undoubtedly the cause of the trouble. It takes many weeks for the fumes from creosote, which are poisonous to plants, to dissipate, so you should always wait before planting. The alternative is to use one of the safe preservers based on copper naphthenate. These are usually green or sometimes cedar brown. It is safe to plant them against fences treated with these materials as soon as they are fully dry. If you are in any doubt, check the instructions on the container before buying.

399

The ivy on my wall has suddenly changed. The leaves at the top have become smaller and much narrower and are flowering and bearing fruits. What is happening?

Ivy goes through two stages—a juvenile stage and a mature stage. While ivy climbs it remains in its juvenile stage, in which it produces no flowers or fruits. When it reaches the top of its support, where there is usually more light, it grows bushier, with smaller leaves, and produces flowers and berries. This is quite normal, but such growths can be cut off if you wish.

400

When I bought my wisteria a good few years ago, it did not grow for a long time. I fed it, and recently it began to grow— but it still has not flowered. Why?

Wisteria is one of those plants that takes a fair while to come into flower. To make the wait even more agonising, it often grows very little in its first year or two. Help to induce flowering by shortening any unwanted long stems in July, cutting them back to about 300 mm (1 ft), and prune the plant again in January, shortening all sideshoots back to three buds. An occasional feed with diluted tomato fertiliser can also coax flowers from reluctant plants. If, after five or six years, the plant is still reluctant to flower (in spite of the fact that you have pruned and fed it regularly) it might simply be that it is from a clone (see 935) which is not free-flowering. If so, remove the plant and start afresh.

401

I have a strange climbing shrub on the wall of my house: at least half of each leaf is green but the tip is pink. Is it healthy, and, if not, what should I do about it?

This is indeed quite healthy and is a pretty, although not very common, climber called the kolomikta vine (*Actinidia kolomikta*). The strange foliage, creamy white flushed with pink at the tip of the leaf (or sometimes entirely pink) is encouraged by planting it in a sunny position. The plant is a vigorous grower, and also has fragrant white flowers.

402

I am having a problem with my virginia creeper. I planted it last year on my garage wall but the stems don't seem able to climb—they just fall on the ground. Have I bought the wrong variety, or what can I do to help it?

The problem is that Virginia creepers (*Parthenocissus quinquefolia*) need a little help before they get the hang of climbing. The simplest way to guide them on their way is to tape the shoots to the wall with small pieces of waterproof sticking plaster. A couple of pieces on each stem, one quite near the tip, should do the trick.

Conifers

403

I have a prostrate silver fir which has suddenly grown a vertical shoot right in the middle. Should I cut it out or leave it?

This is a common problem with prostrate conifers, especially varieties of the silver fir (*Abies*). It is very important to remove the vertical shoot as early as possible. Cut it out with sharp secateurs at the point from which it arises on the horizontal stem. If it is left, more vertical growths will arise, until the plant has lost all its character.

404

I bought some dwarf conifers from my local garden centre a few years ago but they do not seem to be staying very small. Can I prune them?

There is a difference, I'm afraid, between dwarf conifers and slow-growing conifers. Very few stay permanently small, although many will grow very slowly and so remain small for a fair while. Some can be clipped, rather than pruned, but you must never cut out the growing shoot. Those that will stand clipping include yews, junipers and cypresses; but *never* clip firs or spruces.

405

What is the best place in the garden for a bed of dwarf conifers and how should I go about preparing the soil for planting them?

Conifers do best in open situations with sun for at least part of the day. Do not put them under larger trees. Prepare the soil by adding plenty of organic matter and removing all perennial weeds. If you are to grow heathers (*Calluna*) with your conifers, the soil will need to be acid, so dig in peat.

406

I would like to plant a golden conifer as a specimen in the corner of the garden. Can you suggest a variety that will grow fairly quickly but not get too big?

There is no such thing as a conifer that will grow quickly and then stop. However, here are some suggestions. The golden form of the very popular Leyland cypress (× *Cupressocyprais leylandii* 'Castlewellan') is quick-growing— but eventually it will lose its gold; the golden Monterey cypress (*Cupressus macrocarpa* 'Goldcrest') is slower, but will still become fairly large eventually; the Lawson cypress (*Chamaecyparis lawsoniana* 'Lanei') is a stage slower again, eventually reaching about 9 m (30 ft); the variety *C.l.* 'Stewartii' is a good alternative, and 'Winston Churchill', a striking dense gold in colour, is even slower-growing.

407

Can you suggest a good prostrate conifer to disguise a manhole cover?

The junipers are best: the savin (*Juniper sabina* 'Tamariscifolia') is especially flat, while dwarf common juniper (*J. communis* 'Hornibrookii') runs along the ground at first, building up a little later. Two varieties of creeping juniper (*J. horizontalis*) hug the ground very closely: 'Emerald

Spreader', and 'Glauca' with its sea-green foliage.

Bear in mind, that you may have to lift the manhole cover occasionally. In particular if it is in a border I would suggest planting something a little more upright, such as one of the many varieties of Chinese juniper (*J. chinensis;* syn. *J. × media*), with branches arising at an angle of about 45 degrees from the ground. Access to the manhole will then be far easier.

408

I have a Lawson cypress whose branches are beginning to fall sideways, especially after they have been weighed down by snow. What can I do about it?

The first thing to do on winter mornings is to knock any snow off your conifer trees, so that it never has a chance to build up. You can also loop polypropylene twine loosely around the tree every 450-600 mm (18-24 in) to bring the branches closer to the trunk. I have seen plastic pea and bean netting, with a 150 mm (6 in) mesh, tied around a conifer to keep the branches in place. They will eventually grow through the netting and mask it. The problem is especially difficult if more than one main shoot has become established, so it is wise to cut out all but one of the rival leaders on young plants.

Ann Bonar

Horticultural journalist and consultant; a regular contributor to gardening magazines and author of 16 books on horticulture.

Hedges
and
Trees

Boundary hedges

409

Can you suggest a suitable boundary hedge for my country garden? It has a field on the far side which has stock grazing in it, and I am anxious that the hedge plants should be neither attractive nor poisonous to the animals.

Hedges which best suit the style of a country garden are those made of hawthorn, blackthorn, hazel (*Corylus*), field maple (*Acer campestre*), and myrobalan (wild) plum (*Prunus cerasifera*). None of these is toxic, but all are likely to be grazed by stock in adjacent fields, and while still small they should be protected from such grazing.

A hedge formed from a mixture of these plants would be dense and impenetrable and would probably need two or three cuts a season. Yew (*Taxus*) should not be used in such a hedge, as it is poisonous.

410

We have just moved into our first (newly built) house and would like to plant a boundary hedge around the outside of the garden. What are the cheapest types of hedge available?

The least expensive hedges nowadays are those formed from hawthorn (*Crataegus*) or privet (*Ligustrum*), which cost in the region of £30-£40 per 100 plants. Blackthorn (sloe) (*Prunus*) and beech (*Fagus*) come next at about £40-£50. The honeysuckle *Lonicera nitida* and the hedging plums (*Prunus*) are about £60-£70.

Privet is evergreen; beech retains many of its leaves through the winter, but they change in autumn to a warm russet brown; hawthorn and blackthorn are spiny. All these are best trained as formal hedges. They will need at least one cut each season, and privet certainly more than one. Yew and most conifers used for hedges are twice or three times as expensive as the plums quoted above.

411

There is an old wooden fence around the outside of our garden which needs to be replaced, and I am thinking of planting a yew hedge, as it would make a good background to our herbaceous borders. Could you tell me how long it will take to form a reasonable hedge, and how does its cost compare with holly?

Yew (*Taxus*) is a slow-growing plant: it can take five years to reach 1.5 m (5 ft), and some years longer before it is as broad at the top as at the base. However, if given dressings of rotted organic matter early every spring, it will put on

375-450 mm (15-18 in) of growth annually. Holly (*Ilex*) is even slower-growing, although it also makes a good evergreen hedge; its prickliness can be an advantage. Yew and holly cost about the same.

412

Would you recommend a formal or an informal hedge for the boundary of a property?

The choice depends to some extent on the amount of time you have to spare. Formal hedges need a complete 'close shave' at least once in the growing season, and many of them need cutting several times. Informal hedges, because they are usually grown for their flowers, need only one cut, either in spring or mid- to late summer, with secateurs, and then only in the form of spaced-pruning cuts.

Both types are ornamental in different ways, and the choice depends on your personal preference and the style of your garden. Informal hedges can make just as effective a barrier, given the right choice of plants. Some suitable ones are: the barberries, such *Berberis stenophylla* (orange-yellow flowers in spring); *B. verruculosa* and *B. gagnepainii* (yellow flowers in spring); *B. thunbergii* 'Rose Glow' (purple leaves and rose-pink young shoots and leaves); *Fuchsia* 'Riccartonii' (in mild districts); *Rosa rugosa* cultivars; gorse (*Ulex*); and the purple *Rhododendron ponticum*.

413

I want to plant a beech hedge along my front-garden boundary, which faces north, as a protection from the wind. The soil tends to be chalky: is this suitable for beech?

Beeches grow naturally on limestone, and some of the most magnificent specimens are to be found in the Chilterns, where the hills are formed mainly of alkaline topsoil, with a chalk subsoil. The addition of well-rotted garden compost, farmyard manure (if obtainable), or similar material before planting is advisable; use about a barrow-load to each 4.5 m (15 ft) of trench.

Young beech is very vulnerable, and in order to ensure the hedge will be strong when mature it is important to provide a barrier against strong winds for the first three years or so. This need be only of sacking, hessian, hop-lewing, or heavy-gauge plastic sheet; and in late spring and summer each year it may be removed during calm weather.

414

Is there much difference between the type of hedge used for a boundary and that used for an internal barrier?

Boundary hedges generally need to be strong and impenetrable, and they are often also required to provide privacy and protection against cold. With internal hedges the accent tends to be on their decorative qualities and their ability to provide 'surprise' within the garden or to screen off parts which are utilitarian.

Boundary hedges need to be quick-growing and about 1.8-2.1 m (6-7 ft) high; internal hedges need be only 1.2-1.5 m (4-5 ft), or, if used for edging, only 300-450 mm (12-18 in) high.

415

Can you suggest suitable hedging plants for my open-plan front garden, which is constantly overrun by neighbours' cats and dogs? I would want to keep the hedge about 900 mm (3 ft) tall.

A strong and effective hedge can be grown from some of the barberries (*see also* 412), which are prickly, vigorous, and decorative. *Berberis gagnepainii* is excellent for this purpose; it has dense, upright growth, evergreen leaves, and yellow, pendant flower clusters in May. Another good one is the purple-leaved *B. thunbergii* 'Rose Glow', whose young growth is a spectacular pink; the flowers are orange-yellow in April, and the leaves develop reddish tints before they fall.

Hedges for particular purposes

416

What are the best evergreen hedges?

The most ornamental evergreen hedges, which will stand formal training and clipping, are yew and holly. However, hedges of cypress (*Chamaecyparis*) and cherry laurel (*Prunus*) come a close second; and privet (*Ligustrum*), provided it is trained correctly from the time of planting, will supply a satisfactory semi-evergreen barrier.

The honeysuckle *Lonicera nitida* is also dense, with small evergreen leaves, and can be trained easily into a variety of shapes, but it needs clipping several times a year; it can, indeed, be rather time-consuming to maintain, so it is better used as an internal hedge kept to about 1 m (3¼ ft) high.

417

We live in a bungalow near the seashore in Sussex, where the soil is rather sandy. Could I have suggestions, please, for some suitable hedging plants.

There is quite a wide selection, from which I would choose the following: *Griselinia littoralis* (any soil) with thick, yellowish-green leaves forming a dense hedge under a formal clipping; *Escallonia* 'Langleyensis', with red flowers in

June-July; *E. macrantha*, with
deep red flowers in June-
September, *E.* 'Slieve Donard',
with large pink flowers in
June-August; sea buckthorn
(*Hippophaë rhamnoides*), with
silvery grey foliage and orange
berries if both male and female
plants are grown; tamarisk
(*Tamarix pentandra*), with feathery
flowers in August, and the May-
flowering *T. tetrandra; Euonymus
japonicus*, with evergreen shiny
leaves, available in variegated
forms, which stands close clipping;
and the honeysuckle *Lonicera
nitida*.

418

**We need protection from a
fierce north-east wind in
winter and from a south-west
breeze which blows in from
the sea most of the summer.
What do you suggest?**

Here are a few possibilities:
elderberrry (*Sambucus nigra*),
which grows rapidly to 6 m (20 ft),
and its golden-leaved form, *S.n.*
'Aurea', which is less quick-
growing; hornbeam (*Carpinus
betulus*), which grows up to 6 m
(20 ft); mountain pine (*Pinus
mugo*), which grows up to 3 m
(10 ft); Lombardy poplar (*Populus
nigra* 'Italica'), which can be kept
at the height required by annual
clipping; Leyland cypress (×
Cupressocyparis leylandii), which
should be kept at a maximum of
2.7-3.6 m (9-12 ft).

Whichever plants you use, they
will need to be protected against
the winds during their first two
years, while they get established.

419

**We have recently bought an
Elizabethan house, and want
to plant a knot garden at the
front, in keeping with the age
of the house. Can you tell us
what to use for edging the
beds?**

Knot gardens can look enchanting
when well designed, with their
geometrically shaped beds
intensively planted (in the 16th
century mainly with medicinal
herbs), and edged with dwarf
hedges. Plants to use which are
in keeping with the time are
sage (*Salvia officinalis*); hyssop
(*Hyssopus officinalis*); box
edging (*Buxus sempervirens*
'Suffruticosa'); lavender; and
rosemary (*Rosmarinus officinalis*);
the last two are preferably kept
clipped and formal.

420

**I have a hedge of box edging,
which is old and gappy; the
cats have sat in it over the
years, so it is now very
straggly. I would like to
replace it with a similar dwarf
hedge, perhaps a flowering
one. Do you think lavender
would be a good idea?**

Lavender (*Lavandula*) can
produce an excellent low-growing
hedge, about 600-750 mm

(2-2½ ft) tall, with fragrant flowers in July. It needs careful clipping immediately after flowering, or in spring: be sure to cut back only the previous season's growth, *not* any of the older growth.

Other plants you could use include *Senecio greyi*, which has grey felted leaves and yellow daisy flowers in July; southernwood (*Artemisia abrotanum*), with aromatic grey, ferny foliage; *Berberis buxifolia* 'Nana', an evergreen with yellow flowers; cotton lavender (*Santolina chamaecyparissus*), an evergreen with silvery foliage and yellow button-flowers.

421

I like the idea of flowering hedges, but I do not know what sort of plants I should use or how long they will go on flowering. Can you give me some information please?

Flowering hedges are essentially informal—that is, they are not close-clipped like formal hedges but are allowed to grow more or less naturally, although they need to be cut every year to keep them within the space available. This cutting (in effect pruning) is done in spring or summer, depending on the time of flowering (*see below*), and it involves removing the old flowered shoots and cutting back any new shoots which have elongated beyond the selected line of the hedge.

Plants to use are preferably fairly close-growing and evergreen, as well as good for blossom. Some excellent examples are: the hybrid musk roses 'Felicia' (apricot pink), 'Moonlight' (lemon-cream), 'Penelope' (salmon-apricot), and 'Cornelia' (apricot pink); the hybrids of *Escallonia*, flowering in June-August; *Cotoneaster franchettii*, with white and pink flowers in June, and grey-green leaves: firethorn (*Pyracantha* × *watereri*), with white flowers in June, and brilliant red berries; *Spiraea thunbergii*, with white flowers before leaves in March-April; shrubby cinquefoil (*Potentilla* 'Katherine Dykes'), with primrose-yellow flowers in May-August; calico bush (*Kalmia latifolia*), with bright pink flowers in June-July (*note:* this one needs an acid soil); *Hebe* 'Autumn Glory', with violet-blue flowers in August-November; tamarisk (*Tamarix gallica*), with pink flowers in August-October.

Buying hedge plants

422

Can I buy hedging plants from my local garden centre, or do I have to send away to a mail-order specialist nursery?

You should be able to buy hedging plants from either of these outlets. In both cases it pays to order well in advance of when you intend to plant, so as to make sure that they arrive at the right time and that you get your choice of plant.

423

Are plants for hedges sold individually or by the metre-run, and what is the best size of plant to buy?

Hedging material is usually sold in batches of 10, 50, or 100 individual plants; the greater the quantity, the lower is the unit cost. Given the length of the proposed hedge and the distance between each plant, the number of plants required can easily be worked out. Box-edging is sold by the metre-run, and 1 m (3¼ ft) will plant 2-3 m (6½-10 ft) of edging.

As regards size, the larger box-edging plants will obviously achieve the impression of a hedge much more quickly, but they are correspondingly more costly and take longer to establish. The small plants root much more rapidly and are probably stronger in the long term, but they need more protection in the first two years or so. A good average height for the young plants is 450 mm (18 in).

Site & soil preparation

424

Is there such a thing as an ideal site for a hedge?

As with any other type of plant, hedging plants have preferences for aspect, soil, and so on, but in practice the position of a hedge is dictated by necessity. It is more a case of fitting the material to the site, and particularly of choosing the species or variety which is most appropriate to the needs and purposes of the hedge first, and then making sure that it will grow in the soil and aspect.

425

What is the right time of year to plant a hedge?

As with any woody plant, the dormant season is the best time for planting. Plants which are deciduous (whose leaves fall in autumn) can be planted at any time when the weather is suitable between mid-October and March, but preferably before Christmas. Evergreens should be planted in early to mid-autumn or early to mid-spring.

The above remarks apply to bare-rooted plants. If the plants are container-grown, planting can be at any time, though be prepared for frequent watering of summer plantings.

426

We ordered 50 plants for a beech hedge last July and have been advised by the nursery that they will arrive shortly. We are anxious that they should all 'take' and know in general how to plant, but can you give us any special tips?

If the hedge site is not fully prepared when the plants arrive, unwrap them and plant them shallowly for the time being in a sheltered place, so that the roots do not become dry. When you do plant, mark the position of the hedge first with a taut line pegged at intervals to keep it from moving, otherwise the hedge will be a wavy one. Make a measuring stick from a length of batten, to show the distance between plants.

Dig out a trench to a spade's depth and about 375 mm (15 in) wide, or whatever is sufficient to allow the roots to be spread out. Start at one end, put in the first plant to the same depth as it was in the nursery (indicated by the soil mark on the stem), fill in some but not all of the soil over the roots and firm it in with the foot. Use your measuring stick to position the next plant, and continue until the hedge is complete. Then fill in the remainder of the soil, making sure that the line of the hedge is straight as you go. Finally, firm the soil as before. Stakes will not be necessary. If you are planting in dry soil, give the plants a good watering-in at once.

427

Is any special treatment required for the soil before planting a hedge, other than that given to any shrubby plant?

Soil preparation needs to be thorough as the hedge is likely to be there for many years, so double digging is always advisable (*see* 730). The trench should be about 1.2 m (4 ft) wide to give the hedge a good root-run. Dig it out four or five weeks before the intended planting date, and mix in well-rotted organic matter. Add a general compound fertiliser a week before planting if the soil is light and quick-draining.

Before starting, mark out the required position of the hedge with a tightly stretched line that runs down the middle of what will be the trench; there should therefore be 600 mm (2 ft) width on either side of the line. Be careful to dig to an even depth, otherwise you will get uneven growth of the hedge.

428

Is it necessary to trim or cut back hedge plants immediately after planting?

Some, but not all, should be cut back, unless they were planted in late winter or spring, when the trimming described below should be delayed until the following winter. The privets, tamarisk, thorn, blackthorn, and myrobalan plum should have their height reduced to about 100-125 mm (4-5 in). Plants such as beech, berberis, box, cotoneaster, escallonia, *Euonymus japonicus*, gorse, hazel, hornbeam (*Carpinus*) laurustinus (*Viburnum tinus*), *Lonicera nitida*, firethorn (*Pyracantha*), and rosemary (*Rosemarinus*) should have their height reduced by a third and the side growths trimmed to make them tidy. Conifers, holly, laurel—including Portugal laurel (*Prunus lusitanica*) and bay (*Laurus*)—and pittosporum should *not* have their height reduced, although straggling sideshoots can be trimmed.

In the second winter, repeat this trimming on all but the first group mentioned above (privet, etc); they will need only to have the previous summer's *new growth* cut back by half. These methods of training will ensure that the hedge is thick and well-clothed right from the base, and apply to formal hedges.

All informal hedges, except evergreens and brooms, should be cut back to leave 30 mm (12 in) length; the exceptions are left uncut.

429

I planted a cypress hedge in late April, and most of it went brown and appeared to die in the summer. Why is this?

Conifers, and indeed any species of evergreen, continue to transpire (give off water vapour) after planting or transplanting, but the roots will not absorb water from the soil for some time. If dry weather follows planting, the loss of moisture from the plant is much quicker, and results in discoloration and, often, leaf-fall, followed by death.

After planting, therefore, the water supply in the soil *must* be maintained—by artificial watering if need be. Mulches (*see* 706) help to retain the moisture, and overhead spraying to soak the foliage every evening further helps to slow down transpiration.

Some nurseries send out their evergreens coated with a special substance which prevents loss of moisture; the coating dissolves completely in due course. Other important post-planting treatments include firming back into the soil any plants which have been forced up by frost; and supplying shields against strong or cold winds.

Hedge care

430

The garden of our new home has a beautifully cared-for formal hedge of purple-leaved plum alternating with green-leaved plum and beech. What other care will the hedge need besides the annual cutting?

Once a hedge is established and has grown to the height required, little routine care is needed apart from clipping. However, it is important to keep weeds from infesting the roots, particularly perennials such as ground elder and bindweed, so regular weeding should be carried out.

Other common weeds of hedges are nettles, couch-grass, dock, and dandelion, which are all difficult to eradicate once they become established. Watch out also for tree seedlings such as sycamore, hawthorn, and elderberry, which can rapidly grow unnoticed amongst the hedge plants.

You should give the hedge a dressing of well-rotted organic matter (manure or compost) in spring or autumn; and, each spring, clear the hedge bottom of rubbish accumulated during the winter, taking the opportunity also to remove all dead growth.

431

Colt's-foot has encroached around the base of my privet hedge. How can I destroy it without also harming the hedge? Digging it out seems to be impossible, as its roots are inextricably entangled with those of the privet.

When weeds with extensive roots or creeping underground stems invade a hedge, weedkillers are the only remedy, short of digging up the hedge. Even repeated hand-weeding every year is not completely successful, as some of the root always survives to fight another day. Use one of the weedkillers based on glyphosate, painting it on to the leaves of the colt's-foot.

Colt's-foot is one of the most difficult of hedge weeds. Others, which should be dealt with in the same way, are ground-elder, bindweed, couch-grass, horsetail, and creeping thistle.

432

I have noticed locally that hedges which are kept clipped close vary considerably in shape; some of them have a rectangular outline, some a curved top, and so on. Is there an optimum shape, and if so, can you please explain why?

Yes, there are in fact two preferred shapes: the rectangular one with completely vertical sides from base to top; and the other with tapered sides, the base being broader than the top. If the base is narrower than the top it will become bare and badly clothed with growth, and the top-heavy upper part will get damaged by wind and snow.

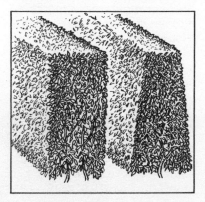

433

Is there any reason why the top of a hedge should not be curved, or cut in some other way than horizontally? Is it detrimental to the hedge?

No, curved and shaped hedgetops are not damaging to the hedge's growth, but they do need more skill in clipping. It is sensible to decide on the shape early in the hedge's life, so that it can be trained accordingly. To alter it when it is mature could produce variations in the hedge's density, and even result in ill-health. Undulating, castellated, curved, pointed, or rounded are all possible shapes, provided the hedge base is not narrower than the top.

434

So many hedges, whatever they are made of, seem to be thin and bare of leaves at the base. Can this be prevented?

Yes. Some of the trouble is due to poor nutrition, but mostly it is due to incorrect clipping from the time of planting. In order to induce good thick basal growth, the height of most hedging plants has to be considerably reduced in the first two or three years. This encourages it to send out side growth low down. If the side growth is trimmed back to tidy it up, the clipped sideshoots will sprout further sideshoots, giving an even denser cover.

435

When is the best time of year to cut a hedge whose leaves fall in the autumn?

There are two kinds of deciduous hedge: those which grow at a moderate rate, and those which grow fast. Those which grow moderately, producing new growth about 300-450 mm (12-18 in) long during the season, should be cut in August. This applies to beech, hornbeam, hazel, and tamarisk. If they are growing particularly well, however, they may benefit from two trimmings—one in late July and another, light one early in October.

Fast-growing hedges, such as blackthorn, myrobalan plum, and hawthorn, will need about three clippings at six-weekly intervals (so too, incidentally, will the evergreens gorse and honeysuckle *Lonicera nitida*).

436

I have been told by a local gardener that the right time to cut my Leyland cypress hedge is in the autumn—but it grows so fast that, if I leave it until then, I find I have to take secateurs to it, and it is now getting rather thin in places. Can you advise me please?

Early autumn is certainly the right time to cut some evergreen hedges, such as spotted laurel (*Aucuba japonica* 'Variegata') and all the other laurels, *Elaeagnus*

pungens, sweet bay (*Laurus nobilis*), and × *Osmarea burkwoodii.* But the fast-growing evergreens, including conifers, are better trimmed either once (in August) or twice (in late July and in early October). This will keep them under control and ensure that they have thick, close growth. Hence your Leyland cypress needs to be cut earlier than you have been advised.

There are one or two evergreens which need even more cutting, notably gorse and *Lonicera nitida* (*see* 435).

437

I want the hedges in our smallish garden to be a definite feature rather than just an enclosing background. I intend to use flowering species of hedging plants, and we will be making our choice from *Camellia japonica,* Mexican orange-blossom (*Choisya ternata*), *Hebe speciosa* hybrids, and *Pittosporum tenuifolium* (the last for its evergreen leaves). What is the correct method of trimming these plants when they are grown as informal hedges?

Plants such as these, which grow slowly or flower from side growths, are very easy to maintain. They simply need any long straggly shoots cut back in autumn or spring to make them tidy, and their dead flowerheads removed.

438

The tiny low-growing hedges that form edgings to beds of summer annuals always look so neat and exact. Is there any special method of clipping them?

The formal edgings you mention need close cutting about once a month from the end of May, until late in August or early September. Use razor-sharp shears, and cut exactly to your guiding line, which should be tightly stretched between supports (see 441).

439

I recently passed a beautiful flowering hedge formed of roses, but I have been unable to discover the name of the variety. Its flowers were salmon-pink, with a strong perfume. Can you identify it, as I would like to grow it?

The hedge you describe seems likely to be one of the hybrid musk roses, called 'Penelope'. It flowers from June to September and has good scarlet hips in winter. There are several other hybrid musks with flowers of different colours, but equally decorative. To be seen at their best, such hedges must be at least 1.5 m (5 ft) wide; if less, they will be rather disappointing. To get this effect, they are pruned late in February by cutting short side shoots back so as to leave three buds, cutting long new shoots from ground level by a third

of their length, and removing entirely some of the oldest growth. In summer, the faded flowers are removed at once to encourage further flowering.

440

I am told that a laurel hedge should not be cut with shears or a mechanical hedge trimmer. Is this true?

Yes, because the leaves will unavoidably be cut in half by these methods, and will turn brown. Eventually this damage may weaken the hedge, as such leaves will fall. Although rather laborious, it is better to use secateurs and cut stems individually.

441

I never seem able to get an even, level cut on my hedge when I give it its annual trim. How can I obtain a really neat appearance?

First, check whether your hedge is one which does indeed need only one clip, or whether it should have several. If the latter, it will be difficult with only one cut to keep it smooth, as so much material will have to be removed. Second, when cutting, stretch a line tightly between two posts along the top, at the height you want the hedge to be, and clip exactly to this level. For the sides, put in canes vertically at intervals along the hedge, and sight along these as you cut.

442

How and when should I trim my informal flowering hedge?

In general this type of hedge needs only to be pruned, rather than cut all over; do this once a year, in spring if it flowers between mid-summer and autumn, and in mid-summer if it flowers in spring or early summer. In either case, take off the shoots which have flowered, thin out the growth if it is crowded, and remove completely any old growth which is straggly and flowering badly.

443

What is the quickest and most comfortable method of hedge-trimming using shears? I find such work very tiring.

Keep the shear blades really sharp, and use shears which are well-balanced, comfortable to hold and of a weight suitable to your strength. Indeed, before you buy shears, check that they have a cutting action which does not jar your wrists. Do not try to reach up or stretch—this is tiring and is one of the causes of unintentionally wavy hedges. Use step-ladders if need be, and keep the hedge of such a width that the middle of the top surface is easy to reach from either side. Cut the sides from the base upwards, otherwise the trimmings will get caught in the uncut hedge below. Put sacking on the ground beside the hedge to catch the trimmings.

444

Can you tell me how to train a hedge by the method known as laying?

Basically the method consists of making a long slanting cut partly through a stem about 300 mm (12 in) above ground-level, then bending the stem sideways and weaving it around stakes already put in position. It is used on old hedges which are overgrown and thin in patches in order to renovate them and encourage new growth from the base of the plants. The stakes are put in behind the hedge at an angle of 45 degrees and the layers (stems) are bent the opposite way across them and at right angles to them. Weak, damaged, and straggling shoots are removed at ground level, and four or five of the straightest shoots remaining on each plant are used for laying. The stakes are bound together along the top for neatness and security while the hedge thickens up.

445

I have a row of overgrown lime trees which originally formed a screen and which I want to cut back and pleach. Are limes suitable for this kind of training and what are the details of the method?

Limes can certainly be pleached: they have pliable growth, and the shoots rapidly grow long enough to be woven in and out. Once the trees have been cut back to the height you require, the lower part of the trunks should be cleared of side-growths; horizontal bamboo canes or wires are now attached to the trunks and placed between the trees. Then shoots are allowed to grow out sideways; any which are produced fore and aft are removed completely. The sideshoots are tied to the canes and, when plentiful enough, are interwoven with one another. As the shoots mature into branches, the canes or wires can be dispensed with and new growth trained amongst the old.

446

What is a 'fedge'?

A fedge is a combination of a fence and a hedge, and usually consists of a wooden fence over which a climbing plant is grown. For instance, the variegated ivy *Hedera canariensis* 'Variegata' (white-variegated) or *H. dentata* 'Variegata' (yellow-variegated) can be trained to cover a fence completely and will need hardly any care. Similarly, the trailing winter jasmine (*Jasminum humile*) and *Forsythia suspensa sieboldii*, with its long pendulous shoots, can be trained in and out of the stakes of a rustic or palisade fence. You can also make a frame to replace the fence component out of thick wire bent to the shape you want.

Pests & diseases

447

A patch of my privet hedge appears to be completely dead: all the leaves are brown and withered, and there are no new shoots. It was quite all right last year. What is the matter with it, and will it recover? If not, can I plant some more privet in its place?

When a section of privet hedge turns brown and does not grow, it is usually because it has been infected with a disease called honey fungus (*see* 960).

You should dig up the dead privet completely, with all its roots, together with one or two apparently healthy plants on each side of it, and burn them; then treat the soil with Bray's Emulsion (which you may also find under its original name, Armillatox). Alternatively, you can remove the soil in which the privet was growing and replace it with fresh soil. You can replant about two years later. This disease can infect all woody plants, and it is a good idea to destroy any dead wood elsewhere in the garden, as this may also be infected.

448

There is a white woolly substance all over the leaves and stems of my beech hedge. What is it, and how should I deal with it?

Your hedge is infected with beech scale (*Cryptococcus fagisuga*), a tiny insect which is covered with white 'wool' for protection from predators. It sucks the sap from the foliage and overwinters in its egg form. Spraying under strong pressure with malathion is a useful control; you should also fork the soil lightly around the hedge, and give it a dressing of well-rotted organic matter in autumn.

449

I have found two of the largest caterpillars I have ever seen feeding on the leaves of my privet hedge. They are about 75 mm (3 in) long, green with red stripes on the sides, with a short erect tail at the end. What are they, and should I spray the hedge?

These are the larvae of the privet hawk-moth, a night-flying species with a wing span of 100 mm (4 in) and brown in colour. The caterpillars are rarely seen nowadays and do little damage; there is no need for control measures.

Improving old or overgrown hedges

450

The boundary hedge of the property I have just bought is badly overgrown. It seems to be a mixture of hawthorn, sloe, nut bushes, and some other plants. Can I cut it back hard without harming it, and, if so, when?

Yes—a hedge made up of a mixture of deciduous plants like this can be cut back by at least half its height, provided it is healthy and vigorous. The time to do this is between October and March, and it will result in new growth appearing from lower down and from the base, thus helping to fill up gaps, as well as making the hedge a more manageable height.

451

Can I cut down hard a conifer hedge which has gradually got too tall over the years?

Conifer (and other evergreen) hedges have to be treated gently when it comes to renovative cutting. It is not wise to cut hard, as this may kill them; this is specially true of the cypress family. Instead, it would be better to cut a little extra off each year when you do the routine clipping until it is down to the height you want.

452

I have cut down hard my rather neglected hedge, which had grown too tall. What should I do now to help it grow well again and fill in the gaps?

Starting at one end, work along both sides of the hedge, removing long side-shoots and any which are broken, dead, or diseased. Then thoroughly clear the base of all rubbish and remove any weeds completely, by hand if possible, but chemically if necessary. Fork the soil along both sides, and apply a dressing of well-rotted organic matter; add a general fertiliser dressing the following spring. Cutting it down hard will encourage new growth from the base to fill in the gaps.

Machinery & tools

453

What are the essential tools for trimming and training hedges in a typical, smallish garden?

Razor-sharp shears are the vital tool, with comfortable handles and a balanced weight. Step-ladders, canes, and a line, a collecting sheet, and a wheelbarrow are also useful or necessary; also secateurs for larger shoots and for laurel hedges (*see* 440).

454

We have a 100 m (330 ft) frontage of a formal mixed hedge of beech and hornbeam. Cutting this by hand now that it is established is time-consuming as well as hard work. What are the pros and cons of mechanical hedge-trimmers?

Mechanical hedge-trimmers have reciprocating blades, and will make 2000 to 4000 cuts a minute; the higher rate produces a lot of vibration and can be very tiring. But even the slower-cutting models do the work very much more quickly than by hand. Electrically powered either by a battery, mains, or a power take-off point, they are easy to use and well-balanced so as to minimize their apparent weight.

They are, of course, much more expensive than shears, but for gardens with a long hedge, or many hedges, they are essential. For extra safety, the electric models have double insulation, and at least one model has an on-off catch which automatically returns to off. Try to test-cut a hedge before buying to make sure that the weight is suitable and the grips comfortable for your hands.

Trees

455

I have acquired a small, treeless garden. Can you suggest two or three attractive trees that will flower in summer and will not ultimately grow too tall?

Most trees flower in spring and early summer; the few which flower later grow too large too quickly for a small garden. A delightful early-flowering one is the Judas tree (*Cercis siliquastrum*), which has clusters of rosy purple flowers in late May and June on bare stems; the leaves unfold *after* the flowers. It is related to the pea family; it will grow about 3 m (10 ft) high and wide in eight years, and will eventually reach a height of about 4.5 m (15 ft) or a little more.

Another delightful early-flowering tree is the hybrid *Laburnum × watereri* 'Vossii' (syn. *L. × vossii*), which bears lovely golden flower racemes 300 mm (12 in) or more long in May. It will eventually reach 4.5-5.5 m (15-18 ft) in height.

Finally, a tree with a fine, wide-spreading head is *Crataegus × prunifolia*, an ornamental thorn or may tree. Its white flower clusters, borne in June, are followed by bright red haws (berries) and brilliant crimson leaves in autumn. Its height and spread willl be about 2.4 × 3.5 m (8 × 12 ft) after 10 years or so, and it will eventually reach about 4.5 m (15 ft) in height and spread. (*See also* 466.)

456

I would like to plant a weeping willow next to my garden pool, but I am worried about the size it may eventually attain. Can you recommend any reasonably small varieties?

Although weeping willows are handsome, graceful trees, the commonest species, *Salix × chrysocoma*, grows much too large for the average garden—it will eventually attain a height of about 18 m (60 ft) or even more, with wide-spreading roots. A better, slower-growing tree is the standard form of the purple weeping willow (*Salix purpurea* 'Pendula') which will reach about 4.5 m (15 ft) in 12 years but will not grow much taller. Its young shoots are a striking purple in colour.

457

To provide winter colour in the garden, I want to plant some trees with attractive bark. Can you recommend suitable species?

The Himalayan birch (*Betula jacquemontii*) is one of the handsomest, especially when well-grown, with its silvery white bark, and in autumn when its leaves turn yellow. *Prunus serrula* is a white-flowering cherry with shining red-brown bark which looks as if it has been polished. *Acer davidii* is a maple whose striking bark is bright green and white striped. All these are small trees growing to about 4.5-7.5 m (15-25 ft).

458

I wish to replace a tree recently blown down in a gale. Can you recommend one with good autumn leaf colour? My garden soil is acid.

The American sweet gum (*Liquidambar styraciflua*) has maple-shaped leaves which turn crimson, yellow, and orange in autumn and give a brilliant display; it slowly grows into a large tree of 15 m (50 ft). (Make sure you buy from a nursery which is known to have a good-colouring form. Some liquidambars have indifferent autumn colour.)

The snowy mespilus (*Amelanchier lamarckii*) is a small tree whose leaves turn various shades of red in autumn; it also makes a charming show with its white flowers in spring.

The flowering cherry (*Prunus sargentii*), with its crimson and orange leaves in autumn, also has a delightful springtime display of pink flowers; it has chestnut brown bark. Both this and the snowy mespilus rarely exceed 6 m (20 ft) in height.

459

I am growing a collection of plants to lighten a dark corner, and for a focal point I would like a tree which has yellow or yellow-variegated leaves. Can you suggest one which does not grow too tall?

Some trees with foliage of this nature are: The 'Winston Churchill' variety of Lawson cypress (*Chamaecyparis lawsoniana*), yellow with a conical shape; *Ilex* × *altaclarensis* 'Golden King', a yellow-margined female holly; *Robinia pseudoacacia* 'Frisia', yellow leaves, which grows at a rate of 450 mm (18 in) a year.

460

What trees are there with well-coloured berries in autumn which are least likely to be damaged by birds?

Suitable small trees include *Sorbus vilmorinii*, with pink and white berries and purple autumn leaves; yew (*Taxus baccata*) with red berries (poisonous); the hawthorn

Crataegus carrierei, with pretty orange-red berries; the mountain ash *Sorbus* 'Joseph Rock', with amber-yellow fruits; and the holly (*Ilex*) 'J. C. van Tol', which has heavy crops of berries every year. Spraying with non-poisonous substances bitter-tasting to birds is a useful insurance; but the substances are usually washed off in a heavy shower of rain.

461

In a local park there is a handsome grey-leaved tree, with dense and rather weeping growth, which makes it look rather like an elongated shrub. Can you identify it, or suggest a similar tree, as I would like to obtain a specimen?

This sounds like the weeping pear (*Pyrus salicifolia* 'Pendula'). Its willow-like leaves are silvery grey; it has white flowers followed by small brown, pear-like fruits, and it grows slowly to about 7.5 m (25 ft).

462

Are there any small trees which flower in August? It seems that most garden trees flower in spring or early in summer, but I would like to get away from the usual cherry/crab-apple/laburnum permutation.

The choice is limited but there are a few: *Eucryphia* × *nymansensis* 'Nymansay' is one, with white saucer-shaped flowers through August and September; it prefers acid-neutral soil and a sheltered site. Another is the golden-rain tree, with bright yellow flowers in clusters; it grows about 9 m (30 ft) tall. (*See also* 468.)

463

How can I prolong the season of my flowering cherries?

You can get a succession of flowers from these beautiful trees by planting the following: *Prunus subhirtella autumnalis* (flowers November-February, with single white blooms); *P. sargentii* (*see* 458) (flowers March-April); and *P.* 'Pink Perfection' (double rose-pink flowers late April-May, with bronze-coloured young leaves).

464

I have a small garden and want to plant a pocket-handkerchief tree. How large does it grow, and does it need special soil?

Davidia involucrata has large, white, paper-like bracts to the flowers, which account for its popular name; but it takes many years to reach flowering size. It has no special soil needs and grows 12-15 m (40-50 ft) tall, so it would eventually be rather large for your garden. It would be better to choose a smaller species (*see* 455, 462); pruning and cutting back large trees which have outgrown their space can be costly and harm their future growth.

465

I have several winter-flowering shrubs in my garden. Are there any winter-flowering trees I could plant to keep them company?

There is the winter-flowering cherry (*Prunus subhirtella autumnalis; see* 463); the strawberry tree (*Arbutus unedo; see* 468); and the cornelian cherry (*Cornus mas*). This last has its branches and twigs wreathed in clusters of bright yellow, spidery-petalled flowers from late January-March; later it has red cherry-like fruit, and red-purple autumn foliage.

Size and shape

466

We have a small garden with little space, but would like a tree to emphasise the vertical dimension. What would you suggest?

A fastigiate form—that is, narrow in growth habit—would be best, and one of the following might be suitable: *Prunus* 'Amanogawa', a flowering cherry with double-pink flowers and good autumn colour; the maidenhair tree (*Ginkgo biloba*) in its fastigiate form, the leaves of which are larger versions of those of the maidenhair fern, and turn yellow in autumn; a

blue-grey form of Lawson cypress (*Chamaecyparis lawsoniana* 'Allumii'); and the yew *Taxus baccata* 'Fastigiata'.

467

We have a large pool in the garden and would like to grow a moderately sized weeping tree (but not a willow) next to it. What can you recommend?

The following grow to about 3-4.5 m (10-15 ft): *Cotoneaster* 'Hybridus Pendulus', an evergreen with red berries; the weeping ash (*Fraxinus excelsior* 'Pendula'); and Cheal's weeping cherry (*Prunus* 'Kiku-shidare Sakura'), with double pink flowers. All form umbrella-shaped heads, reaching to the ground.

468

Can you recommend a small- to medium-sized tree which looks attractive all year round?

The strawberry tree (*Arbutus unedo*) fills the bill: it has shining evergreen leaves, clusters of white flowers in autumn and early winter, and red strawberry-shaped fruits, which change colour slowly through the year until they mature the following autumn; it grows to a height of 3.7-4.5 m (12-15 ft). It needs a mild climate, but will withstand gales.

The ornamental crab-apples (*Malus*), which grow to 3.7-6 m (12-20 ft), are hardy, easily-grown, and attractive for most of the year, with crimson, red, pink, or white spring flowers, yellow or red fruit, and good autumn colour with purple leaves in some varieties.

469

What is a standard tree?

This is a small tree whose trunk measures about 1.8 m (6 ft) from the ground to the point at which the main branches originate to form the 'head' of the tree. A half-standard is a tree with a clean trunk about 1.2 m (4 ft) tall; and a 'bush' tree has a short main stem about 600 mm (2 ft) tall.

Site & soil

470

Suggestions, please, for some trees to provide shelter from salty gales in our seaside garden.

The following are good, hardy trees which will help provide a wind-break; you will need to provide a temporary barrier between them and the wind for a year or two while they get hold: common hawthorn (*Crataegus monogyna*); scotch laburnum (*Laburnum alpinum*)—the commoner *L.* 'Vossii' would soon be damaged; the beach pine (*Pinus contorta*); the pussy willow (*Salix caprea*); and the whitebeam (*Sorbus aria*).

471

We live at the lowest point of a shallow valley, and the ground tends to be boggy in parts of our garden. Is there a tree which will thrive with its roots permanently in moist soil?

The swamp cypress (*Taxodium distichum*) would be ideal for these conditions provided there is room in your garden: it grows eventually to about 24 m (80 ft); it is a deciduous tree, with foliage somewhat resembling that of the dawn redwood. The alders (*Alnus*) and willows (*Salix*) are also good trees for damp situations.

472

I wish to plant a row of cypresses to form a shelter belt, but have been told that the shallow, rather chalky soil of my garden is not suitable. Is this true, and if so what can I plant instead?

It is true that most conifers do best in a well-drained soil, or a well-worked clay. Shallow chalky soils are *not* suitable. For shelter on such a soil you could try hawthorn, beech, spindle-tree (*Euonymus*) ash, laburnum, and whitebeam (*Sorbus aria*). Whichever you plant, shelter them from wind for three years while they become established.

473

Is there a specially good type of soil for trees?

On the whole, most trees will grow in most soils—the deeper the better. So far as general likes and dislikes of particular types of trees are concerned, silver birches prefer a sandy type, beeches thrive on chalky ones, conifers do badly on sticky clay soils, and one or two trees need acid-reacting soils. Your local nursery or garden centre will tell you whether a particular species in which you may be interested has any definite preferences.

Planting & aftercare

474

We have ordered several trees from a local nursery, and they are due to arrive in about three weeks' time. Should we prepare the ground now, or leave it until the trees arrive? What should we do if there is a hard frost when they come?

Ideally, the soil should be double dug as for hedge or shrub planting (see 730). Double digging is particularly important for trees as they put down long anchoring roots and remain in place for many years. Dig out the hole a day or two before the trees' arrival, so that you can plant them without delay. If the ground is frozen, leave the roots in their moist packing material but allow the tops some air until the soil thaws.

475

What are the essential stages in planting a tree?

Make sure the hole is large enough to take the roots when they are spread out around the trunk; they must not be doubled up or bundled together. Put any supporting stake needed into the hole first, make sure both tree and stake are vertical, and fill in soil to the original soil mark on the trunk. Firm the tree well in with the foot, water the soil if dry, and rake the surface lightly.

476

After planting a tree, is there anything to be done to help it get established?

In dry weather, water well every few days until the rain sets in; in addition, spray the foliage of evergreens every morning and evening. Ensure that the young trees are shielded from strong winds. (Conifers that cannot be tied to a stake can be given support by a cylinder of plastic mesh that is attached to two or three stakes.) Push young trees back into the soil if they are lifted by frost, and firm them well in. If necessary protect them in winter from bark-gnawing by rabbits, hares and deer with proprietary tree-guards or wire-netting cylinders.

Pruning & shaping

477

I know that shrubs and fruit trees need pruning regularly to help them fruit or flower better, but does the same rule apply to trees?

No, fortunately most trees do not require regular or formal pruning. They grow naturally into attractive shapes, provided they have the room to do so, so it is most important when choosing trees to find out their ultimate height and spread. If they have to be cut to fit, so to speak, it will be difficult, unsightly, and bad for the tree. While they are still young a little help in shaping can be given, and any dead or diseased growth removed.

478

In a recent thunderstorm one of the poplar trees in our garden was struck by lightning, and a very large branch broke off. How can I deal with the resultant massive wound?

Poplars being large forest-type trees, it would be advisable to call in a professional tree surgeon to repair the damage and treat the tree to prevent rot setting in. It is dangerous for an amateur to attempt such work; but if it is not done, the whole tree could become rotten and ultimately fall.

(For removal of more manageable branches, *see* 1047.)

479

What is the difference between pollarding and lopping a tree?

Strictly speaking, pollarding is the cutting back of a tree to leave only the main trunk, whereas lopping involves cutting the main branches back to within a few feet of the trunk. In other words, lopping is not so drastic, but both procedures result in a forest of small shoots arising at some point on the tree, and are ways of reducing its height considerably without having to remove it. Willows are pollarded to produce shoots used to make baskets and hurdles.

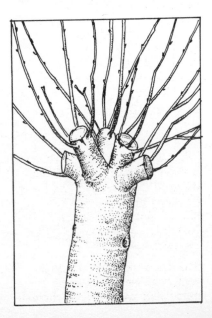

Shade & root problems

480

Part of my garden is in shade for most of the day because of the trees in a neighbour's large garden. Since I cannot remove the trees, what can I do to improve the conditions for my plants? And what plants will grow well?

If the trees grow close to your garden the shade will be dense, and the soil is likely to be permanently moist from overhead drip. Improve the drainage with coarse grit, and plant moisture- and shade-loving plants such as hardy ferns, *Primula* species, violets, and periwinkles. Lighter and more dappled shade is no problem, as there are many plants which prefer this kind of light: lilies, hostas, azaleas, rhododendrons, and blue poppy (*Meconopsis*) are a few examples.

481

The soil beneath my large horse chestnut is very dry for most of the year and the lawn grass will not grow in its shade. What can I grow instead to keep weeds and moss at bay?

The dwarf cyclamen should do well; small-leaved ivies and epimedium will also grow there. If

you mix plenty of peat and some general fertiliser into the soil, many more plants will grow, since this treatment will introduce food and water to the soil.

482

The roots of a nearby poplar tree are showing above the surface of my lawn and are sprouting shoots. If I treat these leaves and shoots with hormone weedkiller, will it kill them—but also kill the tree?

The solution will kill the treated shoots but not the tree. However, more shoots are likely to appear and will also need treatment. Either increase the depth of lawn soil by topdressing to cover the exposed roots, or mow the shoots off regularly.

483

I've heard a lot about the trouble tree roots can cause to the foundations of houses, and am wondering whether the roots of the cedar planted in our front garden are likely to be a problem.

The tree roots which penetrate foundations are mainly those of poplar, elm, and willow—large, vigorous, and widely extending trees—and the trouble occurs most often on clay soils. In general, it is wise to avoid planting a tree within 5 m (16½ ft) of the house. Even if the roots of your cedar do little damage, the branches will eventually cast shade into your rooms; and they could damage the fabric of the house if they broke off in a gale or a heavy snowstorm.

484

What are my legal obligations regarding trees which overhang a neighbour's garden? Do I have to cut them back? And what about the roots?

No, you need not cut overhanging branches back, though your neighbour is entitled to cut them back to the boundary of his garden. Such cut-off branches, however, will still legally be yours, including any fruit on them. Roots which 'trespass' are a different matter, and if they damage walls or foundations you will be held responsible. If you wish to cut down one of your own trees completely, make sure it does not have a preservation order on it for reasons of rarity, amenity, or whatever. In certain cases a tree can be cut down only if it is replaced by one of similar dimensions and appearance. Your local council will be able to clarify the situation on any particular tree you may have in mind.

General

485

To what age does the average tree live? For instance, how long could I expect a tree 6-8 m (20-26 ft) tall to survive? And at what age would it be mature enough to flower?

Small trees of the size you mention vary greatly in the age at which they start to flower; it may be about 5 years, or it may be 10 or more; and they live for 40-50 or more years. The larger forest trees, such as the tulip tree (*Liriodendron tulipifera*), oak (*Quercus robur*) and beech (*Fagus sylvatica*), may live for hundreds of years, but will be slow in starting to flower— perhaps not for 20 years.

486

A horse chestnut in my neighbour's garden has developed curious, brownish plate-like growths sticking out of the trunk, not very far above the ground. What are they caused by?

These hard woody growths are the fruiting bodies of a fungus which has infected the tree internally. They produce millions of spores which can infect other trees, so they ought be sawn off and burnt. There is no cure for the infected tree, which will eventually die; cut it down and destroy it.

487

Can I make use of the piles of leaves which accumulate from trees every autumn?

Yes, they can be used to form humus-supplying material if you gather them into heaps contained in wire-netting or compost bins, and allow them to rot for about a year. Restrict the heap to leaves: do not include twigs or bark, which take many years to decay.

488

A young ash tree in my garden appeared to be growing well until this spring, when the leaves on a couple of branches wilted for no apparent reason. A close look showed holes in the bark, and what looks like sawdust around them. Is there some beetle at work internally?

From your description it sounds as though your ash tree has been infested with caterpillars of the leopard moth. They feed on the wood for about three years; they grow about 100 mm (4 in) long and are cream-coloured with brown heads. Bad attacks by these caterpillars can kill a young tree. Fill the holes with HCH (BHC) solution and seal them with putty; or, if only one or two branches are affected, cut these off and burn them.

Michael Jefferson-Brown

Director of a horticultural bulb firm and nursery; frequent gold-medal winner at the major flower shows; author of eight books.

Bulbs

General

489

What is a bulb, and how does it multiply?

A bulb is a modified bud consisting of a flat base 'plate', from which rise layers of fleshy or scaly food-storing leaves that enclose a bud; roots form on the underside of the plate. Bulbs such as daffodils grow larger, split, form offsets (young plants), and also produce seed. Some, such as tulips, grow for a season and then die, having produced in their place more large bulbs and sometimes several bulblets (miniature bulbs). Care has to be taken when lifting tulips such as *Tulipa kaufmanniana* because, apart from forming bulbs and bulbils, they also produce 'droppers'—bulbs that are pushed much deeper in the soil and are easily broken off. Bulbils are small bulbs that form away from the main bulb. In certain lilies, for instance, bulbils form in the leaf axils; while some alliums develop bulbils in their flowerheads. Bulbils can be grown on quickly to form flowering bulbs.

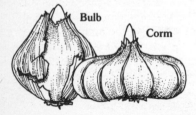

Bulb

Corm

490

What is a corm? How does it increase?

A storage organ like a bulb, a corm is a swollen stem that grows at or just below the soil surface. Usually it lasts one season, new ones forming above it (as in the crocus) or at the side (as in the colchicum). Increase is by these new corms. A crocus may form two or three; a large gladiolus corm may develop only a couple of fresh corms, but it will produce large numbers of cormlets (small corms), which may grow to full size in two seasons.

Corms are normally planted at a depth three or four times their own length; thus, small corms such as those of crocuses will have 25-38 mm (1-1½ in) of soil over their tops, while larger corms such as those of gladioli will have 75-100 mm (3-4 in) of soil over them.

491

Are the biggest bulbs of a particular variety the best?

In principle, yes: large crocus corms, for instance, will give more blooms than small ones; the larger a lily bulb, the more flowers one may expect on the stem. But the size does not always indicate superiority: daffodil bulbs grown in Cornwall or the Isles of Scilly are usually much smaller than those grown in Holland, but will acquit themselves just as well; the difference in size is basically due to different amounts of water in the bulbs. Large corms of anemones, on the other hand, are often old ones that are past their best.

492

Can bulbs be increased by seed?

Wild bulbs depend mainly on seed to maintain their populations. All species fertilised by their own pollen will provide new generations either identical to the parents or showing variation within close limits. Depending on family and species, new bulbs reach flowering size in 15 months to 5 or 6 years. *Narcissus bulbocodium* can be in bloom in 18 months, while the large narcissus hybrids may take 5 years. Tulips and lilies can produce well over 100 viable seeds per pod. Some small bulbs (for instance, bluebells and grape hyacinth) with many flowers to a head will drop several hundred seeds from one flower stem.

493

Some of my daffodils and tulips are developing seed pods. What will happen if I sow this seed?

Seed from wild species will give seedlings more or less similar to the parent provided the flowers were fertilised by their own pollen. Your seedpods are more likely to be hybrid—a cross between two species or varieties. Each seed in a pod will be a unique individual;

some will be good, others less so. If you sow daffodil seeds when ripe (usually late summer) in pots or boxes with 25 mm (1 in) of soil over them, they will produce seedlings early the following year. After four or five years the seedlings reach blooming size. Tulip seed is best sown under glass covered with 10 mm (3/8 in) of seed compost. Depending on type, these seedlings will bloom in three or four years.

494

Can you suggest some autumn-flowering bulbs?

Many varieties of crocus bloom in autumn, as of course do the colchicums, commonly known as autumn crocuses. There is the very attractive pink *Nerine bowdenii* (good in sheltered spot) and the small yellow *Sternbergia lutea* with dark, thick, strap-like leaves and flowers like those of the crocus.

If you can put up with the masses of large leaves they develop in spring, the colchicums are excellent, although some species are of greater botanical interest than garden merit. *Colchicum autumnale* is an easy to grow, with mauve flowers. The hybrids are very good value. 'Lilac Wonder' is a very-free-flowering, quick-increasing pinky mauve kind.

Of the many true crocuses, try *Crocus pulchellus*, which is quite early and has lilac flowers, and *C. speciosus*, which has many good garden hybrids.

495

My garden looks bleak in winter. Are there any bulbs that will enliven it?

We attack the winter by a pincer movement, with late-autumn and early-spring flowers to support the genuine winter ones. Colchicums bloom in September and October, while there are crocus species that bloom from September through October and November into December. Several iris species bloom in winter: the popular *I. reticulata*, with violet flowers, is just 150 mm (6 in) tall; more spectacular is the brilliant blue *I. histrioides* 'Major', only 100 mm (4 in) high but with larger, blue flowers; there are also some good hybrids. Winter aconites (*Eranthis*), with yellow buttercup flowers, are bright on dark days; snowdrops (*Galanthus*) are obvious candidates for the turn of the year. Then, in February, the earliest daffodils arrive, notably the hybrids of the dwarf *Narcissus cyclamineus*.

496

Can you suggest a selection of labour-saving bulbs that will give year-round colour in my garden?

Many small bulbs—crocuses, winter aconites, scillas, and anemones—will provide colour in January and February. Daffodils and narcissi planted in natural clumps in the grass will give you flowers from March into May.

There are some tulips that can be left down for several years, providing colour in April and May. For summertime colour there are some lilies that can be left down for ever, while for the autumn there are cylamen species and *Nerine bowdenii*, which can also be left permanently in the ground.

497

When tidying my borders I often dig up bulbs that I had forgotten. How can I avoid doing this?

Discreetly placed labels are the commonest solution. They must be permanent and not too easily removed, so plastic ones are better than wood or metal types.

The trouble is that, with low-growing plants, even the most unobtrusive labels tend to draw attention to themselves. It is easier to manage bulbs planted in clearly defined clumps, and this is florally more effective than lines or bulbs dotted here and there. These clumps can be located when dormant if you more or less surround them with some herbaceous plants such as polyantha primroses.

498

Do I need to give my bulbs fertilizers?

Normal soils contain all the nutrients bulbs need, but they do benefit from a light dressing of a general fertilizer, such as

Growmore, at planting time or when they are about to start strong root activity. Tests have shown that the most important bulb food is potassium, which is available commercially as sulphate of potash; wood ash and fresh bonfire ash are alternative sources. Several light dressings are better than one big helping: a handful to each square metre of soil is ample. Remember too, that bulbs need plenty of water while growing.

499

Are bulbs prone to attack from pests and diseases?

Bulbs, like most plants, are prey to pests and diseases. Pests range from dogs to organisms visible only under the microscope. Crocuses and tulips make fodder for rodents, while narcissi and some related plants contain a poison that deters them; slugs attack many bulbs, lilies and some smaller bulbs being their favourites; Tulips, alliums (the onion family), and narcissi are vulnerable to attack from different species of eelworms. These microscopic pests eat the cell material, multiply to vast numbers, and reduce the bulb to a pulp.

Eelworms and, more importantly, greenfly are responsible for spreading virus diseases among bulbous plants. The symptoms include mottling, yellowing, spotting, and curling of leaves, and blotches or other marks on flowers. Diseased plants must be taken up and burnt.

500

I have a small garden and need to move my bedding tulips and daffodils out to make room for summer plants. When is the best time to do this?

Some of the stronger-growing tulips can be dug up a few days after flowering and dried off in a cool airy place. Normally, however, the procedure with both daffodils and tulips that need moving is to give them a thorough soaking, dig them up with as much root as possible, and replant them temporarily in an out-of-the-way trench until they die down. To minimise the shock, the bulbs should also be heavily watered after being moved.

501

What is meant by 'naturalising' bulbs?

This is the term used for the practice of planting bulbs so that they look as if they are growing naturally—in lawns, for instance, or in 'woodland' settings; they are labour-saving because they are left down indefinitely. The early-blooming daffodils are the type of bulb most commonly used. Some of the wilder kinds obviously look most at home, notably the Tenby daffodil (*Narcissus pseudonarcissus obvallaris*).

Be cautious about buying so-called 'naturalising mixtures' that are advertised at the end of the season; they may simply

consist of various kinds of bulbs
the dealer has failed to sell. Much
better to go to a recognised
bulb-grower and ask if he has any
lower-priced selections that are
suitable for naturalising.

502

**Part of my garden is more or
less wild, and here I would like
to have snowdrops and
bluebells emulating on a small
scale what nature does more
grandly. Can this be done, and
are there other bulbs that
might fit in with the scheme?**

Clumps of snowdrops can be
divided year by year after
flowering. The wild bluebell
(*Endymion nonscriptus*, syn. *Scilla
nutans*) increases quickly by bulb
and seed; planted fairly thinly it will
colonise the area. (*Endymion
hispanicus* (syn. *Scilla
campanulata*), with many named
varieties, is the larger kind, with
upright spikes; it is a quick
increaser.

Winter aconites, smaller
daffodils, and the 'Old Pheasant's
Eye' narcissus look well in a wild
setting. You might also try Star of
Bethlehem (*Ornithogalum
umbellatum*) and the green
O. nutans; the Star of Bethlehem
has narrow, spreading leaves and
star-like flowers, about 25 mm
(1 in) across, borne in sprays some
150-200 mm (6-8 in) high. Later
lilies such as *L. pardalinum
giganteum* will form attractively
informal clumps.

503

**How often should I water my
bowls of bulbs?**

This depends on the bulbs, the
growing medium, the container,
and the stage of development of
the bulbs. Too much water is as
bad as severe drought: moist
conditions start bulbs rooting;
flowering failures are often due to
bowls drying out. Daffodils and
hyacinths growing in the living
room may need watering every
day. Bulbs to be kept need plenty
of water after blooming.
(Alternatively you can carefully tip
out the bowlful and plant the bulbs
in the garden where they are to
grow next season. Plant them
deeper than in the bowl.) Prepared
bulbs (*see* 541) will adjust
themselves within 12 months.

504

**I am planning to plant bowls
of tulips and wish to have six
to eight tulips in each bowl.
How big should the bowls be?**

Small types you will be able to get
into bowls 150 mm (6 in) wide;
large types may require containers
200 mm (8 in) wide. Use bowls
with drainage holes and plant in
John Innes Potting compost. Bulbs
at the end of their season are then
much better than those from fibre.
Draining holes make watering
easier.

Types to try include: All
T. kaufmanniana and *T. greigii*
hybrids; early double varieties;

species such as *T. praestans,
T. batalinii,* and *T. clusiana
chrysantha*; large-flowered but
relatively short-stemmed
T. fosteriana varieties such as 'Red
Emperor'. The large Darwin
hybrids are unsuitable for most
domestic interiors as they need
large bowls and maximum light.

505

**I grow a few bowls of bulbs
each year. Is it best to grow
them in fibre or in compost?**

The answer depends on whether
you hope to use the bulbs again. If
they are to be planted in the
garden after flowering or used
again, it will be better to grow them
in John Innes Potting compost,
which contains nutrients to help
the bulbs keep or increase their
strength. Fibre merely provides
bulbs with a moisture-retentive
environment; but if the bulbs are to
be discarded at the end of the
season, fibre will be cheaper than
compost.

506

**I have a lovely amaryllis in
bloom in a pot in the house.
What do I do to ensure it
flowers next year?**

This belongs to the genus
Hippeastrum. The varieties and
hybrids should bloom every year.
They are almost evergreen, but die
off for a period. Your bulb should
be planted in a 125-175 mm
(5-7 in) pot with the nose or even

one third of the bulb exposed.
Newly planted bulbs are kept
barely moist, which allows them to
start slowly and produce new roots
before being more generously
watered and fed. Once in full
active growth, the bulbs take lots of
water provided drainage is correct.
Keep your plants growing strongly,
feeding with a liquid fertiliser. After
flowering allow the bulbs to dry off
at the end of the summer, and
then repot them in fresh compost
and start them slowly into growth
again in the autumn.

507

**My rock garden could do with
some miniature bulbs to grow
near thymes and heathers. Can
you suggest some small spring
bulbs that do not have untidy
foliage?**

The winter aconites (*Eranthis*) have
buttercup flowers and attractive
foliage and do not exceed 100 mm
(4 in) in height. The dwarf tulips
are also suitable: try *Tulipa tarda,
T. batalinii, T. praestans,
T. kaufmanniana* and *T. greigii*
hybrids, *T. linifolia,*and
T. marjoletti; the lady tulip
(*T. clusiana*) with narrow pink and
white flowers on tall slender stems,
is particularly elegant. The pale
blue *Hyacinthus azureus* and its
white form are early and look like
very tidy grape hyacinths. The
vivid blue stars of *Scilla sibirica*
'Spring Beauty' make a wonderful
show, as does the related Spanish
bluebell (*Endymion hispanicus*),

which is a sturdier, larger, upright cousin of the English bluebell. *Iriso reticulata*, which rarely grows taller than 150 mm (6 in), and the even smaller *I. histrioides* 'Major', and their numerous hybrids are good value.

508

We have some large pedestals on the patio and by the driveway. Can I grow bulbs in these, and if so which do you suggest?

The basic need for any plants growing in these containers is good drainage; so long as surplus water can drain away, bulbs should grow well in them. Pedestals suggest height and the possibility that plants may be blown about, so you need to choose plants that can put up with wind. However, even lilies are a possibility here: sturdy-stemmed types that can be tried include 'Enchantment' (orange blooms), *L. regale* (white), and 'Destiny' (yellow). Daffodils in spring and tulips a little later will give colour for weeks; in particular a double layer of daffodil bulbs planted in the autumn will give you plenty of colour.

Among many suitable daffodils you could try 'Tête-à-Tête', 'February Gold', 'Foresight', 'Armada', 'Rembrandt', and 'Thalia'; tulips might include 'Red Riding Hood', 'Giuseppe Verdi', 'Toronto', 'Red Emperor', and the early doubles 'Electra' and 'Peachblossom'.

509

I live in the middle of town and have no garden. Can I plant bulbs in growing bags?

Bulbs are packaged plants that are so adaptable that they can be used in many ways. Your idea of bulbs in growing bags is perfectly feasible: just as one can have a double layer of bulbs in a pot to give a double floral effect, so one can do the same in bags. Among narcissi the old double-yellow 'Van Sion' is early, cheerful, and showy; 'Armada' is large and gold and scarlet; 'Royal Orange' is large and white and orange. Among tulips the Darwin hybrids in reds, yellows, oranges, and white are hugely impressive.

510

I am a keen flower arranger and would like to grow some of the more unusual daffodils and other bulbs for cutting. Can you suggest a few?

Try some of the split-corona daffodils, such as 'Baccarat', all yellow with split trumpet laid back onto its petals; 'Congress', with yellow petals almost obscured by a split crown of vivid orange; and 'Cassata', with cream petals and split crown of primrose lemon. Other especially striking daffodils include 'Binkie' in luminous shades of lemon, and the tall triandrus 'Tresamble', with several heads, white petals, and milky cups.

The numerous members of the

onion family are good fresh or dried: *Allium aflatunense* has tall umbels of silver-purple; *A. albopilosum* has huge globes of metallic pinkish-violet stars.

511

I would like to send some bulbs to friends overseas. Is this possible?

Almost every country requires health certificates to accompany imported plant material and has a variety of other regulations. These usually involve inspection of the plants in growth by Ministry of Agriculture officials and again prior to despatch. The easiest way to send bulbs abroad is to find a bulb grower who already exports. He will have his ground cleared for export and his bulbs inspected in growth at least twice a season as a matter of course. He will also be familiar with the forms and formalities involved in sending bulbs abroad.

512

Cut flowers are often expensive. Are there any bulbous flowers that can be dried and used effectively for floral arrangements?

A surprising number of flowers are suitable for this. Many onion species are most effective. *Allium albopilosum* (syn. *A. christophii*) is 300 mm (12 in) tall with 150 mm (6 in) or even larger umbels of starry pink flowers; *A. aflatunense*

is taller. Most other *Allium* species are suitable. They should be cut young in order to keep the flowers and colour, and dried by hanging in an airy place. Alternatively, you can delay cutting: the dried seedheads are also attractive.

Chincherinchees (*Ornithogalum thyrsoides*) can be cut when freshly open and the spikes of silvery white, cream, or yellow flowers dried. The seed pods of some tulips are most attractive. It is worth experimenting with different plants, even small ones like Spanish bluebell (*Scilla campanulata*).

513

We are moving house shortly and want to take some of our bulbs with us. How should we tackle this?

Moving house causes problems for gardeners. Often it is best to be very selective, concentrating only on the most important bulbs and leaving the rest of them behind. Some may be nearly dormant, and these can be lifted, dried, and dealt with normally; remember to label everything clearly.

Bulbs in full growth will reluctantly tolerate some disturbance. Water them thoroughly before lifting with as much root as possible and some soil. Place the bulbs in polythene bags or pots with their leaves protruding, and keep them moist. Replant them as quickly as possible in the new garden, and water them in very thoroughly.

Daffodils & narcissi

514

What is the difference in form or colour between a daffodil and a narcissus?

There is no difference. Daffodil is the English name and *Narcissus* the botanical one. The small-eyed 'Old Pheasant's Eye' narcissus (*N. poeticus recurvens*) is as much a daffodil as a yellow-trumpet variety such as 'Golden Harvest' or 'King Alfred'. (The assumption of a difference between the two has a long history: John Parkinson writing in 1629 complained of the 'great confusion' and rebuked those who differentiated between the narcissus and daffodil.)

515

Why are some new varieties so expensive?

Daffodils take a long time to breed and to increase: seed takes five years to produce a flowering-size bulb, and only one seedling in a thousand will stand any chance of getting into commerce. It will take the breeder 7 to 10 years at least before he has enough bulbs of the seedling to offer a few for sale. The ones he sells have to pay for the five years' work on the 999 seedlings that did not make the grade and for the work of increasing the individual to a saleable-size stock.

516

I find catalogues a bit confusing. Can you suggest where I can see a good range of daffodils, so that I can make a selection 'in the flesh' rather than from photographs, in which the colours are often inaccurately reproduced?

Flower shows are held in different parts of the country at which you may expect to see collections in the spring months. The Royal Horticultural Society shows at the horticultural halls at Westminster, London, are among the best. The society has an Early Daffodil competition and a Daffodil Show each year. The Daffodil Society usually holds a show in the Midlands, and it also holds a competition at the North of England show at Harrogate each spring, where firms show their wares. You will also find daffodils at the Chelsea Flower Show. The RHS gardens at Wisley (near Woking, Surrey) have many old and new daffodils planted and labelled. The Harlow Carr Gardens in Yorkshire also have daffodils, as do all the main public gardens. The Springfields gardens at Spalding (Lincolnshire) have plantings of all bulbs, and there is an early spring show at Spalding too—not to be confused with the carnival later in the year.

Specialised nurseries may welcome visitors, but you should make sure that this is so before setting out.

517

Can you suggest a list of about 10 daffodils which will bloom in a continuous succession from early to late?

There are some 10,000 registered varieties of daffodils, so any selection of 10 will be highly subjective—but here goes: 1. 'Tête-à-Tête, a dwarf variety 100-125 mm (4-5 in), blooms February-March, gold, 1-3 heads to a stem. 2. 'Armada' March, large, gold petals, with large orange cup. 3. 'Ice Follies', March-April, white petals, wide primrose cup. 4. 'Galway', early April, best traditional golden trumpet daffodil. 5. 'Charter', April, tall, lemon petals, goblet crown opens lemon becomes white (an improved version of 'Binkie'). 6. 'Passionale', April, uniform crop of perfect white petals and rose pink cup. 7. 'Tahiti', April, large double, yellow and orange. 8. 'Kilworth', late April, white or cream petals and dark orange cup, often with medium green centre. 9. 'Sundisc', late April-May, dwarf, 100 mm (4 in) yellow circles, flat crowns. 10. 'Cushendall', late April-May, snow-white circle, small cup centred in mossy green.

NOTE The flowering times given above are approximate and apply to southern England. In Cornwall flowers may be two to five weeks earlier in each case; in northern England and Scotland they will be two or three weeks later than in the south.

518

I must have daffodils, but I find their foliage a nuisance in the border after flowering. What do you suggest?

In a border much of the daffodil foliage can be hidden if the plants are carefully sited amidst shrubs and herbaceous plants. In general, however, the answer is to concentrate on early-blooming daffodils. The very dwarf 'Tête-à-Tête' is early and neat. At about 125-150 mm (5-6 in) high, it produces a lot of gold and pale tangerine blooms, one, two, or three to a stem, and its foliage dies down quite early. The same applies to the 200-225 mm (8-9 in) 'Tenby' daffodil (gold), and 'February Gold'. Among the larger varieties, 'Armada' is a bold, cheerful, early daffodil in brilliant gold and scarlet; 'Brunswick' is early, sturdy, and reliable in white and lemon; and 'Ice Follies' is very prolific with large white and primrose-cream flowers. *See* 532 on tying back.

519

I want to enter daffodils in our local flower show. I haven't tried before, so what are some of the points I need to watch?

Make sure your entry form is handed in on time, and that the varieties you show are entered for the correct class (trumpet, large-cupped, small-cupped, double, etc). If your class calls for a certain number of blooms in each exhibit, check that yours are correct.

If possible, cut your flowers the day before the show, selecting fresh blooms unspoilt by wind damage or sun fading. Use the full length of stem, with a little daffodil foliage to the side or behind the flower stems. Arrange the flower stems with moss, oasis, or other material so that the flowers are displayed to best effect. Ensure the vase or container is clean. Prepare a label with the name of the variety at the base of the container.

520

Our local show has classes for daffodils and narcissus. Can you suggest varieties for the main classes (not too expensive, please)?

A brief selection of my personal favourites: TRUMPETS Yellow: 'Rembrandt', 'Kingscourt'. White: 'Mount Hood', 'Empress of Ireland', Reversed bicolor: 'Spellbinder'.
LARGE CUPS Yellow: 'Galway'. Yellow and orange: 'Ceylon', Falstaff', 'Armada'. White and yellow: 'Bizerta', 'Tudor Minstrel'. White and red: 'Prof. Einstein', 'Kilworth'. White and pink: 'Passionale'.
SMALL CUPS Yellow and orange: 'Chungking'. White: 'Verona'. Pale: 'Aircastle'.
DOUBLES 'White Lion', 'Golden Ducat'. Yellow and orange: 'Tahiti'. White and yellow:

'Unique'.
TRIANDRUS White: 'Tresamble'. Lemon: 'Liberty Bells'.
CYCLAMINEUS Yellow: 'February Gold', 'Charity May', 'Bartley'. White: 'Jenny'. White and primrose: 'Dove Wings', 'Jonquil'. Yellow: 'Trevithian', 'Sweetness'. Yellow and orange: 'Suzy'.
TAZETTA White and orange: 'Geranium', 'Orange Wonder'.

521

I like scented flowers. Can you give me the names of some attractive varieties of well-scented daffodils?

Most daffodils have some scent, but some are much better endowed than others. Almost all the true jonquil daffodils have, in greater or lesser degree, the strong perfume of the wild jonquil (*Narcissus jonquilla*) to which they are related; particularly good is 'Trevithian'. Most of the poeticus varieties are very sweet scented; especially evocative is the perfume of old-fashioned 'Old Pheasant's Eye'. The many-headed tazettas are strongly perfumed, the gold and orange 'Soleil d'Or' being particularly pungent. Among daffodils of other groups, pink-crowned 'Louise de oligney' smells of lemon; doubles such as 'Mary Copeland' are more pungent than most carnations; the double, many-headed 'Bridal Crown' is like an improved version of 'Cheerfulness' and has an even finer perfume.

522

I was particularly struck with the miniature wild daffodils I saw growing like buttercups in Spain and Portugal. Any chance of growing these here?

Narcissus cyclamineus, 150-200 mm (6-8 in) tall, and the dwarf *N. bulbocodium,* 50-150 mm (2-6 in), are both native to Spain and Portugal. In the RHS gardens at Wisley these two species increase naturally by seeding themselves in the light grass of the alpine meadow, where the soil—sandy and somewhat acid—suits them well.

Bulbs offered for sale are often collected in the wild while in full growth. They may take a while to establish themselves. Plant with 25-38 mm (1-1½ in) soil over their tops, and keep the area slug-free. *N. bulbocodium* can produce over 100 seeds to a pod. If grown in pots and kept moist, the seedlings may bloom in 18 months.

523

I'm told that some of the smallest species of daffodils are reluctant to get going in the garden. Are there any little species or hybrids that are good growers?

Most of the small hybrids are very much easier to grow than the species; some of them are very fine plants with surprising rates of increase. The very early 'Tête-à-Tête', for instance, doubles

its bulbs each year. Its flowers last for weeks. It stands about 125 mm (5 in) high when it starts to bloom, with one, two or three flowers on a stem. It has yellow petals and a long, pale-tangerine crown.

There are several small jonquil hybrids that grow almost as readily as weeds. 'Sundisc', 125-150 mm (5-6 in) tall, blooms at the end of the season and has perfectly circular yellow flowers with flat disc crowns.

524

How quickly do daffodils increase?

There is considerable variation. On average, daffodils do not double themselves in a year, although some kinds will and the work of breeders is tending to select kinds that increase more quickly. The small 'Tête-à-Tête' usually easily doubles itself, while most of the *N. cyclamineus* and *N. jonquilla* hybrids are quick to increase. A few of the older trumpet varieties are rather slower to increase by weight or number.

525

I want to grow the wild English daffodil in grass in my garden. Where can I get bulbs?

The English daffodil, or Lent lily, of which Wordsworth glimpsed 10,000, is *Narcissus pseudonarcissus*. It is a wild species that relies far more on seed than on bulb division for maintaining and increasing its population. Bulbs of this species put into a normal commercial regime fail to increase satisfactorily; any bulbs offered for sale are likely to have been lifted from the wild, which is against the law and rightly so.

It may be possible for you to obtain bulbs from a garden where *N. pseudonarcissus* is already established. Failing that, you may perhaps be able to get seed, which germinates readily.

The closely related Tenby daffodil (*N. pseudonarcissus obvallaris*) is an alternative suggestion. It is a brighter yellow, somewhat smarter form, and it is available from the trade as it grows easily under cultivation.

526

What daffodils are best for naturalising in grass and rough ground?

Some of the simpler kinds are the most effective. The old early double yellow, 'Van Sion' is good in all sorts of odd spots. Orange-crowned ones are best in the foreground, and 'Armada' is an impressive early example that grows well if left to itself. Avoid orange-crowned ones in groups that will be viewed from a distance; in the green grass the complementary orange becomes visually muddied. The small, yellow-trumpet Tenby daffodil '*N. pseudonarcissus obvallaris*) is bright, early, and reliable; 'February Gold', of a similar size, is

also good.

'Brunswick' is sturdy, healthy, and clean in white and lemon; 'Ice Follies', in white and primrose cream is good; both must be planted with at least 100 mm (4 in) of soil over their nose. The double white 'Mrs Wm Copeland' is sturdy, large, and effective. 'Old Pheasant's Eye' is best grown between shrubs where the grass is not to be mown, the same applies to the newly available double white *N. poeticus flore-pleno*.

527

How often do I need to lift my daffodils?

Some daffodils can be left forever: you have probably seen country churchyards and gardens where 'Emperor', 'Empress', and other varieties, planted over 60 years ago, continue to thrive. To get the maximum increase, however, most commercial growers lift bulbs every other year. In the garden, after three or four seasons, most clumps will have increased so considerably that the competition for space and nutrients is incompatible with good flowering performance. Lift in the second half of June or early July, while the foliage is still present to show you where to dig. After lifting the bulbs, you may clean and re-plant them 100 mm (4 in) apart and 100 mm (4 in) deep immediately, preferably in a fresh location or they may be stored in a dry, airy place and replanted in August, September or October.

528

I envisage sweeps of daffodils in the grass but the work of planting them is daunting. Any suggestions?

The job is best left until the autumn rains have softened the ground—but not so late that the cold makes it all too tempting to plant carelessly. It is very important that the bulbs have 100 mm (4 in) of soil over the noses, otherwise they will split up into lots of small, non-flowering bulbs.

The tools sometimes sold for this purpose may work on some soils. You press a cylinder into the ground, remove a core of soil, insert the bulb into the hole, and replace the soil. It does not work so easily, however, on hard or stony soil. Alternatively, take a spade and cut three sides of a square, each side being the width of the spade's blade. Lever up the turf, put in two, three, or four bulbs, allow the turf to fall back, place a foot on the turf, and move to the next position. Try to avoid 'unnatural' patterns of bulbs in grass: aim for an appearance of natural colonisation.

529

I want to cut the grass where daffodils grow. How long do I have to leave the daffodil foliage?

Up to a point, the longer the leaves are left the better will the bulbs perform. After the flowers have finished, the efficiency of the leaves, working as food factories for the bulb, begins to fail, and by six weeks after blooming the leaves are contributing little to the well-being of the bulb, and can therefore be cut without jeopardising the plant's future. A daffodil blooming in mid-April may have its leaves removed in the first half of June if necessary. It follows that the earlier blooming kinds, which are likely to receive the heartiest welcome, will also earn good marks for being ready for tidying up earlier—possibly before the grass has become unmanageable.

530

Clumps of my double daffodils produce fat buds each spring, but they fail to open. What am I doing wrong?

I wish I had a pound for every time I have been asked this question! You may be doing nothing wrong at all. You may, for instance, be growing the double yellow and orange 'Texas' which often exhibits this deplorable habit. The only course is to dig up the bulbs and put them in the dustbin. Some doubles, like the June-flowering 'Gardenia narcissus' (*N. poeticus flore pleno*), occasionally produce blind buds; this may be caused by a jolt in their development—a severe drought, perhaps, or a sudden burst of very hot or cold weather. Pot-grown doubles, which may be similarly affected, need to be grown with greater care than other types.

531

Most daffodils that I have grown in window boxes and bowls get too tall. What can I do about this?

Daffodils kept in the dark reach up for light. To a bulb, the centre of a living room—or indeed any poorly lit corner—can be a dense, dark jungle. One answer, then, is to keep your bowls of daffodils in the lightest spot as often as possible.

Dwarf types are certainly easier to manage in window boxes and bowls. Of these, the very early 'Tête-à-Tête' is one of the longest in bloom; 'February Gold' is one of the best in bowls. The popular multi-headed double 'Bridal Crown' is very-free-flowering and sturdy, while 'Binkie', in shades of lemon, is unusual and good in window boxes.

532

I have read that one should tie-up daffodil leaves after the plants have finished flowering. Why is this?

I can think of no good reason for this practice. They are no neater than if left to grow naturally, and the twisted leaves cannot function properly: they will not get enough light and air to carry out their work as the bulbs' food factory.

If the foliage is an annoyance—and I cannot see why it should be—it may be wise to plant your bulbs in places where shrubs and herbaceous plants will grow up and obscure the leaves as they fade.

533

When I asked for 'Van Sion' recently, I was offered something called N. 'Telamonius Plenus' and told this is the same thing. Is that true?

Yes. This early double yellow, which has been popular in Britain for over three-and-a-half centuries has several aliases. Two other names for it are 'Wilmer's Double' or simply 'Common Double'.

534

Some of my daffodil bulbs have disappeared. Could they have rotted away?

There is a trouble called basal rot, but in our climate and with present-day varieties this is unlikely to be the cause of the trouble.

Three pests attack bulbs. The narcissus fly lays eggs that hatch into grubs that bore into a bulb and eat out the centre. The grubs are about 13 mm (½ in) long, fat, and a dirty cream colour. One can spoil a bulb. The small daffodil fly produces a lot of small grubs, but these rarely attack a bulb that is not already damaged. The narcissus eelworm, the worst of all, cannot be seen by the naked eye. It enters a bulb and multiplies so fast that millions are soon devouring the bulb, which is left as a soggy, rotten mass. Any bulbs discovered in this state must be destroyed together with any others nearby, and the ground must be

quarantined for three or four years.
Any bulbs with deformed foliage,
twisted stems or flowers just above
soil level should be suspect. A bulb
lifted and cut transversely to reveal
rings of discoloration should be
burnt.

Tulips & hyacinths

535

**Are there any tulips, large or
small, that I would not have to
lift each year?**

Most of the large Darwin hybrids,
such as 'Apeldoorn', are so strong
that they can be left where they
grow for up to five years without
harming the bulbs. After their first
season the huge flowers will be
somewhat smaller, but they remain
gorgeous and impressive.

   Many of the species tulips, given
reasonable sites with good sun and
drainage, can be left indefinitely. In
particular, *Tulipa praestans* in the
rock garden or in the border will
increase year after year, and *T.
kaufmanniana* and *T. greigii* are
equally good.

536

**Which tulips would you
recommend for growing in
pots?**

I have seen most types growing
happily in pots and other
containers. Certainly the early
doubles are easy and showy, with

flowers almost like peonies. The
shorter-stemmed kinds are
obviously more easily managed;
these include all the early-flowering
T. kaufmanniana and *T. greigii*
hybrids. Particularly good are 'Red
Riding Hood' (brilliant red with
striking purple-marbled foliage);
'Stresa' (early; gold and orange);
'Toronto' (neat, pointed buds;
clear rose pink); 'Heart's Desire'
(neat grower, rich pink and white).
I am especially fond of the delicate
T. batalinii 'Bronze Charm'
(miniature series, with grey-green
foliage and exquisitely shaped
broad-based blooms).

537

**Which tulips are best for
bedding?**

The Darwin hybrids are the largest-
flowered, strongest-growing kinds,
and will therefore make the boldest
display. Colours range from white
through yellow to orange, pink,
and red; the red 'Apeldoorn'
and its sports are widely available,
and bloom in April and May.

   Earlier April display can be had
from the double early group. These
are short-stemmed and sturdy,
and look rather like peonies.

   Wallflowers can be associated
with Darwin hybrids to prolong the
display. Forget-me-nots can be
used with the doubles or the
lily-flowered types such as the
favourite 'China Pink'. The dwarf
T. kaufmanniana and *T. greigii*
hybrids are also being used
increasingly for bedding.

538

We have a wind-swept garden. Can you suggest which tulips might be most suitable?

All dwarf species and their hybrids are suitable. Of the older-established kinds, the dwarf early double types make attractive bedding plants. The lily-flowered group, such as 'China Pink' and the red and gold 'Aladdin', are not dwarf but their strong-stemmed flowers withstand rough weather. Absolutely reliable are the *T. kaufmanniana* and *T. greigii* races, available in a wide range of colours. Among species tulips, try *T. tarda*, with prostrate shining foliage, and a nest of green buds opening to white and yellow stars, and virtually stemless; *T. maximowiczii* and *T. linifolia*, which are neat, brilliant red and about 125 mm (5 in) tall; and *T. praestans*, with several brilliant orange flowers, are 125-175 mm (5-7 in) tall.

539

I wish to grow *Tulipa kaufmanniana* and *T. greigii* hybrids but am embarrassed by the vast numbers from which to choose. Could you list five distinct examples of each?

My favourites among the *T. kaufmanniana* hybrids include: 'The First' (white, widely banded red in bud); 'Brilliant' (small early scarlet); 'Stresa' (gold, broadly banded red

outside); 'Gluck' (marbled foliage, flowers cream and pinky red); 'Heart's Desire' (mottled foliage, flowers outside pink and red, inside cream and gold).

From *T. greigii* hybrids I select: 'Lady Diana' (pointed petals, cream and red flowers); 'Mary Ann' (mottled leaves, milk-white and pink flowers); 'Zampa' (dwarf, red and gold); 'Red Riding Hood' (marvellous purpled foliage); 'Mizkodeed' (gold-flushed orange).

540

I want to plant some tulip species with character in the rock garden. Which are best?

The larger the rock garden, the larger-flowered can be the bulbs. Here are a few of various sizes: *T. acuminata* (syn. *T.* 'Cornuta'), 450 mm (18 in), the horned tulip, yellow and red; extraordinary long, very narrow petals; flowers in May. *T. batalinii* 'Bronze Charm' 100-150 mm (4-6 in), a series of hybrids with *T. linifolia*; very neat, broad flowers in shades of bronze, apricot and peach. *T. clusiana*, 200-300 mm (8-12 in) lady tulip, slender, pinky crimson buds, opening white with blue-black base. *T. kolpakowskiana*, 150-200 mm (6-8 in), neat little bright yellow stars when open, buds striped red. *T. linifolia* 100-150 mm (4-6 in), prostrate foliage made attractive with waved margin; large, superbly red flowers; late. *T. praestans* 'Fusilier', 200 mm (8 in), several red flowers

on each stem. *T. tarda*
100-150 mm (4-6 in), polished
prostrate leaves, green buds, white
stars, golden bases.

541

**What is the difference between
'prepared' and 'unprepared'
hyacinths?**

Prepared bulbs have undergone a
regime of temperature control
while in storage. This treatment
simulates the passage of winter,
and so galvanises the bulbs into
early activity: they bloom a month
or more in advance of unprepared
bulbs. The effect is most marked
with bulbs grown indoors. The
treatment needs to be repeated
every year, which is obviously
beyond the scope of most amateur
gardeners; the most sensible
course, after your prepared bulbs
have flowered, is to plant them
outside, where they will bloom at
the same time as unprepared
hyacinths next spring.

542

**I enjoy hyacinths but have
been disappointed recently
with some of my bulbs. Can
you suggest where I might
have gone wrong?**

Grow only one variety in each
container to be certain of
simultaneous flowering, making
sure that the bulbs are even-sized
and undamaged. Use containers
with drainage holes to ensure the
bulbs do not become waterlogged

(expanded mica and poly-granules
are too light and free-moving to
make suitable anchoring media for
most bulbs). Plant with the noses
level with the top of the potting
medium, which may be potting
compost or fibre. Allow enough
space between the compost and
pot rim for watering.

Keep the bulbs moist and cool
for the first six to eight weeks to
encourage growth of an extensive,
healthy root system. Bowls may be
kept in the dark during this period,
but this is not necessary. At the
end of this period bowls should be
brought into a light, warm spot and
be given progressively more heat.

543

**I grow hyacinths every year,
but have been fairly
conservative in my choice of
varieties. Can you suggest
some reliable ones that are
just a little different?**

Strikingly coloured varieties include
'Blue Magic' (a rich blue with white
eyes); 'Gipsy Queen' (unusual
salmon-orange with florets
somewhat frilled); 'Violet Pearl'
(mauve-violet); 'Blue Giant'
(well-formed heads of large,
pale-blue florets); 'Amsterdam'
(rich red). Double-flowered
hyacinths include 'Chestnut
Flower' (large soft-pink flowers),
'General Kohler' (clear lavender
blue); 'Holly-hock' (rich red). You
could also try the multi-flora
hyacinths; these give stems of
loosely arranged flowers.

544

I have a large bowl which I want to fill with hyacinths. Which kind would you recommend?

The rich blue 'Ostara', is one of the best current varieties: 'Pink Pearl' and 'L'Innocence' (white) are equally good. All have the characteristic hyacinth scent.

We find an odd number of bulbs to be more appealing than an even one; we plant in 3s, 5s, 7s, and so on. We have rarely found it successful to mix varieties. Prepared bulbs (*see* 541) produce flowers a month or more earlier than those not prepared.

Crocuses & other spring bulbs

545

Most of the catalogues have long lists of crocus species. Could you suggest a few to start with?

They are often rather arbitrarily divided into autumn- and spring-flowering kinds. Your autumn selection might include *Crocus cancellatus* (syn. *C. nudiflorus*) one of the largest-flowering purple-veined white crocuses; *C. speciosus* in white, blue, and purple, the October variety 'Oxonian' being one of the darkest and largest. One

of the nicest winter-flowering species is *C. laevigatus fontenayi*, violet with purple feathering, which blooms in December and January. In February and March comes armies of crocus: *C. chrysanthus* has many different-coloured varieties; *C. tomasinianus*, in varying shades of purple, is one of the kinds that seed themselves freely; the dark yellow *C. aureus* is another free seeder; *C. imperati*, buff outside and lilac inside, is one of the most majestic; *C. susianus* is the cloth of gold crocus, and the smaller form *C.s. minor* is a little later but free-flowering.

546

I tried growing crocuses in the house last year and they were a dismal failure. Where might I have gone wrong?

Crocuses need to be left for several weeks in the cool to establish a good root system before being introduced into mild warmth. The failed crocuses were probably brought into too warm a room too suddenly. Alternatively, the trouble may have been that the plants were allowed to dry out or to become waterlogged, preventing the flower buds from developing.

547

I seem to have lost a lot of crocus bulbs. Where could they have gone?

The most likely answer is that they have provided a meal for local fauna. Mice and other rodents are partial to crocuses and tulips. How they rate against other foods I am not sure, but they seem to be eaten most in the winter months when presumably there is less food. Narcissi contain a natural poison and so are less prone to attack.

Crocuses survive and increase best in friable (well-worked and crumbly) soil in open areas. They tend to fade away if crowded by stronger-growing neighbours.

548

Some of my crocuses have set seeds. Is it worth sowing them?

Many crocus species set huge quantities of seed, and this grows so quickly that a new flowering generation is present in about 18 months or two years. There is great pleasure in choosing the best out of batches of seedlings from species such as *C. tomasinianus, C. chrysanthus,* and even less-dramatically variable kinds such as *C. imperati.* You could even produce a future winner to carry a name! The other species are all worth growing from seed as the seedlings are fresh, healthy, vigorous stock.

549

Which of the dwarf irises are good garden plants?

The old favourite *Iris reticulata,* 125-150 mm (5-6 in) tall, with violet flowers in February and March, is attractive but rather overshadowed now by *I. histrioides* 'Major', with its royal blue flowers, or by hybrids between these two: 'Blue Veil' is an excellent sky blue; 'Harmony' is becoming popular for the size and colour of the dwarf bloom (clear blue with central yellow flash) and for the tidy habit of having very low foliage at flowering time; 'Joyce' is similar but blooms later; 'Violet Beauty' is like a larger version of *L. reticulata.* The brilliant yellow *I. danfordiae* is of the same neat size and blooms early. The bulbs tend to split and then build up, and so it is wise to repeat planting for two or three years till a succession of flowering bulbs is established.

550

I would like to grow ixias outdoors, but are they sufficiently hardy?

The ixias are a genus of South African bulbs; they are not hardy but most of the garden varieties will survive outdoors in the south and south-west of England. The small corms should be planted in October or November to a depth of at least 125 mm (5 in) in well-drained soil in a sunny, sheltered spot. The flower spikes, which appear in May and June, are 300-450 mm (12-18 in) tall, fragrant, and in brilliant shades of blue, purple, red, and yellow. The corms should best be lifted and dried when the foliage dies down.

551

How do you suggest I grow hardy cyclamens?

If you can get fresh seed, this is the best way of getting stock. Alternatively, you may get growing corms from an alpine specialist. Buy dry, large corms collected from the wild only if all else fails: they are less likely to succeed.

There are several good species. I believe the pink *C. hederifolium* (syn. *C. neapolitanum*) and its white form 'Album' are the best. They produce a huge number of perfect miniature flowers about 100 mm (4 in) high in the autumn. Attractive marbled foliage follows the flowers. The corms are grown with the tops just below soil level. Once planted they can be left for decades in a rock garden, between shrubs, in the border, in troughs, or in light grass.

552

I want to grow some interesting small bulbs in miniature gardens in a series of troughs and sinks. Any ideas?

Here are a few: Spring-flowering *Anemone blanda* in blue, pink, and white, 100-150 mm (4-6 in)

high. Crocus species such as *C. minimus* (April) in white and violet; *C. vernus albiflorus* (March), white, *C. susianus minor* (February), gold. *Muscari azureum,* a dwarf, bright-blue grape hyacinth. *Narcissus asturiensis (minimus),* a miniature 'King Alfred' 50-75 mm (2-3 in); *N. triandrus albus,* 'Angel's Tears', creamy white bells, 75 mm (3 in). The bluebell-like *Scilla tubergeniana* (February-March), pale blue and sky blue. Early tulip species include tiny *T. biflora,* (March-April), with two or three white and yellow flowers, 150 mm (6 in) tall; *T. kolpakowskiana,* with neat yellow flowers painted red outside; *T. tarda,* with its prostrate rosette of leaves, and virtually stemless white and yellow stars, 100-150 mm (4-6 in) in diameter.

553

Every time I try to grow winter aconites they seem to fail. Can you give me some help for one last try?

The problem is to get fresh stock; some corms are very dried up when sold. Try to buy growing plants in March or April. There are two main species, *Eranthis cilicica* and the better-known *E. hyemalis,* both have golden buttercup flowers in February-March, and *E. cilicica* has cut foliage with a bronzy cast. 'Guinea Gold' is a hybrid series between these species; it is much more vigorous and its flowers are larger. The hybrids are sterile and so produce no seeds but they can be divided each spring. *E. hyemalis* will seed itself freely, and has quite often strayed into the wild.

554

I tried some giant snowdrops but they were not very successful. What sorts of snowdrops do you recommend?

I expect you tried *Galanthus elwesii*, which is sometimes difficult to keep going year after year. The common snowdrop, *G. nivalis*, and its double form, *G.n.* 'Floreplena', are probably the most reliable; they will bloom and increase from year to year. Clumps can be divided after flowering or dry bulbs can be planted in the autumn.

There are a number of variants of the common snowdrop: 'Viridapicis', for example, has green spots on the petals. Some varieties, although expensive, are impressively large and grow well; two fairly readily available hybrids are the large 'S. Arnott' and 'Straffan'.

555

I have some grape hyacinths but they seem to have a rather messy abundance of foliage. Are there neater kinds?

Grape hyacinths increase quickly. The kind that you have is probably the variety 'Heavenly Blue', which has masses of floppy leaves.

Altogether better is its parent, *Muscari armeniacum*, with similar but darker blue flowers. More unusual is the double 'Blue Spike', which has large, wide heads of mid-blue flowers.

Distinct species include the tassel hyacinth, *M. comosum*, with purple and olive-green flowers; the feather hyacinth, *M.c.* 'Plumosum' (syn. 'Monostrosum'), with feathery plumes of violet; the Oxford-and-Cambridge hyacinth *M. tubergenianum*, in which the tops of the spikes are bright sky blue, the bottoms dark blue.

You might also try *Hyacinthus azureus*, which looks like a neat, very early grape hyacinth in bright, pale blue; there is also a white form.

556

Those bulbous irises that one sees in florists are very impressive, but are they easy to grow in the garden?

Given well-dug soil in an open situation, they grow well and increase quickly. They bloom in June in what used to be called the 'June gap', when other flowers tend to be sparse. They grow 400-500 mm (16-20 in) high; their foliage is upright, tidy, and sparse. The main group is the Dutch hybrids in white, blues, violets, yellows, tan shades, and bicolors such as white and yellow. The English hybrids have wider petals, bloom slightly later, and are now usually sold mixed.

557

My crown imperials have not turned out to be very 'imperial'. What can I do to improve them?

These plants (*Fritillaria imperialis*) resent disturbance so they may take a couple of seasons to establish themselves. They should not be dug around, as this may cause another setback.

The large bulbs are best planted in very-well-drained soil; they want a place in full sun. By planting them on their sides you prevent collection of water in the central hole left by last year's flower stem.

558

I like freesias. The corms seem cheap, but are they difficult to grow?

Shop-bought freesia flowers will have been grown under glass, with special attention given to three aspects: they will have been given plenty of light; they will have flourished in airy, buoyant, frost-free atmosphere; the corms will have enjoyed a moist but open, gritty, well-drained compost.

Freesias can be grown from corms or seed. There are now several strains; some are stronger in certain colours, others are particularly large, some with double flowers.

For outdoor growing, freesia corms are heat-treated for several weeks; this has the effect of retarding growth until the spring, and then inducing rapid development and flowering.

Lilies

559

Which are the best of the scented lilies?

Many modern lilies have very pleasant scents. Most of the trumpet kinds, such as the favourite *Liliam regale*, are perfumed, as is the greenhouse species *L. longiflorum*, the Easter lily beloved of florists. The trumpet kinds also include varieties such as 'Pink Perfection' and 'Royal Gold', and the Olympic Hybrids; some of the Asiatic hybrids are also scented, though rarely very strongly.

Many of the Oriental lilies have as rich a perfume as any flower. The huge-flowered golden-rayed lily (*L. auratum*) has such a strong perfume that a single bloom can scent a whole room. *L. speciosum* is another with a rich scent.

560

My soil is rather limy. Are lilies out of the question?

Some lilies, notably *L. speciosum* and *L. auratum*, hate lime; others are lime tolerant. Lily species that grow well on lime include the orange *L. henryi*, which when established can have 30 or more flowers on a stem. *L. martagon*, the Turk's-cap lily, is another, and there is a series of hybrids from this species that are excellent on lime and, once planted, can be left for ever. The May-flowering *L. pyrenaicum*, with yellow curled-up bells, grows strongly on lime and can naturalise itself.

Most of the Asiatic hybrids will grow quite well in limy soil if peat or leaf mould is added. 'Enchantment', 'Connecticut King', and 'Sterling Silver' are three excellent examples.

561

Can you give some hints on growing lilies in the garden?

Lilies need well-drained-soil with plenty of humus. They like their faces in the sun and their toes in the shade, so plant them between shrubs or in a mixed border.

American species such as the panther lily (*L. pardalinum*) and othes such as *L. henryi* are not stem-rooting—all their roots come from the base of the bulb. Most of the popular Asiatic hybrids (such as 'Enchantment') and trumpet kinds (such as 'Golden Splendour') are vigorous stem-rooters and particularly benefit from mulching.

Plant with at least 100 mm (4 in) of soil over the bulbs. Depending on the size of the adult plant allow 150-300 mm (6-12 in) between bulbs. If slugs are prevalent use slug killers.

Leave American species and *L. martagon* and its hybrids undisturbed. Modern hybrids may need lifting after 3 years to alleviate overcrowding. Do this a week or so after flowering.

562

How are lilies best grown in pots?

Lilies grow easily even in quite small pots. Three bulbs of the smaller kinds can be grown in a 150 mm (6 in) pot, although a 200 mm (8 in) one would be preferable. Tall trumpet lilies need larger pots.

Use equal quantities of John Innes Potting compost No 1 and peat. About 25-50 mm (1-2 in) of the mixture goes in the bottom of the pot. The bulbs are placed in, and then the pot is filled nearly to the top with more mixture.

Lilies grow quickly. Planted in February-May and kept out of frost, the bulbs will break through rapidly and bloom in a few weeks. Bulbs can be grown again the following year if they are kept watered and some fresh growing mixture is added.

563

Which lilies are suitable for pot culture?

In general, lilies are among the most successful of bulbs in pots, but you should avoid *L. martagon* and the American species and their numerous hybrids. Probably the easiest to grow are the earlier kinds such as 'Enchantment' (orange flowers) and the other Asiatic hybrids. Some of the best are: 'Pirate' (orange/red); 'Destiny' (yellow with spots); 'Connecticut King' (plain rich yellow); 'Sterling Silver' (white with spots).

L. regale (white) and the trumpet hybrids bloom a few weeks later and may be taller; they are normally heavily scented. Some of my favourites are: 'Royal Gold' (yellow); 'Golden Splendour' (yellow); 'Pink Perfection' (pink in various shades); 'African Queen' (orange).

564

Are there any lilies that readily naturalise?

Yes, most of the American species are easy to naturalise even on very heavy soil; try *L. pardalinum* or *L.p giganteum* (syn. 'Sunset', 'Red Giant'). Bulbs of these spread to form one underground creeping root like a thick mat after two or three years. *L.p. giganteum*, particularly, will form ever-larger colonies and give more flowering stems each year; its flowers are an attractive red and gold with dark spots, the petals curling back into balls.

The striking Turk's-cap lily (*L. martagon*) in white, mauve, and pink spotted forms takes a year or two to get established, but in gardens where it can be left undisturbed it will then start seeding itself. It appears in some British floras as a naturalised garden escape. *L. pyrenaicum* will also do this and naturalises easily. Both these species are lime tolerant. In acid soil things are not so easy, but you may be fortunate in getting *L. speciosum* to form persistent clumps.

565

How do I increase my lilies?

There are several ways. Lily bulbs divide and form clumps, which can be lifted and split after flowering. Small bulbs may be found near the large bulbs and on the stem below ground. The tiger lily (*L. tigrinum*) and others produce bulbils in the leaf axils (where leaf and stem meet). Growth of bulbils can be artificially stimulated by removing the topmost flowering part of the stem as the flower buds appear.

The seeds of many lilies germinate freely. *L. regale* can provide flowering bulbs after two years. Hybrid seeds will give rise to new kinds.

To produce one kind artificially, gently break off undamaged scales from a bulb. Place the scales upright in a moist mixture of peat and sand. Bulbs will develop from these and may be grown on in nursery rows until the plants reach flowering size.

566

Can you suggest the best lilies for use as cut flowers?

Most lilies make pleasingly opulent cut flowers; the strong Asiatic hybrids like 'Pirate', 'Enchantment', or 'Connecticut King' make marvellous cut flowers.

If you want the bulbs not to suffer, try to leave perhaps half the stem intact. Be careful when handling the lilies. The brilliant orange pollen can stain hands, face, and clothes.

Species to avoid are *L. auratum* and *L. speciosum*, whose glorious perfume is inclined to be overwhelming in confined spaces; and *L. pyrenaicum*, whose scent is unpleasant.

Gladioli & summer & autumn bulbs

567

Are there any hardy gladioli?

It is possible to kill most gladioli but some will persist even after hard winters. We have a planting of 'Green Woodpecker' that has been left down for eight years and is still on parade. Undoubtedly, however, the plants would have increased better if we had lifted them.

There are some species that usually flourish with good drainage and sun. *G. byzantinus* can be relied on to produce 600 mm (24 in) spikes of rich purple-red flowers of good size. *G. communis* is a somewhat taller species; its small corms produce mauve-pink flowers in June on spikes up to 63-75 mm (2½-3 in) long.

568

What is the best way of storing gladioli over winter?

Lift them after flowering provided they can be kept frost-free until planting time. The plants, with their spawn of cormlets, need lifting and then taking to an airy place to dry completely. The tops must be cut away and all soil removed.

The winter dangers are frost, wet, and rot. Ideally the soil-free corms should be rinsed in a fungicide solution, dried, carefully labelled, and stored in trays or plastic net bags in a well-ventilated, frost-proof, dry place. Remember to label each corm, or group of corms, with its name.

569

My garden is inclined to be windy. Do all my gladioli have to be staked?

The large gladioli often need staking: when the flowers open they offer plenty of sail for the wind to catch. There are, however, races of smaller types that can manage without scaffolding. The Butterfly types are about half to two-thirds the size of their large relatives; they form rather triangular, sturdy flowers into stiff, upright spikes. The Primulinus types are more rounded and informal in shape. The *Gladiolus nanus* varieties are smaller still, sprightly and altogether pleasing. *G. byzantinus,* with maroon-coloured flowers, is fully hardy and can be left down year after year.

570

I have bought miniature gladioli from the florists. Can I grow them myself?

Probably these are *Gladiolus nanus* varieties; typical are 'Nymph' (snow-white with crimson markings), 'Guernsey Glory' (pinky orange), and 'Amanda Mahy' (bright salmon with violet-painted flakes). All these are a quarter to a third the size of the big gladioli. They are usually sold in the autumn and can be grown in a cool greenhouse, where they will bloom in spring before those planted outside. In the garden proper the corms do best in a warm spot in well-drained soil.

571

I would like to plant *Allium*, but I notice that some species seem to be rather weedy and tend to pop up all over the place. Can you suggest some less-invasive kinds?

I have already mentioned the fine *Allium albopilosum* and *A. aflatunense* (see 512); you might also like *A. giganteum*, one of the largest and tallest alliums, with great violet umbels hoisted up 1.2 m (4 ft) or more in July. Earlier, and half the height, is *A. neapolitanum* (syn. *A. cowanii*) with umbels of white flowers. *A. karataviense* is particularly suitable. It has broad, dark, metallic leaves with a purple-reddish cast especially near the margins. These

form a rosette below a 150-200 mm (6-8 in) stem carrying a large globe of white stars, flushed pinky violet, in the second half of May into June.

572

I have been given some big bulbs labelled *Galtonia*. Can you tell me something about the plants?

Galtonia candicans (sometimes incorrectly called *Hyacinthus candicans*) is commonly known as the summer hyacinth. It has a strong bulb and grows 1 m (3¼ ft) or more high. Each spike may carry up to three dozen hanging bells of milky white from July to September, and these look quite imposing against a background of dark foliage.

You should plant your bulbs in March or early April and see that they are covered with 100 mm (4 in) of soil. They do best in a well-drained, sunny position. You will enjoy the scent of the flowers.

573

A friend has some magnificent border plants which he knows only by the name of foxtail lilies. What are they, and are they easy to grow?

These belong to the genus *Eremurus*, and are hardy herbaceous perennials in which tall spikes of star-shaped flowers arise from a ring of narrow, pointed foliage. Among the best and tallest, are the series known as *E.* 'Shelford Hybrids', whose flowers vary in colour but are often a pleasing soft pinky beige. They can reach 2.75 m (9 ft) and bear hundreds of primrose-sized flowers. *E. stenophyllus bungei* is the yellow-flowered parent of these hybrids, and reaches 1 m (3¼ ft) in height; the other parent, *E. olgae*, is late-flowering, bears pink blooms, and reaches a height of 1.5 m (5 ft). Other fine examples are the very tall *E. elwesii* with soft pink flowers (and its white-flowered variety 'Albus'), and the even taller—up to 3 m (10 ft)—*E. robustus* with pinky yellow flowers on spikes up to 1.2 m (4 ft) long.

574

I would welcome suggestions for a few unusual hardy bulbs in our mixed beds. Any ideas?

Here are a few to make the neighbours envious: Foxtail lilies (*Eremurus*), mentioned above. Quamashes (*Camassia*) are easy, attractive, late-spring performers. *C. cusickii* 600 mm (2 ft) tall, has lots of pale blue flowers; *C. quamash* (syn.*C. esculenta*) 250 mm (10 in), has spikes of white to deep-blue flowers; *C. leichtlinii*, 900 mm (3 ft), has white or blue stars; *C.l. semiplena*, with semi-double creamy flowers on sturdy stems, is especially pleasing. *Fritillaria persica* 'Adiyaman' stands 800-1200 mm (2½-4 ft) in May, with unusual, deep-hanging bells

of rich plum-purple. *Leucojum aestivum* 'Gravetye Giant', 300-500 mm (12-20 in), is the best of the summer snow-flakes, and has wide-hanging white bells in April and May.

575

Looking through an old British flora I found an attractive plate showing a snake's-head fritillary. I would like to try growing this plant. It is obviously hardy, but what conditions does it need?

Fritillaria meleagris is a rare native plant, sometimes found in water meadows formerly subject to winter flooding. At one time catalogues listed a dozen or so named kinds of white, pink, and many intermediate shades to deep purple. These show varying amounts of the chequering that gave rise to the common name. Nowadays these plants are most often sold mixed. Their large, square-shouldered bells hang from wiry stems 150 mm (6 in) or so high. They grow well in drained but moist soil.

576

Just as a challenge, I want to grow the giant lily. Are there any special problems?

This is the extraordinary *Cardiocrinum giganteum*, a native of Himalayan woodland. The bulbs like soils that are moist, deep, and rich in leaf mould. The nose of the bulbs should be just below the surface. The stems can reach the amazing height of 3.7 m (12 ft). Up to 20 funnel-shaped greeny white lily flowers 150 mm (6 in) long may be arranged on these stems. After flowering the huge bulbs die; they leave behind a few offset bulbs that will take 3-4 years to build up to flowering size. It is wise to cover the dormant bulbs with a frost-protection layer of bracken or something similar in winter.

577

I was surprised to see some nerines flowering in a friend's border in the autumn. I thought these were exclusively houseplants.

All but one nerine require greenhouse cultivation. The exception is *N. bowdenii*, a plant that is completely hardy—it will survive all but the most severe winters in the British Isles. The most popular form is 'Fenwick's Variety', which is somewhat larger than the species. The plant produces flower spikes through the bare soil in September and October. The 300-400 mm (12-16 in) stems carry several brilliant pink, wide-open flowers in umbels up to 150 mm (6 in) in diameter which last well. The narrow, strap-like leaves appear soon after the flowers.

The bulbs take a while to establish as they do not like disturbance. They should be planted in April or August in well-drained soil with noses just below the surface. A favourable position would be near a sunny wall to help the bulbs get their vital summer baking. Leave the clumps undisturbed until the bulbs have become thoroughly overcrowded every five years or so; then lift, divide, and replant the clumps.

578

Have the colchicums any advantages over the autumn species of crocus?

One advantage is the persistence of their corms, which are large and increase steadily. Crocus corms often increase rapidly, but mice and other pests can be a problem. A possible disadvantage of colchicums is their huge leaves in the spring, which look rather a mess when they begin to wither. For garden effect I would suggest the following colchicum hybrids, all of them bred by crossing *C. speciosum* with other species: 'Lilac Wonder', easily the most free of bloom, with clusters of pinky lilac flowers with white stripes in September-October, 150-175 mm (6-7 in); 'Violet Queen', the earliest with somewhat chequered white-striped purple flowers in September, 125-150 mm (5-6 in); 'The Giant', the largest, with pinky violet flowers, 200-250 mm (8-10 in); 'Water Lily', a fine double with lots of strap-shaped violet-mauve petals, 125-150 mm (5-6 in).

579

Some of my bulbs have become squashy and rotten. A friend has suggested that they have become infested with eelworm. Is he right—and is there any simple cure?

I think your friend is probably correct—which is bad news. The cure for this pest is no simple matter. First of all, any bulbs that are obviously infested must be destroyed without delay. The rest would be given hot-water treatment by a commercial bulb-grower. Eelworm, a microscopic pest, can be killed if the bulbs are immersed in water maintained at a temperature of exactly 44.5°C (112°F) for a period of four hours to enable the heat to penetrate the bulbs completely. It is vital that the water is maintained at precisely that temperature. If it goes one or two degrees higher the bulbs will be killed; if it falls below, the eelworms will survive.

Unless you have the equipment to heat the water to that temperature and maintain it within those fine limits, it would be a waste of time attempting this treatment. In that event, you must destroy (by burning) not only the obviously affected bulbs but all others in the immediate area. Just as important—you should not plant any bulbs in the affected area of soil for a minimum of three years; and take care that you do not move any of that soil to another part of the garden.

John Warwick

Superintendent of the Rock Garden Department at the RHS's garden at Wisley; author of a book on rock gardens and alpine plants.

Water and Rock Gardens

Water gardening

580

What is an ideal site for a pool?

This is rarely achieved, but it should be open, away from trees so that leaves do not fall in it; sunny, to allow the maximum number of flowers to form and open, particularly water lilies; compatible with the landscape of the garden; and fully visible from the kitchen or living room—or from some other vantage point of your choice.

581

What is the best size for a pool?

Basically, the size (and shape) that seems most suitable for the space available. It should not be so large as to overwhelm the space, nor so small as to be lost in it.

Mark out the proposed site with a thick string or rope to allow for the pool area, and again outside that with another piece of string to allow for any additional plantings. Then stand back and look at it from all angles, especially from the house. If you want a formal pool, it should be in a formal setting. The formal pool looks best with no planting immediately outside it, but an informal one can have planting around it according to the space available.

582

I am planning a rock garden and wonder whether I might have a pool to go with it.

Certainly—it will give the rock garden extra size in each dimension, increase the scope for another range of plants, and give a more natural appearance to the whole scene. The pool should be built first, and then the rock garden built around at least one side of it. For details of site and construction, *see* 1056-63.

583

What can I do with the soil that I dig out to make a pool?

There are various possibilities. You could use the topsoil, usually the top 150 mm (6 in), for areas of the garden where it could improve the growing of plants; or you could stockpile it if you intend to build a rock garden alongside the pool—it will enable you to raise the level of the site. The subsoil which underlies the topsoil can be used to make up height and put at the base of the rock garden, with the topsoil placed on top of it afterwards. If you have no use for the subsoil, hire a skip and have it taken away.

584

Which plants are essential for an ornamental pool?

To maintain a clear pond, oxygenators are essential. These

are plants which live almost entirely under water and help to maintain an adequate level of oxygen for the other plants, fish, and other animal life. They also help reduce the level of algae, as do water lilies. The oxygenators include Canadian pondweed (*Elodea canadensis*), which is vigorous; *Egeria densa*, less vigorous; water milfoil (*Myriophyllum spicatum*), with its delightful feathery foliage; and *M. verticillatum*, also with feathery foliage, which prefers calcareous water.

585

Can I grow bog plants around my pool?

Not unless you specially provide the right conditions for them: the pool is waterproof, so no extra water will reach the plants from that source; but you can create the conditions artificially outside the pond by laying a sheet of thick black polythene below the soil surface in a saucer shape, up to 600 mm (2 ft) at its deepest, with a few small holes punched in its base to prevent stagnation. You will have to keep the area permanently soaked if the plants are to thrive.

586

What kind of water-plant container should I buy?

This depends very much on the size and vigour of the plants. If you are to have small ones, a square plastic-basket type, with perforated holes all around and below it, is ideal. If the plants are of a type that will eventually become much larger, a wider and possibly deeper container is essential, otherwise it will be toppled over by wind action on the top of the plant, and its roots will probably outgrow the basket. Almost any container will do, provided that it is at least as broad as it is high; I have used large concrete drains cut in half and placed on end.

587

I need some good water plants that will grow up to 450 mm (18 in) high. Any suggestions?

The following are excellent: water hawthorn (*Aponogeton distachyus*), with white flowers with dark spots throughout the year; *Acorus gramineus* 'Variegatus', for foliage colour in green and gold; bog arum (*Calla palustris*), with white flowers in mid-summer; *Caltha palustris* 'Plena', with double yellow flowers in March-April; *Cotula coronopifolia*, with yellow 'buttons' in July-August; *Hydrocharis morsus-ranae*, with white-flowered floaters all summer; *Mimulus moschatus*, with yellow, and *M.* 'Whitecroft Scarlet', with red flowers all summer; golden club (*Orontium aquaticum*), with yellow club flowers in May-June; and all the medium-sized water lilies (*Nymphaea*), in red, white, pink, and yellow shades throughout the summer.

588

Which plants are mainly ornamental?

There are many species. The most obvious are the water lilies (*Nymphaea*), whose flowers come in a variety of shades of pink, red, yellow, and white and are suitable for various depths of pond. Other plants of various sizes and requiring a constant depth of water include marsh marigold (*Caltha palustris*), brass buttons (*Cotula coronopifolia*), monkey flowers (*Mimulus* species and hybrids), water forget-me-not (*Myosotis palustris*), pickerel weed (*Pontederia cordata*), sweet flag (*Acorus calamus variegatus* and *A. gramineus* 'Variegatus'), and frogbit (*Hydrocharis morsus-ranae*).

589

I have a small pool about 3 × 2 m (10 × 6½ ft) in area and 600 m (2 ft) deep. What sizes and species of plants would be appropriate?

All the plants mentioned in the previous answer would be suitable; then to add some stature and height I would include one or two of the following: *Iris kaempferi*, *I. laevigata* (especially the variegated sorts), *I. forrestii*, and *I. sibirica*; flowering rush (*Butomus umbellatus*), with pink flowers; *Pontederia cordata*, with blue flowers; *Lysichiton camtschatcensis*, with white flowers and spreading leaves.

590

Are there any plants I should avoid in a small pool?

I would avoid the following, all of which are far too vigorous for all but the largest pools or lakes: *Alisma plantago-aquatica*, most species of *Carex* except *C. stricta* 'Aurea', *Cyperus longus*, *Lythrum salicaria*, *Mentha* species, *Lysimachia vulgaris*, *L. thyrsiflora*, *Polygonum amphibium*, *Potamogeton natans*, *Ranunculus lingua*, *Sagittaria* species, and *Sparganium* species.

591

Do I need fish and other water life to maintain a pool?

No, these are not essential. Most pond inhabitants except fish will soon appear, apparently from nowhere. However, enjoyment of a pool is greatly increased if fish are present. Some I would recommend are showy ones such as golden orfe and goldfish, especially the former, which come to the surface more often. As for other water life, I suggest you could add ramshorn snails (the best scavengers amongst the snails), and if you introduce tadpoles into the pond they will reduce the larvae of pests such as mosquitoes but when they turn into frogs you must provide a means by which they can reach dry land—a gently sloping edge to the pool or, better, some water plants by the edge.

592

When is the best time to plant a pool?

In early spring to mid-June, when the weather is warming up—and in any event *before* you add the fish, otherwise the fish will go hungry unless you feed them yourself. You can plant later if the weather is not too hot but there will be a greater risk, especially to the fish, of a failure to adjust to the changing autumn conditions.

593

How far below the surface of the water should I position my plants?

This varies with the type of plant. Water lilies, for instance, need to be at the depth at which their leaves will lie flat on the surface, not stick out of the water. Most plants will thrive if the crown (the point where roots and stem meet) are just covered. Most water-plant nurseries state in their catalogues the planting depth (distance between water surface and crown) of each of the plants they sell.

594

How can I propagate my water plants?

This is very simple for most water plants. You just divide them in the spring after lifting out of the containers any plants you require. Division is achieved by driving in either two handforks (or two larger

forks for larger plants) back to back, then pushing the forks apart to prise away the outermost plants in the clump. Do not use the centre crowns: these are the oldest parts of the plant and should be thrown away. Use a sharp knife to cut water lilies into sections with individual crowns. In some particular cases, as with *Mimulus* 'Whitecroft Scarlet', take soft nodal cuttings. For propagation techniques, *see* 883.

595

How do I plant my water plants and what soil should I use?

Let's take water lilies first. The crowns (tubers or rhizomes) should be planted in a medium to heavy loam with the crown tips exposed and upright—they must *not* be buried. All other container plants can be planted in the same type of soil and to the same depth as they were at the nursery or when you propagated them.

All planting should be firm, with the roots spread out and excessive or damaged leaves removed. Cover over the soil with chippings or shingle to prevent fish from disturbing it.

The oxygenators will need to be weighted if this has not already been done by the nursery. Clumps of 6-12 small pieces should be put on the floor of the pool and held in a group by a lead weight. This will keep them from floating to the surface. Natural floaters like

Hydrocharis morsus-ranae are simply placed on the surface.

596

Can you recommend using a fountain in a pool with water plants?

If the plants are marginals and oxygenators, I would say yes. But if they are water lilies or other plants with leaves floating on the surface, you must not use a fountain: the surface will be disturbed, which they will not like, and even if they survive they will rarely flower. This does not apply in a large pool, where water lilies could be located at one end and the fountain at the other.

597

Which is better, a submersible or an out-of-water pump?

For most small pools the submersible type is preferable. It is easy to instal and produces sufficient power for both the fountain and also a waterfall if you wish to have one. If, however, you want to make a big splash, or have a long connecting pipe, then a non-submerged pump will be necessary; but it is more expensive to buy and to operate. .

598

How do I deal with a leaking pool?

If the pool is made of concrete you should drain it and line it with one of the liners suggested (*see* 1057). Before laying the liner, smooth the concrete surface or line it with nylon netting.

If your pool has a polythene liner, it would almost certainly be best and cheapest to renew it completely. But repair kits are available for repairing the more expensive PVC and butyl-rubber sheeting, and your supplier can advise you on repair procedures.

599

What are the main pests and diseases of pool plants and livestock?

The worst pest of the plants is the water-lily beetle. Its larvae are like small slugs, dark on top and pale underneath. They feed on the leaves of water lilies. The small brown beetles hibernate in the hollow stems of other aquatic plants, which should therefore be cut down in the autumn and burnt. You can control the larvae by laying a double thickness of newspaper over all the foliage from the first appearance of the pest (indicated by holes chewed through the foliage). If this is done in the evening and the papers removed the following morning, and the process is repeated at weekly intervals for at least four weeks, you should find that the beetle larvae will have been eaten by other water life. Remove the worst-damaged leaves. This method of control is also good against the reddish-black aphids which can seriously damage the leaves. Hosing-off the aphids and beetles is also effective—but be careful not to add too much water to the pool (*see* 600).

As far as the fish are concerned, a good balance of water life and a fairly clean pool will go a long way towards preventing most problems; removal and disposal of diseased and injured fish is invariably simpler than treatment. Over-fed fish become constipated and sluggish. Bloated gills, tails, or fins are disease symptoms: remove the fish before the infection spreads. Bloating is due to over-feeding, temperature-shock, or overcrowding. Another disease symptom is a white film that may appear over any part of a fish. This is due to a fungus and usually follows injury. Again, remove the fish from the pool as soon as you see the symptom.

600

There is a thick green scum on the surface of my pool. What should I do?

If the pool has been filled with water for a matter of only days or a few weeks, remove the worst of the scum (which is formed of algae) with a fine mesh net, but do *not* change the water: it goes through this stage every time it is filled before it settles down. The presence of foliage on the surface will help to speed up the process by preventing light getting to all the water.

If your pond has been filled for some time, then the algae growth is most probably due to the fact that you are topping up with fresh water owing to a leak. In this case, mend the leak and do not change the water once you have re-filled the pool.

601

My pool is overgrown with plants and weeds. What should I do with it?

The first thing is to decide which plants you want to keep, and remove some crowns of these to a temporary home (a water-filled liner laid over a low circle of bricks is ideal). Then scrap the remaining plants, (they make good compost) or give them away.

Save the animal life in the same way as you preserve the plants (with a water-filled liner)—but separately, providing them with some degree of shade as well.

Clean the pool thoroughly, check for any leaks by filling it up without plants in it, and replace any damaged containers; renew the soil. Re-stock the pool first with the plants, then with the animals; make sure that the water temperature is the same all the time, otherwise you will risk losing the fish.

602

How often should I change my pool water? I have no pump to circulate it?

Never—unless you have to: the

more often the water is changed, the greater the difficulty of maintaining the balance of life in the pool. Apart from replanting every 5 to 10 years, leave the pool to its own devices.

603

Although in an open site, my pool collects many leaves in autumn from my neighbour's trees. Any advice?

Leaves rotting in a pool build up toxic gas, so they must be removed. The easiest solution is to place a net over the surface of the pond when the leaves begin to fall: it will save you a lot of work and will be there only for a short period. Clear the net periodically to admit light to the pond.

604

When is the best time to clear a pond of rotting and dead foliage?

In early spring from February to March, just as growth is starting; but do not do it during frosty weather. Handle the fish with care and remove them to water of the same temperature as that from which they have come.

605

How long can I keep a pool from the time of stocking it to the time of renewal?

So much depends on the initial stocking and subsequent

maintenance that no hard-and-fast rules apply: it could be 3 or 30 years—though the latter is unlikely for a small pond. An average would be 8 to 10 years.

606

How can I prevent my pool from freezing over the entire surface (I have fish in it)?

The simplest way is to use a weighted plastic bottle, at least 300 mm (1 ft) long, floating so that the rim is about 150 mm (6 in) above the surface. Pour hot water into the bottle to thaw the ice surrounding it, then remove and refill it with a little warm water to thaw out thin ice when replacing it later the same day. This procedure is necessary only if the water has been frozen for more than 24 hours. Do not on any account attempt to crack the ice by hitting it: the shock of pressure would severely injure the fish.

607

Could you suggest a month-by-month programme of work to be carried out on a pool?

January
Keep pool unfrozen in at least one place (*see* 606).
February
As for January. During mild spells, clean up pond if growth has started.
March
As for February. Also carry out propagation and fresh plantings;

instal and start pump.
April
As for March. If pond is new, start removing algae from water surface.
May
As for April. In late May introduce new fish to pool, take lily-beetle precautions (*see* 599) and weed if necessary, especially around margins.
June
Introduce any new fish into pool; weed and take lily-beetle precautions.
July
Weed and take lily-beetle precautions.
August
As for July.
September
Weed.
October
Net ponds against falling leaves.
November
Start to remove leaves from net. Remove pump for the winter and service or clean it thoroughly.
December
As for January.

Rock gardening

608

Do I have to build a rock garden in order to grow rock garden plants?

No. Plants usually grown in a rock garden may be grown in raised beds, sinks, or troughs; but they certainly look best in a well-planned and maintained rock garden. Rock plants require good drainage and, usually, plenty of light; and the better the setting the more spectacular they look—even in a small space.

609

I have decided to build a rock garden on sloping ground at present covered with a rough collection of shrubs. What should I do to prepare the site?

Remove all plants, including perennial weeds, before you start construction. Use the existing soil, adding extra drainage only if it is heavy clay. Start laying stone from the base in a series of terraces, of any shape you like, but preferably simple; the number of terraces is determined solely by the slope of the ground and size of stones, which should match in height at their tops and be of the same type. Make the ends disappear in the ground by 'bending' them into the slope: they should not stand out like sentinels but should lean into the slope for greater stability and better appearance.

610

What type of stone do you recommend for a rock garden?

Preferably any stone with angular faces, which are easier to lay and maintain in position than those with rounded faces. Whatever type of rock you use, stick to it and do not mix with other types. Avoid volcanic granite as this has no strata and different pieces are almost impossible to join together. Where possible use the stone native to your area—it will be cheaper in terms of transport costs—and the individual pieces should be as large as you can safely handle.

611

How large should the stones be for a rock garden about 3 × 3 m and 1.5 m high (10 × 10 ft by 5 ft)?

This site has sides sloping at an average of 45 degrees; it should ideally have three to four layers approximately 450 mm (18 in) high on each terrace. The depth from front to back of each stone will not need to be more than 300-400 mm (12-16 in); they should be as long as possible, but manageable. This may sound horrifically large; you can reduce them in size as long as you do not lessen their height, otherwise there would be nothing but stones on the site!

612

I recently saw a reference to planting rock plants on a scree. What does this mean?

To the geologist a scree is an accumulation of rock, broken up into stones by the action of heat and frost, which collects on the slope of a mountain. You can make a miniature version of this in the rock garden if the slope is not more than 20 degrees. Lay a rock-garden compost in the normal way (see 631) and on top of this put a layer up to 200 mm (8 in) thick of chippings or shingle, with a scattering of larger stones. Planting is carried out directly into the chippings or shingle; the plant roots will soon reach down to the soil below.

613

I would like to build a rock garden, but I have available only a flat site. What do you suggest?

The site must be free of perennial weeds before any start can be made. Then you should consider whether a stone raised bed would be more suitable than a flat site. What I have in mind is essentially a dry stone wall, consisting of two faces sandwiching a core of soil. The total thickness would need to be not less than 1 metre (3¼ ft) to prevent the soil from drying out too quickly. The stones would be laid on top of one another until the required height was reached; the faces of the wall would be built to a batter (leaning inwards) to increase stability. If you decide to build a rock garden instead, make sure that each of the terraces is level all the way around to retain the soil; the structure should be not more than three terraces high.

614

I plan to build a rock garden approximately 9 × 9 m and 3 m high (30 × 30 × 10 ft). Do I need to build steps into the structure?

Yes, I would recommend them for a site of this size, to make access easier and to enable you to show off the whole site to friends. Make the steps wide enough for two people to pass, and lay them on the same strata as the rock garden, remembering to use the same stone type. Make sure that the risers are not higher than those of house stairs.

615

Is there a best time to order stone and build a rock garden?

Any time of the year is suitable, bearing in mind the rest of the work to be done in the garden during the growing season. Ideally, I would suggest you order your stone during the summer and begin building in late summer, aiming to complete by the time of your first spring plantings.

616

I have been lucky enough to obtain, free, some supplies of sandstone and Westmorland limestone. I intend to use them to build two small rock gardens. Any tips about laying these rocks?

Sandstone should always be laid with the strata (the layers which formed the stone) arranged horizontally. Place the stones so that they either join end to end or overlap slightly; this will discourage soil erosion. Then build in a series of terraces.

The Westmorland limestone is more difficult. It should be laid with its largest surface area to the ground and in a series of irregular small terraces. It will need to be fitted like a jig-saw puzzle, with as little space as possible between the joins, into which plants are placed to prevent soil erosion.

Stratified rocks include a number of limestones other than the Westmorland type. Bear in mind that stratified rock, of whatever type, is best for rock gardens: it is easy to lay and holds soil.

617

Do I need help to plan and build a rock garden?

To plan I would always advise at least a second (and preferably an experienced) opinion. To build you ought to have at least one other person, possibly more: two people can deal with stones weighing up to 100 kg (2 cwt); for larger ones, three or four people will be needed.

618

What equipment do I need for building a small rock garden?

Apart from the usual spade and fork, I would recommend at least one crowbar about 2 m (6 ft) long; a sack truck or a builder's barrow (depending on size and weight of stone and the help available); at least four scaffold planks to run the transport on; a baulk of wood to act as a fulcrum for the crowbar and as a stop for the truck; and, for a flat site, a spirit level. All these tools, apart from the spade, fork, and level, can be hired.

619

How do I know what to buy when selecting plants for a small rock garden? I obviously do not want rampant growers.

A visit to specialist nurseries is the best course. Opinions vary as to eventual size attained by many rock plants, but if you give some indication of the life expectancy of your rock garden (15 to 20 years is reasonable) the nurseryman will at least be able to tell you what to avoid. If you cannot visit a rock or plant nursery, send off for catalogues and make your enquiries by post.

620

I have raised beds and a sink garden. What rock plants can I grow in them?

Taking the raised bed first, you can use the same plants as in a rock garden of similar size though you should avoid too many tall, spiky plants: one or two will give an extra dimension, but a lot of them will spoil the whole effect. The sink garden, on the other hand, must be restricted to the slowest growers, so that the display can last 10 or 15 years.

621

What is a crevice plant?

This is simply a plant that will grow in the narrow vertical or horizontal spaces between stones in a rock garden or paving. It is worth remembering that all crevice plants should be placed in position during construction, never afterwards, otherwise the plants will be severely damaged when forcing them in. Some good examples of crevice plants are sempervivums, ramondas, haberleas, *Saxifraga longifolia*, and *Alyssum saxatile*.

622

Can I grow shade-loving plants in a rock garden?

Yes, you can, and very good they are too—but beware of rampant growers. Many ferns are ideal, as are haberleas, ramondas, gaultherias, vacciniums, and many others. Again, you should seek advice from specialist nurseries, which in this case will include those growing woodland plants, especially dwarf rhododendrons.

623

Are ground-cover plants suitable for a rock garden?

Yes, but perhaps not the types usually advertised as such, many of which are rampant growers. The cushion plants, the trailing types, and many herbaceous plants of a dwarf habit are suitable. Bear in mind, however, that rock-garden plants in general grow more slowly than their open-garden counterparts. Maintenance by weeding is still very important.

624

How 'dwarf' is a dwarf conifer?

This is always a problem for the rock-garden enthusiast. Nurseries advertise dwarf conifers in good faith—but dwarf in relation to what? The following dwarf forms are all of a stature suitable for the rock garden: silver fir (*Abies balsamea* 'Hudsonia') and *A.b.* 'Compacta'; Hinoki cypress (*Chamaecyparis obtusa* 'Nana'); *Juniperus communis* 'Compressa'; and the spruces *Picea gregoryana* and *P. mariana* 'Nana'. None of these exceeds 900 mm (3 ft) in height; most are 600 mm (2 ft) or less—but their width may exceed their height.

625

Can I use dwarf shrubs as rock garden plants?

Yes, but again be careful because 'dwarf' is a term used in relation to their larger relatives; they may well be too large for the smaller rock garden. Their eventual size should not be greater than what will be wanted in, say, 15 to 20 years. These shrubs, together with dwarf

conifers (*see* 624) and dwarf rhododendrons in the shade (*see* 622), form the backbone of the planting, especially in winter, and the specialist nursery is the best place to go if you are uncertain about what to select.

626

Are heathers suitable as rock garden plants?

They can be used there, but they would really be better planted elsewhere in the garden. Most heathers grow quite large, especially in spread; and, as there are so many other plants to choose from, the rock garden is better used for those more suited to their culture.

627

What size of plants should I plant in a rock garden?

Planting size is immaterial: it is the size a plant will attain in a given period of time that is important. I normally recommend 15 to 20 years as a good lifespan before the rock garden is completely renewed; though a few plants will be renewed within that time owing to death, or their growing too large, or there being better plants to replace them. The size of rock garden will also, of course, determine the size of plants. In a rock garden 3 × 3 m in area and 1.5 m high (10 × 10 × 5 ft) the conifers and shrubs should not exceed 450 mm (18 in) in height and spread. The remaining rock plants can vary up to 300 mm (12 in) high and of as wide a spread as you wish.

628

How long do rock-garden plants live?

Some plants live for up to 60 years, notably dwarf conifers and dwarf rhododendrons. Some by contrast, are monocarpic—that is, they grow until they flower, and then they die, having produced plentiful seed. Examples include *Saxifraga longifolia* and *Townsendia grandiflora*. The majority, however, have a useful life of 15 to 20 years, which is why I recommend renewing the site after that time.

629

How do I know how many plants to buy?

I would suggest a maximum density of 10 plants per square metre (slightly less per square yard), provided that rampant growers are not used. If dwarf conifers and rhododendrons and shrubs are planted, reduce the number to one to three per square metre. For sink gardens, the number should preferably be increased to 20 plants per square metre, but make sure that only very dwarf plants are used.

It is my experience, however, that after one has completed the work of planting one invariably

comes across plants which one would like to have included. So it is a good idea to leave a few spaces in one's general scheme to accommodate these late-comers.

630

When is the best time to plant rock-garden plants, and how do I plant them?

Almost any time of the year is suitable except mid-winter; but dwarf bulbs should be planted in autumn. Avoid very hot or very cold weather. If plants are bought during weather extremes, plunge them in their containers (most are pot-grown now) in soil up to the rims, and plant them as soon as the weather changes for the better. Plant them at exactly the same depth as they were in the pots; firm them in; then water thoroughly. If more than one of the type is planted, place them closer together within the group, but place the different groups farther apart.

Soil

631

What type of soil do I need for rock-garden plants?

Most rock-garden plants growing in sunny positions require well-drained soil. For those growing in wetter conditions I recommend equal parts by bulk of peat, sterilised loam, and grit (not sand)

and half a part of shingle; the grit should have grains 3-13 mm (⅛-½ in) in diameter, and the shingle approximately 6 mm (¼ in). For drier sites omit the shingle in the mixture. As long as this goes into the top 150-250 mm (6-10 in) of soil, the remainder can be the garden soil you already have. For shadier-area plants, you should either double the peat content or, better, use leaf mould instead of peat.

632

I have inherited a rock garden which has been sadly neglected. How should I set about improving it?

The first task is to propagate any of the plants which you want to keep, then remove and dispose of all but the best of the dwarf conifers, which can be retained to good effect and, hopefully, last a further 15 to 20 years. If there are any perennial weeds, remove them carefully by hand or with a weedkiller. Lastly, remove the stones to a pile well away from the site and re-build, as described in 609-11. If you try short cuts in this process, such as patching up the structure, I am sure you will be disappointed with the results.

633

Do I need to prune any of my rock-garden plants?

Yes, you should remove dead and decayed wood from shrubs and old flower-heads from cushion plants; cut all herbaceous plants hard back in late winter or early spring; and pull off dried bulb foliage (but only when it comes away easily). Use a pair of shears on the stronger growers—trailing plants such as aubrietas and helianthemums—so as to keep them compact and encourage them to produce the maximum amount of flowers next time.

634

How often do I need to water my rock-garden plants?

Frequency will obviously depend on the weather, but never water more than once every five days. However, when you do water, give the plants a good soaking, until the soil is wet to a depth of at least 150 mm (6 in).

635

I am told that rock-garden plants are prone to 'rotting off'. How can I prevent this happening?

This problem affects grey-foliaged and cushion plants, which can retain water in their compact leaves or hairs, and more especially plants producing rosettes. Putting extra grit below the area of planting will help, and in the late autumn I like to put a cover of glass over these plants. This cover must be removed in the spring, when the sun has become warm enough for growth to begin.

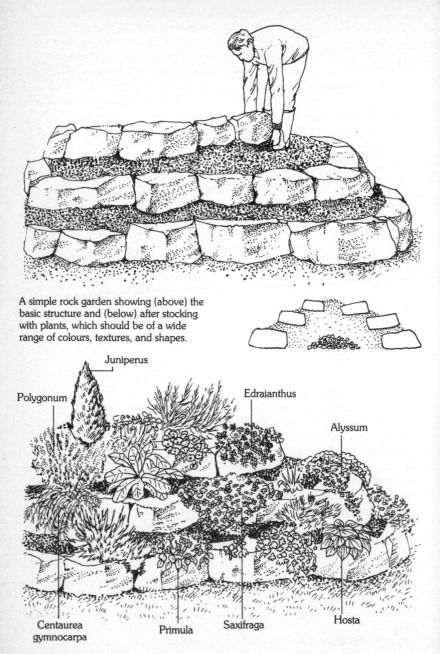

A simple rock garden showing (above) the basic structure and (below) after stocking with plants, which should be of a wide range of colours, textures, and shapes.

Juniperus

Polygonum

Edraianthus

Alyssum

Centaurea gymnocarpa

Primula

Saxifraga

Hosta

636

How do I get rid of perennial weeds?

On a rock garden in otherwise good condition, use a brush to paint the leaves of perennial weeds with a suitable weedkiller when they are in full growth in June. If the weeds persist repeat the dose in July, provided that the ground is moist and the weeds are pulled away from any plants.

On a site which is otherwise in disrepair, follow the procedure outlined in 632. Then leave the site for 12 months before starting from scratch.

637

Can you give me a summary of the main work, month by month, in the rock garden?

January
Remove any remaining loose leaves. Check glass covers (*see* 635). Prune any herbaceous plants covering any bulbs.
February
Weed on mild days. Prune remaining herbaceous plants. Apply pre-emergence weedkiller on paths and steps.
March
Weed. Remove glass covers. Begin planting programme.
April
Prune dead and straggly growths from shrubs. Weed. Scratch the soil surface with a hand fork.
May
Water as necessary.

September
Weed and hand-fork. Apply insecticides. Remove old flower stems, unless decorative. If you are starting from scratch, this is the time of year to plan, prepare, and begin building the new rock garden.
October
Remove loose leaves. Apply slug pellets if necessary. New rock garden: complete building work.
November
As for October. Place glass covers over grey-foliaged, cushion, and rosette plants (*see* 635).
December
Check glass covers. Remove loose leaves. Check for slugs.

J. R. Escritt

Freelance writer; formerly Director of the Sports Turf Research Institute at Bingley; author of two books on lawns and turf care.

Lawns

New lawns

638

The builders have left an awful mess just where I want to put a lawn. How do I start?

The first thing to do is to collect the rubbish and take it all to the council tip, unless the broken bricks can be used for making a drainage soakaway. You may then discover that there is enough topsoil (builders are much better than they used to be)—otherwise you will have to buy some. If there are marked ruts and much unevenness, collect all topsoil into a temporary heap so that you can adjust levels in the subsoil and ensure the deep cultivations which are important for drainage.

639

What is the best way to level out a considerable slope to make a lawn?

It will be necessary to remove the topsoil and carry out sufficient levelling by 'cut and fill' in the subsoil. Compaction caused to the subsoil should be relieved by cultivations before or after the topsoil has been returned. If it is a small job done by hand the subsoil can be dug over and smoothed out before replacing an even depth of topsoil. On larger jobs, done by machine, the subsoil cultivation is best accomplished by special

subsoiling equipment *after* the topsoil has been returned because the machines spreading the soil themselves compact the subsoil.

640

How do I prepare the ground for a lawn?

You need to create a smooth, thoroughly dug and raked, fine seed bed which has been well firmed. The firmness helps establishment and minimises the risk of the soil settling unevenly, which would lead to a bumpy surface on the new lawn. A roller is not very good for achieving the right kind of firmness since it rides over air pockets. These are best

got out by 'heeling'—progressing slowly over the site in very short steps, with one's weight on the heels so that soft spots are firmly filled. After this, rake over the soil and repeat the heeling operation. Collect all stones during the final raking and smoothing out. The seed bed should be free from weeds and a good way of achieving this is by digging followed by regular raking and hoeing throughout the summer, with a view to sowing, say, at the end of August—the best time for the job. For turfing (ideally done in the autumn) the same preparations are needed, though cultivation need not be quite so thorough.

641

Is it necessary to pre-treat the soil with fertiliser when making a new lawn?

On land which has been well fed for vegetables, fertiliser is probably unnecessary. In most other circumstances a dressing of general fertiliser, such as standard Growmore, or one of the special pre-seeding or pre-turfing lawn fertilisers is beneficial.

642

What kind of grass seed should I use for my new lawn?

Three main types of lawn seed mixtures are available. Type 1 – high-quality mixtures for first-class turf usually contain only fine fescue and fine bent grass; they require

expert maintenance. Type 2 – general-purpose mixtures for the average lawn usually contain a selection (in varying proportions) of rough-stalked meadow grass, smooth-stalked meadow grass, and timothy, plus fine fescue and bent. Type 3 – general-purpose mixtures are similar to Type 2 but also include perennial ryegrass, which is very quick growing and sometimes rather coarse; these mixtures are used on football pitches.

Several good new varieties of each of the grasses in each of these types are available. The good varieties cost more than less-good ones, but it is worthwhile paying a little more to ensure you get certified seed of the best grasses, especially those of Type 1.

643

What is the best way to sow grass seed?

First divide the lawn area into a number of equal squares and measure out the right amount of seed for each square. Scatter this by hand, preferably after first dividing it into two portions to spread in two directions at right angles. Finally, rake in the seeds very carefully and lightly.

644

What is the best way of preventing birds from attacking a new-sown lawn?

Seed pre-treated with bird repellent is of some value, but the main trouble is not the amount of seed they eat but the disturbance they cause in dust-bathing. An effective deterrent is nylon netting stretched between sticks that keep it 75-100 mm (3-4 in) above the ground. Cotton can cut the feet of birds and should not be used.

645

How do I ensure that I get good turf for my new lawn?

Obtain high-quality samples and ensure that the delivered material is as good as the sample selected. The turf should have a predominance of fine grasses, it should be weed-free, and it should not be too fibrous, although each turf should hold together satisfactorily. The soil present should be reasonable (not heavy clay, for instance), and the turfs should be of even thickness—about 38 mm (1½ in).

646

Could you advise on how and when to lay the turf?

Well prepared land (see 640), fertilised if necessary (see 641), and good turf (see 645) are essential. Individual turfs should be laid out flat in a staggered pattern (like that of bricks in a wall). Move in a forward direction. That is, work from planks resting on previously laid turf so as to avoid damaging the prepared bed. Correct any unevenness in the turfed area by levelling the

underlying soil, *not* by tamping down the turf. On completion lightly roll the turfs and add a top-dressing of sandy compost (see 667 and 673).

The best time to lay turfs is in October and November; do *not* lay it later than December.

647

How do I set about making a chamomile lawn?

Common chamomile (*Anthemis nobilis*; syn. *Chamaemelum nobile*) is a ferny non-grass plant which has found some favour for small lawns for several hundred years. It forms a dense mat of feathery fronds and emits a pleasant aroma when trodden on. Chamomile is advertised in gardening columns of newspapers; be sure to get a non-flowering variety such as 'Treneague'. You can buy a relatively small quantity and grow it on in boxes before planting out sprigs on the site. The ground should be prepared as for an ordinary lawn (see 640) and you must take special care to eliminate weeds because it is impossible to get a selective weedkiller that will not also kill the chamomile.

648

My new lawn, sown a few weeks ago, is coming along well. How do I ensure continued success?

Aim to get a good cover of the sown grasses as soon as possible so as to keep out invaders. Important points: (1) watch out for damping-off disease (see 649); (2) collect surface stones; (3) then lightly roll to firm up the surface and push down uncollected small stones out of reach of the mower; (4) mow after rolling but before the grass gets too long—50 mm (2 in) for Type 1 lawns and 75 mm (3 in) for Types 2 and 3—the final cutting height being reached only in stages; (5) keep the grass growing by applications of nitrogenous fertiliser. For weed treatment, see 650.

649

On my recently sown lawn of chewings fescue and browntop bent there are lots of small brown and dead patches, and around these seedling grass tends to have a red or purplish colour. What should I do?

The grass seems to be affected by damping-off disease, which seems to affect these two species more

than others. The disease is usually restricted to new swards sown in cold, wet conditions and/or at excessive seed rates. It may be possible to prevent further damage by spraying with a turf fungicide such as one based on chlorothalonil, or by treating with Cheshunt compound in water. Bare patches will need to be over-seeded.

650

My newly sown lawn is full of weeds. What can be done about it?

Most of the weeds are probably annuals which will disappear with regular mowing. The rest can be treated with selective weedkiller when the grass is sufficiently well established—perhaps in August after a spring sowing or in April after a late-summer sowing.

If the weeds are so rampant in the first weeks after sowing that the grass cannot establish itself properly, apply one of the proprietary weedkillers containing ioxynil which are sold for use on new lawns. Follow the instructions on the label exactly.

Lawn care

651

What is the best kind of mower to buy?

Buying mowers is like buying

cars—there is a choice of many kinds and many prices. For a domestic lawn of say, 100 m² (120 sq yd) a good quality 300-350 mm (12-14 in) hand mower of the traditional cylinder type and fitted with grass box is suitable. You may have to shop around for this: the fad nowadays is for powered motors (with petrol or electric engines) and with rotary cutting blades, and among these the hover types have been especially heavily promoted. Some machines, of whatever type, have grass-collecting attachments and some have not. From the various types of mowers available you make your choice and pay accordingly. First-class lawns, however, need a cylinder mower (roller type with grass box) which gives 100 cuts or more per metre (yard) run.

652

How is the height of cut measured?

It is not practicable to measure the actual height of the grass because fixed points are difficult to establish. Instead heights are described in terms of the mower setting. With a cylinder mower the height of cut measured is the distance between a straight edge laid from front to back roller and the cutting edge of the bottom blade. With side wheel mowers and some rotary mowers the straight edge is laid from roller to side wheel.

653

How often should I mow my lawn?

The aim is dense turf with an attractive appearance, so the grass should be cut whenever it visibly exceeds the norm: see next answer. For very fine lawns this may mean mowing two or three times per week at the height of the growing season, though once per week suffices for the average lawn. When growth is slow, less frequent mowing is needed—a good reason for not using too much fertiliser.

654

Is there a best height at which to mow a lawn?

For each kind of lawn (see 642) the answer is probably yes. The heights of cut suggested are: finest quality (Type 1) lawns, 6-13 mm (¼-½ in); average quality (Type 2), 13-19 mm (½-¾ in); and general purpose (Type 3), 19-25 mm (¾-1 in).

655

I do not have a grass box on my mower. Should I remove the cuttings from the lawn after mowing?

There are pros and cons to removing cuttings. Leaving them on the lawn means that mineral nutrients are returned to the soil, and the organic matter of which they mainly consist helps drought resistance. However, they release their mineral nutrients only as the organic matter decomposes—and decomposing organic matter is good earthworm food; so leaving the cuttings encourages earthworms with their unpleasant casting. It also helps to spread weeds, and may encourage disease. So, on balance, it is better to remove the cuttings.

656

It seems to be common practice to put away lawn mowers from October to April. However, since my lawn grows during some parts of this period, should I cut it occasionally?

If the grass gets much beyond its normal height it may be harmed if you do not cut it. Provided the weather is right—look for a mild and preferably dry spell—it is beneficial to mow whenever there is grass to mow; but do not cut it as short as in the summer.

657

Can I use growth retarders on my lawn instead of mowing it?

Available growth retarders (based on maleic hydrazide) are apparently quite effective on privet hedges but only moderately successful on lawns. Their use has to be skilfully organised to achieve any kind of success; they often cause considerable discoloration, and the turf does not look as smart as when it is mown. Reducing

grass growth helps weeds to flourish, so if you use a growth retarder you may need to combine it with a selective weedkiller.

658

Should I roll my lawn occasionally?

If possible, no. Rolling is harmful because it causes soil compaction, which spoils the drainage qualities of the soil, and it restricts aeration, which leads to poor root development and a weaker turf.

659

Do I need to rake my lawn?

Most lawns benefit from brushing with a stiff broom or raking with a wire rake about once a month to remove debris. In spring and summer, this should be done before mowing. In autumn, scarifying (vigorous raking out of debris) is also beneficial. Remove rakings with a stiff broom if your mower has no grass box.

660

How do I maintain neat lawn edges?

The main needs are regular trimming with shears or special edge trimmers, avoiding treading on the lawn edge, and siting plants in adjacent beds far enough away to avoid them overhanging the lawn.

Long edges should be given permanent support. Metal-strip

edging is cheap and effective; timber and concrete are longer-lasting. The top of such edging should be a little lower than the surface of the lawn so that you can mow right up to the edge. If no edging is used, you can maintain straight edges by trimming with a spade or 'halfmoon' against the edge of a long plank.

661

Can I grow bulbs such as daffodils and crocuses in my lawn?

Bulbs will certainly grow in a lawn and can be very attractive in the spring. Unfortunately, their growth conflicts with mowing requirements: if the turf is not mown regularly it deteriorates, and if the bulbs are mown they cannot thrive. Planting the bulbs in not too plentiful groups or drifts minimises the area of lawn affected.

662

Should I water my lawn?

Watering is beneficial if done properly and not overdone. In really dry weather give the lawn a good soaking and then allow several days partial drying out before repeating.

663

How often should I apply fertiliser?

Fertiliser requirements vary depending on soil, grasses present,
whether cuttings are removed, and so on. Good, fine grasses such as fescues and bents are poverty grasses: in nature they typically occur on areas of low fertility such as moorland. Making the grass grow faster increases the amount of mowing you will have to do. Lawns receiving little wear may require a general lawn fertiliser only once every 5 to 10 years. Heavily worn lower-grade lawns may require feeding with balanced fertiliser at least once a year; so too may fine-grade luxury lawns.

The chief mineral nutrient required by turf is nitrogen. If there is reason to suppose that the other main nutrients (phosphate and potash) are in reasonable supply but that the grass is not growing vigorously enough, especially in the spring, you should give it a dressing of nitrogenous fertiliser, such as sulphate of ammonia at 18 g/m^2 (½ oz/sq yd), diluted with a spreading agent (see 664).

664

How can I ensure that the fertiliser is spread evenly?

For many people spreading by hand is simplest and best. The fertiliser should be well mixed with a spreading agent such as compost, allowing about 280 g/2 m^2 compost (8 oz/sq yd). If the total amount is halved then one half can be spread lengthways and the other crossways. Alternatively, especially for large lawns, the area can be divided into a number of measured squares and the material rationed out equally for each square.

Fertiliser distributors are of two types: linear distributors, which use rollers to transfer fertiliser from a hopper to a broad band of turf; and spinners, which spread by means of a quickly revolving plate. With either type it may not be strictly necessary to dilute proprietary fertiliser with compost but it is still a good plan. It is also wise to divide the fertiliser into two and spread it in two applications at half rate. With a linear distributor the two applications should be at right angles; with a spinner they should be in the same direction but overlapping because the spinner applies more fertiliser in the middle than at the edges of its spread. With any distributor particular care is needed during filling and turning.

665

The quantity marks on my fertiliser distributor do not seem to match the amounts it applies. Why is this?

Materials vary in density and in ability to flow, so the marks on the distributor aim at an average. The best way to calibrate the distributor for a particular material is to fill the hopper and run the machine at working speed over a measured sheet or tray. The amount distributed can then be weighed and any necessary adjustments made to the machine setting before lawn use.

666

What are the advantages of applying fertiliser in solution?

Except for convenience, very few. The need for solubility restricts the kind of fertilisers which can be used and those which are compatible and suitably soluble are not necessarily the best for turf. If it is applied as a spray the solution has to be applied very carefully to avoid the grass being scorched. If it is watered in, the dilute solution tends to find the lower and softer spots least in need of fertiliser.

667

I have been advised to apply lawn sand to my turf. What exactly is this material?

Lawn sand is a mixture of chemicals and sand used to promote grass growth and burn out weeds, including moss. A typical formula is 3 parts sulphate of ammonia, 1 part calcined sulphate of iron, and 20 parts fine sand. This mixture would be used at a rate 140 g/m^2 (4 oz/sq yd). Proprietary lawn sands are very useful, although the advent of selective weedkillers and the new mosskillers has much reduced their popularity. Unfortunately the term 'lawn sand' is used to describe the sand used (without chemical admixture) as a top-dressing to smooth out the surface of the lawn. Top-dressings are used at heavy rates—2 kg/m^2 (4 lb/sq yd) is typical—and the use of a true lawn sand at this concentration would ruin the lawn.

668

Where the chalk lines are marked out on my lawn tennis court the turf seems much greener and more vigorous than the rest of the lawn. Does this mean that my lawn needs lime?

It does not follow at all. If you have a good lawn it is probably wise to leave well alone since lime encourages coarse grass, weeds, worms, and disease! You may see evidence of this near the chalk lines if you examine those areas carefully. It *is* possible that your lawn needs lime, but a laboratory soil test is the best basis on which to form an opinion. Most good lawns are found on slightly acid soil.

669

There is a bewildering range of selective weedkillers available for treating lawns. Is any one type better than the other, or are they all effectively the same?

They are all useful if used strictly in accordance with the instructions on the labels; but they are by no means all the same. There are at least four chemicals used in these weedkillers either singly or in combinations (usually of two). Each of the chemicals is effective against some weeds but not others, so that combinations deal with a broader range of weeds than do single-chemical formulations. Different combinations deal with different ranges of weeds, so read the labels carefully to make sure which weedkiller most nearly answers your needs.

670

What is the best way to apply selective weedkillers to a lawn?

For a typical small suburban lawn apply the prepared solution by means of a watering can fitted with a fine rose or with a dribble bar. For large lawns you could try a roller-type applicator, which feeds the diluted weedkiller from a tank mounted on the frame so as to wet the special roller which in turn wets the foliage as it passes over the turf. Spraying is not recommended because of the risk of spray drifting onto the rest of the garden (and even into your neighbour's).

Combined fertiliser/weedkiller powders or granules used carefully are often useful—they produce two effects from one effort!

671

My large lawn has only a few scattered weeds. How can I get rid of these without treating the whole lawn with selective weedkiller?

There are various ways of doing this—including hand weeding! The safest chemical way is probably to make up a correctly mixed watering-canful of a broad-spectrum selective weedkiller and, using the rose, to sprinkle each weed lightly, trying to avoid excess. You can always repeat the treatment a week or two later, whereas grass damaged by excess weedkiller may take many weeks to recover.

So-called touchweeders are useful against many lawn weeds—they consist of weedkilling chemicals in a piece of softish wax with which the weeds are touched quite lightly; rubbing them hard results in very brown or dead grass. Small pressurised containers of selective weed-killer are also available—but again it is very easy to apply an overdose. Spot treatment involves only small patches, so that excessive applications do not kill off the whole lawn; but there is less danger of excess if the correct amounts of weedkiller are measured out and applied to the whole area.

672

What is meant by the term top-dressing?

In horticulture top-dressing usually means applying a fertiliser, particularly a nitrogenous one, to the surface of soil bearing a crop, usually in concentrations of about 18 g/m^2 (½ oz/sq yd). In lawn management top-dressing means the application of suitable bulky material to the surface of the lawn at the rate of 1-3½ kg/m^2 (2-7 lb/sq yd), and then working it in by means of suitable equipment such as a drag brush with a view to making the surface smooth.

673

What kind of material should I use for top-dressing my lawn?

Although some gardeners use them, pure sand and peat are both unsatisfactory because they produce layers which form moisture and root breaks. Make up a synthetic compost if you are unable to buy suitable stuff ready-made. For this the sand should be of medium grade, with a particle size range of 0.5-0.125 mm, it must be stable (not break down into smaller particles, for example) and it should be lime-free. A suitable mixture would be 6 parts of this sand, 1 part granulated peat, and 3 parts topsoil.

674

From my garden waste I have made a heap of compost resembling well-rotted farmyard manure. Would a top-dressing of this be good for the lawn?

No: it would be far better used for vegetables and flowers because it would encourage worms and weeds in the lawn.

675

How often should a lawn be aerated?

Regular aeration is usually essential for sports turf since the top soil becomes compacted by heavy use and possibly by rolling. Many lawns receive very little treading and no rolling so that they seldom need any mechanical aeration at all. If a particular lawn or part of a lawn, does get well trodden, spiking by hand or machine could be beneficial two or three times a year. For such areas hollow tine forking, which is very efficient at relieving top-soil compaction, could be done at a frequency of once in three years—over frequent hollow tining leads to excessive softness and to weed invasion.

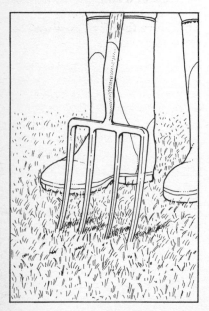

Lawn troubles

676

My turf seems to dry out very quickly. What can I do to keep it going in long, dry spells when the use of garden hoses is prohibited?

Grasses are difficult to kill and although the lawn may go very brown it will usually recover from even the worst British drought. If you must not water the lawn, it helps to raise the height of cut when mowing and to let the cuttings remain on the lawn. Compost is also useful—a light dressing will act as a mulch during the drought and regular heavier dressings each autumn will help to build up the moisture-holding capacity of the top soil. Remember that a reasonably fertile lawn withstands drought better than a hungry one!

677

What is the best way to drain a lawn which tends to hold water?

The trouble may be caused by impermeable top-soil. In that case monthly aeration with solid-tine aerators and/or hollow-tine forking at, say, 3-year intervals to help excess water through the soil may do the trick. If sub-surface drainage proves necessary, a soakaway constructed in the lowest corner should help. The soakaway might be a metre or yard cube filled with stones, topped with gravel and/or coarse sand, and finished off with top soil and turf. If this is not sufficient a diagonal land drain could be laid 600 mm (2 ft) deep to empty into the soakaway. Only rarely is it necessary to instal a full herringbone system of drains, and there could be difficulty in obtaining a suitable outfall for such a system.

678

My cylinder-type mower produces an uneven cut—in the bands across the lawn there are variations in grass length. What is the explanation?

The cause may be the mower or the lawn. The cutting height should be checked at various parts of the mower's bottom (fixed) blade. It may need to be adjusted to ensure an even height of cut right across the blade. The trouble may, on the other hand, arise from the lawn. If it is cut across a slope the weight of the machine can result in a shorter cut at the lower side, especially if the surface is soft.

679

Part of my lawn is so short of light owing to nearby trees that it is very difficult to keep grass on it. What can I do about this?

If you *must* have a lawn under trees, let the grass grow quite

long—up to 50-75 mm (2-3 in)—because this helps all lawn grasses to survive. Some people sow wood meadowgrass (*Poa nemoralis*) for its shade-tolerance, but unfortunately it does not tolerate any mowing at all. Shortage of light may not be the only cause of trouble. The combination of shade and drip can keep the surface overmoist for long periods, while in dry weather tree roots compete for nutrients, and for moisture, too. Possible action might therefore include tree-root pruning, aeration, extra watering in dry weather, and even applying a little extra fertiliser.

680

In my fine lawn there are patches of a soft, broad-leaved grass which I am told is Yorkshire fog. Can anything be done about it?

Yorkshire fog (*Holcus lanatus*) is the commonest and most noticeable invader of lawns. On utility lawns it probably does not matter much, but it looks bad in a fine lawn. Unfortunately there are, as yet, no selective grasskillers. If the patches are small and few, hand weeding or replacing them with good turf is the best answer. The alternative is regular, severe scarification of individual patches of the unwanted grass using a garden knife to cut into the surface at close intervals in one direction and then across the cuts in other directions before collecting up the debris. If you persevere with this treatment you should at the very least thin out the Yorkshire fog, and so make it much less conspicuous.

681

How do I get rid of yellow suckling clover patches?

This weed has proved difficult to eliminate but it is moderately susceptible to proprietary weedkillers containing the chemicals ioxynil and mecoprop. Even with these, repeated applications (at monthly intervals) may be necessary. A few other problem weeds, hitherto difficult to kill, respond to similar treatment.

682

Can I treat my lawn with selective weedkiller during the winter?

The selective weedkillers used on lawns contain plant-growth regulators. These are absorbed mainly through the leaves and are distributed throughout the plant, causing growth inhibition or modification. The process of distribution works best when the weeds are actively growing. In winter, when there is little growth, distribution is sluggish at best, so the effects of the weedkillers will be greatly reduced.

Apart from that, the calm, dry days necessary for spraying weedkillers are much rarer in winter than in the rest of the year.

683

How can I prevent moss invading my lawn?

Good lawn management to produce a healthy vigorous sward is the best defence against moss. The conditions that encourage moss include: wetness; dryness (for instance on bumps or ridges where the grass becomes weak); cutting too close; poor surface smoothness leading to 'scalping' (slicing off the surface of bumps) when the grass is mowed; a soft spongy sward with a thick fibrous layer; low fertility (caused by, for instance, deficiency of lime or plant food, or a shortage of top soil); compaction of the top soil (giving poor aeration and drainage); constant shade.

684

The shaded part of my lawn has developed a slippery surface scum varying in colour from green or blue-green to black. Is there an easy method of getting rid of it?

The description is typical of an invasion by algae, and the affected area is probably very damp because of the shade and possibly of the soil conditions. If you can get rid of the surface moisture by aeration and alleviation of the shade, and then apply a little fertiliser to promote vigorous growth, the algae will probably disappear. It may help to water in a solution of sulphate of iron at the rate of 50 g in 8 litre/4 m^2

(1½ oz in 1½ gallon/4 sq yd) or by using a dichlorophen-based moss killer.

685

How can I eliminate moss from my lawn?

There are several proprietary moss killers based on dichlorophen or chloroxuron. It is better to treat the whole lawn rather than just the obvious patches, although this is expensive. Somewhat cheaper, if perhaps not so effective, are the products based on lawn sand (see 667). Before treating the moss, however, try and find out *why* it is there (see 684): unless the cause is removed, moss will return even after using moss killer.

686

Patches on my lawn become discoloured when the ground starts drying, and then stay yellowish no matter how much water is applied. How can I deal with this?

Such patches are often found on raised parts of the lawn, where water just runs off the surface. Alternatively or additionally, there may be a shortage of good soil below them. Sometimes 'droughty' patches are caused by the presence of tree roots, in which case root pruning or even removal of the offending tree is the answer. There are, however, dry patches which, it is believed, are due to a fungus (possibly no longer present)

which has produced material that effectively waterproofs the soil.

In any case, once soil has completely dried out it can be very difficult to wet. Spiking or forking helps to let water in, and it may also be beneficial to use a wetting agent because very dry soil often repels water. Some people use a mild (bleach-free) washing-up liquid suitably diluted as a wetting agent, following this immediately with a thorough sprinkling of plain water. There are also several proprietary soil penetrants for use in a similar way.

687

What is the cause of brown patches on my lawn and how can I get rid of them?

Brown patches are due to a variety of causes including: (1) scorch by chemicals (including fertiliser); (2) scorch from animal urine; (3) drought; (4) spilt oil or petrol; (5) fusarium patch disease.

The remedy depends on the cause. The immediate answer to the first three and possibly to the fourth is to apply plenty of water for a time and ultimately to overseed any bare patches. With petrol or oil damage, it may be necessary to excavate contaminated earth and replace it before reseeding. The first four causes are unlikely to spread. Fusarium, however, can spread rapidly and cause extensive damage, so immediate treatment is necessary (see 688).

688

Numerous brown patches, 75-100 mm (3-4 in) across, have suddenly appeared on my lawn. They seem to start as small yellowish spots, which get larger and browner, or reddish brown, finally turning dark brown. The grass appears to be dead in the middle of some of the patches. What's the trouble?

It sounds very much as if you have an attack of fusarium patch disease, which typically occurs during mild, moist weather in spring and autumn although it can come at other times when weather conditions suit it. The matter is urgent but perhaps you can get positive identification from local parks staff before treating the whole lawn with fungicide (see 689). The fungicide, of course, will not bring the dead grass to life, so some re-seeding or re-turfing may also prove necessary.

689

Some years ago I successfully treated an attack of fusarium patch with a mercurial fungicide. I now have a fresh outbreak of the disease, but mercury fungicides seem to be unavailable. What can I use instead?

EEC regulations ban the use of these fungicides (mercury compounds are very poisonous). Readily available, however, are a

number of excellent proprietary fungicides based on organic chemicals, some of them quite new. They are usually produced for application with added water by means of a suitable sprayer or with a watering can fitted with a fine rose or dribble bar.

690

My lawn, consisting mainly of fine grasses, is producing small yellowish tufts of grass above the surface. Can this be cured?

Your lawn seems to be affected by yellow tuft disease, which attacks fine bent grass. This is not a common disease and its cause is not fully understood. It may be due to physiological disturbance started by injury of some kind, and it is sometimes associated with wet surface conditions which can be helped by aeration. Scarification, employed in conjunction with mowing, eliminates the tufts, which seldom recur.

691

My old-established lawn, cut regularly at about 6 mm (¼ in), has developed several sunken patches about 150 mm (6 in) across. How should I deal with them?

There is probably a pronounced layer of fibrous material (mat or thatch) at the surface, and the likely cause of the trouble is a fungus attacking the fibre. This fungus feeds on the accumulated fibre, breaking it down and so producing the depressions. Killing the fungus is difficult; it may be worth trying close forking of the areas, and then applying a turf fungicide at double the normal rate, followed by clean water to wash it well in. Often such fungal attacks die out of their own accord, and the patches neither grow big nor spread. In such cases all that is necessary is smoothing out the depressions with sandy compost. Sometimes, however, patches of replacement turf may be needed.

692

I am worried that the toadstools on my lawn may be poisonous. How can I get rid of them?

Toadstools usually arise from fungi in the topsoil which may be treated with fungicide (see 693).

693

How can I control the fairy rings in my lawn?

Treatment depends on the type of fairy ring. In one type the rings show up as dark green ribbons or circles of grass on which puff balls or mushrooms may appear. Any of several different kinds of fungus may be responsible for them, and since their effect is so small most people tolerate the ring. Another type has no visible effect on the grass but is revealed as rings of toadstools which can easily be

swept or mown off. Both types can sometimes be controlled by watering in a turf fungicide after sprinkling.

The worst types are those which appear as two concentric dark green rings with a brown or bare zone between them. They may be quite small (less than a dinner plate in diameter) or very large indeed (some have been observed to stretch over several fields). Tan-coloured toadstools are produced from the white mycelium which can be found in the top soil. The only reliable treatment until recently has been to dig out all the affected turf and earth completely and replace it with clean soil, after sterilising the dug area with formaldehyde solution.

A new chemical however, called oxycarboxin is now sold in proprietary form for dilution with water. The makers claim that it is effective against all types of fairy rings, and it has shown promise in independent tests.

694

My lawn looks very poor this summer. Overall it has a brownish appearance with something of a mottled effect. The 'mottles' have peculiar bleached but rather brownish appearance, and some of the individual grass leaves are pink and red. What is the cause?

This is almost certainly due to corticium disease; although

disfiguring, it only rarely kills the grass. Before taking any action, however, try to get positive identification of the trouble by a member of your local parks staff. If indeed it is corticium, a light dressing of sulphate of ammonia to the whole lawn of about 9-18 g/m² (¼-½ oz/sq yd), diluted with sand or compost and watered in if the weather remains dry, should cause the grass to grow away from the disease satisfactorily. Only rarely is corticium serious enough to require treatment with a fungicide.

695

On damp days in spring and autumn my lawn becomes covered with earthworm casts. I would like to get rid of them but am told that worms are beneficial. What should I do?

There are many species of earthworm but not all of them make casts. Earthworms are useful for mixing and aerating soil, but those which cast cause trouble by making the surface muddy and uneven and by encouraging weeds—their casts make good seed beds for weed seeds.

Earthworm activity is encouraged if cuttings are left on the turf and by the use of alkaline or organic fertiliser dressings. Improved management, especially removing cuttings and brushing away the casts in dry conditions, help to alleviate the problem.

It is, however, sometimes necessary to use more drastic

means. The main wormkillers used by groundsmen are based on chlordane (highly poisonous) or carbaryl (much less poisonous). A fairly safe but messy treatment involves the use of permanganate of potash. Watering this in at the rate of 17 g in 5.4 l/m² (½ oz in 1 gal/sq yd) brings the worms to the surface, where they can be swept up. Treatment against worms is carried out when they are working at the surface in spring and autumn (preferably the latter). Proprietary products have recently appeared which claim to combine good disease control with selective worm control, and these hold out hope for better worm control in the future.

696

I suspect that my lawn is affected by some kind of grub. Is there an appropriate treatment?

Lawns are seldom attacked by pests. I suggest that you excavate a few holes to see what you can find. You should certainly avoid using pesticides unless they are absolutely necessary. The most common grub to attack turf is probably the leatherjacket, which is the larva of the crane fly (daddy-long-legs). Sporadic outbreaks of trouble from this source occur on golf courses but seldom, if ever, on lawns. If the presence of leatherjackets is established, treat the lawn with a suitable soil insecticide.

On the continent of Europe and occasionally in southern England cockchafer grubs cause damage and require eradicating with a soil insecticide.

697

Mole hills keep appearing in my lawn (and elsewhere in the garden). How can I stop this? The farmer next door does not seem to bother much about those in his field.

As long as there are moles next door there will be reinvasion of your lawn. You may be able to use traps, handling them with old gloves to minimise human odour, and placing them in the main mole run. It pays to enquire for a local mole catcher—there is usually one somewhere near, although they are getting increasingly rare. You may also be able to get help from the local Pest Officer.

Moles need a constant supply of earthworms for food and you can reduce their activities on your lawn by killing off the worms with suitable wormkiller (*see* 695). Do *not*, however, try killing the moles by placing worms treated with highly toxic strychnine in the runs. Gassing with proprietary products or with exhaust pipe fumes from the car is usually impracticable and rarely successful.

Restoring really bad lawns

698

My lawn seems to be worn out! There is a lot of moss and assorted weeds (especially cat's-ear), but very little grass, and what there is grows so slowly that it is rarely worth mowing. Advice, please!

You may well have to dig the whole thing up and start again. You may, however, get quite dramatic improvement by liming (if soil tests show over-acidity) and generous fertiliser treatment. Such a treatment often reveals that there is more grass (probably fine grass) present than had been thought; in which case it becomes worthwhile to keep the turf and improve it further with more fertiliser, moss killer, selective weedkiller, and possibly scarification.

699

Recently widowed at the age of 75, I have just moved into a smaller house with a very thin and extremely weedy lawn growing in clay. My neighbour is willing to mow it for me, but he thinks I should dig it up and start again. Is this necessary?

Starting again would be a good idea if you could arrange for it to be dug up in the winter, cultivated regularly in the summer to eliminate weeds, and sown on a well-prepared seed bed in late-summer (or turfed in the autumn). This, however, would mean the absence of a green lawn for about a year, so I suggest a different approach.

A spring dressing of a fertiliser-cum-selective weedkiller in granular form will encourage the grass and kill *some* of the weeds—killing all the weeds at once would leave you with mainly bare ground! Follow this up about a month later with a dressing of sulphate of ammonia, mixed with sand to facilitate spreading, at the rate of 18 g with 280 g sand/m^2 (½ oz with 8 oz sand/sq yd). This will further encourage the grass, so that a further 7-10 days later you can water on a good selective weedkiller with the confidence that you will almost certainly have a weed-free, well-grassed lawn by the end of July.

700

I have just acquired a property in which the old lawn has been neglected for years. There are in fact only a few weeds (which I can deal with) and the grass is quite fine, but there is a wad of springy fibre 100-150 mm (4-6 in) thick at the surface and very little growth. How can I make this into a good lawn?

There are three possible approaches. (1) Start again.

Remove the turf and fibre for making into garden compost and prepare the soil for re-establishment. (2) Since the turf seems potentially good, you can lift and relay it. Hire a turf cutter and cut the turf about 25 mm (1 in) thick in uniform pieces of, say, 300 mm (12 in) square. Lay the turf flat on spare ground and prepare the site for re-turfing. The fibrous material is probably best removed, but may instead be dug in. Excessive fibre (thatch) formation is sometimes caused by over-acidity, so have the soil tested to check whether lime is required. (3) Embark on a long-drawn-out process of improving what you have. Correct any lime deficiency, give occasional dressings of fertiliser, and, above all, carry out severe scarification, repeated each autumn. It is scarcely possible to achieve enough with a wire rake: you will need a mechanical scarifier. It will probably take at least five years to solve the problem by this method of improvement.

701

I have acquired a real jungle of a lawn. The grass is 300-450 mm (12-18 in) high and tufty. Weeds are not too numerous, but they include some very flourishing ragwort. Is it worth trying to bring it round by intensive care?

It may be worth a try. First, get the grass down to a reasonable height in stages. The first cut (to about 50 mm (2 in)), could be made by scyth or the type of grass cutter with reciprocating knives; these and other coarse grass cutters can be hired. The mown grass should be removed. Since the turf is to be progressively checked by being mown over closer, a good dressing of fertiliser is called for in due season. The height of cut should be lowered gradually over a period of several weeks until it is about 13-19 mm (½-¾ in), and the grass maintained at this height until it appears strong enough to be mown shorter (that is, if you want it shorter). Ragwort does not like cutting, so it may present few problems. Selective weedkiller will, of course, prove necessary, but if possible it should not be used until the area begins to look like a real lawn. Scarification from time to time may be required to improve the turf: a careful raking may be appropriate at first, but later more vigorous treatment, perhaps with a mechanical scarifier, might be needed.

Patrick A. Johns

Technical Adviser in the Garden Products
Department of ICI at Farnham (Surrey);
has written four gardening books.

Soil

Formation

702

What is soil made of?

Garden soil consists of many different ingredients. These include varying proportions of clay, silt, and sand. A soil containing a high proportion of clay is considered to be heavy and it is often difficult to cultivate, especially when wet. Sandy soils, on the other hand, are light and easy to cultivate, even after rain. Decomposing plant remains, air, and water are other important soil constituents. Microbes by the million are also present; some can be seen only with the aid of a microscope. Other organisms, such as the earthworm, can be seen easily.

703

How does soil form?

During the course of millions of years, weathering reduces different types of rock to small particles. Freezing, for instance, causes rock to shatter and crack, allowing plant roots to penetrate; their expansion causes further crumbling. Wind blasts the rock fragments into smaller pieces, and rain swirls them together. Rainwater contains carbonic acid, which causes chemical reactions to take place in rocks. Carbonic acid is also produced by small plants that attach themselves to rocks. The plants die and, in turn, provide food for other plants. Running water also plays a part by grinding rocks and transporting fragments from one place to another.

704

Why do different soils vary in colour?

The colour of soils depends considerably on the minerals present. Various oxides of iron, for instance, are responsible for red, yellow, blue, and grey tints in different soils; and most people have seen the effect of chalk on down-land soil. Humus (see 708) makes the soil darker, which helps soil to warm up faster in spring.

705

What is a soil pan?

When certain minerals are washed down through the soil by rain, they usually lodge some way below the surface. This often happens in sandy soil containing a high proportion of iron. Over a period of time the minerals weld together to form a hard layer impervious to water. This layer restricts the downward spread of plant roots, so that poor growth results.

A similar situation can occur if a rotary cultivator is used regularly and its tines are set at the same depth on each occasion: the action of the tiller blades causes soil compaction at that depth. This 'mechanical pan' is avoided by varying the depth of rotovation.

Improving the soil

706

The soil in my borders dries out rapidly whenever we get a spell of fine weather. Is there anything I can do to prevent this happening?

There may be a mineral or mechanical pan below the surface that restricts the upward movement of moisture from below (it could also cause waterlogging in heavy rains). Dig down and, if a pan is present, break it up by forking or, if it is very hard, by use of a crow-bar. Light sandy soils, and those containing gravel, often drain too rapidly. If this is the case, dig in plenty of bulky organic material such as well-rotted garden compost or farmyard manure to help retain moisture.

A layer of the same sort of material, or of peat, leaf-mould, or composted bark, can also be placed on the surface around plants before the soil dries out. Such a layer is called a mulch. It also helps to retain heat, especially if a dark-coloured mulch is used, and discourages weed growth. Other materials that can be used as mulch include polythene, bracken, spent-mushroom compost, straw, spent hops, and grass clippings, although the last should be used sparingly. Organic mulches of plant materials can be dug in during the autumn to enrich the soil.

707

How can I stop moss from growing over my soil?

Moss will grow over any bare surface, particularly if the surface is compact. Hoeing and raking off is a temporary cure, although the problem is often worse afterwards because small pieces of moss come away and grow faster than ever. The best remedy is to encourage an open, well-drained soil surface by laying a bulky organic mulch over the ground. Extremely acid soils (*see* 738) are especially plagued by moss; the application of lime will reduce the acidity, but do *not* put it on at the same time as bulky manure. Moss also favours soils that are in the shade.

708

What is humus?

Humus forms when the remains of dead plants and animals decompose as a result of the action of soil bacteria. A well-matured garden-compost heap is well on the way to becoming humus, and when such compost (or any other bulky organic material) is dug into the ground it will decompose further. Sooner or later, depending on soil moisture and temperature, the material will become a dark brown colour and sticky, and then it will turn black.

Humus constantly releases nutrients into the soil that are taken up by plants. It greatly improves the structure of soils: it enables the particles of light sandy soil to stick together to form crumbs, so that moisture and plant foods are conserved for the use of plants, rather than draining away; and it opens up the structure of heavy soils such as clay, so making cultivation much easier.

709

How can I make a compost heap?

Good garden compost results from careful stacking of vegetable and other organic waste. The heap should be kept moist without being too wet, so that conditions favour the requisite bacteria. Bacterial action in the heap increases its acidity, so a sprinkling of lime is necessary over each 300 mm (1 ft) depth as the heap is made. Bacteria require nitrogen, so the heap should also be sprinkled with sulphate of ammonia. Keep these two additives apart by treating each 150 mm (6 in) depth with one or the other. (You can,

alternatively, buy special compost activators that trigger the bacterial process.) Enclose the heap in a 1.2 m (4 ft) square frame of wire netting, timber slates, or corrugated iron, and provide a cover to keep out heavy rain. Special composting bins are available for smaller gardens. The compost will be ready for use in about six months.

710

What is the value of farmyard manure?

A sample of farmyard manure typically contains straw saturated by animal urine and droppings. If stacked in a heap, it will heat up by bacterial action and eventually rot down to a friable (crumbly) texture. Farmyard manure contains some plant foods, but its main purpose is to improve soil texture. It binds light soil particles together, making them more retentive, and it opens up heavy soil.

If you have bought some farmyard manure, shake out the heap from

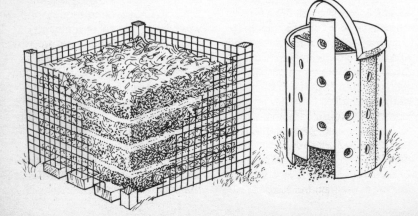

time to time and add water to keep it moist. When you turn the manure over, the outside of the heap should be placed in the centre and vice versa to ensure even rotting. Never apply manure straight from the stable to your soil. If the manure was already well-rotted when bought, however, it should be shaken out with a fork and dug into the soil as soon as possible. For deep-rooting plants it should be dug well down.

711

What is green manuring?

Seed of a quick-maturing crop such as mustard and rape is sown thickly on vacant ground, and the resulting crop is dug into the soil while it is still soft and before it forms seed. For the small garden, grass is an ideal plant for this purpose, although grass seed is rather expensive.

Green manuring is beneficial because it takes up residual fertiliser which might otherwise be leached from (drained out of) the soil; the root action of the growing crop improves soil structure, and its foliage rots down to make humus.

712

Is seaweed a good manure?

Provided it is unpolluted by oil, seaweed is a valuable source of plant foods, especially trace elements such as iodine. Although it may be dug straight into the garden in small quantities, seaweed is better mixed with other plant debris and decomposed before digging in . If sufficient quantity is available, seaweed can be dehydrated by spreading it over the ground and turning it over with a garden fork from time to time. When dry it is burnt, and the resulting ash makes a very good fertiliser used at the rate of 112 g/m^2 (4 oz per sq yd).

713

Can I add straw directly to the soil?

Undecomposed straw can be dug into the soil provided nitrogen is added at the same time. Straw contains less nitrogen than that required by bacteria to decompose it, so 0.4 kg (1 lb) of sulphate of ammonia should be added to each 50 kg (110 lb) of straw. Lime is also required at the rate of 2.5 kg (5.5 lb) ground limestone per 50 kg of straw.

Straw is a valuable source of humus and is more usually rotted down with lawn clippings and other vegetable matter in the compost heap; the heat generated will kill some of the unwanted seed left in the straw.

714

Which is the best kind of animal manure to use?

All animal manure is beneficial. Poultry and pigeon droppings contain the highest concentration of plant foods, and great care is needed to use them sparingly or they may scorch plants. They are best dried and used as fertilisers. Sheep manure is also a rich source of plant foods and used to be mixed with water to make a liquid feed. Horse manure is next in order of plant-food value, and when mixed with straw bedding it is ideal for digging in. Cow and pig manure contain relatively little plant food and tend to be too moist for use in all but sandy soils.

715

Can I dig established turf straight into the ground?

Yes—the fibrous roots of grass plants are excellent for improving tilth, while plant remains at various stages of decomposition will also be present; the grass top-growth too, will add humus to the soil.

If turf is dug in to the soil during active growth, it may re-grow (and so become a weed). If this happens, use one of the quick-acting total weedkillers that become inactive as soon as they touch the soil, before digging in the turf. The turf must be chopped up and turned grass-side down.

716

How can I prevent the soil surface from becoming hard after heavy rain?

Soil containing a high proportion of clay packs down during rain. The minute soil particles cement together, and they will prevent

seeds germinating and also hinder the growth of established plants because the soil will lack oxygen. The hard surface 'pan' is caused by the lack of organic material in the soil. The remedy is to fork peat, composted bark, or other bulky organic material into the surface. A surface mulch of the same material will also help.

717

What can I do to prevent deep cracks from appearing in the soil during dry weather?

Evaporation of moisture from clay causes the soil to shrink. The trouble is cumulative because the deep cracks will allow further moisture loss from the subsoil reservoir. Mulch the surface with a bulky organic material. This is best carried out during the spring when the soil is still moist; worms will eventually carry the material down into the soil. Take every opportunity to incorporate compost when cultivating the soil.

Soil types

718

What is meant by soil 'texture'?

Garden soils contain particles of varying size. Clay particles are minute and tend to clog together (which is why clay is so heavy and difficult to work). At the other end of the scale, gravel consists of very large particles; this type drains very easily and so is known as a hungry soil. Between these two extremes will be found comparatively small soil particles, known as silt, and larger particles of sand. The majority of soils consist of mixtures of the different-sized particles. The proportions of large, medium, and small particles in a given soil determine its texture.

719

I know that a soil's quality depends greatly on its structure. What makes for good structure?

A soil has good structure if it contains a balanced range of particle sizes that provide air pockets of a size to accommodate the right amount of air and moisture for healthy plant growth; drains well; and contains adequate humus and organic material. One way of encouraging good soil structure is to incorporate sufficient garden compost and other bulky organic material. Over-cultivation, especially with rotary cultivators, tends to spoil structure.

720

What is tilth?

When a soil has been forked and raked and its clods have been broken down to a fine, workable texture it is said to have good tilth. This quality is particularly important when small seeds are being sown, because it enables them to make good contact with the available soil moisture. Too fine a texture does not make a good tilth because such a soil's surface will cake in the first shower of rain. Heavy clay soils are often difficult to rake down to a fine surface because the particles clog together and bake hard in dry weather. Such soils are best dug and left rough in autumn; winter frosts crumble the heavy lumps of soil, which are then much easier to bring to a fine tilth in spring.

721

What is the difference between clay and silt?

Both are types of soil. Clay consists of particles less than 0.002 mm (0.0001 in) in diameter. It is very sticky when wet, smears, and shines without any feel of grittiness when rubbed between finger and thumb. A clay surface cracks as it dries out and the soil is difficult to manage. Silt particles are slightly larger than those of clay (0.002-0.02 mm), but are equally liable to give a poor-draining soil, although silt's presence in fast-draining sandy soils can be beneficial. Silt feels smooth and silky when rubbed between finger and thumb. Unfortunately silt particles do not flocculate (join together) to form crumbs when lime is mixed with them as do clay particles.

722

How can I improve the drainage of my soil?

The first thing to do is to dig one or two holes 1 m (3¼ ft) deep to find out why drainage is poor. A mechanical or mineral pan may thus be fractured—and that would probably solve the problem.

If there is no pan, it may be necessary to lay land drains (see 1021). Poor surface drainage can sometimes be overcome by simply improving soil tilth.

723

How can I improve water-retention in a stony soil?

Owing to excessive drainage, stony soils are always hungry: they tend to be warmer, and their humus is burned up very quickly. Dig in well-rotted manure, garden compost, peat, or other bulky organic material to improve retention, while a mulch of the same sort of material will lessen evaporation from the surface.

Soil water

724

Why is soil moisture important?

A plant can take up foods from the soil if they are in liquid form—as when fertilisers, for instance, are dissolved in the soil moisture. It

can happen that plants starve because, although sufficient fertiliser is present, the soil is too dry to make it into solution and thus make it available to the plants.

The moisture taken up by the roots enables a plant to transport foodstuffs internally. Moisture is also circulated, rather like water in the engine of a motor car, to help keep the plant cool. Water in the form of vapour is passed out through pores in the leaves. If there is not enough moisture in the soil the leaves flag or, in severe cases, shrivel. Moisture is also necessary for bacteria and other soil organisms to function properly.

725

How often should I water the garden?

Too much watering will wash plant foods out of the soil and will cause excessive leafiness and poor root action. Too little water will cause starvation, stunted growth, and poor crop yield.

Plants need more watering than usual during long (summer) days when they are making active growth, especially when the weather is warm. Soil moisture can be lost by evaporation from the surface as well as by drainage. The amount of evaporation will depend on the size of the plants: if leaves cover the ground, less evaporation will take place. The same applies to soil covered by a mulch (see 706).

A good rule-of-thumb test for moisture is to take a handful of soil from around the root zone of a plant and squeeze it. If it binds together well and feels as moist as a wrung-out face-flannel, it is moist enough for the plants. If it refuses to bind and is dusty or barely moist, it needs watering. Give it a really good soak by leaving a lawn sprinkler running over it for up to two hours.

726

What is meant by the water table?

When soil is saturated by rain or irrigation, the water drains downwards until it reaches a common level, known as the water table. This may be at a depth of several metres or only just below the surface. The level may vary from time to time, depending on the season: in winter (the wettest season) it is usually much higher.

If the level is so near the soil surface that plant roots would be immersed in water for most of the time, it would be necessary to lower the water table by installing a drainage system if you were planning to make a garden on such a site (see 1021). A high water table can lead to a cold, stagnant soil unfavourable to most plants.

727

Is soil temperature important?

Soil temperature is vital to the health of plants at every stage of growth. Seeds sown in soil which is too cold for them will fail to germinate and in many cases will rot. The same applies to plants set out before the soil has had time to warm up. Bacteria are sluggish when the soil is too cold and so may fail to convert fertiliser into a form which can be taken up by plants; the fertiliser may then be washed out of the soil by rain before the soil has had time to warm up. On the other hand, low temperatures are required by some seeds to break their dormancy, so that germination can take place. Seldom is the soil temperature too high in the open ground for normal spring sowings. Dark-coloured soils tend to be warmest; light, sandy soils are warmer than heavy clay. A shallow mulch helps to keep the soil warmer than a bare surface in early spring. But a mulch put on ground already cold will prevent it from being warmed by the sun.

Cultivation

728

I find digging very hard work. Is it really necessary?

Digging the soil helps to aerate it—although in a fertile soil earthworms do that task anyway. Digging is also necessary if you wish to incorporate bulky organic material and bury weeds. Perennial weeds are more readily removed from the soil as digging proceeds.

Some gardeners do not dig at all. They rely on vast quantities of organic material placed on the surface to smother weeds, and a high earthworm population to take the organics down into the soil. Total weedkillers, which become inactivated when they touch the soil, are useful if soil is not dug.

729

My soil turned into lumps like housebricks after digging. What went wrong?

You have a clay soil, and it sounds as if you dug it over during late spring or summer. The sun and drying winds made the lumps go solid, and they became very difficult to break down. Clay soil should always be dug in autumn, before heavy rain sets in to make the clay sticky. Turn the soil over and leave the surface rough so that frost will shatter the clods. If your soil is too acid, you should apply lime (also in the autumn). Garden compost or other bulky organic matter is useful, but do *not* apply

lime and manure at the same time. (Do not, of course, use lime where lime-hating plants, such as rhododendrons, heaths, and potatoes, are to be grown.

730

How deep do I need to dig?

Generally one spit is sufficient: that is, the depth of your spade blade or the tines of your fork. If the topsoil is less than one spit deep, then dig more shallowly: you must avoid bringing the subsoil to the surface. Deep-rooted plants benefit from deep digging if the subsoil is compacted, and it may be necessary to dig deep to remove a pan (*see* 705).

In order to dig the subsoil, or second spit (a method known as double digging), first dig out a trench one spit deep to gain access to the lower level. The subsoil is then forked over and the topsoil from the next trench to be dug is placed on top of it. The subsoil

Double digging

from the final strip is filled with the topsoil from the first trench.

731

There is one particular area of soil in my garden where plants never seem to grow. Can you suggest why?

Dig down into the soil to see if there is an obstruction, such as a piece of concrete. During the time before refuse collection in the country, many gardens had a refuse tip; you might find a collection of old bottles and cans just below the surface! Residues of old sump oil and other persistent liquids can linger in the soil and inhibit growth for many years. Chicken wire and galvanised iron release toxic levels of zinc as they rust away. The only remedy is to remove the old soil and replace it with fresh, although a good liming may 'lock up' sufficient zinc in the soil to allow plants to grow.

732

We have just moved into a newly built house. Is there anything we need to do before sowing and planting?

First dig over the site and remove any bricks or other unwanted debris. While digging, check for a mechanical pan which may have been caused by the wheels of vehicles used in building work. Make a note of the position of drains and other services. Check the depth of your topsoil. If it is less

than 150 mm (6 in), try to obtain more. Rake over the soil after digging and then wait to see the type of weeds that germinate. Annual weeds can be hoed off; perennials can be treated with the appropriate herbicide.

733

Weeds are growing on my soil. Can I dig them in, or must I remove them?

Weeds are a useful source of humus, provided they are dug in *before* they flower. But you would be well advised to remove completely all deep-rooted perennial weeds, and those with creeping roots or stems.

734

Is hoeing really necessary?

Hoeing is carried out to cut through weeds, to loosen a caked soil surface so that air will circulate in and out of the soil, and to create a mulch of dry soil to conserve soil moisture below. It is an effective way of incorporating fertiliser into the soil; and soil pests are often chopped up as hoeing proceeds.

On the other hand, in a well-stocked bed, border, or vegetable plot, hoeing can easily damage the stems and surface roots of plants unless it is done very carefully. In such cases, a surface mulch is the better alternative. It will suppress weeds, conserve moisture, avoid caking of the surface, and will not bring weed seeds to the surface to germinate, as often happens with hoeing.

735

Is mechanical cultivation better than digging by hand?

On a plot of any size, mechanical cultivation is obviously quicker and far less tiring. But often it results in perennial weeds being chopped up—and thus effectively being increased. Soil structure can be harmed if the soil is tilled too frequently, and there is the possibility of creating a mechanical pan if a rotavator is used at the same depth each time.

736

Should soil be firm before sowing and planting?

As long as you have created a fine tilth, the soil should preferably be firm: loose soil is inclined to dry out too quickly in windy weather, especially in strong sun, and most plants require firm soil to establish their roots properly. In fact, certain vegetables, such as brassicas (the cabbage family), should be planted so firmly that it would be difficult to pull them up after planting without snapping off the leaf.

Seed beds should be firm enough to enable the seed to make good contact with the soil and to prevent it drying out. It is also far simpler to draw out a straight shallow seed drill in firm soil. The best way to firm the soil uniformly

is to tread it over without leaving spaces between foot marks. Do *not* firm wet soil, otherwise tilth and structure may be spoiled.

737

How can I level a sloping site?

You will need a digging fork, a spade or shovel, a wheelbarrow, several long stakes, a straight edge, and a spirit level. First remove the topsoil and place it to one side, preferably away from the site to be levelled. Next drive the stakes into the ground all over the site, the distance between each being slightly less than the length of your straight edge. With the aid of the spirit level, make the top of each stake level with the others. You now have a guide to work to. Move the subsoil around the site until it is level in comparison with the stake tops. The topsoil is then returned.

Acid and alkaline soils

738

How can I tell whether my soil is acid or alkaline?

The easiest method is to buy a simple soil-testing kit from your local garden centre. It will include an indicator solution, which you mix in a test tube with samples of soil from your garden. The solution will turn a certain colour depending on the acidity or otherwise of the mix. Compare the colour with that on the chart supplied with the kit to discover whether your soil is acid, neutral, or alkaline. Soil-testing kits usually supply a table so that you can work out how much lime (if any) is necessary for each crop on your soil.

739

What is the meaning of *p*H?

This is the logarithmic scale which defines the acidity or alkilinity of a solution. The *p*H scale ranges from 0 to 14. A *p*H of 7.0 is neutral; above 7.0 is increasingly alkaline and below 7.0 is increasingly acid. A *p*H of 5.0 is ten times more acid than *p*H 6.0; *p*H 9.0 is ten times more alkaline than *p*H 8.0.

Different groups of plants require a different soil *p*H: rhododendrons and most heathers, for example, like acid conditions, and so cannot thrive in alkaline (chalky or limy) soils: cabbages, on the other hand, like a neutral or alkaline soil.

740

Why do brassicas not grow well in my sandy soil?

Sandy soil is often rather loose and, as we have seen (see 53) the cabbage family needs firm soil. Another reason is that brassicas prefer soil with lime present. Unless lime has been applied within the past year or two, your sandy soil will probably be too acid because lime can readily be leached out

(washed away) from such soils.

741

How can I lower the *p*H of my soil?

Avoid using lime. Use acid-reacting fertilisers like sulphate of ammonia and sulphate of potash. Sulphur can also be used to reduce alkalinity; a suitable rate would be 135 g/m^2 (4 oz per sq yd) while acid sphagnum peat can be employed as a bulky organic material.

742

I have read that peat is acid, and yet a sample I tested was clearly alkaline, with a *p*H 7.5. Can you explain this?

Not all peat is acid. Sedge peat, for example, is likely to be alkaline if it is dug from areas which are fed by rivers flowing through chalky (alkaline) soil.

743

How can I raise the *p*H of my soil?

The soil is made more alkaline by adding ground limestone, chalk, hydrated lime, or marl (clay with a high level of calcium). Dolomitic limestone can also be used; it adds magnesium as well as lime.

744

Why is it important to apply lime to the soil?

Lime neutralises acidity, and this enables bacteria to become more active. The majority of plants require a soil which is either neutral or very slightly acid (a pH of 6.8 to 6.4). There is a natural tendency, however, for the soil to become increasingly acid with time. Lime corrects this tendency and also makes available essential plant foods. Clay soil is often improved by an application of lime, which flocculates the particles to form crumbs.

745

I am told that beech leaves should not be used to mulch lime-hating plants. Why is this?

The leaves of many trees can make a valuable contribution to your compost heap. Beech leaves, however, contain a considerable amount of lime in the form of calcium, so they should not be used as mulch or compost in association with rhododendrons, azaleas, ericas, and other lime-hating plants. Continual use of such leaves will raise the alkalinity of the soil.

746

When should I apply lime?

Lime should be applied to the soil only if a pH test indicates that it is

necessary. If too much lime is present in the soil, certain plant foods such as magnesium, manganese, and iron become locked up in the soil and so cannot be absorbed by plants. When liming is necessary, it should be applied to unplanted soil during autumn, so that winter rains wash the powder into the ground and it becomes fully incorporated into the soil in time for spring sowing and planting.

747

Why do some of the plants in my chalky soil have unhealthy, yellow leaves?

Although a certain amount of lime in the soil is required by many plants, an excess will make certain plant foods unobtainable to their root systems. Iron deficiency causes young leaves to go yellow (a condition known as chlorosis), while magnesium deficiency causes older leaves to go yellow, with the veins usually remaining green. Iron sequestrene can be used to correct the first deficiency, while Epsom salts is used to control magnesium deficiency. The remedies should be applied according to label instructions for the type of plant in question.

748

Why should lime be added to the compost heap?

The vegetable material added to the compost heap is fermented and converted by the microscopic bacteria present in the heap. Bacterial activity, however, causes an acid reaction, and unless lime is added, satisfactory composting will not occur. Proprietary activators recommended for use on the compost heap usually contain lime. Otherwise a dusting of lime should be applied and watered in every other 150 mm (6 in) depth of material as the heap is built up.

749

Can I apply lime and fertiliser at the same time?

It is better not to do so unless it is already formulated together in a compost activator. Lime and some fertilisers (for example, those containing sulphate of ammonia) react together and the nitrogen content is lost to the atmosphere. This occurs in the soil application as well as in the compost heap.

Soil fertility

750

How can I improve the fertility of my soil?

Soil fertility is built up over a period of time by adding the correct fertilisers in the required amount. Bulky organic material such as garden compost, farmyard manure, composted bark, and peat all help to promote fertility by

encouraging bacterial activity in the soil. The correct amount of each major fertiliser to apply can be ascertained by carrying out a soil test. It will be necessary to sample the soil in various places to determine the treatment required.

751

How can I test my soil to see if it needs feeding?

Soil-test outfits are simple to use. They can be purchased from garden stores and will test for nitrogen, phosphate, and potash. Charts supplied with the kit indicate the amount of each nutrient to be used for particular types of crops.

752

Is organic fertiliser better than inorganic (chemical) fertiliser?

Plants are unable to distinguish between either type: soil bacteria convert both into a form which can be taken up by the plant. Organic and inorganic fertilisers can be purchased in slow-release and fast-acting forms; organic fertilisers usually cost more. *See also* 9.

753

Can I use poultry manure around my plants?

Poultry manure on its own is very concentrated and would certainly scorch plants if used fresh. It is better to dry it and use it sparingly around the plants, or to rake it into the soil before planting. Alternatively, it can be soaked in water and used as a liquid feed. Poultry manure collected from deep-litter houses is usually mixed with wood shavings and should be added to the compost heap or dug into the ground.

754

I can obtain large quantities of spent-mushroom compost. Is it beneficial?

Used in moderation spent-mushroom compost is very useful because it is full of plant food. It is light in weight and for that reason is unfortunately often used to excess. A 50 mm (2 in) layer dug into the top 200 mm (8 in) is adequate for most soils. It can also be used as a mulch.

Bear in mind that mushroom compost often contains a high level of chalk, so it would tend to raise the pH of the soil and harm lime-hating plants.

755

I have heard gardeners referring to NPK. What does that mean?

The letters stand for the chemical elements that plants need in greatest abundance if they are to thrive: nitrogen (chemical symbol N), phosphorus (P), and potassium (K). These chemicals are often mixed together as a compound fertiliser, which is generally referred to as NPK. *See also* 11.

756

What are trace elements?

Plants require a balanced food supply consisting of many different chemicals. Some, such as nitrogen, phosphate and potash, are required in large amounts; others, called trace elements, are needed only in minute quantities; for example, a soil concentration of 1 ppm (1 part per million parts of soil) of boron is sufficient for most plants. Other trace elements include magnesium, manganese, zinc, molybdenum, iron and copper, all present in fertile soil.

757

What is the nitrogen cycle?

When plants take up nitrogen from the soil, they convert it to proteins. These proteins within the leaves of plants are eaten by animals, which convert them into forms of nitrogen. The animal droppings return to the soil to nourish bacteria, which complete the cycle by converting the nitrogen into a form that can be taken up by plants. That is a simplified version of the nitrogen cycle.

758

What is a base dressing?

An application of fertiliser made before seed is sown or before plants have been set out in the soil is known as a base dressing. Fertiliser applied after sowing or planting is known as top dressing.

759

How should fertiliser be applied to the soil?

The easiest way to apply dry fertiliser before sowing seeds or planting is to measure out the quantity required, then halve it so that one half is broadcast by hand in one direction over the plot. The remaining half is then broadcast at right angles to the first half. In this way, the coverage will be more uniform.

Supplementary feed as a top dressing for established plants can be trickled alongside. Fertilisers can scorch plants. When applying dry fertiliser take care to avoid plant leaves and soft stems; root scorch is avoided by applying fertiliser to moist soil and watering it in.

760

Is it true that sawdust and wood shavings starve plants?

Any raw material which does not contain sufficient nitrogen to feed the soil bacteria will cause starvation in plants. Such material is better added to the compost heap to ferment and rot down before it is added to the soil.

761

Seeds do not seem to thrive in my garden. A neighbour thinks the soil may be sick. What exactly does this mean?

Seeds and plants need moisture, air, and warmth together with food to grow properly, and the correct soil pH is important for most plants, too. It is possible that your soil contains too much fertiliser, or pests and diseases may be present. It would be a good idea to test your soil (see 738-9).

762

When should I apply fertiliser?

Fertiliser often takes a few days to become available to the plants' root system, depending on soil temperature. A base dressing should, therefore, be applied 7 to 10 days before planting. Established plants require feeding from time to time, usually during spring and again in the summer. In addition to dry-fertiliser dressings, liquid fertiliser is beneficial.

763

Should earthworms be encouraged?

Worms can be a nuisance in lawn maintenance because their casts can give the lawn a hard, bumpy surface. Apart from that, worms are largely beneficial: they help to cultivate the soil by burrowing and distributing organic material; and they help water and air percolate through the soil so that they become available to plant roots.

Ron Menage

Horticultural journalist; runs a trials garden with six research greenhouses; has written or co-written 16 gardening books.

Greenhouse Gardening

Choosing a greenhouse

764

Will my local rates be increased if I buy a greenhouse?

The average small home greenhouse should not affect rates—especially if it is of the type that can be considered 'portable' by being easily erected and dismantled. Consult your local authority, however, if you wish to erect a greenhouse of more than about 28 m³ (1000 cu ft) capacity: permission may be needed and sometimes a rate may be charged. You should certainly tell your local council if you propose to build a structure of any size on to your house—a lean-to greenhouse or conservatory is an example. In this case a small rate may be charged and you will have to comply with certain building regulations.

765

Do you have any general advice about greenhouse size?

In general it is wise to buy the largest greenhouse that you can afford and that will fit into the space available. But if you propose to instal artificial heating, the cost of running this must be borne in mind when considering the size. For an unheated greenhouse, size does not matter and plenty of space will be an enormous advantage. In all cases, adequate width is helpful for working and makes it less likely that plants will get knocked over. A greenhouse with a high capacity (or air volume) is easier to manage than a small one: in a small house the atmospheric conditions and temperature are liable to fluctuate more widely and suddenly—and most plants do not like this. Most beginners soon find the need for more space as they gain experience, so it may be worth getting a design that can be extended. A survey has revealed that the average home greenhouse size is about 3 × 2.4 m (10 × 8 ft).

766

Will I need expert help to erect a greenhouse?

The typical home greenhouse of the prefabricated type can be put up in a matter of hours, single handed, and without any special tools. Full instructions are supplied by the manufacturers, and the glass is usually already cut to size. Metal frames sometimes take more time to put together, but anyone who likes playing with constructional toys would derive enjoyment from seeing the structure gradually taking shape. You may need professional help if a greenhouse or lean-to requires much brickwork or concrete construction, and when it is to be built on to a dwelling. However, even in these cases, most handymen will be able to cope easily. For laying concrete foundations, *see* 770.

767

Which of the many greenhouse shapes are the best?

For most practical purposes the square or rectangular greenhouse allows the best exploitation of space. However, a round or many-sided structure, especially if ornamental, can make an interesting garden feature for the display of decorative plants.

A greenhouse with sloped sides, called the Dutch-light shape, lets in more of the sun's radiation than a vertical sided one. For commercial growers this is an advantage with early crops, but it matters little to the home gardener. In any case, avoid greenhouses with very sloping sides: their shortage of headroom restricts the convenient working area.

768

Where and how should I site my greenhouse?

In a small garden there may not be much choice, but try to find an open, bright position, and not too far from the house if you wish to connect to gas, water, and electricity supplies. An open site means plenty of free heat from the sun: shading is easy enough to provide when it is needed. A rectangular greenhouse should preferably be positioned with its longer axis running east-west; this will allow it to get the greatest benefit from winter sunlight. If the ideal site cannot be found, it is always possible to find *some* types of plants that will be happy in the conditions the greenhouse provides—but the choice may be restricted by such conditions.

769

I have space for only a very small greenhouse. Is it worth buying?

To make the most of a very tiny greenhouse make sure it is glazed to ground level (*see* 775). If you fit it with shelves you will be surprised at how much it can accommodate. A tiny house will make a good home for quite a large collection of the smaller cacti and other succulents, or alpines (with good ventilation) if you wish to specialise. Not much room is needed for seed-germination and mist-propagation work, so even a small greenhouse can make a dramatic difference to the garden in growing plants for it. A small greenhouse will cost relatively little to heat if you wish to grow exotic plants, plenty of which are not space-demanding.

770

I'm a bit daunted by the prospect of laying a foundation and floor for a greenhouse. Is it difficult work?

There is no need for elaborate foundations for a small

greenhouse. Follow the supplier's recommendations, and if ready-made foundation curbing or the like is available (usually as an 'extra') it is well worth having it. Framework designs are now available with 'ground-anchor' fittings for alloy greenhouses. The foundations of these are especially easy to arrange, with the minimum of work and concrete mixing. You can easily make an excellent floor by levelling and firming the soil and strewing it with shingle. This will hold moisture to maintain humidity during summer.

771

How does a conservatory differ from a greenhouse?

A conservatory is a greenhouse used to display ornamentals and is also an extension to a sitting room. Obviously, direct communication with the home is desirable, so conservatories are almost invariably lean-to structures. A decorative floor, which can be quarry-tiled or laid with vinyl sheet or tiles on a flat surface, is an advantage. Plants should also be displayed artistically and in suitable planters. Hanging plants, the use of evergreens and foliage, and good planning for year-round colour, are important to effective conservatory management. What you can grow depends on how much light the conservatory receives. A northern aspect is not a disadvantage since a wide range of conservatory plants like cool, shady conditions.

772

What are the advantages of a lean-to greenhouse?

It is ideal as a conservatory or garden room when attached to a dwelling, especially if there is a communicating door or French window. It may also help to keep a home warm and eliminate draughts. Lean-to structures make excellent vineries and fruit houses if built along a sunny garden wall. A south-facing house also acts as an efficient solar greenhouse: a brick or masonry wall holds the sun's warmth during the day and radiates it at night. Under these circumstances a lean-to greenhouse can be used for any warmth-loving plants, and is also, of course, more economical to heat artificially.

Materials of construction

773

Most of the greenhouses on sale locally have metal frames. Are they better than timber-framed models?

Although metal is a better heat conductor than timber, the area of frame in proportion to glass is so small that this can be discounted. The metal is stronger than timber, so the frames of metal houses have much thinner members than those of timber—and thus more of the sun's radiation can enter, giving extra free heat. Most greenhouses for the amateur are now made of aluminium alloy, which is virtually maintenance-free, will not corrode, and needs no painting or other treatment (although it can be given a decorative finish if desired).

Timber, in contrast, may be subject to rot, insect attack, warping, and other problems, although a good-quality cedar greenhouse regularly treated with preservative can last a lifetime. In general, alloy-framed greenhouses are cheaper than cedar ones and are probably a better buy for most amateurs, although it can be argued that cedar-framed structures look better in older cottage gardens.

774

Which is better material for glazing—glass or plastic?

Plastic is not a substitute for glass: it does not trap the sun's warmth so effectively, it will not retain artificially created warmth so efficiently, and it will not weather so well or remain unaffected by time. In short, it is not recommended for *permanent or long-term* glazing. On the other hand it is useful for light-weight portable structures, especially where crops are grown in the ground soil and can be rotated. On sites subject to trouble from vandals, many plastics are suitable due to their unbreakability.

775

Which is the more useful—a base-wall structure or glass-to-ground?

A glass-to-ground house is the most versatile and is the better choice if size has to be limited; a base wall may be preferable if the greenhouse is heated and is sited in a cold area, if it is sited alongside a pathway where low glass could get broken, or if it is used to store materials under staging which might be an eyesore if visible from outside. A structure with a base wall, often called a 'plant house', is usually fitted with staging—wide shelves at waist height. Some kinds of conservatory may be better with a base wall if overlooked by neighbours—the wall gives a certain amount of privacy. Base walls may be timber boarded as well as of brick or concrete block.

776

Would it be worthwhile to design and build my own greenhouse?

It might well be considerably more expensive for the ordinary handyman to build his own greenhouse. It is not possible to compete with the bulk-buying of raw materials and mass-production methods of the leading greenhouse manufacturers. The time spent on the work would also have to be taken into account: a prefabricated structure can be erected very quickly. In general, building your own deserves serious consideration only if you need a specially designed structure or one of an out-of-the-ordinary shape or size.

Fittings

777

How many ventilators do I need, and what associated fittings must I buy?

Good ventilation is essential. The typical small greenhouse should have at least two vents—one in the roof and one in the side. More will be an advantage, since you do not have to open them all at the same time, and they enable you to allow for wind direction so as to avoid draughts and sudden gusts of air blowing through the greenhouse and causing damage. Few other fittings are essential, but a maximum-and-minimum thermometer is very important: it allows you to see how the temperature is behaving, so that remedial action can be taken to avoid rapidly fluctuating temperatures.

778

What is the best design for staging?

For the home greenhouse some form of slatted-top or mesh-topped staging is the most convenient. In winter this allows free circulation of

air, which is greatly beneficial, as well as more light to the area below, which may be useful. In summer it can be covered with plastic sheeting and strewn with a moisture-retaining material such as grit or vermiculite (there are several proprietary aggregates that are kept moist to maintain humidity).

779

Are automatic aids worth the expense?

A thermostat is an essential money-saver for all heating systems. For those who have to leave the greenhouse to fend for itself for long periods, automated watering of some kind is a great boon, and a form of capillary watering is usually the most adaptable. Automatic ventilation arms are self-operating, very useful and reasonably priced. For larger greenhouses, electric-fan ventilation may be more practical.

780

What exactly is capillary watering?

This depends on the natural tendency of liquids to rise against gravity when absorbed by fine particles of fibres—as happens in the operation of a wick in a paraffin lamp. Traditionally, a layer of wet sand was spread onto the staging, and pots with unobstructed drain holes were firmly pressed down upon it so that the moisture in the sand could rise up into the compost in the pots. As the plants depleted the moisture in the compost, more water was automatically taken up by 'wick action' from the sand. Modern refinements include automatic moistening of the sand. More recently a synthetic fibre matting has replaced the sand; it is more convenient, lighter, and easier to keep clean.

Temperature control

781

Is it worth installing and running artificial heating?

If you are taking up greenhouse gardening seriously, some form of artificial heating is extremely worthwhile. It widens the scope of operations enormously and renders the greenhouse productive all the year round of an extensive range of food and decorative plants. Most of the 'specialist' plants—flowers such as carnations, orchids, chrysanthemums, and sometimes even alpines—need some degree of artificial heating for perfection.

782

Is a greenhouse useless without artificial heating?

Certainly not—there is a host of plants that need only weather protection and are hardy or semi-hardy as regards temperature. With the right choice of plants an unheated greenhouse can be useful and interesting all the year round—winter can be quite colourful, too. By late February the sun's radiation will be keeping temperatures high enough for early sowings and propagation of many plants.

783

Will heating my greenhouse involve me in huge fuel bills?

There are three generally recognised greenhouse temperature regimes: cool, with temperatures ranging from frost-free to about 7°C (45°F); intermediate; with a minimum overall temperature of 12°C (54°F); and warm, with a minimum of 18°C (65°F). It must be said at once that the cost of maintaining any of these temperatures varies widely, depending (a) upon the size of the greenhouse and (b) upon the area of the country in which you live. In general, however, to maintain an average-sized home greenhouse at temperatures from frost-free to about 7°C (45°F) should not prove beyond your means, especially if you take care to conserve heat. However, to heat even a small greenhouse above this level *will* prove costly—even one or two degrees above would make a dramatic difference to your fuel bills. It is possible to calculate roughly the cost of heating, given the price of the fuel and the dimensions and materials of construction of the greenhouse; most suppliers of heating equipment will do this for you.

784

Can you list some of the more popular plants for growing in a heated greenhouse?

All the most popular pot plants can be grown in a greenhouse with a temperature minimum between frost-free and 7°C (45°F). Some typical examples are fuchsias, pelargoniums of all types, cinerarias, calceolarias, primulas, as well as innumerable tender bulbs and other storage organs, and greenhouse annuals. There are also many tender greenhouse shrubs and perennials that are easy to cultivate if the temperature is right, and these include cool-house orchids such as cymbidiums. All kinds of propagation can be fitted in, too, and bedding-plant production for the garden is unlimited—as is the growing of all the popular edible crops, many of which can be had early or out-of-season.

785

Which fuel would you recommend?

Nowadays the costs of the various fuels usually work out much the same in terms of the heat energy they can produce. However, some are much more convenient to use

than others and are more suited to the home greenhouse. Electricity, usually regarded as expensive, is ideal—especially if used to power a fan heater; with thermostatic control there is no waste, and the atmospheric conditions created are excellent for plant health. Natural gas is also much used and can similarly be controlled by thermostat. If burned in a non-flued heater, however, it makes the air extremely damp in winter (as does a paraffin heater). Both electricity and gas need the minimum of attention, and are especially suited for greenhouses that have to be left unattended for long periods. The various forms of hot-water-pipe heating are better suited to use in larger greenhouses heated to higher temperatures.

786

How can I avoid wasting heat?

Make sure that all vents and doors are draught-free and that there are no gaps in the greenhouse structure. The temperature should never be higher than absolutely necessary, and as noted, some form of thermostatic control is desirable if heat waste is to be avoided. Lining the greenhouse with thin transparent polythene so as to enclose 12-25 mm (½-1 in) *static* air between the plastic and the glass will reduce heat loss—and your fuel bill—by about 40 per cent. It is the air layer, by the way, that forms the insulation. The lining must allow as much light to pass as possible, and should be taken down at the end of the winter.

787

One hears a lot of talk about solar greenhouses. What are they, and do they offer any advantage over conventional types?

The term 'solar greenhouse' has recently been applied rather loosely to a number of new models of various fancy shapes. In fact, a true solar greenhouse—one that can store the sun's heat on completely sunless days—has not yet been invented. The storage of solar energy is difficult without elaborate, bulky and expensive equipment.

All glass greenhouses are 'solar' to the extent that glass traps the sun's warmth. Some of this warmth can be absorbed during the day by the floor, staging, and (in the case of lean-to) rear wall, and given out overnight. There seems little point in buying one of the fancy, costly designs. In any case, in summer, keeping the temperature *down* is usually more of a problem that providing warmth; while in winter most conventional designs, if well-sited, will trap any of the sun's warmth that may be available.

788

What is 'bottom heat'?

This is an old term meaning heat applied from below. It is usually recommended for propagation, particularly to speed up the rooting of cuttings, but also to aid seed germination and the starting of roots or storage organs (bulbs and the like). Nowadays the heat can be conveniently supplied by electric soil-warming cables (*see* 853) covered with moist sand, which is overlain by moist peat. The propagation containers are then plunged in the peat. However, any similar arrangement comprising a peat plunge with warmth applied from below can be employed; and where cuttings are to be rooted directly into a propagating frame, a mixture of equal parts peat and sand can be laid over the base layer of peat. Most electric or paraffin propagators available to amateur gardeners also provide bottom heat. Since most of these usually have covers there is no need for a peat plunge because adequate warmth is retained in the container as a whole.

Pots, potting & composts

789

I am told I should not grow crops in the greenhouse soil. Why is this?

It is certainly best to avoid doing this if possible. For edible crops, tomatoes in particular, it is extremely risky to use the ground for more than one year when the greenhouse is first put into use (*but see* 826). Most gardeners know how important it is to rotate crops whenever possible. If the soil is constantly employed for the same crop it will become 'sick' and various disease organisms may take hold. Far better results can be obtained by growing crops in containers or growing bags containing potting compost.

790

Are different types of compost available for different purposes?

Yes. The seed composts and potting composts used for sowing and growing plants in containers differ from each other, and are carefully formulated and prepared mixtures with the required texture, the right balance of plant nutrients, and relative freedom from pests, diseases, and weed seeds. They are quite different from the garden compost made by rotting down vegetable waste—this should never be used for pot plants. Instructions for making your own composts can be found in many gardening books, but most people now prefer to buy them ready-made. The John Innes composts were the first to be introduced and are still excellent, but they are based on special loam now not easy to come by. Most modern proprietary composts are based mostly on peat.

791

Which are better, clay pots or plastic pots?

The advantages of plastic pots are that they encourage hygiene because they are easy to clean and to sterilise; they are not so easily broken as clay pots; and they are lighter in weight and easier to store. The fact that plastic pots retain moisture better than clay, and that plants growing in them tend to need less-frequent watering is also an advantage, although for people used to clay pots there is the danger of overwatering. Plastic will usually deteriorate with age, so it is still a wise investment to buy large clay pots, especially if they are to be stood outdoors and exposed to sunlight, which causes many plastics to become brittle. Finally, of course, most people would agree that clay pots—especially the larger sizes—are better looking than plastic ones.

792

Can you outline potting procedure?

Always use a pot size in correct proportion to the size of the plant to be potted, moving on into a slightly larger pot at intervals as the plant develops; a sequence called 'potting-on'. This keeps the compost fresh and lessens loss of nutrients. An approved potting compost is essential. It must be nicely moist but *not* soggy before use. With modern composts, potting does not have to be too firm, and usually 'crocking' is unnecessary unless the pot-drainage holes are very large. (Crocking involves covering the holes with some clean stones or pieces of clay pot to ensure that the holes do not become clogged). After potting leave a gap of 25 mm (1 in) or so between the compost surface and the pot rim; this is the 'watering space'. It helps to assess quantity when applying water, and also prevents the water from running off the surface.

793

Is there any difference between potting-on and re-potting?

Yes. Potting-on, which involves annual plants and perennials in their younger stages, is carried out as the plants increase in size (*see* 792). Perennials to be saved for future years, however, will need re-potting, which should be carried out when the plants are dormant or just about to make new growth. Re-potting involves removing a plant from its pot, reducing the size of its root-ball, and returning it to its pot, or to another of the same size, which is partly filled with fresh compost. Very large plants do not lend themselves to this treatment. Deal with them by removing the top layer of compost and replacing it with fresh or with a dressing of balanced fertiliser. This treatment is called 'top-dressing'.

794

What is a 'plunge-bed'?

It is used for starting hardy bulbs and similar storage organs into growth. It is made from a container or a pit with very good drainage filled with a clean, moisture-retaining material, usually peat or sand. The plunge-bed should be outside the greenhouse, but covered to protect it from waterlogging. Planted-up containers are put into the plunge-bed until the plants are well rooted (usually after about 8 weeks), before being taken into the greenhouse. When making a plunge-bed bear in mind that it must be sufficiently deep that the pots will be covered by 50-75 mm (2-3 in) of the moisture-retaining material.

795

Am I likely to be troubled by weeds in my greenhouse?

Modern seed and potting composts are relatively weed-free, but they can become contaminated with weed seeds if left about exposed to the air. Ground not used for growing can be treated with a total weedkiller such as a mixture of paraquat, diquat and simazine applied with a watering can and dribble bar. Hormone weedkillers should *not* be used in the greenhouse: they may become airborne, and even in minute traces are extremely damaging to plants.

General maintenance

796

What are the basic essentials for environmental control?

Maintain the temperature range required by the type of plants grown and do *not* mix plant types with widely differing needs. Good ventilation is vital in winter, whenever weather permits, and a low humidity level should be maintained throughout the cold months. In summer, shade the greenhouse when necessary, and remember to ventilate it to avoid scorching temperatures.

Avoid erratic watering at any time, especially in summer, and keep conditions generally on the dry side in winter when temperatures are low. In summer, damp-down (*see* 799) frequently to raise the humidity. Prompt attention to any pest or disease is vital. Make sure that the plants do not lack essential nutrients by using recommended quantities of the appropriate balanced fertilisers; but always avoid over-feeding as well as over-watering. As a guide to watering always aim at moist roots, as distinct from absolutely dry or waterlogged compost.

797

How critical is humidity?

It has a considerable effect on the well-being of plants. In summer,

when temperatures are high and plants are making active growth, a moist atmosphere reduces the rate at which plants lose moisture (and therefore the frequency with which they have to be watered), and they grow better and more vigorously as a result. In winter, when outside temperatures are low, the presence of excessively moist air in the greenhouse—especially if it is stagnant—is generally harmful: it encourages moulds and mildews, which attack the plants and can become a nuisance; hence the importance of winter ventilation. So watering must be kept to the minimum—and do not carry out damping-down (*see* below).

798

What is the best type of shading?

For greatest cooling efficiency the shading should intercept the sun's rays *before* they pass through the glass. This means either exterior blinds or a shading paint applied to the outside of the glass. Blinds should preferably be slatted to allow for degrees of shadow. They must be of substantial construction, or they will be liable to catch the wind and blow off. These requirements and the possibility that the equipment may have to be custom-made to fit specific areas, means that blinds are rather expensive. Most people prefer a shading paint. This must be coloured white—*not* green, as is so often seen. A recent development has been the electrostatic type of shading fluid which can be diluted from an easy-mix concentrate to give almost any degree of shading required. It can be applied by brush or spray, and it will not wash off with the rain; yet it can be instantly removed by friction with a dry duster at any time. But note that it is difficult to remove completely from certain plastics.

799

What is meant by the term 'damping-down'?

This involves thoroughly sprinkling the greenhouse floor and staging with water, and, if necessary and recommended, spraying the plants with a mist of water from time to time if they are high-humidity lovers. The purpose is to elevate humidity, but it may also help to keep down temperatures in summer if done in combination with judicious ventilation. This is because water absorbs heat from its surroundings in the process of evaporation. Damping-down is rarely, if ever, done in winter, but may occasionally be needed then if tropical plants from hot and humid climates are being grown.

800

How can I prevent my greenhouse from overheating in summer?

Many beginners at greenhouse gardening fail through letting excessive temperatures develop.

Ventilation combined with damping-down is only part of the answer; if the vents are wide open, a sudden gust of wind may blow over or damage the plants. Special care must be given to satisfactory shading. Indeed, only very rarely is a summer so bad that your greenhouse will not need to be shaded at some time or other. On the other hand, the shading must not be such that it casts a perpetual gloom: it must protect the plants from scorching rays and reduce the amount of heat trapped by the greenhouse, but at the same time allow adequate light for the plants to remain sturdy and keep a good colour. In inadequate light, plant growth will be poor, weak, spindly, and pale.

801

Should I use mains water for my plants or is rain water better?

Rainwater that has been collected from roofs and stored in open butts can be a 'soup' of insect pests, diseases, organisms, weed seeds, and algae slime—and as such is likely to be a menace to all plants grown in the greenhouse. It is senseless to use such water if you are using carefully prepared, reasonably sterile composts. If your mains water is very hard or limy it is possible that some plants that are lime haters may not grow so well if it is used. If necessary, then, clean rainwater can be collected in clean containers and stored in closed vessels especially for use with these plants. There are now available, however, special fertilisers in a form that can be absorbed by plants despite alkaline conditions resulting from soil or water. These are known as 'chelated' preparations. Plants known to be lime hating, such as azaleas, many primulas, citrus, and many ericas, should be potted in a special ericaceous (lime-free) potting compost available from good garden shops.

802

Can you give me a basic guide to feeding greenhouse plants?

Crude animal manures must never be used: they would introduce all manner of pests and diseases. All properly prepared composts contain enough nutrients in the right proportions to take the plants to an advanced stage. Further feeding can be done using a proprietary balanced feed—that is, the right proportions of nitrogen, phosphorous, and potassium (N, P, and K: see 11 and 755), and trace elements such as iron, manganese, and other minerals. Soluble feeds that can be dissolved in water and applied when watering are the most efficient, but slow-dissolving feeding tablets that are pressed into the compost within the pot are also useful. An important time to feed is when flower buds are just beginning to form. Do not feed dormant plants, and try to regulate the degree of

feeding according to the vigour and growth of the species or variety. Over-feeding, like over-watering, is harmful; and do not feed plants when they are dry at the roots. The special proprietary foliar feeds, applied to the leaves by spraying, are also effective on greenhouse plants.

803

Is pest control more difficult in the greenhouse?

No—it is considerably easier. There are now a number of modern pesticides that control almost all the common pests without the necessity of having a 'medicine chest' of chemicals. Most of these work by systemic action and remain effective for a long period on plants protected from the weather. Fumigants (in the form of aerosol sprays or 'firework'-like canisters) are also an efficient way to control many greenhouse pests, as well as moulds and mildews.

Remember that pesticides and fungicides are poisons. Always follow carefully the manufacturers' instructions for their use, wash thoroughly any equipment after use, and keep the containers out of reach of children and pets.

804

What is sterilisation and how should it be carried out?

In the greenhouse this means the destruction of all living things that could jeopardise the culture of the plants. It must, of course, be done when the greenhouse is *empty*. The safest method of sterilising the home greenhouse is to use one of the proprietary preparations based on cresol and to follow the instructions on the label exactly. Usually the greenhouse has to be left empty for some weeks after treatment, so planning of the operation, especially with regard to plant accommodation, is necessary. If possible the greenhouse interior structure and floor should be sterilised at the beginning of each annual growing period; early February is a good time. Seed and potting composts are also 'sterilised' and are in this condition when bought as proprietary brands or as approved John Innes types, so always seal bags of unused composts.

805

Can you give me any hints to help me ensure that my plants survive the winter?

See that their minimum temperature requirement is maintained at all times, and be very cautious when watering, especially on the colder days: plants on the dry side are more likely to survive the cold. Plants not making any active growth or in the dormant state should not be watered or fed. Ventilate when the outside temperature allows it, so as to get the air moving freely; this discourages mould or mildew.

Growing & training

806

Where should I buy my greenhouse plants?

Greenhouse plants should preferably be bought from specialised nurseries—there are many long-established and reliable firms. The same applies to seed. Plants are ideally obtained as young specimens or rooted cuttings, or they are grown from seed. Such plants are usually more vigorous than old mature specimens, which are not only more expensive but can be temperamental after a change of environment. Many greenhouse plants that are commonly raised as house plants are sold at Marks and Spencer stores.

807

Have you any general advice on sowing and tending seeds?

Buy only the best-quality seed, and sow it as soon as possible. The catalogues of seed firms usually give guidance as to the optimum temperature needed for germination. For tender species and half-hardy plants you may need a propagator. Always use a proper seed compost for sowing, and do not sow deeply; very fine seed should not be covered with compost. Water in by spraying with a fine mist of water, and make sure drying out does not occur at any time after sowing. Cover the sown containers with clean white paper and then with a sheet of transparent glass or plastic: the paper will prevent condensation from waterlogging the seed, and the glass helps the compost to retain its moisture. Always sow thinly to make pricking out easy, and prick out as soon as the seedlings can be safely handled—the sooner the better for minimum root disturbance. After sowing, keep the containers out of direct sunlight but not in the dark. Give the seedlings good light to ensure sturdy growth and avoid excessively high temperatures, which will cause them to become drawn, pale, and weak.

808

I wish to raise plants from seed. Can many greenhouse plants be grown in this way?

Seed is an exciting source of new plants. Even the ever-popular 'geranium' (*Pelargonium*) can now be grown to produce superb flowering plants in only about three months from F_1 hybrid seed. Nearly all the most showy popular pot plants are grown from seed, and many long-term perennials can also be cheaply obtained this way. Some firms specialise in unusual and rare seeds from many parts of the world. Germination of these may sometimes be a gamble, but if you get results it can be a source of great satisfaction.

For propagation of plants from seed, *see* 860-77.

809

I have noticed a reference to 'stopping' a plant in a gardening magazine. What does this involve?

It means snipping off the growing tip of a shoot or stem in order to halt development at that point and to encourage growth of shoots from below—usually in generous numbers. Thus, when stopped, a plant develops a branching, bushy shape. In a flowering plant each shoot will usually carry flowers and a much more showy effect is obtained by stopping. Many greenhouse and pot plants have to be stopped at some time, often at the seedling stage, to keep them compact and improve their decorative effect or cropping performance. Sometimes the new shoots that form after the first stopping are themselves stopped to develop an even bushier specimen.

810

What is the point of disbudding?

Some plants develop numerous buds at the end of a flowering shoot. If these are left undisturbed they will eventually become overcrowded and form a tangle of undersized, poor-quality blooms. Disbudding involves removing at the earliest possible stage all but the leading bud(s)—which are usually at the tips of stems and are slightly larger than the others—so that the full resources of the plant can be directed to developing the bud or buds remaining. Typical plants needing to be disbudded are carnations, chrysanthemums, begonias (removal of the female flowers with their winged seed capsules) and camellias (to prevent bud overcrowding).

811

What are standard plants and how are they grown?

A standard is, essentially, a plant in which a bush growth forms atop a tall, non-branching stem. Standards are usually started early in the year from seed or rooted cuttings and are grown on as a single stem, all side shoots (but not foliage) being removed promptly. When the required height is reached the stem is stopped (see 809). This encourages a number of side shoots to form at the stem's top and these can be further stopped if necessary to form a bushy 'head'. Then, and only when the head is well formed, can the foliage on the supporting stem be removed. The growing on may take more than a year. If so, in winter, enough warmth must be provided to maintain growth and so prevent dormancy or die-back. If the latter occurs, the roots may survive but the top may die. This means that growth will recommence from the base and the previous work of growing the

supporting stem will have been to no avail. Popular plants grown as standards are fuchsias, pelargoniums, heliotropiums, some coleus varieties, datura species, and a number of greenhouse shrubs and marguerites.

812

How can greenhouse work help to increase my stock of garden plants?

A greenhouse can help you to save a great deal of money because you can raise all your own bedding plants very cheaply in wider variety and often of better quality than if you bought them in shops. Many tender garden plants can be over-wintered in the greenhouse, and it is also invaluable for all kinds of propagation jobs. It can be used to raise vegetable seedlings to ensure early crops, and to grow plants for sub-tropical bedding to give the garden a look of distinction. It can also house numerous quite tender plants grown in pots for standing out on patios, window sills, and the like during summer.

813

How can I best use the space under my staging?

This depends on light conditions. With a glass-to-ground greenhouse, the space will probably be bright enough for a wide range of purposes; it is, for instance, a good place to site a propagator or those plants liking slight shade. If there is considerable shade, as there may be if your greenhouse has base walls, only shade lovers can be put there—but there are lots of these. Many of the most popular house plants like the under-staging area (and may even be raised there); so, too, do many sub-tropical plants and exotic-foliage subjects if warmth and humidity is adequate. Good crops of mushrooms can be grown and, if an area is blacked out, it can be used for blanching and forcing crops such as chicory, rhubarb, and seakale.

The area should not be used to store 'junk', which will harbour pests and diseases, but it can be a useful place for keeping tools that are used regularly in the greenhouse and also containers of seed and potting compost as long as these can be effectively sealed.

814

I have 'inherited' a greenhouse, but the only available space for it in my garden is generally shaded. Is it worth the trouble of moving it to my place?

Certainly; the great majority of popular greenhouse and pot plants prefer shady conditions when in the decorative stage—but good light, which does not mean *direct* sunlight under glass, is essential for them in their early stages of growth. If there is too much gloom, growth will be weak, straggly, and pale. If your greenhouse is going to

be very shaded, the use of garden frames in a more open, sunny position might solve the problem of the early growing stages of some plants.

There are also many plants that revel in considerable shade, apart from the low growers suitable for placing under the staging. Examples include many ferns for both cool and warm conditions; Norfolk Island pine (*Araucaria excelsa*) in its juvenile form; the climbers Chilean bell-flower (*Lapageria rosea*) and *Hoya carnosa*—both with attractive flowers; many ivies; the *Schefflera* foliage species; camellias, which flower very well in pots when young; streptocarpus, gloxinias, and many of the *Gesneria* family; the 'forest cacti' such as schlumbergera and rhipsalidopsis; the annual *Exacum affine*, which is sweet smelling; *Anthurium crystallinum*; and various palms. There are many more possibilities to choose from, depending on the temperature maintained.

815

I would like to grow some plants for winter colour. Any suggestions?

Winter colour is one of the chief delights for the greenhouse gardener. Suitable plants include the following: Cinerarias (*Senecio*); calceolarias; *Primula obconica* (many fine varieties) and *P. sinensis*; numerous hardy bulbs and other storage organs if potted early, such as narcissi (daffodils), hyacinths, and so on; the winter cherry (*Solanum capsicastrum*) for its scarlet fruits; cyclamen; *Erica hiemalis*; Christmas cactus (*Schlumbergera*); *Browallia speciosa*, including dwarf varieties; chrysanthemums, perpetual-flowering carnations, gerberas, winter-flowering pansies and stocks grown in pots, and the new multi-coloured primroses. A number of shrubby plants, such as camellia (suitable varieties) and various *Acacia* species, also give good winter colour.

816

A friend has offered me his small greenhouse free. I have space to spare—but I have one greenhouse already. Apart from extra capacity, what are the advantages of a second greenhouse?

The chief advantage is that you can create two quite different environments—one, perhaps, devoted to a special purpose or to growing plants such as orchids, alpines, carnations, and the like which would not thrive in the sort of environment you create in your present greenhouse.

A second greenhouse would also be useful to keep as a conservatory for the display of decorative plants, and quite separate from the place used for the vital visually less interesting jobs of propagation and growing-on. Bear in mind, however, that even if you have

room (or time or the money) for only one greenhouse, you may be able to create at least two different environments by dividing the structure into two compartments.

817

How can I keep my greenhouse 'in production' all the year round?

There is a very large number of possible permutations, and the main thing is to plan well in advance. A typical example of a schedule is to start in spring by sowing bedding plants and planting summer- and autumn-flowering bulbs. Cuttings can be taken of summer- to autumn-flowering pot plants, and crops such as tomatoes, sweet peppers, cucumbers, and melons can be grown. With the approach of autumn, chrysanthemums can be moved in; and the winter can continue to be colourful from sowings of suitable plants made during summer. There is also a number of useful winter salad crops, lettuce being most important.

818

Can you explain some of the tricks involved in growing plants out of season?

The fact that a greenhouse gives weather protection and generally elevated temperatures is sufficient to give out-of-season results in many cases without resorting to trickery. However, a number of decorative plants do lend themselves to flowering-time control by manipulation of the length of daylight. This can be reduced by blacking-out or extended by using special artificial lights. The procedure is rather complicated and needs experience and expertise, and is more suited to commercial nurseries. A number of bulbous plants can be bought in a specially 'prepared' form for early out-of-season forcing, but these may need rather more warmth than is maintained in the average greenhouse.

819

Can you suggest some shrubs that won't crowd out my greenhouse?

There are a number of dwarf forms of shrubs that can be grown in 125 mm (5 in) or slightly larger pots. Examples include miniature roses, pomegranate (*Punica*), lantanas, and *Lagerstroemia indica*—all of which can be grown from seed. Young camellias flower extremely well in small pots, and there are numerous colourful azaleas (both these are ideal for cold conditions), and several pretty *Acacia* species. Hydrangeas can be kept fairly compact in pots; and so, with careful management and proper pruning, can many other popular shrubs, including the oleander (*Nerium*), the calamondin orange (*Citrus mitis*), *Daphne odora*, coral tree (*Erythrina*

crista-galli), *Plumbago capensis* (which with drastic pruning can be pot-grown instead of being grown as a wall shrub), and *Tibouchina semidecandra* (syn. *T. urvilleana*); fuchsias, too, should not be forgotten as shrubby subjects with a long flowering period.

Generally the pruning, shaping, and cutting back to maintain neat, compact development should be done soon after flowering is over.

820

I thought it might be nice to grow some plants for use as gifts at Christmas. Any ideas?

Special dwarf, compact, and early varieties of cineraria (*Senecio*) and calceolaria are colourful favourites; of the latter, the new variety 'Anytime' is particularly easy. *Primula obconica* is a fine pot plant, too—but it gives some people a rash if they have sensitive skin. The Christmas cherry (*Solanum capsicastrum*) has bright red berries, and so have some forms of the red pepper (*Capsicum annuum*), which are often easier to grow. All these can be raised from seed.

The popular poinsettia, with its colourful bracts, cannot be grown for the Christmas period without special artificial-light treatment. It should be fully enclosed in a thick, black plastic dustbin liner every night (from about 6 pm to 8 am) from late September to late November to give it long nights. Flowering and bract coloration will then be initiated.

821

Are there any general rules for the over-wintering of plants?

The great enemy of plants when temperatures are low in winter is dampness or over-watering. During very cold spells it is usually best to withhold water entirely (plants that are dormant or resting should in any case be watered only very rarely—perhaps just enough to prevent complete drying out). Plants with fleshy roots, and bulbs, corms, tubers, rhizomes, and other storage organs, must be kept quite dry and frost-free or they will rot. They should be stored in containers of clean, dry sand or peat. The greenhouse atmosphere must also be kept on the dry side, and should be ventilated when the general temperature allows. If you have a heating problem due to an extra-cold spell, you can protect your plants to some extent against frost damage by covering them with dry newspaper on bubble plastic anchored with stones.

Fruit and vegetables

822

What vegetables can be grown in the greenhouse?

Edible crops usually called 'vegetables', although some are botanically fruits, include the following: tomato, cucumber, sweet pepper (capsicum or pimiento), courgette, aubergine, French bean, climbing French bean, new (early) potato, lettuce, radish, beetroot, carrot, and mushroom. Various herbs can be grown for winter use, and a number of crops such as asparagus, rhubarb, chicory and seakale, can be blanched or forced (*see* 78). Mustard, cress, and more recently a wide range of sprouting vegetables, are also popular if there is enough warmth. Many of the basic vegetables of the outdoor plot can be harvested earlier if they are started under glass before planting out.

823

What fruits are suitable for growing in the greenhouse?

The melon is easy for most home greenhouses, and the cape gooseberry (*Physalis edulis*) has also recently become a popular crop. Strawberries are often grown, although frames are also suitable. Suitable varieties of a number of stone fruits, such as peach, apricot, and nectarine, are ideal for training on the rear wall of a bright lean-to. Figs can be treated similarly, but they also make a good tub plant. Oranges and other citrus fruits need only frost-free conditions and are often grown for their sweet smelling blossom as much as for the fruit. Most big houses of the past had an 'orangery', although the plant tubs were usually stood outdoors for the summer.

824

I have heard that tomatoes and cucumbers cannot be grown together. Is that true?

Not any more. Modern varieties of cucumber—especially the F_1 hybrids—are extremely vigorous and very easy to grow. They are not nearly so exacting as to temperature and environmental conditions as the old varieties, and usually do well if grown in the same greenhouse as tomatoes and under similar conditions. Another factor that makes this practical is the introduction of pesticides that can be used on *both* crops. At one time the cucumber family was prone to damage by many of the chemicals used to control tomato pests.

825

I cannot spend as much time in my greenhouse as I would like. It seems that ring culture might be just what I need for my plants. Can you explain how it works?

It is used mostly for tomato-growing, but it can be adapted for other crops, particularly cucumber and any especially vigorous grower. It is especially useful for gardeners who have to leave the greenhouse unattended for long periods since, when properly set up, it can maintain even root moisture. The plants are grown in bottomless flowerpots or cylinders—usually made from fibre and about 225 m (9 in) in diameter—filled with a suitable potting compost (John Innes No 3 is ideal, but any equivalent proprietary compost will do if recommended by the maker of the equipment). The cylinders are placed on a bed of aggregate consisting of clean shingle or peat kept nicely moist. The water can be applied from a can or hose or, preferably, by one of the automatic watering systems. Diluted liquid fertilisers are applied to the compost within the cylinders where the fine nutrient-absorbing roots will form. The water-absorbing roots form low down and will take up moisture from the aggregate.

826

What are the basic environmental conditions needed for quality greenhouse tomatoes?

Firstly, select a good variety from the seed catalogues of the leading firms. Do not, if possible, grow in the ground soil (*see* 789); or, if you have to, graft the seedlings on to what the seedsman calls KNVF rootstock, also grown from seed. (The letters 'KNVF' refer to various root pests or disease organisms against which this type of rootstock has good resistance).

Try to maintain even environmental conditions: wide fluctuations are the cause of many troubles, such as poor pollination, flower and fruit drop, under-sized fruit, and cracking skins, as well as fungus troubles such as blossom-end rot. Attend to de-sideshooting promptly, removing any shoots growing between the leaf stalks and stem. While the fruit is developing, the greenhouse temperature must not exceed 28°C (80°F); otherwise the red pigment of the fruit fails to form and your tomatoes will suffer from blotchy ripening, greenback, and other ripening problems. Shade your glass with white electrostatic shading if necessary, but avoid heavy shade.

827

Can you recommend some different types of tomato varieties?

'Moneymaker' has had such powerful and persistent publicity that it is sometimes difficult to get people to try the many newer and superior introductions. There are improved forms of 'Moneymaker', and it remains an outstanding cropper; but there are also many varieties with a much greater resistance to the many diseases that attack the tomato. The F_1 hybrid varieties are all worth considering first; the following are fine examples of the many different types. 'Alicante' has become a favourite for general culinary use in recent years. 'Big Boy' is a very large-fruited variety with firm flesh but excellent flavour. 'Sweet' is an excellent small-fruited variety, producing masses of cherry-sized tomatoes. 'Golden Sunrise', with

its excellent flavour and general quality is overcoming the British prejudice against yellow varieties. Finally 'Ida', a very new variety, is especially recommended for growing in *unheated* greenhouses.

828

Do I need to feed my tomatoes?

Yes. Special proprietary tomato feeds are available; these are usually formulated to give the high concentration of potassium which the crop particularly needs. It is more useful in the early stages of the plant's development, and towards the end of the season it is best to replace the high-potash feed with an ordinary balanced pot-plant feed. Tomatoes often show a deficiency in magnesium by the foliage yellowing from the edge inwards with perhaps only the veins remaining green. This can be corrected by watering or spraying with Epsom salts (magnesium sulphate) at the rate of 6-12 g/l (1-2 oz/gal) of water.

829

I have heard that cucumbers are a difficult crop. Is that true?

To grow this crop out of season needs warmth and care, but it is easy to produce excellent greenhouse cucumbers for picking from about late May to autumn. The modern varieties are excellent; look especially for the *all-female* varieties you will find in the seed catalogues of leading firms. These can often be left to grow as they will, with the minimum of interference. Even if left untrained they are very productive as young plants, but proper training will ensure continuity of cropping.

830

Can you explain the basic technique for growing cucumbers?

The seed usually germinates quickly if sown on edge at a temperature of about 15-18°C (60-65°F) in a propagator during March or April. Transfer to 88 mm (3¼ in) pots, and later plant in 225 mm (9 in) pots or grow bags

when well rooted. Place these containers on the greenhouse staging and train the plant as a single stem up the greenhouse side to the eaves by removing any side shoots that may form. When this stage is reached, run strings or wires along the roof from end to end or from the glazing bars to cover the area above where the plants are sited and a few feet beyond either way. Space the strings 150-200 mm (6 to 8 in) apart and train the stems under them. Sideshoots (laterals) can then be allowed to grow and should be led along and tied to the strings. When a fruit forms, stop the lateral about two leaves further on. Secondary laterals will form and should be treated similarly. For

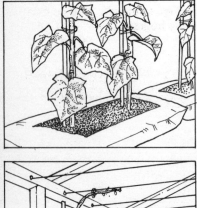

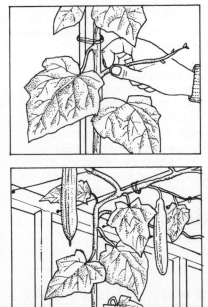

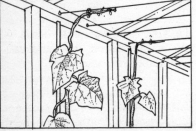

varieties that are not all female, the male flowers without a tiny cucumber attached must be promptly removed as a routine before they open—otherwise the fruit will become club-shaped, seedy, and possibly bitter.

831

I am fond of sweet peppers and would welcome advice on how to grow them.

These have become very popular in recent years (they are widely but incorrectly known also as capsicums, the correct name, of Spanish origin, being pimiento). They are easy to grow, especially the newer hybrids. Culture in the early stages is similar to that for tomato, but they can be grown in 175-200 mm (7-8 in) pots quite well. They usually need no support or special treatment, but the number of fruits that form sometimes need restricting, by picking some off at an early stage, so as to give the rest enough space to swell and develop properly. The fruits can usually be gathered green or through any stage of ripening to a full gold or red colour from summer to autumn; they are eaten raw or cooked.

832

Are melons really a suitable proposition for the greenhouse?

A number of good greenhouse varieties will be found in the seed catalogues. They should be sown and trained exactly as described for cucumber except that the supporting strings should be spaced about 250-300 mm (10-12 in) apart. A vital difference in growing is that the melon flowers must be pollinated. Pick off a male flower and transfer the pollen to the female flowers, which have a tiny fruit attached. When pollination is successful the little fruits will soon begin to swell. Do not permit more than about three or four fruits to grow on for each plant. Any others should be picked off. The large fruits may need support with nets which can be improvised from net curtain or string shopping bags. Do not harvest them until the fruit is properly ripe: the end should be springy to the touch and emit a fruity fragrance.

833

Is it possible to grow lettuce all the year round in my greenhouse?

Yes—but it is more sensible to regard lettuce as a greenhouse or frame crop for the colder months of the year, since in the heat of summer greenhouse-grown lettuces tend to 'bolt' (run to seed) and fail to form nice crisp hearts. It is very important to sow varieties specially developed for the purpose—not all lettuce will grow well under glass. Examples of good varieties include 'Kwiek', 'Kloek', 'Sea Queen', 'Emerald', and 'May

Queen'. Sowings can usually be made from August to March for cropping from about November to late spring.

834

I want to improve the output of vegetables in my greenhouse. Can you tell me something about catch-crops and how and when to grow them?

These are crops that take up very little space and can be grown in between main crops, such as tomatoes or lettuce. They are usually salad crops, such as early carrots, pulled in the very young state, and radish, which can be sown almost the whole year round.

835

I would like to grow grapes, but I have heard that growing and maintaining a grape vine is difficult. What do you suggest?

The vine is certainly one of the less easy crops, and ideally it should be given a house of its own. In old-fashioned greenhouses, with brick sides to waist-level, the vines are planted immediately outside and led in through a specially made hole. In a modern glass-to-ground structure you can plant a vine in the greenhouse border; but take care that the roots do not dry out—as tends to happen in a small greenhouse. A vinery offers conditions that are not liked by most other plants—notably shade from the vine itself and lack of heat in winter—but I have successfully grown camellias in pots in a vinery. If you wish to grow a vine and have only little space, it is possible to get good results by using pots or small tubs. However, this does mean that the useful life of the vine is limited and a fresh start has to be made from time to time.

Decorative plants

836

Can you give me a brief guide to growing pelargoniums?

Named varieties of all the popular pelargoniums are best bought from a specialist nursery in early spring in the form of rooted cuttings. From then on you can propagate from plants you have overwintered in the greenhouse; cuttings can be taken either during late summer or spring (see 191 and 902). The recently introduced F_1 hybrid geraniums (*Pelargonium*) are very easy to grow from seed sown in late February. Fine-flowering plants will then be obtained by June, with quality and colours equal to, or even better than, the named types. Generally, the plants like good light conditions and ventilation, need to be kept frost-free and must be kept on the dry side in winter, with moderate watering in summer. Do not allow plants to become straggly: cut them back severely if necessary; they will probably be of better shape and flower more profusely. Do this pruning early in the year, just before the plants start into new growth.

837

Can you recommend some other easy-to-grow greenhouse pot plants?

Few of the most popular pot plants are difficult to grow in the average home greenhouse, given reasonable care. The exceptions are mainly those plants that are artificially dwarfed or brought into flower out of season, such as some chrysanthemums, poinsettias, kalanchoes, and *Rhododendron simsii* (the so-called Indian azalea). Many greenhouse annuals and biennials are extremely easy to grow from seed; subjects like schizantus, salpiglossis, *Phlox drummondii* (a good pot plant as well as a bedder), busy lizzie (*Impatiens*), the wishbone flower (*Torenia fournieri*), and the cigar flower (*Cuphea ignea*) are several that will give colour a few months after sowing.

838

Have you any hints on growing fuchsias?

These are best bought as rooted cuttings. It is not very practical to raise them from seed unless you are an enthusiast: the named types are usually far superior. Fuchsias can be grown in numerous ways—brush, trailing, standard, and fancy shapes—but some varieties are more suited for a particular growing habit. Fuchsias that are being trained should not be allowed to suffer chill in winter, as this may cause the top growth to die back. Propagation is easy from suitable stem cuttings taken in spring. The plants like good light conditions, but need slight protection from bright sun with white shading during summer to prevent scorch. Stopping the plants (*see* 809) encourages more generous flowering, but they should be left untouched from about eight weeks before the time the flowers are required to give the best show.

839

What bulbs are specially suited to the greenhouse?

By 'bulbs' people usually include all storage organs, such as corms, tubers, and the like. For the greenhouse these fall into two categories: the hardy types autumn-planted for spring display, and the tender kinds started from late winter to spring for summer to autumn colour. The latter include achimenes, begonia, canna, cyclamen, eucharis, eucomis, freesia, gloriosa, gloxinia (*Sinningia speciosa*), haemanthus, hippeastrum (the so-called amaryllis), hymenocallis, nerine, tuberose (*Polianthes tuberosa*), smithiantha, Jacobean lily

(*Sprekelia formosissima*),
Scarborough lily (*Vallota
speciosa*)—all of which are quite
easy to grow given normal cultural
attention.

840

Can I raise my own houseplants in the greenhouse?

Numerous permanent houseplants
can be cheaply and easily raised
from seed sown in spring. They
include *Begonia rex*, the so-called
asparagus ferns (not true ferns),
the polka-dot plant (*Hypoestes*),
Schefflera species, the cabbage
palm (*Cordyline terminalis*),
various *Eucalyptus* species, the
well loved African violet
(*Saintpaulia*)—grown from F_1
hybrid seed, which is easy to
manage—and a vast range of cacti
and other succulents. Many
houseplants are also easily
propagated from cuttings, either
stem or leaf (*see* 897-926), if you
can get material from friends who
have plants you like.

841

I would like to try growing some exotic greenhouse plants. Can you suggest a few that are not too difficult?

One of the most highly prized
greenhouse plants is the bird-of-
paradise flower (*Strelitzia reginae*),
with flowers like an exotic bird's
head. This can be grown well in
barely frost-free conditions in
winter—although it is often
described as a 'stove' plant! The
new hibiscus F_1 hybrids, such as
'Southern Belle', have immense
flowers like dinner plates, yet they
are extremely easy to grow from
seed, flowering in a few months.
The butterfly flower (*Schizanthus*),
in the form of modern hybrids,
calceolaria, and salpiglossis all have
extremely exotic flower form and
colouring, and are also easy to
grow.

Bulbs also provide a source of
some flowers amazing for size and
form; notable examples include
hippeastrum and the related
sprekelia, gloxinia (*Sinningia
speciosa*), nerine, foxglove-like
smithiantha, and hymenocallis.
There are some very showy
shrubby subjects too, like
callistemons, with their crimson
'bottle-brush' flowers; *Erythrina
crista-galli*, with large wax-textured
red flowers; and tibouchina, with
its blooms resembling giant
pansies.

842

What are the best permanent foliage plants for the greenhouse?

Palms immediately spring to
mind—but there are few suitable
hardy types. Remember to select
only those that will thrive in the
minimum temperature of your
greenhouse: you would do well to
seek advice from a specialised
palm nursery. For the home
greenhouse look for foliage that

gives an impression of warmth, but is in fact fairly cold-resistant; *Fatsia japonica*, with large glossy palm-like leaves, is a typical example. Many ferns, too, are cold resistant, but not all may retain their fronds in winter. *Hoya carnosa* is an exotic-looking climber with some good leaf variegation, and it also bears flowers. Among those grown from seed are the popular shrubs *Grevillea robusta* and *Jacaranda mimosaefolia*; both have very graceful, ferny leaves but they may eventually outgrow the space available.

843

Is there any way in which I can adapt my cool greenhouse to grow warmth-loving exotics without running up prohibitive fuel bills?

Provided you select modest-sized plants you can grow these plants in large warmed frames that have been brought into the greenhouse; alternatively, you can partition off a section of the greenhouse to reduce the amount of space that has to be given the extra heat; for frames or cases, electric soil-warming cables are the most convenient means of heating. Some plants to consider include cattleya orchids, and evergreens such as marantas, calatheas, aglaonemas, *Cissus discolor*, codiaeums, anthuriums, saintpaulias, dieffenbachias, and fittonias.

844

What special conditions, if any, do I need to provide for cacti and other succulents?

Maximum light is important for most species, although there are a few exceptions such as the forest cacti. Frost-free conditions are important for most too, although there are some hardy species. It is wrong to assume that this type of plant can go without water indefinitely (no plant can); they are, however, well equipped to withstand short periods of neglect and so they are ideal plants for those who have to be away from home and the greenhouse from time to time. During active growth the plants can be well watered, but in winter they should be given hardly any or even left dry. With proper care many plants flower beautifully and become extremely showy. A free-draining compost is essential; most modern potting types will be satisfactory if you add extra grit to them.

845

How are greenhouse chrysanthemums grown?

There are many types including the 'cascade' and 'charm' kinds, with masses of small daisy flowers, as well as those used for cutting with giant 'football' blooms. In all cases the training is vital to success and can be rather involved, although it is not difficult. The most popular large-flowered types with incurved or reflexed petals should be bought as rooted cuttings in spring and grown on in large pots outside the greenhouse during summer. They must be stopped (see 809) and a limited number of shoots that then form are allowed to produce buds. The shoots are subsequently disbudded to permit only one bloom to develop on each.

846

I like the idea of growing carnations all the year round. Can you tell me how it's done?

For this purpose grow the PF (perpetual-flowering) type. They are bought as rooted cuttings of named varieties in early spring, and the plants will flower from summer onwards in 175 mm (7 in) pots. To get the best blooms in winter, give the plants a bright position and do not let the temperature fall below 10°C (50°F) except for short periods. The young plants must be stopped (see 809)—the supplying nursery will often do this before despatch—and the stems that develop must be disbudded to allow only one large flower to develop on each.

847

Can you suggest some other flowers I might grow for cutting?

Try the Christmas rose (*Helleborus niger*), which needs only weather protection: stocks (*Matthiola*) of the 'column' type and snapdragons

(*Antirrhinum*) grown as single spikes; many other annuals sown in autumn, grown on for early flowering, and chosen for long, strong stems. The various hybrids and varieties of *Gerbera* are highly prized for flower-arranging; and so too are the various types of gladioli; suitable rose varieties (grown in pots for early flowers), and most of the long-stemmed spring-flowering hardy bulbs, are other good examples.

848

I have a small greenhouse but I would like, if possible, to try my hand at climbing plants. Are there any that might be suitable?

Many climbers can be rampant and take up lots of room, but they can usually be managed if they are grown in containers which confine the roots. Some good plants to grow in this way are the passion flowers (*Passiflora*), *Abutilon megapotamicum*, Chilean bell-flower (*Lapageria rosea*), *Hoya carnosa*, *Stephanotis floribunda* (which needs warmth), *Plumbago capensis* (as a wall shrub), *Bougainvillea* (as a wall shrub), and *Jasminum polyanthum* —all widely available. There are also some pretty climbers to grow as annuals such as black-eyed Susan (*Thunbergia alata*), morning glory (*Ipomoea*), Chilean glory flower (*Eccremocarpus scaber*), *Maurandia barclaiana*, glory lilies (*Gloriosa*), which are grown from tubers that can be saved, and the balloon vine (*Cardiospermum halicacabum*).

849

I have heard that, with various adjustments, my greenhouse would be suitable for growing alpines. Could you tell me what would be involved?

Very many alpine or rock plants are relatively hardy, but they resent wet and humid conditions in winter, and are often better if given just a little frost protection. Their dainty flowers will also look better if they are given some protection from the damaging effects of the weather. An 'alpine house' is designed to provide plenty of air, light, and protection, and to bring the plants nearer the eye on extra-high staging. Most alpines are spring flowering and can be kept in frames during the rest of the year if preferred. This allows the alpine house to be used for many ordinary summer- to autumn-flowering plants.

850

Is orchid-growing beyond the scope of the average greenhouse gardener?

Not at all: few orchids are really difficult to grow, and if you can provide the correct temperature and conditions they are extremely rewarding. The best for the beginner and the home greenhouse are the *Cymbidium*

species, most of which need temperatures of only 5-7°C (40-45°F) in winter and about 16°C (61°F) in summer. There is also no need for a special greenhouse. A catalogue from a specialist nursery will give useful hints for growing and information regarding the special compost required.

851

Which among my greenhouse plants are most suitable for use in hanging baskets?

Trailing varieties of fuchsia and the ivy-leaved pelargoniums are great favourites; Pendula type of tuberous-rooted begonias are also beautiful. Modern trailing lobelias can be grown from seed and are now very showy; they come in a wide range of colours, and are useful for mixing with other subjects. The bell-flower (*Campanula isophylla*), columneas, some achimenes, *Aeschynanthus speciosus, Hypocyrta glabra*, petunias, schlumbergeras, *Lachenalia bulbifera, Lobelia tenuoir,* and some of the annual climbers (which will also trail) are also popular.

Adrienne Wild

Technical writer on the staff of *Practical
Gardening* magazine; formerly a propagator for a municipal parks department.

Propagation

Tools & equipment

852

I would like to propagate from cuttings a few plants on my window sill, but do not want to go to the expense of a propagating unit. Can I get round this?

The main problem you need to solve is that nearly all cuttings need a humid atmosphere: in dry air their leaves soon shrivel and die because there is as yet no root system to replace the moisture lost through rapid evaporation. Place four canes in the pot of cuttings and drape a polythene bag over them, securing it to the pot with a rubber band. Place the pot in a bright spot, but out of direct sunlight, in a room where a temperature of about 18°C (65°F) is maintained. Rooting will take a few weeks: its occurrence will be indicated by new growth, so the cuttings should not be disturbed until this is visible.

853

I will need a heated propagator to start off my seedlings during the winter months. Proprietary models seem to be very expensive, so I wondered if it would be feasible to make my own. Could you tell me what materials I would require?

First you will need to make a box about 150 mm (6 in) deep. Line the base with approximately 50 mm (2 in) of sand. Lay on the sand an electric soil-warming cable (which needs to be thermostatically controlled) in loops about 75 mm (3 in) apart across the full length of the bottom of the box. Cover this with a further 50 mm (2 in) of sand.

Complete your propagator by

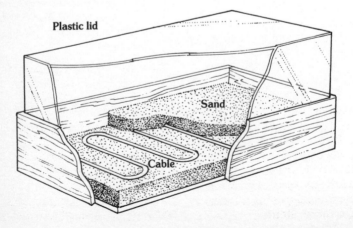

Plastic lid

Sand

Cable

making a close-fitting plastic or glass lid to help maintain a warm, humid atmosphere. Alternatively, for a slightly greater outlay, you could buy a proprietary heating panel. Most types made for the amateur gardener will fit under a standard plastic seed tray, which is equipped with a clear-plastic cover.

854

I'm a keen gardener and would like to start propagating my own plants, especially from cuttings. Could you please advise me on the best sort of propagating knife to buy? There are many different types available.

It is important to choose a knife with a good-quality steel blade which can be sharpened to a keen edge. Poor quality steel (or that which is highly chromed) will soon become blunt and will wear down quickly when sharpened. For general propagation choose a medium-weight knife which opens easily and is comfortable to use. Go for one with a straight blade which is set well back into the handle, so that it will not become loose with wear. (Knives with a curved blade are best avoided as they are difficult both to use and to sharpen). If you buy a knife with a blade which is honed only on one side of the edge, check that it suits you, for it is either left- or right-handed. Keep your good knife for propagation only; use a cheap pen knife for cutting string.

855

My propagating knife needs sharpening quite often, and I have not yet been able to master this task. I have a carborundum stone, but all I seem to do is wear down the blade. Could you explain how I should use it?

Slightly moisten the carborundum stone with a little clean mineral oil and gently push the whole blade along the full length of the stone. If it is a two-sided blade, hold it at a very shallow angle and push it in a forward direction only. Do this several times, then repeat the operation on the other side of the blade. If it is a flat-ground blade, with only one sharp edge, lay it horizontally on the stone, exerting slight pressure towards the sharpened edge, and push it gently in a forward direction as before.

856

Is it all right to use garden soil for sowing seeds in pots? Plants I grow outside seem to germinate well.

Your garden soil will grow outdoor plants; but it is unsatisfactory if used in pots. This is mainly because it is not sterile and can harbour pests and diseases which will compete directly with the plants being grown. Neither will it contain all the essential nutrients at the right strength for pot-grown plants. Even light soils can drain badly in pots. Instead, use one of the proprietary seed composts. These are specially formulated for containers, are essentially pest and disease free, and include all the foodstuffs necessary to grow good plants from seed.

857

As an economy measure, can I use yoghurt cartons instead of clay or plastic pots?

Clean yoghurt cartons and the like make excellent pots. Remember, though, to pierce plenty of holes in the base of the cartons to allow for drainage.

858

I have read that mist propagation guarantees better results. What is it and can it be done in a small greenhouse?

Mist propagation is a system which keeps the plant material moist throughout the rooting period. Proprietary kits, which are widely available, consist essentially of a water-supply stand-pipe surmounted by a nozzle and an automatic on/off switch that is triggered by the humidity level within the propagator. When the switch is on, the nozzle emits a fine spray. Mist propagation creates a humid atmosphere that allows maximum light to reach the cuttings; combined with the extra warmth provided by the propagator's heating unit, it creates an ideal environment for the young

plants to root in. The propagators in which the mist units are installed are available in various sizes, most of which are compact enough to be used in a small greenhouse. If you are thinking of buying a mist unit, however, bear in mind that you will need to have both electricity and water supplies to the greenhouse.

859

I would like to use artificial lighting in my greenhouse to supplement poor daylight in winter. What type of lamps should I use?

Fluorescent tubes specially made for indoor gardening are available; these give out light in the red to blue wave-lengths that plants enjoy. If you prefer to use ordinary tubes, choose those described as 'cool white'. For each 300 × 300 mm (12 × 12 in) of growing area allow 15-20 watts of light, and set the tubes 300-450 mm (12-18 in) above the plants.

Seeds

860

I would like to collect the seed from plants in my garden. How can I recognise the right time to do this?

Collect seed only from good plant specimens: the resultant plants may not be identical but they should at least have some desirable characteristics. Choose a dry, preferably sunny day to gather seeds contained in pods or capsules (it does not matter if fleshy fruits are wet when collected). Collect only *ripe* seed heads, which can be recognised by the change in colour (in most cases from green to brown). Pods and capsules should be harvested just before they open to disperse their contents. Spread them out on a sheet of paper in a warm dry place indoors to complete the ripening process. This will encourage the pods to open and release their seeds.

861

How do I prepare a 'guaranteed weed-free' seedbed outside? I would like to grow some hardy ornamental plants so that in a few years time I can extend my borders.

By far the best time to prepare a weed-free seed-bed is in the autumn. Preferably make a raised bed, to allow for better drainage, with a maximum width of 900 mm (3 ft) so that you do not need to stand on it at any time to work. Thoroughly dig the bed in autumn, adding a soil conditioner such as peat or compost in the bottom of each trench created by the spade, and let the winter frosts break the soil lumps down. In spring, rake the bed level and leave it fallow to

allow any weed seeds to germinate; then spray them off with a contact herbicide containing paraquat. Continue to do this until the seedbed appears to be sterile of weeds. Before sowing, apply bonemeal at 100 g/m^2 (3 oz/sq. yd); this will help root development of the young seedlings.

862

I want to grow an avocado plant from seed. How should I go about this?

Pierce the avocado stone with three cocktail sticks and suspend it in a jar of water so that the bottom of the seed just touches the water. If you place the jar in a propagator (or on a warm windowsill) at a temperature of 21°C (70°F) the seed should germinate within a couple of months. Once several strong roots have developed transfer it carefully to a pot of moist compost, and gradually harden the plant off so that it can be put in a well-lit, draught-free position in the house.

863

I have collected some pine cones. How do I extract the seeds?

If the cones are fully open the seed will already been dispersed. If they are tightly closed, put the cones in a bag and store them in a warm place (such as an airing cupboard) so that the scales will open to expose the seed. Shake the bag from time to time to separate the seeds.

864

I have tried growing sweet peas on several occasions, but have had little success in getting the seeds to germinate. I have heard that you should cut them with a knife, but wonder if this treatment might damage them. What is your opinion?

Sweet peas and many other seeds which have a very hard seedcoat are sometimes unable to absorb the water that is necessary to make the seedcoat swell and rupture, so that the root and shoot can emerge safely. An easy way to tackle this problem is to soak the seed for 24 hours in warm (but not hot) water to help soften the seedcoat. Alternatively, you can carefully nick the seed with a sharp knife to expose the fleshy part within. Seeds which are too small to handle in this way can be scratched by shaking them in a jar lined with sandpaper.

865

I have read that the fleshy fruit of some trees and shrubs requires chilling before the seed will germinate. Why is this, and how do I go about it?

Many fleshy fruits (such as holly, cotoneaster, berberis, mahonia, pyracantha, and sorbus berries) have a hard stone, within which is the seed. This stone, or seedcoat, will need a period of chilling before it becomes soft enough to absorb water and allow germination. Crush the fruit with a wooden presser to expose the seed, then add it to a 50:50 mixture of moist sand and peat. Place this in a container, stand it outdoors in an exposed position, and cover it with a piece of slate to prevent damage by mice. It may be 6 to 18 months depending on the type of fruit, before the seed is ready for sowing.

866

How can I tell when clematis seeds are ripe and ready for sowing?

The feathery seeds turn a silvery colour when ripe. They should be sown in March in pots filled with a sandy compost. Place them in a cold frame and keep them in the dark. Germination may take as long as 12 months, so be patient.

867

I have never had much luck growing *Begonia semperflorens* from seed. The germination results are always poor, even though I provide optimum conditions in my heated propagator. What could be the cause?

Begonias have tiny seeds and no covering is required. If they are buried it is likely that they will not germinate—and if they do shoot up they will probably damp-off (*see* 875) before they have a chance to reach the surface.

868

Every year when I have completed my sowing programme, I have some seed left over. Can these be kept and used the following year or is it best always to buy fresh?

You can save seed from one year to the next provided it is kept cool and in an airtight container. One thing to note, though, is that germination results may not be as good in subsequent years. The viability of some seeds deteriorates rapidly after they have ripened to maturity: the seed is using its store of food in order to survive, so that less food will be available for the embryo at germination.

869

Do ferns produce seed or will I have to divide them to get more plants?

Ferns do not produce true seeds as such. They are propagated from spores which grow on the back of the leaf fronds. If a cloud of dust-like spores appears when a frond is tapped, the spores are ripe and ready for sowing. Collect a ripe frond and put it in a dry paper bag in a warm place, so that the spores are released. Prepare a pan of seed compost, then sow the spores onto the surface; do *not* cover them with compost. Place a

sheet of glass over the pan to keep the humidity high, and maintain a temperature of about 21°C (70°F). Stand the pot in a tray of water from time to time to keep the compost evenly moist. Within six weeks a mossy-growth will be seen: this is the first stage in fern development. Keep it moist at all times and when, after a further four weeks or so, the first fronds appear, remove the glass to harden the plants off (*see* 28) before they are pricked out in clumps into trays. Attempt to separate the individual fern plants only when they can be handled easily.

870

I would like to grow some bonsai forms of trees. I intend to collect my own seed in the autumn, but are there any which cannot be stored over the winter?

Yes—the ripe seeds of oak, horse-chestnut, and sweet-chestnut will usually lose their viability if they are not sown immediately they are collected.

871

I have poor eyesight and find sowing small seed difficult. Are there any tricks of the trade that will make it easier for me to sow thinly and evenly?

When sowing fine seed, such as begonias and lobelias, add to them a small amount of dry silver sand so that you can handle them more easily and see where you are sowing them. Shake the mixture from a paper bag on to the surface of the compost.

872

I have noticed that some seed is sold in pelleted form. What are the advantages of sowing this type?

Pelleted seeds are coated with a water-soluble soil-clay mixture. They make sowing much easier because they are large enough to handle individually. You can sow the exact number of seeds you require, so you waste less. Thinning the seedlings is unnecessary, so the plants can develop without checks. But before you sow pelleted seeds you must thoroughly moisten the seed bed, so that the coating will quickly disintegrate to allow germination. If the soil dries out at all it is most likely that the seeds will fail to germinate.

873

I would like to grow lilies from seed, but I gather that they take quite a while to germinate. Is this the case?

Lilies are best sown in the autumn, when the seed is fresh. If they are left until spring, it is probable that they will remain dormant (fail to germinate) until the following spring, when they will be chilled into action by the winter frosts.

874

I have some tree peony seeds. How should I sow them?

Seeds of tree peony (*Paeonia lutea* and *P. suffruticosa*) are best sown as soon as they are ripe, normally about October. Plant them 25 mm (1 in) deep and 50 mm (2 in) apart in a deep seed tray of John Innes seed compost. Water the soil from below, so as not to disturb the seeds, and place the tray in a cold greenhouse or frame. Protect the seeds from mice, otherwise you may lose them all. Frost will not harm the seed; indeed, it is beneficial. Check the seeds regularly, but it may be some months before there are any signs of germination.

As soon as the seedlings are large enough to handle, prick out the strongest directly into a well-prepared nursery bed. Plant them 300-450 mm (12-18 in) apart and leave them undisturbed for 3-4 years before planting them out in their permanent positions.

875

How can I prevent seedlings from damping off? Every year I seem to spend pounds on seeds which produce nothing.

Damping-off is caused by a fungus disease which thrives when conditions are far from ideal. To prevent attack, always use freshly made compost, provide optimum environmental conditions (especially good ventilation), and use water which is clean and uncontaminated. Seeds should be sown thinly and evenly, as overcrowding will encourage the disease. Other preventive measures are to water the seed trays with a solution of Cheshunt compound fungicide or use a proprietary seed dressing.

876

When is the best time to sow alpine plants? I understand they require a cold period. Does this mean that I will not need a heated propagator?

Most alpines should be sown when fresh because their ability to germinate deteriorates. Alternatively, they should be sown in autumn or winter in pots and kept outside to expose them to a period of cold to overcome dormancy; it may take 6-18 months. With this treatment they should germinate easily in the spring months as soon as the temperature rises.

877

What is fluid sowing, and is it worth trying at home?

Fluid sowing is an excellent method to use with outdoor-sown seeds, especially early in the year because they will have been given a head start. The seeds are germinated on moist tissue paper in a sealed container kept at a temperature of about 21°C (70°F). As soon as the roots and shoots emerge the seeds are collected in a sieve and rinsed before being transferred to a jelly fluid, such as wallpaper paste. The germinated seeds are carefully mixed with the paste and then sown from a piping bag into prepared drills in moist soil. Sowing is usually even, which eliminates the need for later thinning, and the plants emerge much sooner than those sown in the conventional way. Fluid sowing is, however, a fiddly method, so that it should best be used only if you have had poor results from normal sowing techniques.

Division

878

What methods are used for propagating orchids? I have a small collection but would like more.

The method you use depends entirely on the type of orchids. Cymbidiums, for example, have squat, fattened stems called pseudobulbs and these can be removed and potted up individually. Vandas and pleiones are increased by offshoots, which are removed from the parent plants and potted individually. Dendrobiums can be increased by plantlets growing on the parent. These can be carefully removed when they start to put out roots, and transplanted into small pots. I would suggest that you invest in a good orchid book for beginners.

879

How do I take a cutting of an aspidistra?

Aspidistra and other clump-forming houseplants such as popular mother-in-law's tongue (*Sansevieria trifasciata*) are most effectively propagated by division. Remove the old plant from its pot and split it up. A single leaf with a bud and a few roots attached will grow if potted into a small pot of sandy compost.

880

When is the best time to divide pampas grass?

Old clumps are best divided in the spring when they are just starting into growth. They have a better chance to establish than plants divided in autumn. The crowns of old clumps may be exceptionally tough and these will need to be cut off with a sharp knife.

881

I have a large New Zealand flax (*Phormium tenax*) in my front garden which is getting a little too large for space available. It appears to be made up of several plants. Can these be divided and transplanted elsewhere?

Yes—in spring lift the plant and clean the soil from around the roots. Remove the offsets together with their own roots and plant them individually as soon as possible in their new positions.

882

A friend has asked me for some cuttings from plants in my garden. He has told me that I can divide herbaceous plants, of which I have plenty. Is he right? I would not like to spoil them.

Division is an easy way to propagate herbaceous plants, and is best done as a matter of course every three to five years to keep plants vigorous. It can be done in the autumn, but plants with fleshy crowns are best divided in early spring so that the largest buds can be seen. Large clumps are lifted and separated with the aid of two garden forks, which are pushed into the centre, back to back, and forced apart; or with a knife. Each piece should have several buds and plenty of young roots, or it may fail to establish itself.

Tubers & rhizomes

883

I have a garden pool which is so full of water lilies that the other plants are being swamped. Can I divide and repot them or is it necessary to start afresh?

You can remove the plants from the pond at any time between April and June. Cut the tubers into smaller pieces so that each contains a number of 'eyes' from which the new leaves are produced. Trim back the long, straggly roots and plant them individually in large baskets to help contain their growth.

884

I bought some dahlia tubers last year, and at the end of the season I lifted and stored them in a dry shed as recommended. I have been told that the best way to get more plants is to take cuttings from the old tubers. Please explain how I should do this.

Place the dahlia tubers in boxes and cover them with moist peat to just above their necks. Start them into growth in a greenhouse with a temperature of 7-10°C (45-50°F) in February. As soon as they begin to sprout, look out for good cuttings: select only strong, healthy shoots and trim them to just below

a pair of leaves so that they are about 75 mm (3 in) long. Dip the bases of the cuttings in a hormone rooting powder and put them individually in small pots of sandy compost. Keep them warm and transfer them to larger pots when they are rooted. Harden them off (*see* 28) in a cold frame or porch in May before planting them out in June.

885

I grew some achimenes from seed last year and have now dried off the plants for the winter. How do I start them into growth again in the spring?

Knock the dried-off plants out of their pots in spring and break up the rootballs to separate the brittle young tuberous rhizomes. Re-pot five or six of them in a 125 mm (5 in) pot in February or March. Use an ordinary potting compost and bury the rhizomes just below the surface. Place them in a temperature of 16°C (60°F) to boost them into growth, and keep them moist at all times.

886

I have heard that one can propagate tuberous begonias by division as well as from seed. Is that true, and, if so, how is it done?

Yes, they can be divided when they start into growth. Cut each tuber into several pieces, each with a bud, dust the cut edges with a fungicide, and leave your 'divisions' to dry overnight in a warm, dry room. Then plant them on the surface of some moist compost in trays. As soon as there is plenty of top-growth, transfer them individually to 125 mm (5 in) pots.

887

When is the best time to divide flag irises? I have a large border of them and a friend would like some.

Lift a clump of rhizomes with a fork immediately after the plants have flowered. Choose the younger parts on the outer edge of the clump (this is where most new growth is formed). Cut away the old part of the rhizomes to retain only a small portion of the current season's growth, with some roots and a small fan of leaves attached.

Bulbs & corms

888

Can hyacinths be propagated at home? I would like to grow some to give friends at Christmas.

Hyacinth propagation is a long-term pursuit, but the bulbs can be encouraged to produce bulblets quite simply by two methods, called scooping and scoring. They

are carried out at the end of the summer; and as their names imply, they involve cutting into the basal plate of the bulb. After the base has been scooped or scored to expose the inner scales, the surface should be dusted with a fungicide to prevent rot. Place the bulbs upside-down in a tray of dry sand and maintain a temperature of 21°C (70°F). New bulblets will develop in two or three months, and at this stage the bulbs should be planted, still upside down, to just below compost level in a pot. Place them in a cold frame for the winter.

In the spring the bulblets will shoot, while the old bulbs will die off. The small bulbs can then be re-planted and will flower in about three to four years. They will *not*, however, flower in time for Christmas: hyacinths need to be specially prepared by the bulb merchant or grower in order to flower so early in the season.

889

How can I increase the lilies I have in my garden, so that I can plant in drifts rather than in regimented lines?

Lily bulbs have loose scales which can be pulled off and propagated. The job is best done in October and November and strong healthy bulbs should be used. Gently remove the scales (they must be completely intact) and dust them with a fungicide powder. Mix them with damp peat and grit in a polythene bag and store them in a warm place. In about eight weeks, when bulbils have appeared at their base, the scales should be planted in pots of sandy compost so that their tips are just above the surface. Keep the young plants warm. The following spring the bulbils will produce leaves. Harden off the plants (*see* 28), and transfer them to their permanent position in the autumn.

890

The *Lilium* × *maculatum* in my garden have produced tiny bulbs in the leaf axils. If I pick and pot them on how long will I have to wait before they are ready for planting out?

The bulbils should be picked when mature; this is indicated by their changing in colour, and also by the leaves of the parent plant turning yellow. Place them on the surface of trays of a sandy compost, cover them with grit, and put them in a cold frame. They must remain there for at least 12 months before you plant them. They will probably flower the following year.

891

I have been told that some lilies can be propagated from bulblets. Where on the plant can I find these and how will I recognise them?

The bulblets (small bulbs) grow from the parent bulb of some species, such as the tiger lily

(*Lilium tigrinum*). The best time to look for the bulblets is in late summer, when the plants are dying back after flowering. Bulblets should not be confused with bulbils, which are found in the leaf axils of some species.

Layering

892

If I plant heathers too deep will the stems root? If so can I then divide and transplant them?

Yes, but this method is normally used only to propagate straggly plants which do not have much cutting material on them. They are usually lifted and planted deeper in the spring, just before growth begins. By the following autumn the branches will have rooted and individual plants can be cut off and transplanted. This operation is known as 'dropping'.

893

I have a rather large clematis which is bare at the base. I would like to propagate it, but do not want to cut out all the shoots in one go. What do you suggest I do?

You could try air-layering it. Choose a strong healthy shoot towards the top of the plant. Remove the leaves about 250 mm

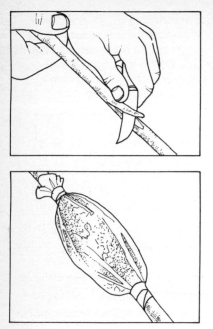

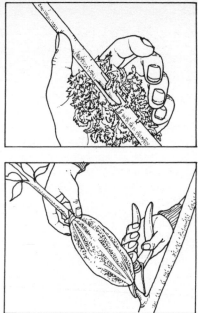

(10 in) below the tip and make a 50 mm (2 in) slit upwards into the stem, behind a leaf joint. Dust the wound with a hormone rooting powder, then pack behind the slit with some moist sphagnum moss. Place a sleeve of polythene over the area and seal it at top and bottom. Keep the moss moist at all times. When roots become visible sever the rooted plant from the parent and pot it on.

894

What is the best way to propagate rhododendrons? I do not have a greenhouse, only a cold frame.

The simplest way is to layer the plant *in situ*. Prune some of the lower branches of your rhododendron in the winter to induce vigorous growth. Fork over the soil, adding some peat, in a circle around the plant. In the following summer remove most of the leaves about 100 mm (4 in) below the tip from a few of the strongest new shoots. Bend the stems down to ground level and peg them to secure them in the bottom of individual trenches 100-150 mm (4-6 in) deep. Firm the shoots in and water them well. The following autumn the new plants can be severed from the parent. Nip out the tip of each shoot to encourage a bushy habit. One year later lift the plants and transplant them to their permanent growing sites.

895

What is French layering? I have been told that you can easily propagate a number of shrubs in this way.

This is a good method to use to propagate shrubs such as the dogwoods (*Cornus*), which are normally cut hard back each year to encourage growth of their brightly coloured young stems in the winter. In the spring, reduce the number of new shoots on each shrub to 9 or 10 and trim the tips so that each shoot is about the same length. Peg these stems horizontally on the ground. The buds will shoot and grow vertically, and when they are 50-75 mm (2-3 in) long, bury them 50 mm (2 in) deep, leaving just the shoot-tips exposed. Continue to earth up the shoots as they grow until the mound is about 150 mm (6 in) high. In the autumn remove the soil to expose the rooted shoots. They can then be cut into individual plants and transplanted.

896

My neighbour's blackberry bush is trailing over the fence into my garden. She has told me that if I stick the shoot tips into the ground, I will get some plants of my own. Is she right?

Yes. Select strong new stems in July and August and peg them down in the bottom of a 100 mm (4 in) deep hole, replacing the soil

on top of them. Keep them well watered. In autumn sever the old stem from the newly developing plant. By the following spring your new plants will be well rooted and ready for transplanting.

Stem & root cuttings

897

How do I go about selecting the right plant material for cuttings?

Cuttings should always be taken from clean healthy plants which have strong vigorous growth. The type of cuttings you can take will generally depend on what facilities you have to root them.

Softwood cuttings are taken in the spring and root most readily if given heat from below. Semi-ripe cuttings (those prepared from the current year's shoots) are a little more tough, being woody at the base and soft at the top, and they will usually root well in a cold frame. Hardwood cuttings are taken in the autumn and winter months and will root slowly outdoors in the open ground.

898

Why are most cuttings taken below a leaf joint?

The area of stem around the leaf joint (node) is much harder and more resistant to rot, so it is usually suggested as the site for taking very soft cuttings. It is also the point at which root-inducing chemicals are most effective.

899

Is it possible to take cuttings of *Magnolia grandiflora*?

The magnolias are not the easiest trees and shrubs to propagate, but the simplest way is to take cuttings of semi-ripe wood in the summer. Such cuttings should be about 75-100 mm (3-4 in) long, preferably with a 'heel' (*see* 904) of old wood. While it is best to root these in a heated frame, they will probably root outdoors if you give them a sheltered place and a soil which is both well-drained and yet not likely to dry out.

900

Can I store cuttings for any length of time before inserting them?

Yes, but be sure to collect only strong, healthy cuttings from pest- and disease-free plants. Place the cuttings immediately into a labelled polythene bag. Keep the bag in a

cool place such as the salad drawer of the fridge. Here the cuttings will remain fresh for a few days.

901

Why is it necessary to wound cuttings to encourage rooting? I always though this treatment would attract disease.

Wounding the base of woody cuttings is beneficial especially with those which are difficult to root, such as rhododendrons. It seems to stimulate root formation, and the cut area allows the roots to emerge from the stem more readily. For the greatest benefit the cuttings should be treated with a hormone rooting compound after wounding.

902

Last year I got very few cuttings from my pelargoniums, which were bedded cut in the garden. How can I encourage more growth so that I can produce more plants next year?

Take your first cutting in the summer from non-flowering shoots or from those which have just flowered. This will encourage the plants to bush out and produce a second flush of cuttings at the end of the season. Lift the plants before the first frost and pot on any which are healthy and not too woody. Bring these into the greenhouse to gently force more shoots for cuttings in spring. The plants produced from cuttings in the summer will be quite large by March and can be robbed of more cuttings which will produce small rooted plants for bedding out in June.

903

I have a large rubber plant which is starting to lose its lower leaves. Is it possible to propagate it to get several plants or is the only way to air layer it for one?

To get several plants, cut the softer part of the stem (avoiding the extreme tip) into 25 mm (1 in) pieces each with a leaf attached. Roll each leaf into a tube and secure it with a rubber band. Dip the cut stem base in a hormone rooting powder and insert your cuttings individually in small pots filled with a sandy compost. Support each cutting with a cane through the centre of the leaf roll to keep it upright. Place all the cuttings in a warm, humid environment until they are well rooted. At a soil temperature of 21-24°C (70-75°F) rooting will take four to six weeks.

904

I have read that some cuttings should have a 'heel' of bark at the base. What are the advantages of this?

Semi-ripe or half-ripe cuttings are often taken with a 'heel' of older wood. Although older wood is slow to produce roots, it dries out more

slowly than younger shoots and will not rot so easily. You can also root these tougher cuttings in a closed cold frame rather than in a heated propagator.

905

I want to propagate a large berberis in my garden so that eventually I can make a people-proof hedge around my house. What is the most reliable method to propagate it?

You can take half-ripe (firm but bendy) cuttings at the end of the summer from side-shoots of current year's wood. Cut the shoots 150 mm (6 in) long, each with a plug of hardwood at the base, so that it resembles a mallet, and trim off the soft tip. Insert the cuttings around the edges of pots of sandy compost and root them in a closed cold frame.

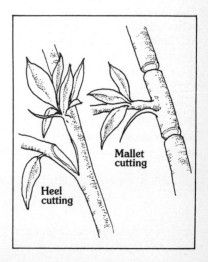

Mallet cutting

Heel cutting

The following spring, line out the rooted cuttings in nursery rows outdoors. Grow them on for a couple of years before transplanting them to their permanent positions.

906

Some conifer cuttings I took during the summer have produced a hard, nobbly base but no roots. What has caused this, and will it affect rooting?

This is called callus and usually develops around a wound when favourable conditions for rooting are provided. It appears to be essential in the process of forming roots. The acidity of the soil can affect the production of callus: if there is too much lime, the callus may be hard and prevent roots from breaking through. I wonder if you have been checking for root-growth too often? Each time you lift the cutting, another tiny wound is made which has to callus over before rooting occurs. I suggest you remove the hard callus with a sharp knife and start afresh.

907

I would like to grow houseplants by the hydroculture method. Is this possible and can I take cuttings from soil-grown plants and insert them immediately in water?

Yes—hundreds of different kinds of houseplants have responded well to hydroculture—even cacti. Vegetables, especially tomatoes and cucumber, can also be grown by this method. Cuttings are taken in the normal way. Stand them in water (supported by an 'inert medium' such as clay granules), and root them in a warm, humid environment.

Plants tend to establish quicker by this method; oxygen reaches the roots easily, and there is no competition from pests or toxic substances sometimes present in compost. The main advantage, however, is that it is virtually impossible to kill the plants by over-watering; and since they will thrive for a month or longer without more water needing to be added, they present no worries if you are going away on holiday. Special soluble fertilisers are available for adding when you top up the water.

908

What are pipings? I have read that carnations and pinks are propagated this way, and would like to try the method.

Pipings are softwood cuttings taken from the very tip of a plant. They are not trimmed with a knife but simply pulled off with a finger and thumb. Each cutting should have two or three leaves and be about 75-100 mm (3-4 in) long. Dip the base of each cutting in a hormone rooting powder, then insert them 25 mm (1 in) apart around the edge of a pot of sandy compost.

Rooting will take 6-8 weeks at a temperature of 16-18°C (61-64°F). Carnations and pinks do respond particularly well to this method.

909

I am worried that a bamboo plant in my garden might die as it has not looked at all well lately: its leaves turn yellow and then fall, and new growth appears to be stunted. Can I propagate the few remaining canes?

You could try taking cuttings if there are any two-year-old canes left; these are found on the outer edge of the plant, and will still be fairly flexible. Cut them into sections 300 mm (12 in) long and insert them in a deep pot of compost. Root them in a warm greenhouse.

910

What is the difference between softwood and greenwood cuttings? I have read that chrysanthemums are propagated from greenwood.

The difference between softwood and greenwood cuttings is slight. Softwoods are taken from the first flush of growth in spring. Greenwoods are taken slightly later, when the wood at the base of the cutting is a little firmer, so that they will not root quite so quickly; they should be used to propagate only plants such as pelargoniums and delphiniums that root readily.

911

How do I take rhododendron cuttings? I have several large-flowered hybrids in my new but untidy garden. I would like eventually to replace them all with young plants.

Cuttings can be taken from mid-July to August. Make them 100 mm (4 in) long, remove the lower leaves, and pinch out the soft tip; cut the large remaining leaves in half to reduce their surface area. Make a wound 25 mm (1 in) at the base and dip the cuttings in a hormone rooting powder before inserting them in trays of lime-free compost. Root them in a heated propagator with a bottom heat of 21°C (70°F).

When they are rooted and new shoots are seen to be growing, pot the cuttings into 75 mm (3 in) pots of peaty compost. Grow them on in a frost-free greenhouse, and then in spring harden them off in a closed cold-frame. Pot them on and stand them in a cool, shady part of the garden for the summer. Plant them in their permanent positions at any time between September and April.

912

Is it necessary to have a greenhouse to propagate junipers from cuttings?

No, you can root these and any of the hardy shrubs in a closed cold-frame—but it will take much longer than if they were in a heated propagator. Cuttings are taken in the summer, before the new growth has had time to toughen. Make the cuttings 50-100 mm (2-4 in) long and dip their lower ends in hormone rooting powder. They may take anything from one to six months to root.

913

I would like to take some conifer cuttings so that I can increase the length of my existing hedge. What is the best time to do this, and how should I take the cuttings?

Take the cuttings between July and September. Select vigorous shoots with a strong growing point, and make the cuttings 100-150 mm (4-6 in) long with a heel of older wood. Apply a hormone rooting powder to the base of the cuttings and root them in trays of free-draining compost in a heated propagator or an unheated frame. When they are rooted, which may take six months, pot them individually into 75 mm (3 in) pots. The following autumn, if the plants are full of roots, transplant them to their final positions.

914

When is the best time to take cuttings from evergreen plants, and how do I go about it?

Evergreen cuttings are usually taken from ripe wood in early summer and autumn and rooted in a cold frame. They can be anything from 50 to 150 mm (2-6 in) long, depending on the size of the plant, and preferably with a heel of older wood. Strip off the lower leaves, and if there is no heel make a wound about 13 mm (½ in) long at the base of the cuttings. Apply a hormone rooting powder and insert the cuttings to half their depth in soil, inside a cold frame, that has been forked over, manured, and fertilised a week or two beforehand. Water them well and close the frame completely. Inspect them regularly, and harden them off during the summer to prepare them for planting out the following autumn.

915

I have tried several times to grow forsythias from hardwood cuttings without success. I usually take cuttings 250-350 mm (10-14 in) long during the summer, and I have tried rooting them both in a frame and in the open ground. The last batch dried up. What am I doing wrong?

It is certainly possible to propagate forsythias from hardwood cuttings in October. One problem, however, is that they have a soft centre, which means they will rot or dry out quite easily. An easy way to overcome this is to seal the ends of the cutting with melted candle wax. Drying out will also be discouraged if you make the cuttings slightly shorter than normal—about 150-200 mm (6-8 in) long—and insert them so that only 25 mm (1 in) is exposed above the ground.

916

I have been given a tall, spindly plant called dumb cane (*Dieffenbachia*). It has very few leaves remaining and these are turning yellow. Can I propagate it, or should I admit defeat and throw it out?

First I would suggest you cut the plant right back to encourage new shoots. The stems removed can then be used for cuttings. Cut the leafless stems into 50 mm (2 in) sections, each below a leaf joint at the base and above a leaf joint at the top. Place them upright in a pot of sandy compost. Keep them in a heated propagator until roots are formed and the latent buds develop into shoots. After the cuttings have rooted and are showing signs of growth, move them from the propagator to the greenhouse staging, maintaining a temperature of about 13°C (65°F).

917

Can heathers be propagated from cuttings? I have tried to root some on several occasions but have not had much success.

Take heel or nodal cuttings about 38 mm (1½ in) long in August from non-flowering shoots. Root

them in a sandy compost in a closed cold frame. Harden-off the cuttings gradually once they have rooted. This will take about two months, after which they are lifted for potting or planted where they are to grow.

918

When is the best time to propagate plants from root cuttings?

During the dormant period of the plants concerned. This is usually the winter, but for some (the spring-flowering alpines particularly) the end of autumn is preferable.

919

I understand that my drumstick primula (*Primula denticulata*) can be propagated by root cuttings. Could you explain the method?

The root cuttings are taken in December and January from the

strongest and healthiest roots. Cut them into 50-75 mm (2-3 in) pieces and lay them horizontally in boxes filled with compost. Cover them with some finely sieved soil and place them in a cold frame or greenhouse, where they will form shoots and new roots. Plant them out in spring.

Other plants that can be propagated successfully from root cuttings include anemones, pulsatillas, mulleins (*Verbascum*), poppy (*Papaver*), phlox, and eryngiums.

920

I have just removed an untidy specimen of stag's-horn sumach from my garden. Now I notice lots of miniature sumachs growing around the same spot. A friend has suggested they are roots bursting into growth. Is he right?

Yes—stag's-horn sumach (*Rhus typhina*) can be propagated from root segments. The severed roots will have been induced into growth and to get rid of them you will need to fork out the young plants as they arise.

921

Which is the best way to insert root cuttings—vertically or horizontally?

It depends on the roots. Slender ones are best laid horizontally on the compost, as they are likely to

break if pushed in vertically. Thicker roots lend themselves to vertical insertion, but you must be certain which is the top and which is the bottom of the cutting. The best way to ensure this is to make a flat cut at the top of the cutting (the end farther from the stem) and a sloping cut at the lower end.

Leaf cuttings

922

I was recently given a plant the donor referred to as umbrella grass. Its leaves are now turning yellow. Can I propagate it before it dies?

This species (*Cyperus alternifolius*) can be divided during the summer months, but in your case the method may not be satisfactory, so I suggest you take cuttings. Remove a head of leaves complete with a short piece of stem. Place this *upside down* on some wet compost and maintain a temperature of 16°C (61°F). Roots and shoots will soon develop, and when the young plant is established pot it on.

923

I would like to grow-on the leafy top of a pineapple fruit that I bought recently. How do I go about it?

First, make sure that the leaves are

fresh—if they are too dry they will not grow. Slice off the top of the fruit 38 mm (1½ in) below the leaves, and trim away most of the fruit flesh so that only the hard core remains. Let this dry out for a couple of days, then pot it into a moist, sandy potting mix. Cover with a glass dome (or a polythene bag supported by two canes) and maintain a minimum temperature of 18°C (64°F). Roots should form within a couple of months, and then they can be potted on into a 150 mm (6 in) pot of loamless compost and grown on in a warm temperature. Do *not*, however, expect your plant to produce fat, luscious pineapples in the British climate!

924

I have grown some cape primroses from seed, and a friend tells me I can propagate them by chopping up a leaf and laying the pieces on top of some compost. Is this true?

Yes, these plants (*Streptocarpus*) will propagate quite easily from leaf cuttings. Choose good strong leaves and, with a sharp knife, cut them into segments about 50 mm (2 in) long. Insert them shallowly on their edges into compost—in a seed tray, (making sure that the sap flow runs upwards), and put them in a heated propagator with a bottom heat of 21°C (70°F) with a humid environment. Young plantlets should appear within a couple of months, and as soon as

they are large enough to handle they can be potted on individually. The popular Rex begonia hybrids can be propagated in much the same way. Cut a large leaf into squares and place each, lightly weighted down, on the surface of the compost.

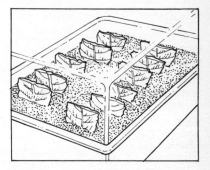

925

Are African violets easy to grow from cuttings? I have a large healthy plant but would not like to spoil it by taking cuttings if they have little chance of rooting.

African violets (*Saintpaulia*) are quite easy to grow from cuttings, which can be taken at any time of the year. Select fully mature healthy leaves and remove them from the plant complete with their stalks. With a sharp knife trim the stalks to 50 mm (2 in) in length, and insert them to just above the base of the leaf in a tray of rooting compost. Water them in, and place in a heated propagator with a bottom heat of 20°C (70°F). Within two months tiny plantlets will develop. As soon as these are large enough to handle, pot them on and harden them off before putting them on the greenhouse staging.

926

Why have the rooted cuttings of my variegated (yellow-and-green) mother-in-law's tongue turned out to be all-green?

The variegated mother-in-law's tongue (*Sansevieria trifasciata* 'Laurentii') is what is called a periclinal chimera, which refers to a genetic condition in which two completely different and incompatable cells are found in layers. If propagated from leaf sections the new plants will revert—as in your example—to all-green. The only way to perpetuate your striped form is to propagate it by division.

Wait until your plant has plenty of leaves and the pot is full of roots. The shoots required arise from underground rhizomes, and those pieces of shoot that have two or three leaves attached can be severed from the parent and potted individually.

Budding & grafting

927

Why are some plants grafted? Can this be done at home?

Grafting is the name given to the process of joining the root system of one plant (called the rootstock) with the top of another (called the scion), so that they form a solid union and grow as one plant. It is often done to plants which do not grow well on their own roots, but is used mainly to transfer the desirable characteristics of the rootstock to another plant. Such a roostock usually controls the plant's vigour or size, but it may also imbue the scion, or top half of the plant, with pest- and disease-resistance.

There are many different techniques. Whip-and-tongue grafting is the method most often used by nurserymen for grafting fruit and ornamental trees. Splice grafting is a simplified version of this. The easiest method for amateurs is known as cleft grafting. You cut a wedge-shape in the top of the rootstock with a clean, sharp knife, then trim the base of the scion so that it fits snugly into the wedge. Now bind the graft securely with raffia and seal it with wax to prevent the graft from drying out.

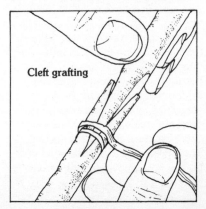

Cleft grafting

928

I would like to try budding some roses in my garden. How should I do this?

First you will need to buy suitable rootstocks from a specialist rose grower. Plant these in the autumn and earth them up around their necks to keep the budding area supple.

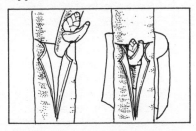

In the following summer select a shoot from a large or cluster-flowered rose which has just flowered, remove any thorns, and trim back the leaves. Clear the soil from around the rootstock, make a T-shaped cut in the neck and slightly peel back the flaps of bark.

Now remove the bud from the selected 'bud stick' by cutting out a piece of stem about 25 mm (1 in) long. Insert this behind the flaps of bark on the rootstock and trim it neatly to the top of the T-shape before covering it with a rubber budding patch. The bud will probably knit into place before the end of the season. In late winter, cut back the rootstock to just above the bud and allow the new bud to develop. Transplant the bush the following autumn to its flowering position.

929

I would like to try my hand at grafting cacti. Which varieties are best and what do I do?

Good stock for most grafted plants are the hardy cereus-type species, opuntia, and echinopsis. The best time to graft is in spring and early summer. Cut the stock flat across the top, make a similar-sized cut on the base of the scion and place the two together so that the tissues match as nearly as possible. Hold them closely together with rubber bands and leave them in a warm dry place until the stock and scion have united.

Offsets & runners

930

Is it best to cut strawberry runners off the plant and root them in a greenhouse?

No. Keep the runners attached to the parent plant so that they can sap energy from it while they form their own roots. Sink pots of John Innes No 1 potting compost into the earth around each plant to be propagated, and peg the runners into the compost. When the young plants grow away and have increased considerably in size, with plenty of new growth, sever their 'umbilical cords'. Remove them from their pots and plant them out about 450 mm (18 in) apart.

931

I have noticed small plantlets appearing on the leaves of a potted asplenium fern I bought last year. Can these be removed and potted on?

The fern *Asplenium bulbiferum* does produce plantlets on its leaves. To propagate, the whole leaf should be removed and pegged flat on a tray of compost. The plantlets will then establish their own roots and within a couple of months may be detached and potted on.

932

A large yucca in my garden has some smaller plants growing from it. Can these be removed and rooted, so that I might use them elsewhere to fill a gap?

Yes—sever them from the parent plant and pot them up in containers of sandy compost. Keep them in a warm greenhouse so that they can establish their own roots, then harden them off before planting them outside.

Miscellaneous

933

How do I harden-off plants which have been recently propagated in the greenhouse?

If plants are being moved from one

temperature to another they need to acclimatize slowly so that they suffer as little check as possible. In progressing from the greenhouse to the garden, plants need to be put in a cold frame as a sort of halfway house. For the first few days, keep the frame completely closed; then gradually apply a little ventilation, at first during the day only, until finally the glass can be removed completely. The plants are then ready for planting out.

934

As an inexperienced gardener I'm interested in trying my hand at plant propagation. Could you suggest a check-list of easy subjects?

The following are all easy to propagate by the various standard methods. Check with previous answers for details of technique.

SEED
Columbine (*Aquilegia*), sown outdoors in late spring; pot marigold (*Calendula*), sown outdoors in spring or autumn; flame nettle (*Coleus*), sown in greenhouse in January-April; Persian violet (*Exacum*), sown in greenhouse in spring or autumn; Transvaal daisy (*Gerbera*), sown in greenhouse in March-April; polka-dot plant (*Hypoestes*), sown in greenhouse in spring; marigold (*Tagetes*), sown in greenhouse, February-April.

CUTTINGS
Softwood cuttings taken from new

growth in spring and rooted under glass: chrysanthemums, dahlias, dianthus, fuchsia, busy-lizzie (*Impatiens*), regal, zonal, and ivy-leaved geraniums (*Pelargonium*), wandering jew (*Tradescantia*).

Semi-ripe cuttings taken from growth just starting to turn woody in summer and rooted in cold frame: berberis, cotoneaster, elaeagnus, erica, hebe, hydrangea, honeysuckle (*Lonicera*), potentilla, syringia.

Hardwood cuttings taken from mature woody growth in winter and rooted outdoors: dogwood (*Cornus*), deutzia, privet (*Ligustrum*), flowering currant (*Ribes*), willow (*Salix*), tamarisk (*Tamarix*), weigela.

Leaf cuttings taken in summer when plant is in active growth: begonia (*B. rex* and *B. masoniana*), sinningia (*Gloxinia*), mother-in-law's tongue (*Sansevieria*), cape primrose (*Streptocarpus*).

Root cuttings taken when plants are dormant in winter and rooted in cold frame: anchusa, aralia, eryngium, limonium, phlox, drumstick primrose (*Primula dentata*), stag's-horn sumach (*Rhus typhina*).

LAYERING
Done with new growth in spring and summer, outdoors: clematis, dianthus, erica, jasmine (*Jasminum*), honeysuckle (*Lonicera*), Virginia creeper (*Parthenocissus*).

DIVISION
Done outside in autumn or spring: herbaceous perennials, erica, rose of Sharon (*Hypericum*), kerria, pernettya, butcher's broom (*Ruscus*).

OFFSETS & RUNNERS
Naturally produced, can be removed and transplanted when large enough: spider plant (*Chlorophytum*), mother-of-thousands (*Saxifraga stolonifera*), house leek (*Sempervivum*), pick-a-back plant (*Tolmiea*), urn plant (*Vriesea*).

935

How are plants cloned, and what are their advantages? Plants produced this way are always slightly more expensive, and I often wonder if it is worth paying the extra cash.

A clone is a group of plants which originate from a single specimen, which has been grown from seed or produced as a mutation from another plant. Cloned plants can be reproduced only by vegetative means, such as cuttings, layers, and grafts; and every plant is identical to its parent. Plants are cloned because they have desirable characteristics which are better than those in other available varieties and which cannot be passed on through the seeds.

Dr Joe Stubbs

Freelance writer; formerly a research scientist on plant pathology and the control of weeds; author of a book on garden pests.

Pests
and
Diseases

Flower problems

936

My chrysanthemums are infested with reddish-brown insects which look like greenfly. What are they?

These are indeed aphids. Although we talk about greenflies and blackflies, in reality these insects range in colour from pale yellowish-green through pink and dark brown to purplish-black. They are all sap feeders, weakening and distorting the plants. In addition they transmit virus diseases and deposit sticky honeydew which becomes covered with sooty moulds, further disfiguring the foliage. Some control is provided by predators such as ladybirds, lacewings, and hover flies but it is usually necessary to spray the plants with a greenfly killer or general insecticide. Sprays based on pirimicarb are specially valuable because they kill the aphids but have no ill effect on the predators.

937

Many of the plants in my garden are disfigured with white, spittle-like foam in the leaf and flower axils. Is this due to a pest or is it a disease?

The masses of foam, sometimes called 'cuckoo spit', are produced by the sap sucking larvae of the common frog-hopper. Attacked plants are weakened and their growth may be distorted. Light attacks can be dealt with by picking off the larvae. Heavier attacks are best controlled by using a forcible spray of general insecticide.

938

The young leaves on my annual asters and hydrangeas are showing numerous small brownish spots and some of the older leaves are becoming ragged. What is the cause of this trouble?

These symptoms are typical of capsid attack. These bugs are difficult to spot since they drop off the plants when disturbed. The damage spots are caused by them piercing the plant tissue to feed on the sap. Heavy attacks cause distorted growth and may even result in 'blind' shoots. Many types of plants are subject to attack. Control by repeated spraying with a general insecticide, and also spray the ground under the plants.

939

Caterpillars cause quite a lot of damage in my garden but I don't like to kill them as I love to see the butterflies. What do you advise?

Caterpillars on garden plants are mostly the larvae of moths. Indeed the only butterflies which commonly cause damage are the large and small cabbage whites. These species are still all too common in spite of the control measures taken by most gardeners. Killing a few caterpillars in your garden will not seriously reduce the moth population since they also breed on a wide range of wild plants. Caterpillars can be controlled by hand picking or by spraying with a general insecticide. Permethrin-based products give particularly long-lasting control.

940

Some of the young shoots of my delphiniums have been bitten through, and similar damage has appeared on my tulips. Can this be slug damage?

Slugs or snails are indeed the likely cause of the trouble. These pests also eat large ragged holes in plant leaves. Both pests, however, generally feed at night and hide during the daytime. Slugs and snails are fairly readily controlled by the use of slug pellets. Alternatively, they can be caught in special traps if you do not want to use a pesticide.

941

Could you identify the tiny, dark-coloured, slender insects which have begun to infest the shoots, leaves, and flowers of some of my plants?

These are almost certainly thrips (thunder-flies) which feed by scratching the surface tissue and sucking up the sap. Damaged

leaves show a fine, pale yellow mottling, while flowers develop white flecks on the petals. Thrips also exude small liquid drops which get covered with a brown mould. Not only do they weaken and disfigure the plants but they also transmit some virus diseases. Thrips are readily controlled by general insecticides.

942

Deep notches have developed in the leaf margins of several of my shrubs but there is no sign of any pest. How and when does this damage occur?

This type of notching is characteristic of vine weevil damage and can occur on a wide variety of shrubs. Other weevils eat holes in leaves and also gnaw the young stems. These small, wingless beetles live in the soil and feed only at night. Control them by repeat sprays of a general insecticide applied to both the bushes and the surrounding soil.

943

What is the cause of the thin yellow, twisted lines which have developed on the leaves of many of my plants?

These 'mines' are produced by the caterpillars and maggots of leaf-mining moths and flies. Some species of leaf miners, however, produce rounded blister-like blotch mines. Established plants are weakened and disfigured by these pests, while young plants may be killed. Carnation fly, which produces blotch mines on carnations, pinks, and sweet williams (all species of *Dianthus*), is particularly damaging since the maggot may migrate into the stem, killing the shoot. Here the best approach is to remove and burn the affected leaves. In other cases spray with an insecticide at the first signs of attack.

Flowers

944

My wallflowers seem to be very stunted this year and are tending to wilt in warm weather. What can have caused this?

From your description of the trouble it seems likely that your wallflowers (*Cheiranthus*) have been attacked by cabbage-root fly (*Delia brassicae*). You can easily confirm this by digging up one of the wilted plants and examining the roots for the presence of the fly maggots. Incidentally, this pest can also attack aubrieta and stocks (*Matthiola*). Prevent future attacks by dressing the seed rows and the transplants with a soil-insecticide powder. Apply also a heavy soil-drench of insecticide based on pirimiphos-methyl or trichlorphon.

945

Brown powdery spots have developed on the undersides of the leaves of my antirrhinums and the plants are not doing at all well. What is the cause of this trouble?

Your antirrhinums have become infected with antirrhinum rust (*Puccinia antirrhini*), which can be very destructive. If the infection is still fairly light you should start a programme of sprays at intervals of 10-14 days using benomyl or thiram. If, however, most of the leaves are infected it is better to cut the shoots back hard and then protect the new growth by repeat sprays. Rust-resistant varieties of antirrhinums are now available from nurseries and should be used for future plantings.

946

As my Brompton stock plants were showing poor growth I dug one up and found that the roots were swollen and distorted. Could this be a form of clubroot?

Yes. It is not generally appreciated that clubroot (*Plasmodiophora brassicae*) not only attacks brassicas (the cabbage family) but can also infect stocks (*Matthiola*) and wallflowers (*Cheiranthus*). For long-term control the beds should be limed before sowing or planting out and a clubroot-control powder applied to the seed drills and planting holes.

947

The flowers of my chrysanthemums are beginning to rot. Some show browning only of the inner florets, while others are completely brown. Can you tell me what has caused this damage?

Since the damage starts in the centre of the blooms, this rot is caused by an attack of the fungus disease called ray blight (*Mycosphaerella ligulicola*). The disease is favoured by hot, humid conditions, so the risk of attack is reduced if plenty of ventilation is given. It is also worthwhile applying a protective spray of benomyl, mancozeb, or triforine before the blooms open.

948

The outer florets of my chrysanthemums are beginning to rot. What is the cause, and is there a suitable treatment?

Chrysanthemum flowers are prone to a number of diseases. Since, however, the damage is showing up first on the outer florets the probable cause is petal blight (*Itersonilia perplexans*). The first sign of this disease is the appearance of small water-soaked spots on the outer florets. It then spreads inwards to spoil the bloom. This disease is favoured by wet weather and can be prevented by repeat sprays of fungicides containing benomyl, mancozeb, or thiram.

949

Some of the shoots of my peonies are rotting at the base and are becoming covered with a grey mould. Nearby leaves have brown patches. What can I do to cure this trouble?

Your peonies (*Paeonia*) have been attacked by wilt (*Botrytis paeoniae*) and you need to take immediate action to save them. Cut out the infected shoots well below ground level and apply a copper dust to the crowns. Follow this treatment by applying repeat sprays of benomyl or thiram to the foliage.

950

My dahlia flowers are being notched and chewed up by some pest. What action can I take?

Dahlia and chrysanthemum flowers are commonly attacked by earwigs, which can also damage the foliage. This not only spoils their appearance but increases the risk of grey mould invading the blooms. Regular spraying at fortnightly intervals with a general insecticide is one way of controlling these pests. An alternative approach is to trap the earwigs in inverted flower pots filled with straw or dried grass and placed on top of the plant support. Petroleum jelly smeared around the stems will also prevent the pests getting to the flowers, provided that it is renewed regularly.

951

The foliage and stems of my chrysanthemums are beginning to get covered with a white powdery deposit. How do I deal with it?

This trouble is caused by a powdery mildew (*Oidium chrysanthemi*). The initial infection is usually on the underside of the lowerleaves, and the upward spread of the disease can be checked by repeat sprays of a mildew fungicide such as benomyl, bupirimate, carbendazim, or thiophanatemethyl. These should be applied every 10-14 days.

952

This year there were quite a few gaps in my established bed of daffodils, and some bulbs developed only a circle of grassy leaves. What produced this effect and how can I prevent it in future?

Assuming your bulbs are well fed and in a spot that suits them, the likeliest cause is an attack by narcissus flies (*Merodon equestris*). These flies lay their eggs on the neck of the bulb, and the emerging maggots bore into the base of the bulb, destroying the central parts. When the foliage has died down you should dig up the bulbs and reject any which are rotten or show tiny entrance holes in the base. From the end of April protect freshly planted bulbs by repeat applications of an insecticidal dust.

953

What is the cause of the angular brown and black areas which are showing on the lower leaves of some of my chrysanthemums?

This damage indicates that the plants are infested with chrysanthemum leaf and bud eelworm (*Aphelenchoides ritzemabosi*). Infested plants must not be selected for propagation as this will only spread the disease. They can, however, be saved from further damage by ringing the stem above the topmost damaged leaf with petroleum jelly every week or two. This pest can also attack asters, delphiniums, phlox and pyrethrums, for all of which the treatment is the same.

954

The young flower buds on my sweet peas are turning yellow and dropping off instead of developing into flowers. Is there any way of preventing this?

This type of bud drop on sweet pea (*Lathyrus odoratus*), which can also occur on camellias and wisterias, is caused by unsuitable cultural conditions, not by a pest or disease. The commonest cause is shortage of water during bud formation. Shortage of potash and phosphate fertilisers, coupled with an excess of nitrogen, may also be contributory factors. Liquid feeding with a well-balanced fertiliser and regular watering should relieve the problem; surface mulching also helps.

955

Checking over my planting of Solomon's seal, I found that many of the leaves were completely shredded but I could see no trace of any pest. What coud have caused this damage?

The pest which has attacked your Solomon's seal (*Polygonatum × hybridum*) is the Solomon's-seal sawfly (*Phymatocera aterrima*). This fly lays its eggs in early summer and the caterpillars which hatch out then start feeding on the undersides of the leaves in June. When fully fed they drop off onto the soil to pupate. You can protect your plants next year by applying an insecticide based on longlasting permethrin in early June.

956

Some of my pansies are dying from a stem rot. Could this be due to the fact that the soil is heavy clay?

Pansies (*Viola × wittrockiana*) are liable to suffer from stem rot in heavy soil which is poorly drained. You should therefore improve your soil by digging in plenty of sharp sand, grit, or bulky organic matter such as compost, peat, or composted bark. Several fungi are associated with this rot, so I would advise you to sprinkle calomel

(mercurous chloride) dust in the planting holes.

957

Some of my tulips emerged looking very distorted and stunted. Nearby bulbs are now developing yellowish streaky spots on their foliage. What action should I take?

Your tulips have been infected with the disease called tulip fire (*Botrytis tulipae*). In moist conditions this can spread very rapidly throughout the planting. First dig up and destroy any badly affected bulbs. Then spray the remainder with one of the fungicides based on benomyl or thiram.

958

Brown ring-like powdery growths have begun to appear on the undersides of the leaves on my geranium plants. Could this be a form of rust and, if so, what can I do about it?

The brown powdery rings on the leaves of your geraniums (*Pelargonium × hortorum*) indicate that the plants have become infected with pelargonium rust (*Puccinia pelargonii-zonalis*). Heavily infected leaves should be removed and burnt and the plants then sprayed with a fungicide containing mancozeb, thiram, or triforine. Repeat sprays at 10-14 day intervals will be needed to protect the new growth effectively against this disease.

Shrub problems

959

One of the shoots of my clematis suddenly wilted and died back to ground level. The remaining shoots are still apparently healthy. What can have caused this dieback?

The situation you describe is typical of an attack by clematis wilt, caused by the fungus *Ascochyta clematidina*. This is a poorly understood disease, but I can assure you that the trouble is not likely to spread to the remaining healthy shoots. If you cut off the dead shoot you will probably get re-growth from its base. No further remedial action is called for.

960

Last year the foliage on a branch of my blue atlas cedar (*Cedrus atlantica* 'Glauca') turned grey and then became brown. This year the whole tree has suddenly died. What can have caused this loss?

The most likely cause is an attack by honey fungus (*Armillaria mellea*). This soil-borne fungus disease penetrates the tree roots and then grows upwards to the base of the trunk, causing the tree to die. You can easily check for the presence of honey fungus by chipping off some bark from the base of the trunk: you should find a sheet of white fungal growth on the surface of the wood. Most types of trees and shrubs, involving hedging plants are subject to attack. Dig up and burn the dead tree, including as much of its roots as possible; then sterilise the soil with a special tar oil emulsion, specially designed for use against honey fungus before replanting.

961

The tips of some branches of my flowering cherry seem to have died back. The branches were girdled by rough cankers. How can I prevent further damage?

Your tree is infected with cherry bacterial canker (*Pseudomonas mors-prunorum*). Protect against further attacks by applying a series of three sprays with a copper fungicide applied at intervals of three weeks from the end of August.

962

The foliage of my pyracantha, which earlier produced a splendid crop of flowers and looked perfectly healthy, has gradually turned brown and now the whole bush seems to be dead. What can have caused this collapse?

The disease affecting your pyracantha is called fireblight and is due to infection by the bacterium *Erwinia amylovora*. This disease enters through the flowers and then progresses down the shoots. Fireblight can also attack apples, pears, cotoneaster, hawthorn, whitebeam, and mountain ash as well as pyracantha. Report any suspected attack to your county horticultural officer or to your park superintendent, who will advise on what action to take.

963

The leaves of my Oregon grape have become covered with a grey powdery growth. What is this, and how should I deal with it?

Your mahonia is infected with powdery mildew (*Microsphaera berberidis*). If tackled in its early stages, this disease can be controlled by repeat sprays of fungicides containing bupirimate, carbendazim, or dinocap.

964

Many of the flower buds on my rhododendrons turned brownish-black this spring and failed to open. What is the trouble?

The buds have been infected with bud blast, a disease caused by the fungus *Pycnostysanus azalaea*. This is believed to enter the buds through wounds caused by the rhododendron leaf hopper (*Graphocephala coccinea*) when depositing its eggs in the buds.

First of all you must pick off and burn any infected buds, and protect against future attacks by

leaf hoppers by spraying the bushes with a general insecticide in August and September.

965

Some of the young leaves of my evergreen azaleas are turning reddish and are swelling into galls. Is this caused by a pest or disease?

This is azalea gall, caused by the primitive fungus *Exobasidium vaccinii*. Although the galls are reddish at first, they turn a waxy white when spores are produced to spread the disease. To prevent the disease spreading, pick off the galls and then spray the bushes with a copper fungicide.

966

Some of the buds on my broom bushes have become very swollen, with the bud scales opened out so that they look rather like miniature green roses. What is the cause of this abnormal growth?

This strange growth is broom bud gall, which is produced in response to an invasion of the buds by minute gall mites (*Aceria genistae*). These galls usually have little effect on the health and vigour of the brooms. Very heavy infestations, however, can cause some suppression of flowering. Normally, therefore, no control measures are needed, although it is helpful to remove and burn as many galls as possible.

967

Abnormal growths, resembling small pineapples, have appeared at the ends of some of the branches of my sitka spruce tree. What is the cause of this abnormality?

The spruce is infested with spruce-gall adelgids (*Aldelges viridis*). These insects are related to aphids but are much smaller and look like darkish speckles on the host plant. To control them, remove and destroy all the galls; in early April give the tree a thorough spraying with a general insecticide.

Vegetable problems

968

Some of my cabbages and other brassicas were very stunted and generally making poor growth, so I dug one up and found that the roots were thickened and distorted. Could this be club root?

The symptoms you describe are typical of an early attack of club root (*Plasmodiophora brassicae*). Later attacks are visible above ground as a discoloration of the leaves and wilting in hot weather. Club root is encouraged by poor drainage and acid soil, so bulky organic matter should be dug in and lime applied. Crop rotation, coupled with good weed control, reduces carry-over of the disease. A proprietary club-root powder should be dusted on to the open drills and in the planting holes; or the roots of the young plants can be dipped in a made-up paste at planting time.

969

The leaves of some of my brassicas are turning bluish, their growth seems to be rather poor, and they tend to wilt in warm weather. Can you explain this condition?

It seems likely that the plants have been attacked by cabbage-root fly (*Delia brassicae*). Dig one plant up and examine the roots and base of the stem for the presence of fly maggots. Early attacks by this pest can be prevented by dusting a soil insecticide on to the seed drills and around the transplants. Later attacks can be dealt with by applying a heavy soil drench of spray-strength pirimiphos-methyl or trichlorphon.

970

Some tiny, white, moth-like insects are attacking my brassicas, and the plants are becoming covered with a sticky liquid which is going mouldy. What is this pest and how do I deal with it?

This is the cabbage whitefly (*Aleurodes proletella*), which weakens the plants by sucking the sap and also disfigures the leaves with a sticky honeydew that supports sooty moulds. It is difficult to control because the eggs and some larval stages are resistant to most insecticides. Use a special whitefly killer such as permethrin, applying a series of sprays at intervals of 5-7 days.

971

When I dug up my carrots I found that the surface of many of the roots were scarred and that they were infested with small maggots. How can I prevent this trouble in future?

Carrot fly (*Psila rosae*) is a major pest of carrots and may also attack parsnip, parsley, and celery. Attacks generally occur in May and again in August-September. Consequently, carrots sown at the end of May and lifted in August normally escape damage. Even so, whenever sowing carrots, apply a soil insecticide to the drills. Carrots which are not to be lifted until autumn should be watered in mid-August with a spray-strength solution of pirimiphos-methyl or trichlorphon.

972

Some of my onions have begun to look very sickly. The outer leaves have yellowed and wilted, and when I lifted one I found some maggots in the base. Is this onion fly?

Yes. Onion fly (*Delia antiqua*) is one of the most damaging of onion

pests and the crop should be protected from attack by applying a soil insecticide when sowing or transplanting onions. Repeat the treatment a few weeks later.

973

Some of my onions have started to die off. The leaves are yellowing and the young bulbs are rotting and developing a white fluffy growth. How can I prevent this trouble in future?

Your onions have been attacked by white rot caused by the soil-borne fungus *Sclerotium cepivorum*. Guard against future attacks by moving the onions to a fresh site each year. The seed drills and planting holes should also be dressed with a calomel (*mercurous chloride*) dust.

974

For several years I have been growing peas successfully in the same area of my garden, but this year many of the plants are yellowing and wilting. What is the trouble?

Your peas are almost certainly suffering from a foot rot or wilt caused by a soil-borne fungus (*Fusarium*). Populations of these disease organisms build up if peas are grown continuously on the same site for year after year. Crop rotation is the answer to your problem, but make doubly sure by using a captan-based seed dressing.

975

The foliage of my broad beans is becoming covered with small chocolate-coloured spots. Is this some sort of disease?

The symptoms you describe are typical of the early stage of chocolate-spot disease (*Botrytis fabae*). This type of infection seems to have little effect on cropping, but in a wet spring the disease can cause whole areas of the leaves to rot. Improving the soil so as to give good plant growth reduces the risk of attack, as does the control of blackfly. In gardens where the disease is a regular problem, however, the young plants should be sprayed with a copper fungicide.

976

Until recently my sweet corn plants looked perfectly healthy, but now large, white, lumpy growths have appeared on the ears and stalks of some of the plants. Cutting a gall open, I found that it was filled with a black, greasy mess. What caused this trouble?

Your sweet corn has become infected with maize smut (*Ustilago maydis*), and the white galls are filled with the black spores of this fungus. Remove and burn the galls before they open and release the spores; burn any infected debris, and do not grow sweet corn in the same place for several years.

977

A white powdery deposit has begun to appear on the leaves and stems of my cucumbers and marrows. Is this powdery mildew and, if so, what action should I take?

Clearly your plants have been attacked by cucumber powdery mildew (*Sphaerotheca fuliginea*), which also infects marrows. If this disease is left unchecked the plants will suffer badly and the cropping will be greatly reduced. Start a programme of repeated sprays at 10- to 14-day intervals, using a fungicide based on benomyl, bupirimate, or thiophanate-methyl; also, ensure that the plants are kept well watered.

978

Some of my lettuces, which were just beginning to heart, have suddenly wilted and collapsed. I find that the tap roots have been cut through just below soil level, but I can find no sign of slugs or other pests. What has happened?

Your lettuces have been damaged by cutworms. These are the large, dingy-coloured caterpillars of various moths which live in the surface soil: check the soil near adjacent, healthy plants and you will probably be able to find and destroy the culprits. Protect against future attack by applying a soil drench of spray-strength pirimiphosmethyl or trichlorphon.

979

When lifting my parsnips late this autumn I found that many of the roots had a reddish-brown rot of the shoulder tissue. Can you identify this disease and advise how I can prevent the trouble in future?

Your parsnips have been affected by parsnip canker (usually caused by the fungus *Intersonilia pastinaceae*), a troublesome and widespread disease. Crop rotation reduces the risk of attack, while improving the soil by the addition of bulky organic matter such as compost, peat, or composted bark also helps. Next year, try growing one of the many canker-resistant varieties introduced in recent years, such as 'Avonresister'.

980

One of my marrow plants is much smaller than the rest and its leaves are puckered and yellowed in patches. Is this due to some pest or disease?

The stunting and mottling indicates an infection of cucumber mosaic, which produces similar effects on cucumbers. There is no cure, and the disease is likely to spread by aphids to adjacent healthy plants. So dig up and destroy the affected plant at once. As this disease is extremely common it is good policy to start with more plants than you really need to allow for possible losses.

981

The leaves of my peas and broad beans have had semi-circular notches cut out of the margins. What pest is responsible for this damage?

The pest involved is the pea-and-bean weevil (*Sitona lineata*). This small beetle lives in the soil and feeds only at night. Fortunately the damage usually has little effect on cropping.

982

Following recent wet weather, many of the lower leaves of my potato plants have blackened and are rotting away. What causes this rot?

Your potatoes have become infected with potato blight (*Phytophthora infestans*). This can spread with alarming speed in damp weather, killing the whole of the haulm and infecting the tubers with a wet rot. Tomatoes can also be infected with potato blight, which kills the foliage and causes a black rot in the fruits. The answer is to spray the crop immediately with a copper fungicide and, if necessary, repeat the treatment.

983

When shelling my peas I found that many of the pods contained small grubs. How can I prevent this next year?

This is typical damage caused by the pea moth (*Cydia nigricana*).

Caterpillars hatching from eggs laid during the flowering period tunnel into the young pods and feed on the developing seeds. Early pea varieties usually escape damage, but it is good policy to spray maincrop peas with a general insecticide 7-10 days after the start of flowering. Permethrin, which is non-toxic and long-lasting, is particularly effective against these damaging pests.

984

Some of my tomatoes have developed a circular brown or greenish-brown sunken patch at the bottom end of the fruit. What is this caused by?

Blossom-end rot of tomatoes is caused not by disease but by irregular watering in the early stages of development of the fruit. The answer to your problem is to ensure that the soil is not allowed to dry out completely at any time. If you do this, later-developing fruit should be free of the trouble.

Fruit problems

985

What causes some of my apples to turn brown and rot while still on the tree?

Brown rot of apples is a fungal disease (caused by *Sclerotinia fructigena* and *S. laxa*) which enters the fruits through wounds made by insects or birds. It cannot be controlled by spraying with fungicides, but you should remove and burn any infected fruits on the tree or on the ground. Apples showing even slight signs of rot should be trimmed of their damaged areas and used immediately and not stored; apples in store must be inspected regularly for signs of rot.

986

This summer clumps of white woolly mould growth have developed on the branches of my apple trees. Can you identify this disease?

These are clusters of woolly aphids (*Eriosoma lanigerum*), the greenfly being covered with a waxy material which looks like a mould; the pest is sometimes called American blight. The aphids feed by sucking the sap and cause warty growths to develop on the branch, which may split and become cankered. Control them by applying a forcible spray of general insecticide.

987

The young leaves on the tips of the shoots of my cherry tree have become curled and distorted. What causes this trouble?

If you examine the shoots you will find that inside the curled up leaves are colonies of cherry blackfly

(*Myzus cerasi*). These hatch from eggs laid near the buds in the previous autumn, so the pest can be controlled by applying a tar-oil winter wash in December or early January. Alternatively, a systemic insecticide should be sprayed on the trees at bud burst. It is most important to control this pest as it stunts the new growth and affected branches may die back.

988

Dull olive-green patches have appeared on some of the leaves of my apple trees and dark brown scabs are showing on a few of the young fruits. What caused this trouble?

Both disfigurements are caused by apple scab (*Venturia inaequalis*), which not only infects leaves and fruits but can cause small cankers on young twigs. If left unchecked it can ruin the appearance of the fruit and also lead to early defoliation. Control it by a programme of sprays of benomyl, sulphur, thiram, or triforine, which should be applied when the green flower buds first appear, at the pink bud stage, at petal fall, and again three weeks later.

989

The leaves on one of the branches of my 'Victoria' plum tree have turned silvery. What can be causing this effect?

This branch has become infected with silver leaf (*Stereum*
purpureum). The fungus invades the branch, staining the wood purple and producing a toxin which moves upwards in the sap, causing the leaves to become silvered. Later the infected branches will die back and small bracket-shaped fruiting bodies may develop on the dead wood. Cut back the infected branch to well below where the wood is stained and then paint the wound with a canker plant.

Before taking this drastic action, however, make sure that the trouble is not due to *false* silver leaf. This physiological disorder can be distinguished from true silver leaf by the fact that most of the leaves become silvered at the same time; moreover, there is no staining of the wood. False silver leaf is caused by a combination of malnutrition and fluctuating water supply. The immediate first-aid is to apply a foliar feed. Next season, feed, mulch, and water the tree as necessary.

990

This year I found that the cores of many of my apples had been eaten away and become rotten. In some fruit there were small caterpillars. How can I prevent this happening next year?

Your apples have been attacked by the caterpillars of the codling moth (*Cydia pomonella*). This moth lays its eggs on apple leaves and fruitlets, and the young caterpillars tunnel into the developing fruits. They leave the fruits in mid-August to pupate. Codling moth can be controlled by applying a general insecticide in late June and again in early July. The non-toxic, highly persistent insecticide permethrin is particularly effective against these pests.

991

Some of the emerging shoots and flower trusses on my apple trees are covered with a greyish-white powder. What caused this trouble and how should I deal with it?

The shoots are suffering from apple mildew (*Podosphaera leucotricha*). The infection will have occurred last summer, but it does not show up until the buds begin to grow. The infected growth will remain stunted and unfruitful. Your first job is to cut off and burn the diseased growths, otherwise they will be sources of infection for the rest of the tree. Follow this up by applying a series of sprays at fortnightly intervals using fungicides based on benomyl, bupirimate, dinocap, thiophanate-methyl, or thiram.

992

Rounded holes have appeared in the leaves of my plum tree but there is no sign of caterpillar attack. What's the explanation?

This trouble is almost certainly

bacterial canker (*Pseudomonas mors-prunorum*), which also attacks cherries. Infected leaves first develop brown circular spots, and then the centres drop out leaving the shot-holes you mention; cankers, exuding gum, also appear on the branches, which may die back. To protect them against this disease, spray the trees with a copper fungicide in August, September, and October. Any branches which die back should be removed.

993

Many of the youngest leaves on my peach tree have developed reddish blisters, while the slightly older ones are swollen, distorted and covered with a whitish bloom. What is happening?

Your peach tree has been infected by peach-leaf curl (*Taphrina deformans*), which not only distorts the leaves but also causes them to fall prematurely, thus weakening the tree and seriously reducing cropping. Spray the tree with a copper fungicide in late January and again in early February.

994

The appearance of some of my apples has been ruined by a spiral, ribbon-like scar leading towards the eye of the fruit. What is the cause, and how can I prevent it in future?

Your fruits have been attacked by

caterpillars of the apple sawfly (*Hoplocampa testudinea*), which hatch from eggs laid on the flowers. They not only cause this surface damage but, if they penetrate the fruit, they will bring about early fruit drop, thus reducing the crop. Control them by applying a general insecticide after the blossom has fallen.

995

The foliage towards the centre of my blackcurrant bushes is being eaten away by large green, black-spotted caterpillars. What spray should I use to control them?

The caterpillars are larvae of the blackcurrant sawfly (*Nematus olfaciens*). They are somewhat resistant to chemical control, but try spraying them with an insecticide based on permethrin or trichlorphon. The alternative is hand picking. I suggest that next year you examine the centres of bushes regularly in May and June and, if necessary, spray them when the caterpillars are still small.

996

Many of the buds on my blackcurrants have become rounded and swollen. They have either failed to open or have produced only small, deformed flower trusses. What caused this trouble?

This condition is known as 'big bud' and is due to the buds becoming infested with a tiny gall mite (*Cecidophyopsis ribis*). In early summer the mites leave the old buds and invade new ones on the current season's growth. Not only does this pest greatly reduce the harvest you are likely to obtain from your bushes, but it can also transmit a weakening virus disease known as 'reversion', that will threaten the production of currants in future seasons; so it is important to take control measures. Pick off and burn any enlarged buds during January to March and then apply a series of sprays with the fungicide benomyl, starting when the first flower buds begin to open.

997

Returning from holiday I was shocked to find the leaves on my gooseberry bushes completely eaten away apart from their mid-ribs. What can have caused such severe damage?

Your bushes have been attacked by caterpillars of the gooseberry sawfly (*Nematus ribesii*). These large green, black-spotted caterpillars start feeding in the centre of the bush so although they are very conspicuous, they are not easy to spot at first. To avoid this kind of damage in future you should inspect the bushes regularly during April and May, picking off any caterpillars you find. Alternatively, spray in April and again in May with an insecticide containing permethrin.

998

Blackish scabs are developing on the young fruits of my pear trees and dull olive-green patches are showing on the leaves. Can you identify this disease and advise on its control?

Your pear trees have been attacked by pear scab (*Venturia pirina*), which has symptoms similar to those of apple scab although it is a different fungus. Like apple scab it damages the fruit, causes early defoliation, and can produce small cankers on the young twigs. Control it by spraying with benomyl, sulphur, thiophanate-methyl, or thiram at bud burst, when the flower buds show white, at petal fall, and finally three weeks later.

999

Small yellow spots have appeared on the upper surfaces of the leaves on my plum tree and on the undersides of the leaves there are small orange-brown powdery dots. Is this some form of rust?

The symptoms you describe are typical of the early stages of plum rust (*Tranzchelia prunispinosae* var. *discolor*). Later, the powdery spots turn dark brown or black and the leaves generally fall prematurely. Rake up the fallen leaves and burn to reduce carry-over of the disease. Next year keep a close watch on the tree and spray it with a fungicide based on mancozeb or thiram at the first sign of attack.

1000

A few shoots on my blackcurrant bushes have died back and now small raised orange spots are appearing on the dead bark. How can I prevent this disease from spreading?

This disease, known as coral spot, is caused by the fungus *Nectria cinnabarina*, which enters the plant through small wounds and pruning snags. Remove and burn any dead branches cutting them several inches below the dead growth and sealing the cut surfaces with a proprietary wound paint. It is also a good idea to clear away and burn any woody debris such as old pea sticks as these are often infected with this fungus.

1001

The leaves, shoots, and fruits of my gooseberries have developed a white powdery covering. Is this some sort of mildew?

The symptoms you describe are typical of American gooseberry mildew (*Sphaerotheca mors-uvae*), an all-too-common disease that not only weakens the plants but spoils the fruit. Prune the bushes to keep the stems well spread, taking care to remove and burn any diseased shoots. Next spring, starting just before the flowers open, apply 2-3 sprays at fortnightly intervals using a fungicide based on benomyl, bupirimate, or thiophanate-methyl.

1002

On picking my raspberries I found that many of the fruits were infested with tiny white maggots. How can I avoid this trouble in future?

Your fruits have been attacked by the raspberry beetle (*Byturus tomentosus*), which can also infest blackberries and loganberries. The beetles lay their eggs on the flowers and the grubs hatching from these feed on the developing fruits. Spray with an insecticide based on derris, malathion, or permethrin. Raspberries and loganberries should be treated when the first fruits are colouring, but blackberries should be sprayed as soon as the first flowers open.

1003

The tips of some of the new canes of my raspberries have died back and I now find that the canes have developed oval greyish spots which are splitting in the middle. Can I take any action to remedy this trouble?

Your raspberries are infected with raspberry-cane spot disease (*Elsinoe veneta*). The infection shows up from early June onwards as small purple spots, which later

run together and give the effects you describe. Cut out and burn any badly spotted canes. Next spring give a series of sprays with benomyl, copper, or thiram from bud burst until just before flowering.

1004

In recent years the cropping of my raspberries has become very poor. The canes are stunted and the leaves distorted and mottled with yellow. What should I do to improve the cropping?

Your raspberries have clearly become infected with one or more virus disease or by mycoplasmas. Unfortunately there is no cure for this type of infection so you should dig up and burn your present plants. Replace them with certified healthy stock, planting these on a fresh site well away from the previous planting.

1005

Something seems to have eaten the seeds and some of the flesh from many of my strawberries, completely spoiling their appearance. I can see no sign of any pest and would like to know what is causing this damage.

The culprit is a shiny black beetle called the strawberry-seed beetle (*Harpalus rufipes*), which hides under plant debris. Keeping down weeds and removing dead leaves reduces their numbers. Further insurance against attack is given by spreading slug pellets based on methiocarb among the plants.

1006

Purplish patches have appeared on the leaves of my strawberries; the edges are beginning to curl upwards, while the undersides have turned greyish in colour. Is this some type of disease?

Your strawberries are showing the early stages of infection by strawberry mildew (*Sphaerotheca macularis*); it can also occur on the flowers and fruits, giving them a dull and shrivelled look. Repeated sprays of benomyl, bupirimate, or thiophanate-methyl should be applied at 10- to 14-day intervals until the fruits begin to change colour. Cut off and burn the old leaves after harvesting.

Greenhouse & indoor plants

1007

Small cottony growths containing insects have appeared on my parlour palm (*Neanthe bella*). Can you identify these pests?

Your plants are infested with mealy bugs (*Pseudococcus*). These are sap-sucking insects which not only weaken the plants by their feeding but also secrete a sticky honeydew which later becomes covered with sooty moulds. Various species of this pest attack a wide range of greenhouse plants. Light infestations can be wiped off with a damp cloth, but heavy attacks are best dealt with by repeated sprays of malathion or a systemic insecticide.

1008

Whitish powdery spots are developing on the young foliage of the 'Black Hamburgh' grapevine in my cold greenhouse. How can I prevent this from spreading?

Your vine is showing the early stages of infection by vine mildew (*Uncinula necator*). To prevent further spread of the disease, apply immediately a spray based on either benomyl or dinocap. Give repeat treatments but do not spray after thinning. Since the disease flourishes in stagnant air, good ventilation and adequate watering make disease-control easier.

1009

When raising seedlings in my greenhouse I sometimes get poor emergence and suffer further loss of seedlings both before and after pricking out. How can I prevent these losses?

Both poor emergence and the later loss of seedlings can be attributed to attacks by soil-borne fungi. The first essential is to use clean seed trays and sterile John Innes Compost or one of the peat-based products. Dressing the seed with a proprietary fungicidal seed-dressing also helps. These measures, coupled with thin sowing and sensible watering, should prove successful. If damping-off occurs, the trays should be watered with Cheshunt compound.

1010

Some of my potted primula plants seemed to be growing badly so I knocked one out of the pot and found that the roots were infested with insects like greenfly. What should I do?

These pests, which are root aphids, can be troublesome on a wide range of greenhouse plants. Ideally, you should wash the roots free of soil and then dip them in a spray-strength general insecticide before repotting. An easier method is to give the pots a heavy watering with the insecticide solution.

1011

The stems of my vine are encrusted with reddish-brown barnacle-like scales up to 6 mm (¼ in) long. Can you identify this trouble?

Your vines are infested with brown scale (*Parthenolecanium corni*), sap-sucking insects which remain fixed to the bark; like aphids, they produce sticky honeydew which becomes covered with sooty moulds. They can be scraped off the dormant rods in winter, but even so it may be necessary to apply summer sprays of malathion or pirimiphos-methyl. Various other species of scale insects attack a wide range of greenhouse plants.

1012

Tomatoes planted in my greenhouse border showed poor growth and began to wilt, so I dug one up and washed the soil off the roots. The root system was poor, and I found numerous small insects floating on the water. Could these be the cause of the trouble?

Yes. Glasshouse centipedes (*symphylids*), which are white, wingless insects with 12 pairs of legs, can be very damaging. They feed on roots and may also damage leaves touching the soil. Apply either a soil insecticide before replanting or a heavy soil drench of spray-strength general insecticide.

1013

Whitefly are attacking most of the plants in my greenhouse. I have tried spraying with a general insecticide but without success. What should I do?

Whitefly are difficult to control because their eggs and larval stages are resistant to most insecticides. The new pyrethroid insecticides permethrin and resmethrin, however, are effective against most stages. Even so, it is necessary to make three to four applications at 4-7 day intervals. Proprietary spray preparations of these insecticides are available; better still, use permethrin-based smoke cones.

1014

One of my potted cinerarias grew badly and began to wilt, so I knocked it out of the pot and examined the roots. Amongst these I found a fat white grub with a dark head. What is this pest?

The grub is the larva of the vine weevil (*Otiorhynchus sulcatus*), a common pest of many plants, which not only feeds on the roots but may also tunnel into bulbs, corms, and tubers. You can guard against attack by working a soil insecticide into the compost; alternatively, apply a heavy soil drench of spray-strength insecticide based on HCH, malathion, or pirimiphos-methyl.

1015

The leaves of various plants in my greenhouse have turned a sickly yellow colour and on some plants fine cobwebs are showing. What's the trouble?

It looks as if your greenhouse is infested with red-spider mites

(*Tetranychus urticae*); if you examine the lower-leaf surfaces carefully you will find that they are covered with tiny insects just visible to the naked eye. The mites spin silk threads to move around the plants. Control them by repeated sprays with systemic insecticides or with a greenhouse smoke based on pirimiphos-methyl.

1016

Some of my house plants seem to have stopped growing and are tending to wilt in sunlight even when well watered. The only possible pests I can see are small dark-coloured gnats flying round the plants.

The small gnats are almost certainly fungus gnats (sciarid flies), which lay their eggs in the compost; the small maggots then feed on the plant roots, seriously affecting the plant growth. They can be controlled with a soil drench of a spray-strength insecticide such as HCH, malathion, or pirimiphos-methyl.

1017

After planting out, my cucumber seedlings grew badly and began to wilt. On digging one up, I found large numbers of tiny grey insects jumping around in the soil. Could these have caused the damage?

From your description it seems that your cucumbers have been attacked by springtails (*Collembola*); some species of these soil-living wingless insects feed on plant roots, on stem bases, and also on any leaves touching the surface of the soil. Before replanting, work a soil insecticide into the top layer of compost, alternatively, apply a heavy soil drench of spray-strength general insecticide, such as those mentioned in 1013 above.

Aquatic plant problems

1018

My water lilies have become infested with greenfly. However, there are goldfish in the pool, so I dare not use an insecticide. What can I do to control these pests?

Water-lily aphids (*Rhopalosiphum nymphaeae*) attack not only water lilies but also a wide range of other aquatic plants. Since you cannot use insecticides I suggest you weigh down the foliage of the lilies and other plants and keep them submerged for a few days, to allow the fish to feed on the aphids. As this aphid species overwinters as eggs on various species of *Prunus* (peach, plum, cherry, almond, etc.) you can reduce the risk of infestation next year by applying a tar-oil winter-wash to these trees, if you have any, in mid-winter.

1019

Irregular holes have appeared in some of my water-lily leaves and a few of the leaves have become ragged and rotten. What caused this damage?

If you examine the undersides of the holed leaves you will almost certainly find oval-shaped 'cases' made of pieces of leaf. These cases are made by the caterpillars of the brown china moth (*Nymphula nymphaeata*) which are eating your water lily leaves. The best method of control is to pick off these cases by hand.

1020

Narrow linear holes have appeared in some of the leaves of my water lilies. Could these be caused by the small dark-brown beetles which are present on the leaves?

These water-lily beetles (*Galerucella nymphaeae*) are indeed the culprits: both the adults and the dark-coloured, soft-bodied larvae feed on water-lily leaves. One method of control is to hose the leaves to wash the beetles into the water, where the fish can feed on them. Alternatively, keep the infested leaves submerged for a few days.

David Stevens

Garden designer; landscape consultant to *Homes & Gardens* magazine; author of three books on garden DIY and other topics.

DIY
Projects

Hard surfacing

1021

Having moved into a new house, I find that parts of the garden become waterlogged after heavy rain and take three or four weeks to dry out. Is there anything I can do about this?

Many new gardens on housing estates are poorly finished, with a layer of topsoil deposited over ground that has been compacted by building work and heavy machinery, and so has formed a hardpan some inches below the surface. As a result water is slow to drain down to the water table (*see* 726). Thorough cultivation to break through the pan can often solve the problem.

If ground water is still persistent, land drains may be necessary in order to lower the water table. Trenches should be dug in a herringbone pattern sloping at a gradient of 1 in 40 to terminate at a soakaway filled with builder's rubble. Clay pipes 100 mm (4 in) in diameter are laid on gravel at a depth of about 1 m (3¼ ft), with broken tiles over the joints. Topsoil, which should be stacked separately, must be replaced last.

1022

I have several jobs to undertake, including laying a patio and building two brick walls. How do I estimate the quantity of materials needed?

Materials these days are expensive and you can make considerable savings if you estimate accurately. A simple scale drawing on graph paper will quickly tell you the number of square or rectangular

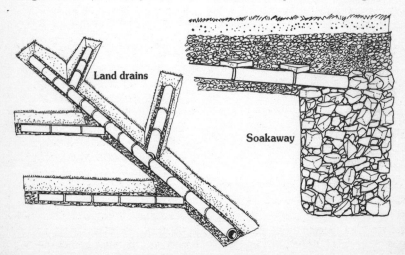

Land drains

Soakaway

slabs of given size needed for a patio. For 1 m² (10.8 sq ft) of a wall that is 225 mm (9 in), or two brick-widths thick you will need 100 clay bricks. Where other shapes are involved, remember that the area of a triangle is half the base times the height, and the area of a circle is the square of the radius multiplied by 3.14.

1023

I want to build a patio using precast concrete slabs, but I am bewildered by the vast range available. Can you offer any advice?

When choosing a slab think of the overall design of the area. Close to a building, 'architectural' shapes look best, so choose squares or rectangles. Away from a building more informal shapes such as crazy paving, pentagons, and hexagons may look better, blending well with grass and plantings. Avoid conflicting colours for what should essentially be a simple surface, and for strength and durability choose slabs 38 or 50 mm (1½ or 2 in) thick.

1024

What is the best method of laying rectangular slabs of old York stone?

There are three methods of laying slabs, whether they be precast concrete or natural stone. The simplest is to level and compact the ground and rake out a 50 mm

(2 in) layer of soft sand, the slabs being bedded onto this. Rain can, however, quickly undermine the surface, making it unsafe. A more durable finish involves laying 100 mm (4 in) of well-compacted hardcore or crushed stone. The slabs can be bedded on five blobs of mortar made up from 3 parts of sand and 1 part cement. This technique is suitable for virtually all garden situations. Where heavy wear is expected, as with a drive, 150 mm (6 in) of hardcore will be necessary, the slabs being bedded onto a continuous layer of mortar. But bear in mind that any services (water mains, etc) underlying the site will be difficult to reach.

1025

When I park my car in front of the garage I get ugly oil stains on the tarmac drive. Is there any way I can disguise this?

Oil drips are unsightly and, on tarmac, destroy the surface. An interesting solution involves laying an area of cobbles in the affected part; this also adds interest to an otherwise dull expanse of hard surfacing. The cobbles should be bedded in mortar over hardcore and must be packed as closely together as possible. The surface will be durable and could form part of a larger composition of paving and planting, the irregular shapes of the cobbles masking any drips.

Oil stains on surfaces other than tarmac can be removed with a proprietary paraffin-based solvent.

1026

The steep ramp up to my garage needs relaying. Is there any way that I can provide a non-slip surface that will be safer in bad weather?

The cheapest way of doing this is by using concrete. Lay a firm base of consolidated hardcore to the required slope or 'fall'. Boards should be used as forms (shuttering) down either side, and if the slope is steep a relatively dry mix should be laid to prevent the surface moving; a board tamped across the surface will give a ribbed, non-slip finish.

An attractive but more expensive ramp can be laid in hard bricks, stable pavers, or granite setts, which should be 'haunched' (set up at a slight angle) to provide a

good grip for tyres and shoes alike.

1027

Can you tell me the right concrete mix to use for laying a strong, durable garden path?

There are three basic mixes for concrete work in the garden. Mix A, consisting of 1 part cement, 2½ parts sand, and 4 parts coarse aggregate by volume, is suitable for 'footings' or floors of garden buildings, lightly used paths, and hard-standing areas. Mix B, 1 part cement, 2 parts sand, and 3 parts coarse aggregate by volume, is a stronger mix suitable for most drives, heavily used paths, concrete paths, retaining walls, and steps. Mix C, 1 part cement and 3 parts sand by volume, is the strongest mix, suitable for

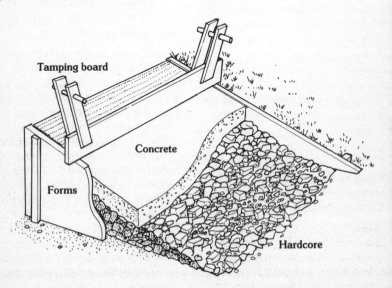

Tamping board

Concrete

Forms

Hardcore

bricklaying and bedding slabs on a prepared surface.

1028

I am bored with my present patio of grey precast slabs. Can I improve its appearance without lifting the entire surface?

A large single-colour surface can often seem heavy and overpowering, and the introduction of a second material—for instance, brick (a possible link with the house), granite setts, stable pavers, or even planting—can make all the difference. Lift a number of slabs, adjust the foundation levels by excavating to the required depth, and insert panels of the new material, making sure that the surface is level with the surrounding paving.

1029

I like the idea of brick paving but have been told that this may break up in frosty weather. Is that true? I have also seen a number of traditional paths in different patterns. Is there any particular merit in using one or another?

Bricks come in a wide range of types and finishes and the main criterion for their use as paving is their strength. To prevent the surface shattering in freezing temperatures the brick must be hard and well fired. Engineering bricks are hardest of all, having a glazed surface, but they can look a little clinical in a garden setting. Many 'facing' bricks are suitable; they come in a wide range of finishes and standards of durability. If in doubt, check the characteristics of your preferred bricks with the supplier.

There is a number of traditional patterns of laying. Stretcher bond and soldier courses lead the eye on if laid along the line of a path; basket weave and herringbone are more decorative, but the latter involves a certain amount of cutting of the bricks at the edges of a path.

1030

I want to make a gravel drive. Is there any way of laying one that will avoid that annoying problem of treading the stones into the house?

Gravel is a cheap, practical surface that blends well into most situations, and thorough preparation is the key to a sound surface. For a drive, a well-compacted hardcore base at least 150 mm (6 in) thick is essential. A 50 mm (2 in) layer of coarse gravel comes next, followed by a similar thickness of hoggin (a clay binder). The latter should be slightly damp and thoroughly rolled to fill and bind the underlying surface. Finally top it off with a 25 mm (1 in) thick layer of 10 mm (⅜ in) size gravel, rolling again to consolidate the surface.

1031

I have a tarmac drive and I wish to extend this surface in the form of a path around to the back door. Is this a difficult job?

No. Asphalt and bitumen are the two tarmac surfaces available, the latter requiring rather more work and being suitable for drives or a path expecting heavy wear. For your purpose asphalt should be fine. Lay a well-compacted 100 mm (4 in) layer of hardcore and spread ash over this to fill in the cracks. Asphalt can be bought in bags and is laid cold by raking out and then rolling. Finally a dressing of gravel or chippings should be rolled into the surface. Remember to lay the path to a slight camber or fall so that water will run off it.

1032

I want to lay a large patio area but find that slabs would be too expensive. Is there a hard-wearing but cheaper alternative?

Why not use a concrete, which can be laid to a number of finishes? Use a good base of hardcore 'blinded' with a weak mix of concrete to level the surface. Above this the concrete patio should be laid in panels no larger than 3 m (10 ft) square to avoid it cracking. The 'expansion joints' inserted between the panels can be decorative as well as practical; they should consist of wood planks 10 mm (3/8 in) thick and as wide as the depth of the concrete. Why not build up a grid of paving stones, woodstrips, or courses of brick, and infill these with concrete?

Expansion joint

The concrete surface finish can be varied, a wooden float giving a rough finish and a steel float a smooth one; perhaps most attractive of all is 'exposed aggregate', which involves sprinkling the surface with water and carefully brushing it with a stiff broom just before it sets, to expose the small stones.

Boundaries

1033

Should I incorporate a damp-proof course and coping into a garden wall?

A damp-proof course (DPC) prevents dampness rising up a wall, while coping protects the top. Both will prolong the life of a wall. A DPC should be about 150 mm (6 in) above ground level; a strip of bituminised felt is easy to lay and effective. Bricks on edge make an effective coping for a brick or concrete-block wall; so will stone if it is widely used locally, and precast concrete slabs or strips also provide a neat finish.

1034

The joints of my old brick garden wall seem to be crumbling away. What can I do about this?

This wall needs repointing; it is very likely that lime mortar was originally used, which deteriorates after prolonged exposure. Rake all the old mortar out with a pointing chisel to a depth of about 13 mm (½ in) and brush the wall down to remove dust. A pointing mixture is made up from 1 part cement, 6 parts soft sand, and 1 part plasticiser. Don't make up too much at a time, and dampen approximately 1 m² (10¾ sq ft) of the wall before you start. Point in the vertical joints first and, if you are patching only part of the wall, match the type of pointing profile to the rest: it may be weathered, flush, or rubbed back, the latter providing emphasis to each brick. A board laid along the bottom of the wall will catch pointing waste.

1035

I have a long, narrow garden and I wish to divide it into sections to alleviate the effect. Walls would be too expensive and hedges need too much maintenance. Are there any other solutions?

Why not use a screen of old scaffold poles that would act as support for a variety of climbing plants? The poles should be cleaned with a wire brush and sandpaper, and painted with metal primer; the tops should be plugged with a timber bung. Mark out the line of the screen and dig a trench 450 mm (18 in) deep and 300 mm (12 in) wide. Set the poles 150 mm (6 in) apart and hammer them about 200 mm (8 in) into the bottom of the trench, carefully checking their alignment. Then fill the trench with concrete, and finally gloss-paint the poles, bearing in mind that white or a pale colour will make the screen harder to see through.

1036

My front gate keeps on binding. I have planed it off but the problem soon recurs. What should I do?

Although you do not mention the type of post, I suspect it is timber; and almost certainly it is the hanging post rather than the gate that is at fault. First check the part of the post at and below ground level. If it is rotten it will need replacing. If it is simply loose, remove both the gate and post, separating the two. Concrete the

post back into position, following the same procedure as for fence posts (see 1037). Take this opportunity of checking the hinges, and rub the gate down prior to repainting, paying particular attention to the bottom, which often gets missed. Rehang the gate, if necessary using longer screws into the post.

1037

I have bought a panel fence to replace an old, untidy privet hedge. How should the fence be erected?

Panel fences are quickly erected and should last a long time if they are maintained with regular coats of timber preservative (not creosote, which is poisonous to plants). The most important job is the firm positioning of fence posts.

Mark out the fence run with a line and dig the first hole just over 600 mm (2 ft) deep. Fill the bottom with broken hardcore and ram this down. Concrete will make the most durable fixing and should be worked in around the post; check the latter frequently for height and vertical alignment.

Use reasonably substantial battens to buttress each post while the concrete is drying; this will prevent the post from moving when the fence catches the wind. The top of the concrete should be brought just above ground level and sloped off to prevent water standing around the post bottom, which would allow rot to set in.

As the lengths of the panels may vary slightly, mark each one separately and offer up the first to determine the exact position of the second hole and post, the erection procedure being repeated.

Allow at least a week for the concrete to set before fixing the panels to the posts with galvanised nails. Concrete posts, which have a groove on either side into which the panels can quickly and easily be inserted, are a more efficient but less attractive alternative to timber ones.

1038

Although my fence is basically sound and well maintained, a number of the posts have rotted. Can I repair these?

First of all, prevention is better than cure, so give all fence panels,

boards, and posts an annual coat of timber preservative. If the base of the post is rotten but that above ground level is sound, a ready-made concrete spur can be fitted. Saw off the bottom of the old post (making the cut through sound timber) and dig the rotten section out. The spur should overlap the retained upper section by at least 300 mm (12 in), and is concreted into the already prepared hole. Bolt the spur to the post when the concrete has set, using nuts and washers.

If the entire post is rotten, remove the panels or boards on either side, cutting through the arris rails flush with the post if the fence is close boarded. The old post should then be removed and the replacement positioned at exactly the same height, preferably set in concrete. If the arris rails are rotten, cut them back to sound timber and fix new sections with scarf joints.

1039

I want to build a boundary wall about 1.8 m (6 ft) high. What would be the best material to use and what foundations will it need?

New structures in the garden should match or complement existing ones in design and materials. Brick and stone may well reflect the character of a house, but so too will concrete if it is sensibly used; smaller cottages often look better with a fence or hedge. The

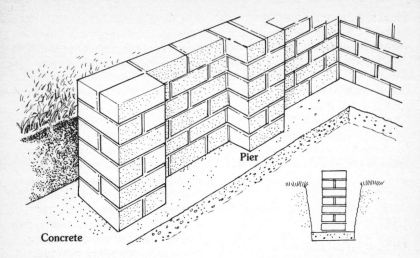

Pier

Concrete

depth of the foundation (footing) for a wall depends on site conditions and should be dug down to solid ground, usually to a depth of 450-600 mm (18-24 in). The width of the footing should be twice the width of the wall. Any wall over 1.5 m (5 ft) high should be 225 mm (9 in) thick for brick and rather more for stone.

Changes in level

1040

I have felled two elm trees that died recently. Is their timber suitable for building steps in an informal part of the garden?

Elm is an ideal timber for many garden projects as it is highly resistant to rot. Log steps can be built in a number of ways, the easiest of which is to use lengths of trunk or stout branches set across the slope. Strip all bark and remove any snags or projections. Simply bed the timber to form risers, driving two stakes into the ground on the lower side to provide a secure anchor. The treads can be gravel, rammed soil or grass edged with tough ground-cover plants such as an ivy or rose-of-sharon (*Hypericum calycinum*) flopping over the edges and softening the outline.

1041

I wish to build a retaining wall about 1 m (3¼ ft) high between two levels, the upper one to be planted with shrubs. I have a good supply of old railway sleepers. Would these be suitable?

Railway sleepers are almost indestructable and blend well into virtually any garden setting. Normally, foundations are minimal: simply excavate a trench the width of the sleepers and lay these end to end. Continue to build the wall in a simple stretcher bond so that vertical joints are avoided and drill holes through the sleepers as work progresses so that lengths of reinforcing rod can be passed through and driven securely into the ground when the wall is complete.

1042

Although the patio at the rear of my house is well laid, the slabbed steps that descend from it have become unsafe. Can I repair these or should they be rebuilt?

If the problem is simply that the treads have become loose and wobble on the risers, the slabs can be carefully lifted and repositioned on a fresh bed of 3:1 mortar, making sure that there is a very slight cross-fall or slope so that the surface will shed water.

If the risers have deteriorated, however, the entire flight should be taken down and rebuilt. If the flight projects out from the patio, retaining walls in brick, stone, or blocks will be needed on either side, and these must be built on sound footings whose depth will depend on the type of ground. The risers should be about 150 mm (6 in) high, and the first riser in the flight should be built off a similar foundation, the space behind it being filled with compacted hardcore topped with a weak concrete mix. Bed each slab on mortar so that it overhangs its riser by about 50 mm (2 in); build the second riser off the rear of the first tread, the whole operation being repeated until the patio level is reached.

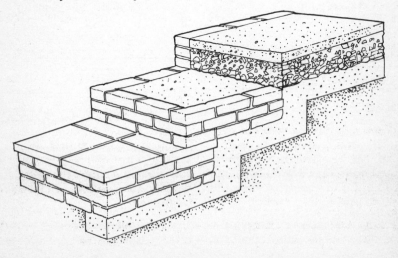

1043

My patio is made of solid concrete and seems stark and uninteresting. As I cannot break through it to create planted areas, is there some other way I can soften the outline?

Planting is undoubtedly the answer, and pots and tubs filled with annuals would certainly give you instant, if rather shortlived, colour. Raised beds are a better alternative, helping to give the area definition as well as acting as occasional seats. As a general rule the bigger the bed the better, as this will prevent excessive drying out. Timber, brick, stone, or concrete blocks would all be suitable, though the last would tend to increase the existing monotony. As your patio has a firm base no footing will be necessary, but remember that you should leave a number of weep holes just above ground level for drainage. Put a 150 mm (6 in) layer of hardcore at the bottom of the bed and top up with good-quality topsoil.

1044

I have a retaining wall 1.2 m (4 ft) high, but over the years the weight of soil has virtually pushed it over. I wish to rebuild it but I do not want the same problem to recur.

This is a common problem and nearly always means that the foundations are inadequate or that the wall is not thick enough. Take the old wall down and cut the bank back 600 mm (2 ft) from the face of the new wall, making sure you stack subsoil and topsoil separately. A wall 1.2 m (4 ft) high will need to be at least 225 mm (9 in) thick for safety and if the area tends to get waterlogged a 343 mm (13½ in) wall—the width of three clay bricks— will be safer. The foundations must be twice as thick as the wall and should be at least 450 mm (18 in) deep.

In order to give the wall added strength it can be built to a batter (leaning inward slightly), and the foundations can be finished at an angle to match this. If using brick, choose a hard well-fired variety and leave open joints (weep-holes) at regular intervals along the bottom course to allow drainage. When backfilling, a layer of hardcore should be placed first, followed by subsoil and at least 450 mm (18 in) of topsoil.

Plants

1045

I have two young flowering cherries, but they were planted too close together. I do not want to lose either, so can one be moved?

Certainly, but moving of a deciduous tree should be

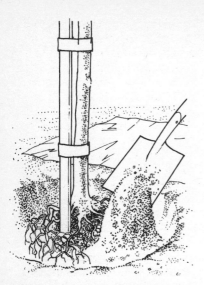

undertaken only during the dormant season, from November to April. The first job is to prepare the new site by digging a hole of ample size and forking the bottom over, incorporating well-rotted manure. Choose a spell of mild weather and place a sheet of tarpaulin or heavy-gauge polythene by the tree. Dig carefully around the base, about 600 mm (2 ft) from the trunk, and then gently slide the tree and its root-ball onto the sheet.

Drag the sheet to the freshly prepared site and reposition it at the original depth. Before replacing the soil, drive in a stout stake between the roots close to the trunk. Backfill the soil and secure the tree to the stake with two plastic ties. Complete the job with a thorough watering. For moving an evergreen shrub, see 375.

1046

I have a conifer 1.8 m (6 ft) high which will be in the way of a new garage. Will the tree survive removal to a site nearby?

Conifers can be particularly difficult to move, but the success rate is good if the job is tackled in the right way. First, make sure the tree is well watered and spray the foliage with an anti-dessicant to prevent the leaves from losing too much moisture. Prepare a planting hole. Now gently lift the tree by digging around the base, then slide a large square of hessian under the root-ball to retain as much soil as possible. Plant the tree in its new position as soon as possible and, as newly planted conifers tend to fall over, place stakes around the tree and attach plastic mesh to them in order to break the force of any wind.

1047

I have a Scots pine with a large limb that is dead. What is the best way to remove this?

Branches can be deceptively heavy and, in order to prevent a limb from ripping bark down the main trunk, as much weight as possible should be removed before sawing through the limb. This means lopping off smaller side branches and also shortening the limb itself. Before making the main cut, rope the limb to a stout branch above. Undercut the branch about

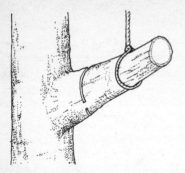

300 mm (12 in) from the trunk and then make a second cut above the first to remove it entirely, making sure to stand clear as the branch swings free. Lower the branch to the ground and trim the stub as close to the trunk as you can, finally applying a wound paint to the cut surface.

1048

I have felled a large sycamore that was dominating one end of the garden, and now wish to remove the stump. How should this be done?

When felling a tree make sure that you leave enough stump to provide leverage. Dig around the base to expose the main roots and sever these with an axe or bow saw. Snap the minor roots by rocking the stump backwards and forwards, and then lever the stump over in order to expose the tap root, if it has one.

If the stump has been cut right down to ground level it will be difficult to remove, and it can be killed by using chemicals poured into specially bored holes. These chemicals are poisonous and the holes must be plugged securely to make them child- and animal-proof.

1049

My untidy heap of decomposing vegetation is getting out of hand in the corner of the garden and I want to construct a simple but efficient compost bin. Advice, please.

Compost bins should ideally be situated out of direct sunlight and cold winds. A simple bin can be made by driving four 100 × 100 mm (4 × 4 in) section posts into the ground and stretching heavy-duty plastic netting around them to form a cage, making sure that the front can be opened to allow removal of the compost. A more permanent bin can be built from concrete blocks, but remember to leave gaps at the back and sides to allow the circulation of air. The compost should be built up off a simple platform of boards resting on bricks.

1050

My blackcurrant and other soft-fruit bushes are constantly raided by birds. How can I make a cheap but effective fruit cage?

Plastic netting has revolutionised fruit cages. Simply mark out the boundaries of the area and dig a trench 150 mm (6 in) deep on all sides, but leaving a gap for the entrance. Drive 75 × 75 mm (3 × 3 in) section posts or poles about 600 mm (2 ft) into the ground and 1.8 m (6 ft) apart at a height to allow you headroom. Stretch galvanised or plastic-coated wire between the poles, fixing it with staples. Now use plastic netting to form the roof and sides of the cage. The side netting should hang down into the trench. Secure the netting to the poles and wires with garden twine, and anchor it at the base by backfilling the trench.

1051

I have a small garden and wish to grow espalier fruit trees. Unfortunately all my fences and house walls are already clothed with climbers. Any ideas?

Espalier and cordon fruit trees (*see* 90, 137, 166) are great space-savers in a garden, and practical too. They can make an ideal screen or division within the garden and in your case can be simply trained on posts and wires. 100 × 100 mm (4 × 4 in) section posts will be necessary, and these can be concreted into position 1.8 m (6 ft) apart, with the tops all at a height of 1.4 m (4½ ft). Three horizontal strands of galvanised wire should be stretched between the posts at equal intervals, the bottom strand 450 mm (18 in) above the ground. Treat the posts with timber preservative (*not* creosote).

1052

The front of my house is built in an attractive but rather overpowering red brick. I wish to train climbers up it but do not want to use trellis. Is there an alternative?

Yes, wires stretched horizontally along the wall provide an ideal host for climbers and are sensibly unobtrusive. Drill and plug the wall (in the bricks rather than in the mortar joints), and insert round-headed galvanized vine-eyes, the bottom row about 1.2 m (4 ft) above the ground and the holes 1 m (3¼ ft) apart horizontally and 600 mm (2 ft) apart vertically. Wires can be threaded through the eyes, and climbers are simply tied back to the wires as they develop.

Electricity

1053

I wish to mount a number of lights in the garden, some close to the house to illuminate the patio and some at a greater distance to highlight shrubs and trees. Is electricity safe in this context, and can I do the work myself?

Lighting can transform a garden, but this is one of the areas where you will need to enlist professional help. Modern garden lighting systems operate a 12-volt system that works off a transformer. You must get a fully qualified electrician to wire your transformer back to a separate 13-amp fuse in your consumer unit (fuse box). The 12-volt systems are completely sealed and consist of up to six lights, usually on ground spikes, and associated cables. They can be easily positioned and, as the voltage is low, the cable need not be buried. NOTE: Outdoor equipment to operate at mains voltage *must* be installed by the Electricity Board or a qualified electrician.

1054

I would like to enliven my rather drab garden pool with underwater lights. Is it safe for me to instal them?

Here again there are 12-volt systems that are taken back to the safety of a transformer in the house. The cable is usually laid under the coping around the pool and buried well beneath the mower blades if it crosses a lawn. The lamps can be weighted to sit firmly on the bottom of the pool or mounted in polystyrene so that they float; some even rotate, but these look garish if over-used.

1055

Can you advise me of the best ways to heat my home-made propagator and cold frame?

There are many sophisticated greenhouse systems available that will automate virtually all routine operations. Electrical equipment for these and for the purposes you envisage normally uses mains voltage, so that expert help will be necessary to run power from the house to the greenhouse.

Propagators are usually warmed by cables buried in coarse sand at the bottom of the box, while frames usually have the cables running around the sides above soil level. There are several kits available for both air and soil warming. Make sure that any you buy conform to safety requirements.

Water

1056

I plan to instal a pool in my garden. Are there any general rules about siting?

Pools should be sited in an open, sunny position where plants and fish can flourish. Shady areas are not suitable and leaves and other vegetation blown into the water may produce gasses that can kill many of the fish.

1057

What constructional materials are available?

Concrete involves a lot of work and for DIY purposes has been largely superseded by plastic of various types. Glass-fibre pools are fairly small and quite expensive, but being pre-formed are simple to instal. Vacuum-formed pools look rather like glass-fibre but are cheaper; they are somewhat fragile and can have a short life. Flexible liners are now by far the most popular constructional material; they are available in polythene, which is the cheapest and least durable; laminated PVC, which is far stronger and ideal for most domestic pools; and butyl rubber, the toughest and most expensive, which is especially suitable for large projects such as lakes.

1058

I want to make a liner pool, but how do I calculate the size of sheet needed?

The size is calculated by taking the greatest length and greatest width and adding twice the maximum depth to both these figures. This gives the total liner area.

1059

Should a pool be all of one depth? And how deep should it be?

In any pool you need to create a balanced environment of plants and fish. To achieve this both shallow- and deep-water plants should be grown. These are placed in baskets either on a 'marginal' shelf around the edge of the pool or on the bottom. The shelf should be 225 mm (9 in) below water level and as much wide. Contrary to popular belief a garden pool no deeper than 600 mm (2 ft) is quite sufficient to grow a wide selection of lilies and other deep-water plants.

1060

How can I construct a pool using a liner in the central part of my lawn?

After calculating the size of the liner, mark out the shape of the pool and surrounding coping. If curves are involved these can be set out by swinging a line from a stick acting as a radius point. Lift the turf and stack it for use elsewhere in the garden. Dig out the entire area within the marked shape to a depth of 225 mm (9 in) sloping the sides slightly. Next mark out the marginal shelves and dig the remaining area out to a depth of 600 mm (2 ft), again sloping the sides; you can make a simple template to check the angle, which should be approximately 20° from the vertical.

Remove any sharp stones from the bottom and sides and cover all the inside surfaces with a 13 mm (½ in) layer of damp, soft sand. The liner can now be gently positioned and the edges weighted down with bricks, water being run into the pool to mould it to shape. When the pool is full, slit any wrinkled edges of the liner to lay it flat and trim it to size so that a 225 mm (9 in) border is left all round the edge of the pool. Coping should be finally laid on a bed of 3:1 mortar.

1061

I have a small sunny corner in the garden, about 3 × 3 m (10 × 10 ft). Is this big enough for a pool?

In general terms the bigger the pool the better, as a large volume of water supports a balanced environment more easily than a small one. A pool of 9 m² surface area is quite adequate, but remember that you will need some form of coping around the edge, which will reduce the overall size. As a rule a pool 2 m (6½ ft) square is a practical minimum to support plants and fish.

1062

With young children in the family, I am concerned about having a pool at ground level. Are raised pools practical, and how should they be built?

A raised pool is inherently safer than one at ground level and can be constructed in a similar fashion to a raised bed. In order to avoid rendering the inside, which can often lead to leaks, fit a plastic water tank so that the top is 50 mm (2 in) below the level of the coping. Fill the space between the tank and the sides with soil: this can later be planted up to provide a softening influence. A submersible pump can be fitted to feed a small bubble fountain, the cable being hidden by surrounding foliage and taken through a hole in the surrounding walls.

1063

I have seen an attractive millstone fountain in a local garden which was most attractive. Can I make one?

Millstones, boulders, and large thick pieces of slate, marble, or granite can all be used to make most attractive water features.

They should be drilled to accept a 13 mm (½ in) diameter copper pipe. A sump forms the basis of the composition and this can be made from a plastic or galvanised water tank. Excavate a hole to accept the latter so that the top is flush with the ground surface, removing sharp stones or other projections from the bottom. Make sure the tank is level. Now build two brick piers off the tank bottom. These are finished just below the top of the tank so that the millstone, when it is positioned on them, projects above ground level. A submersible pump is placed between the piers at the bottom of the tank and is connected to a pipe that passes through the stone and is cut off flush with the top. A circular water tank can usually be obtained to fit the diameter of a millstone, but if there is a gap this can be bridged by large loose cobbles or bold foliage, the latter making an attractive contrast to the hard stone. Finally, fill the tank and switch on the pump.

Tools

1064

I have bought a hand-propelled cylinder mower for my small lawn. Will it need any particular maintenance?

Routine maintenance involves lubrication of moving parts and wiping of surfaces with an oil rag after use. From time to time you will need to adjust the cutting cylinder, which should be able to cut a stiff piece of paper across the full width of the bottom (fixed) blade. Such adjustment involves turning a screw or bolt on either side of the machine. To adjust the height of the cut, the small wooden roller at the front or rear of the machine can be raised or lowered by simple bolts at each end.

1065

I have a chain saw which I use to cut logs and other timber. Can I sharpen it myself and are there any tips to keep it in peak condition?

General maintenance is similar to that of any 2-stroke machine, the plug being particularly susceptible to oiling up. Blades *can* be sharpened at home, but you will need to buy a purpose-made jig that clamps over the blade and cutting bar. A special file is drawn over each blade at an angle set by the jig, the whole operation being simple. Finally, check the chain tension and adjust it in accordance with the handbook instructions.

1066

My son has punctured a new rubber hose in the middle of its length. Is there an easy way to repair it?

Apply a coat of appropriate adhesive (water-insoluble) right around the hose at the site of the puncture, and bind a strip of cloth tightly around this. When the adhesive is dry apply a second coat of adhesive *over* the bandage. A plastic hose can be repaired by cutting out the damaged section and joining the two halves by inserting a simple jointing device obtainable from most hardware stores and garden centres.

1067

The wooden shaft of my spade has broken, but the shank (lower half) is riveted to the blade. How can I get this out and fit a new handle?

To remove the rivet, strike it smartly with a hammer and centre punch, and drill the head out. The shank can now be tapped out. The new handle will be ready-tapered but will probably need whittling down to make an exact fit. Tap it into position and mark through the old rivet hole with a bradawl, finally fixing the shaft with a round-headed screw.

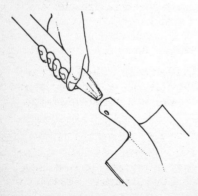

1068

I always have trouble starting my petrol-driven mower, particularly after winter storage. Is there any way of improving matters?

Correct winter storage involves removing all petrol, disconnecting the fuel line and draining down. Then start the engine and run it dry, so that the carburettor is empty and the jets cannot become blocked. Now turn the engine, so that it is on the compression stroke. In this position the valves are closed and exclude damp from the cylinder; the points are closed, too. Always keep the plugs and points as clean as possible, paying particular attention to 2-stroke engines, which build up carbon deposits especially rapidly.

1069

I am new to gardening and having bought a set of hand tools, I wish to keep them in the best possible condition. Should I undertake any special maintenance?

Maintenance, although simple, is vital to keep tools effective. Spades should be rubbed down after use and wiped with an oily rag; the tines of forks and rakes will need tapping straight with a hammer if they become bent. Cutting tools should always be kept sharp and well adjusted. Shears need a few strokes from a file once or twice a year to remove burrs; they may need to be reground by a professional every few years. Secateurs benefit from a drop of oil, while saws can be set and sharpened with a simple jig and file set. Always clean carefully any equipment (secateurs, shears, lawn mowers, etc) that has been used to cut plants. Nothing takes the fine edge off a blade quicker than plant sap left on such equipment.

Projects

1070

My tools are always jumbled in the shed and I would like to construct a very simple rack to hold them.

A straightforward rack can be made from offcuts of timber probably already in your possession. You will need a length of softwood to form the back, say 1-1.5 m (3¼-5 ft) of 100 × 25 mm (4 × 1 in) section. Into this you can fit 25 mm (1 in) diameter dowels about 100 mm (4 in) long and about 100 mm (4 in) apart—a spacing that will accommodate virtually all garden tools. When making holes (with a spade bit or a hole-saw) to accept the dowels, bore them at a slight downward angle, so that the dowel pegs will slope upwards when the rack is in position. Bore the holes right through the timber to prevent glue pressure building up when the

dowels are tapped in. When complete the rack can be neatly screwed into position.

1071

The front of my house is rather stark, and window boxes would help to cheer things up. What is the best size for these, and how can I make them?

Most off-the-peg boxes do not fit the window sill, and look awkward as a result. A box should fit snugly between the reveals. Invariably a simple design looks best, and a box should be a minimum of 200 mm (8 in) deep to sustain plant growth. The bottom, ends, and sides should be made from 25 mm (1 in) thick timber, and the legs from 50 mm (2 in) square section, which is chamfered off to compensate for a sloping sill. Bore a number of 13 mm (½ in) holes in the bottom for drainage, and glue and screw the whole box together, either painting it with wood primer, undercoat, and topcoat or treating it with timber preservative (*not* creosote) for protection.

1072

The felt on my shed roof has deteriorated and is now letting in rain. Is it easy to replace?

First remove all the old material. The heads often snap off old galvanised nails, so make sure no sharp points are left oustanding. Check the boards underneath and

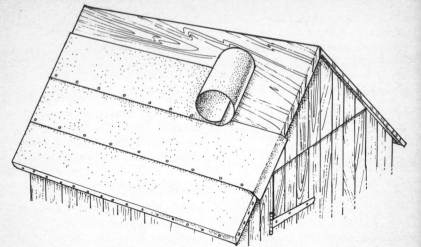

replace any that are rotten, treating both new and old timber with preservative. Bituminous felt should be laid in wide sections, the strips nearest the eaves first so that subsequent lengths overlap these. Fold the edges under before nailing with 13 mm (½ in) galvanised clout nails. Use a strip at least 375 mm (15 in) wide to go over the ridge.

1073

I want to build a sandpit. Does this need any foundation, and what sort of sand should I use?

Sandpits are irresistible to small children, and so they should if possible be sited within view of the house. The pit should be dug 450 mm (18 in) deep in ground that is not subject to waterlogging. Ram a 150 mm (6 in) layer of hardcore into the bottom. In order to prevent the sides crumbling they should be lined with boards; elm

wood is ideal. Cover the hardcore with a 50 mm (2 in) layer of washed pea-gravel and finally top up the pit with silver or washed river-sand. In order to discourage nocturnal visitors, a cover is essential; a waterproof one will keep the sand dry, and if it is firm and strong it can double as a play surface.

1074

I have a fine old ash tree that would make an ideal host for a swing or tree house. Do you think I could fit these safely?

Ash has a tendency to snap under load, so check that the limbs are really stout and in first-class condition (this would be a good opportunity to carry out any necessary tree surgery). A simple swing can be made from a single nylon rope, securely attached to a limb and passed down to an old car tyre.

Tree houses should not be built too high off the ground; in any case the lowest forks are both strongest and most accessible. The floor should be made from a simple framework of 100 × 50 mm (4 × 2 in) section softwood timbers, topped with a sheet of 19 mm (¾ in) thick exterior-grade ply.

This is an excellent project for the young do-it-yourselfer under supervision. Fit the floor into position and bore 13 mm (½ in) holes in the floor supports so that nylon ropes can be passed through and tied to adjacent branches. A simple knotted rope ladder can be provided for access, while an old tarpaulin or tent makes an excellent roof.

1075

We have just moved to a house with a tiny backyard. We are completely repaving this and I would like to incorporate a paddling pool. I do not want the usual plastic type stuck in the middle.

As you are making a clean sweep select a sunny spot close to a house wall, and leave a gap in the paving approximately 1.2 m (4 ft) square. Dig this out to a depth of 225 mm (9 in) and ram 75 mm (3 in) of hardcore into the bottom. In the remaining 150 mm (6 in) form a dish with a maximum depth of 100 mm (4 in), using a 4:1 mix of mortar, finished with a wooden float to give a non-slip finish. The

water splash can either be filled by hand or served by a pipe and stopcock from the adjacent house wall.

1076

I wish to extend the growing season in my greenhouse without heating. I have seen that there are double glazing systems available, but can I fit them myself?

A simple system can be made up at minimal cost using PVC or polythene sheeting. With a timber framed house sheets can be fixed with drawing pins and joined with clear adhesive tape, while suction pads are available for aluminium houses. Make sure there is a gap of at least 13 mm (½ in) between the glass and sheet; and remember that, although the system will retain heat, it will also cut down the intensity of light available to your plants.

Index

S

Sage (*Salvia officinalis*) 50, 333, 338
St John's wort (*Hypericum*), to prune 381
Saintpaulia: see African violet
Salad vegetables 6, 21, 47, 75-76
Salix: see Willow
Salsify 6, 63
Sambucus: see Elder
Sandpit, to make 1073
Sansevieria: see Mother-in-law's tongue
Savory, summer 85
Savory, winter 50, 85, 86
Saws: care of 1065, 1069
Saxifraga stolonifera: see Mother-of-thousands
Scale insects 1011
Scented flowers 242, 267
  shrubs 338
Schizophragma hydrangeoides 363
Schizostylis coccineum: see Kaffir lily
Scilla 496
  Scilla sibirica 'Spring Beauty' 507
Scorzonera 6, 17, 63
Sea buckthorn (*Hippophae rhamnoides*) 395
Seaside: hedges for 417, 418
  plants for 243
Secateurs 251, 1069
Seed bed: to prepare 201, 736
  to sow 202
  weed-free 861
Seedlings: damping off 875
  hardening off 28, 199, 933
  loss of 1009
  to transplant 202
Seeds: collecting 860
  compost (for container growing) 790
  of fleshy fruits 865
  fluid sowing 877
  pelleted 872
  plants propagated from 934
  soil for 856
  sowing fine 871
  storing 868
Sempervivum: see House leek
Shade-liking plants 241
Shallot (*Allium*) 3
Shears 443, 1069

Shed: to camouflage 235
  to replace roofing felt 1072
Shrubs 325
  for acid soil 330
  with all-year-round interest 341
  for autumn colours 340
  for badly drained conditions 334
  bee-attracting 352
  for berries 348
  butterfly-attracting 347
  where to buy 328
  for catkins 350
  in containers 351, 364, 379, 380
  for cutting 343
  dead-heading 376
  colourful evergreens 341
  fertilisers for 367
  long-flowering 341
  to protect from frost 371
  for greenhouse 819
  for hard soil 331
  with silver fur on leaves 344
  for limy soil 329
  mulching 377
  planting 364-7
  poisonous 395
  pruning 381
  for rock gardens 625
  scented 338
  for the seaside 335
  for shade 332
  with colourful shoots 345
  for sunny conditions 333
  transplanting (evergreens) 375
  for troughs 337
  variegated 342
  for walls 346
  for windy conditions 335, 336
  winter-flowering 339
  wounds 370
Silver leaf (fungus) 989
Silver-leaved plants 245
Sink gardens, plants for 620
Sinningia (*Gloxinia*) 934
Skimmia 332
Slabs, concrete 1023, 1024
Slugs 940
Snails 940
Snake's-head fritillary (*Fritillaria meleagris*) 575

Drawings
by Chris Forsey